Processing the Past

Processing the Past

Contesting Authority in
History and the Archives

FRANCIS X. BLOUIN JR.
and
WILLIAM G. ROSENBERG

OXFORD
UNIVERSITY PRESS

Oxford University Press is a department of the University of Oxford.
It furthers the University's objective of excellence in research, scholarship,
and education by publishing worldwide.

Oxford   New York
Auckland   Cape Town   Dar es Salaam   Hong Kong   Karachi
Kuala Lumpur   Madrid   Melbourne   Mexico City   Nairobi
New Delhi   Shanghai   Taipei   Toronto

With offices in
Argentina   Austria   Brazil   Chile   Czech Republic   France   Greece
Guatemala   Hungary   Italy   Japan   Poland   Portugal   Singapore
South Korea   Switzerland   Thailand   Turkey   Ukraine   Vietnam

Oxford is a registered trade mark of Oxford University Press
in the UK and certain other countries.

Published in the United States of America by
Oxford University Press
198 Madison Avenue, New York, NY 10016

Library of Congress Cataloging-in-Publication Data
Blouin, Francis X.
Processing the past : contesting authority in history and the archives / Francis X. Blouin Jr.,
William G. Rosenberg.
p.   cm.
Includes index.
ISBN 978-0-19-974054-3 (hardcover : alk. paper); 978-0-19-996408-6 (paperback)
1. Archives—Methodology. 2. Archives—Technological
innovations. 3. History—Methodology. 4. Historiography. 5. Information resources management.
6. Knowledge management. I. Rosenberg, William G. II. Title.
CD950.B56   2011
027—dc22   2010029638

1 3 5 7 9 8 6 4 2

Printed in the United States of America
on acid-free paper

For Joy and Elie
Patient, Supportive, Loving

CONTENTS

Acknowledgments   ix
Introduction: On the Intersections of Archives and History   3

PART ONE   THE EMERGENCE OF THE ARCHIVAL DIVIDE

1. Authoritative History and Authoritative Archives   13
2. The Turn Away from Historical Authority in the Archives   32
3. Archival Authorities and New Technologies   50
4. The Turn Away from Archival Authority in History   63
5. Archival Essentialism and the Archival Divide   85

PART TWO   PROCESSING THE PAST

6. The Social Memory Problem   97
7. Contested Archives, Contested Sources   116
8. The Archivist as Activist in the Production of (Historical) Knowledge   140
9. Rethinking Archival Politics: Trust, Truth, and the Law   161
10. Archives and the Cyberinfrastructure   183
11. Can History and Archives Reconnect: Bridging the Archival Divide   207

Notes   217
Index   243

ACKNOWLEDGMENTS

We are particularly grateful to the Andrew W. Mellon Foundation and to the many offices and departments of the University of Michigan that helped fund a year-long seminar in 2000–2001 that explored in the broadest terms problems in archives, documentation, and institutions of social memory. Over one hundred presentations were made in the course of the year. We are grateful to all participants for their insights in broadening our sense of the parameters of the issues involved.

There are a number of thoughtful archivists and scholars who have probed these issues in their own writings and from whom we have learned a great deal. Verne Harris, Elizabeth Yakel, Paul Conway, Terry Cook, Helen Samuels, Eric Ketelaar, Roger Schonfeld, Tom Nesmith, Ben Alexander, David Wallace, Rand Jimerson, and Margaret Hedstrom, among others, have contributed much to the discussion with the archival community. Nancy Bartlett has been a wonderful supporter of our efforts, as well as a constantly constructive critic. Her insights into the complex roles that archivists play in "mediating" the past have greatly informed our own understanding of these complex processes. Galina Lisitsyna, our good colleague in Russia, helped us explore a number of theoretical, as well as practical, issues at several seminars she organized at the Archival Training Center at the European University at St. Petersburg. For one of us, the distinguished historian and dear friend Leopold Haimson first opened the secrets of Soviet archives. For us both, Boris Anan'ch, eminent Academician, sometime airport chauffeur, and unofficial tutor to many western scholars, encouraged our efforts from the start and was always eager to engage us on the issues.

We have also learned much about archival practices in other national frameworks from Paule René-Bazin, Du Mei, Eric Ketelaar, Christoph Graf, Vladimir Lapin, Sergei Mironenko, Olga Leont'eva, Jennifer Milligan, Beatrice Bartlett, William Kirby, Jeffrey Burds, Robert Donia, Paul Eiss, Alf Lüdtke, Atina Grossman, Alessandro Portelli, and Frank Mecklenburg, among others; and we have relied on Joan M. Schwartz for understanding the particular problems of photographic archives.

Recent scholarship on archives and history by Ann Stoler, Nicholas Dirks, and Carolyn Steedman has set a very high standard of insight and understanding. We have borrowed liberally from Stoler's rich conceptualization of the archival "grain," which she has used with such imagination in exploring colonial archives; and while we do not agree with Steedman's view of what actually happens—or more precisely, does not happen—in an archive, we have found her work, and that of Nick Dirks, extremely stimulating. Among historians, we are indebted to the work of our Michigan colleagues Geoff Eley, Rebecca Scott, and Rudolf Mrazek, as well as our former colleague Robert Berkhofer and the collective efforts of Joyce Appleby, Lynn Hunt, and Margaret Jacob in exploring the many recent conceptual "turns" in historical understanding.

We especially appreciate the contributions our friend and colleague Phil Pochoda, editor of the University of Michigan Press, has made in helping us think through a number of thorny analytical questions and the steady support he has given us in bringing our efforts to what we hope is a successful conclusion. Phil was instrumental in assuring the proceedings of the Sawyer Seminar were published in a handsome volume as well. In his tenure at the Press, Phil has contributed greatly to the intellectual vitality of the University as a whole. We know he regrets our decision to publish with Oxford in connection with its new series on History and the Archives. We are very appreciative indeed of the grace with which he has allowed us to do so. Nancy Toff at Oxford has also been unstinting in her encouragement and the intelligence behind the new Oxford series. All academics should be as fortunate with their editors.

Finally, we want to thank our students from history, anthropology, sociology, museum studies, and information science whose contributions to our graduate seminars greatly helped us clarify our own understanding of the issues at hand, as well as how to present them with what we hope is a reasonable degree of clarity. Teachers are only as good as their students allow them to be. We are grateful for our years in the most excellent of companies.

Processing the Past

Introduction

On the Intersections of
Archives and History

This book began with a casual encounter between a historian and an archivist, much like the ones that occur when scholars come to the archives. The historian wanted to discuss some general problems about accessing materials, the archivist more than willing to offer counsel but somewhat amused by how little the historian seemed to know about what the archival process was really about. In this instance the doors that swung open were not the often imposing entrances to historical repositories, but those of a prolonged and increasingly interesting conversation. And somewhat to our surprise, as is often the case with archival scholarship, the result turned out to be the book that follows.

One might say that a historian enters the archives in a similar way: the doors open, whether physically or virtually, and a "conversation" begins. The scholar comes with questions to a place of imagined and unexpected possibilities, the archivist usually ready and willing to help. Things begin routinely, perhaps by storing a backpack, signing in, and finding a comfortable place in the reading room. The scholar meets the archivist; the scholar's questions meet the resources of the archives and the experience and understanding of the archivist. First the finding aids, then perhaps an impatient wait, finally the files themselves, in old boxes or pristine electronic formats. The historian begins to process the vestiges of the past into some new form of understanding, rarely giving any thought to the fact that the "vestiges" themselves—letters, memos, reports, all sorts of documents—have already been processed by archivists into what the scholar will hopefully think are interesting materials. The historian uses the materials to process historical information and understanding; the archivist processes the materials to allow this information and understanding to be "uncovered." This processing takes place at many levels and on the basis of a variety of professional and conceptual assumptions.

What the two of us discovered in our own initial conversations was that the scholar's encounter with the archives—so fundamental to the formation of historical understanding—has rarely been examined in any informed way. What has mattered to the scholar is simply whether the visit to the archives was useful in terms of answering his or her questions, and to the archivist, whether the documents provided were useful in appropriate ways. In fact, as we began to probe this seemingly simple encounter, we discovered that the complex conceptual frameworks of contemporary historical research were actually encountering changing conceptual understandings in the administration and definition of archives. Quite complicated processes seemed to be at work on both sides of the archival research transaction.

In the broadest terms, we came to see the relationships between the discipline of history and the discipline of archival administration to be located very much at the intersection of humanities and information science. New technologies of information creation, storage, retrieval, and the nature of the dependency of scholars on these new digital possibilities raised questions about the nature of scholarly communication among humanists generally. How would the ever-changing frameworks of humanistic understanding come to rely on the extraordinary quantity of documentation left for "posterity" in both paper and digital form? How would institutions that hold research resources in this rapidly changing environment intersect with scholars who rely on those resources? And indeed, how have scholars and archivists—history and the archives—actually intersected in the past? How, in other words, have the practices of archival institutions shaped historical knowledge? What will these interactions be like in the archives of the future?

Archives, Archivists, and Historians

As we know, the word "archive" itself has now come to mean a number of things: from simple repositories conventionally referred to by archivists in the plural as "archives" to complex notions of cognition, memory, and the processes of uncovering, where "archive" in the singular connotes its conceptual elements. The most common understanding of an archive would describe it as a body of records generated by the activities of a specific individual or organization and commonly located (although not always) in a repository housing similar or related collections. The Boston City Archives holds records generated by the bureaucracy of the city of Boston. The Archives Nationales in Paris and the U.S. National Archives in Washington hold essential records of the modern French and American states. A university archive is largely composed of records generated by a particular educational institution. The relationship between the individual or institution and an archive, whether in a fancy building, closet, or computer hard drive, is what archivists would call an "organic" one: archives reflect or should reflect in their holdings the evolving nature of the organization or in the case of an individual, his or her personal records. How these often diverse materials then become "historical" depends on the extent to which they capture some aspects of an earlier processed past.

In some cases, both individuals and institutions will not maintain their own records, delegating "archival" tasks to another person or collecting institution along with the responsibility to maintain the record. Like many such collecting institutions around the world, the Immigration Research Center at the University of Minnesota, to take just one example, holds the records of a number of mutual aid institutions. In some cases these organizations no longer exist; in others they have designated the Center as the repository for their older records. Like individuals who "dump" their hard drives periodically into backup computers or other kinds of storage, the organic relationship between record and activity is not broken here. A similar relationship exists between the activities of the repository, in this case the Minnesota Center, and the task of choosing what materials to accept and preserve, and which to reject, discard, or delete. For most collecting institutions, the archives of significant and relevant individuals are also commonly involved. The transfer from study, office, or closet to formal repository does not itself disturb the organic relationship between the person and his or her records. Consequently, when we refer to "the archives" in this volume we will have in mind institutional archives, public and private, as well as what we call "collecting archival institutions." These include "special collections" within larger library establishments, as well as those independent archival institutions that have a particular collecting mandate. We are not considering the library or the museum as archives (that is collections of catalogued books and collections and displays of artifacts), or archives that are sometimes conceptualized practically or metaphorically in complex ways in the psychological and electronic worlds, although we will occasionally bring some relevant connections into our discussion. For us, the organic relationship of record to the generator of that record, whether in paper or electronic form, is what largely defines the conceptual boundary of our exploration.

Like our conversations themselves over the past few years, our primary focus here is not only on archival institutions, as we have just defined them, but on the changing intersections between history and the archive and the corresponding change in relationships between historians and archivists. Here we use the word "archive" as an abstraction of the processes by which archival institutions and collections come into existence. Our hope has been (and remains) that by looking at these relationships as a historical problem in itself, and then by examining their more recent aspects, we could come to some better understanding of what might be needed for both scholars and archivists to understand the impact of information technology on the humanities. Our focus soon came to rest on the importance of "authority"—in a variety of meanings and forms that we will discuss in detail—in conveying a sense of the past as well as an understanding of its documentary residues. This led us to such issues as the role of identity and experience as "authorities" in forming both historical understanding and the structures of archival collections; the activism of archivists themselves in these processes; and the forms and often contested natures of archival and historical sources. We also looked at questions of law and politics in documentary access and preservation. Finally, with an eye to the future, we examined the possible role of computer technology as an agent of change in facilitating research and processing archival documentation, a constantly changing issue we have explored not in any highly technical way, but in terms of its relation to future historical archives and historical understanding.

Each of the chapters that follow blends our thoughts and perceptions on these critical issues. In them we hope to show that at least from the mid-nineteenth century through the mid-twentieth century, historians and archivists occupied what might be thought of as the same conceptual and methodological space. The authority attributed to holdings in the archive underlay a set of arguments about authoritative history that were based on what was mutually understood by historians and archivists as objective and scientific. Historians and archivists shared professional training in the sense that preparation to be an archivist was thought to be firmly rooted in historical knowledge and methodology. They had a mutual appreciation of scientific rigor and a shared notion of how the past should be processed in conceptual terms, as well as through the ordering of documentation. They knew, or thought they knew, the language of citation. And as professionals sharing the same sense of what was historically important, they focused together on the roles of institutions, prominent actors, national boundaries, great ideas, and seminal events in structuring the processes of historical change, as well as the processes of acquiring, classifying, and preserving historical documentation.

As our own work together developed, we discovered that this fundamental connection has now altered dramatically. A sense of partnership joined by shared assumptions about the nature of historical authority and the evidentiary power of archival documentation has given way in history to radically different ways of understanding the past. The various linguistic, cultural, and other "turns" that have recently shaped new historical understanding have been complemented in the archival community by a sharp turn from historiographically based authorities themselves, in a variety of forms, to those more strictly archival or based on practices of records management. Historians now ask important questions not easily answered or understood through an examination of archival documents alone. Archivists now confront an almost unimaginable mass of documentation both in paper form, typically measured in large numbers of linear feet, and in new and potentially unstable digital forms whose very nature seems to dissolve any limits on what might be preserved. As a consequence, historians and archivists no longer share common professional training or historical understanding. Rapid changes have taken place in archival practices that have little or no relevance to current historical conceptualizations. In a phrase, historians have become increasingly uninformed about what archivists have done and now do, and how past and future historical documentation has been and will be acquired and preserved.

Our own conversations about these issues brought together a historian with experience in using western, Soviet, and post-Soviet archives on Russian and Soviet history who had become increasingly aware of the forces and changing conceptualizations shaping the archive and an archivist with long experience administering a university archive and a state historical collection who had become increasingly interested in new forms of their scholarly use and understanding. Although both of us were by background very disposed to the notion of historical archives, we were struck by how much one of us did not know about archives and the other did not know about new directions in historical understanding. This book, then, is both an exploration of the changing elements of historical and archival practice and an examination of the increasing distance between the work, training, and outlooks of historians and archivists that we have come to call the "archival divide." It focuses on contested and changing notions of authoritative history, on the diminished role of historical authority as the governing premise of archival administration, and on the new divergence in the ways historians and archivists now process the past. It is intended to explore for historians how historically centered processing of archival documentation has yielded in the digital age to the demands of records management and administration; and for the archival community, how new concepts like social memory have changed historians' understanding of how the past can be processed analytically. It thus speaks in one voice to what have now become two very different audiences.

For historians, anthropologists, macrosociologists, and other scholars of history, we raise the problem of how historical documentation in both the past and future may be accessible and usable, and how changing archival technologies are affecting how we understand the production of historical evidence. For archivists in both public and private archives, we raise the problem of how to address the needs of present and future historical scholars. For both audiences, we suggest how new historical approaches, new technologies, and massive amounts of contemporary information may affect how societies in the future may process their pasts through historical archives now coming into being. Our book thus raises questions about how the past itself has and will be processed in the archives and how as a consequence historical knowledge has and will be shaped.

Some Background

Since antiquity, archives have been the place where socially important records have been housed. The very notion of *arkheion*, as Jacques Derrida has famously argued in *Archive Fever*, signifies a locus of social and historical authority, the place where those who guard the records of the past create and recreate social order.[1] Over time, as notions of political authority migrated ideologically to other spheres, archives were increasingly regarded as locations of authentic records. Their materials may or may not have been used to support state order. With the introduction in the seventeenth century of the principles of "diplomatics" (the study of the origin, form, and function of specific documents), archivists became identified with the practices of documentary verification. Their repositories were soon privileged as places of "authentic" records and documentary "truth."

In the process, a new conceptualization of archival authority emerged, embedded in authentic archival records. Archives became privileged locations for determining historical truth. European archives soon became a critical element in Rankean positivism and the new "objectivity" celebrated in R. G. Collingwood's idea of history. Authority in understanding the past came to rest on an acceptance of archival rationality and a faith in the authenticity of archival holdings. While that faith could be shaken by a false or falsified document, the fundamental link between the purpose of the archive and the purpose of history took firm root.

Our exploration shows that in the course of the nineteenth century, the space mutually shared by archives and history was defined collectively by historians who saw the archive as a window to real pasts and by archivists responsible for archival processes. This unified conceptual space represented a shared interest in the importance of institutions, prominent actors, and great events, as well as a shared sense of national boundaries and definitions. And, these interests were translated into the "authorities" that the archivists used in selecting, appraising, classifying, and preserving documentation. Once assembled and developed, this documentation in many ways then defined in turn the boundaries of historical scholarship, encouraging its focus on state formation and national definition. Archives themselves became actual, as well as figurative monuments to national pasts and future purpose.

This conceptual and methodological partnership, grounded in a shared epistemology, as well as sense of scholarly purpose, remained strong throughout much of the twentieth century. The first Archivist of the United States was an accomplished historian nominated by the American Historical Association. In Western and Eastern Europe, training as an archivist also involved comprehensive education in national history. Historians and archivists shared outlooks and a familiarity with each other's work. Beginning in the 1960s, however, and then accelerating rapidly in the last twenty or so years, the conceptualization of authority in history spread from institutions, agents, ideologies, and events to embrace broader social and cultural phenomena. For a new generation of historians, texts became objects of critical study, as well as modes of expression. Cultural forms and processes as much as historical events were understood to inform the history of identity formation and both formal and informal relations of power. In some scholarly circles, the "new historicism" in literary studies mirrored the historian's new interest in the roles of narrative forms themselves in shaping the ways societies processed their pasts. A new understanding emerged about how individual and social subjectivities might also affect how historical experience is processed. The complex problem of "social memory" became a central issue here. So did new understandings of power and politics, gender, ethnicity, identity, language, the nature of texts, and what might properly constitute a historical source. All of these issues also imply a multiplicity of historical pasts and empha-size their contested nature.

In and of itself, this expansion in the range of historical enquiry posed difficult problems for archivists. To what extent could one maintain that archivists were professionally obligated to incorporate these new fields of enquiry into the pro-cesses of document selection and retention? If so, were archivists also obligated to anticipate future areas of enquiry? Was this even possible? And what were the consequences for great state repositories of a shifting focus from clearly defined national narratives to more vaguely bounded cultural and social ones? At the same time, if society and culture are also central prisms of historical under-standing, does not the archive itself also reflect certain social and cultural pro-cesses? Who actually should determine what archives retain, and by what criteria? What is identified and processed as being of "historical interest" in the archives, and how do these materials get there? By what sociocultural and sociopolitical constructs are "authentic" records assembled, and how do they give certain his-torical narratives particular kinds of authenticity? Indeed, what kind of "au-thority" itself is embedded in records deemed "historical" and how does this validate particular kinds of historical understanding? These questions (and others) have moved archives from a place of enquiry to a subject of enquiry, from a locus for research to an object of research. In many places they have also pushed archivists away from their traditional partnership with historians, and, we main-tain, would have done so even without two new developments that threaten to rupture their relations completely.

The first has been the geometrical expansion of documentation—the problem of "bulk." Even the most historically minded archivists have been overwhelmed in recent decades by the exponential rise in the amount of records produced. As result, archivists have been pushed from their traditional custodial positions into uncharted "post-custodial" seas, as the archivist F. Gerald Ham has termed the new era, in which even major repositories like the U.S. National Archives have become limited in the amount of documentation they could preserve.

While struggling with these matters, archives and archivists were struck by another virtual tsunami, this time an epistemological one with its origins in new technology. On one hand, digitization offered extraordinary new possibilities in the ways archives could be described and understood. On the other, the very me-dium of documentary creation was transformed from paper records readily ame-nable to authentication to multiple and ubiquitous varieties of digital documents whose very stability, authenticity, and origin was subject to question.

We believe that this "technical turn" in its broadest conceptual sense has radi-cally reshaped archival practice, and in ways well beyond the view of most scholars in the humanities and social sciences. Archivists have suddenly had to be trained to understand the technical processes by which electronic records were generated, described, and preserved in the institutions or agencies that created them. While many scholars were moving away from the essentialist notions of historical processes that informed traditional political and institutional history, archivists have found it necessary to embrace what we will describe below as the essentialist categories in their understanding and description of the archival record: the "essential" relationships embedded in records that link them to the processes by which they were created.

But what in these new relationships has become of historical considerations, or even the broader traditional goals of preserving something commonly thought of as social memory, or the role of archives as the "custodians of the past"? Within this essentialist construct, the archive is no longer able to incorporate conceptualizations drawn from the ever-shifting boundaries of historical understanding, while history and its related fields can no longer affect the ways records are appraised and maintained. Moreover, given the interests of historians and others in a range of complex new social and cultural issues, the new divide between history and the archives threatens to affect the very ways future historical research can be done.

Our book is organized in two parts. Part I examines the historical relationships between archives and approaches to history, and how archivists and historians commonly processed the past. It concentrates on the issue and nature of authority in history and the archives, and analyzes in historical terms the opening of the "archival divide." Part II takes up new approaches to historical understanding in terms of their relationships to archives and their implications for changing archival practices. Because we emphasize the separations, what historians and archivists do and how they respectively think about what they do, the archivists among our readers will undoubtedly be familiar with some of the issues we raise in chapters 2, 3, and 8, and the busiest among them may prefer to concentrate on our discussions about historical scholarship (chapters 4, 6, 7, and 10). Historians, on the other hand, may be familiar with the various "turns" we discuss in chapters 1 and 4, as well perhaps as the "social memory problem" that we examine in chapter 6. For them, a quicker reading of what follows would pay closer attention to our discussions of activism and politics in the archives, the historical relationships between archivists and historians, the new material we present on "cyberinfrastructures" and digital archives, and the opening of the archival divide (chapters 3, 5, 7, 8, 9, and 10).

In our view, however, any visit by a historian to an archival institution is now an exercise in interdisciplinarity. We hope our efforts will allow scholars and archivists both to better understand the changing relationships between authority, history, and documentation that we explore throughout this volume.

FXB

WGR

PART ONE

THE EMERGENCE OF THE ARCHIVAL DIVIDE

1

Authoritative History and Authoritative Archives

Ten years after the collapse of the Soviet Union, the history faculty of one of Russia's leading new independent universities gathered to discuss its curriculum. Its members included distinguished senior figures, as well as a complement of younger scholars who had published extensively since 1991. The head of the department, one of the younger group who was also a prized student of a venerable senior, presented plans for realigning the curriculum to reflect more fully those offered by leading history faculties in Europe and North America. One new course was to incorporate the approaches of historical anthropology. Two others were to explore the symbolic language of political culture and the comparative semantics of historical understanding, focusing on works by Reinhart Koselleck. Still a third was to examine directly the full complexities of the "linguistic turn," offering students fourteen lectures and a series of associated seminars.

The plan created a furor, especially among the department's celebrated elders, who had managed to distinguish themselves through years of struggle against crushing restraints and repression by producing internationally recognized works of genuine erudition on prerevolutionary Russia, all marked by intensive archival research. They had achieved scholarly distinction in part by relegating theoretical prescriptions to conforming introductions designed to be ignored by all but the party hacks, but mostly, both within Soviet Russia and abroad, by scrupulous attention to the archives. One revered academician who mentored this group even made a practice of regularly dropping into the archives simply to make sure his acolytes were dutifully hunched over their archival files. His former charges learned their lessons well. They still talked about the anxieties of this scholarly attendance-taking with nostalgic fondness and pride.

The irony of Soviet-era historians defending authoritative archival research against the onslaughts of postmodern theory bespeaks the degree to which authoritative history itself, like the whole Soviet project, was (and is) a thoroughly modern enterprise. Like the initial efforts to build a modern Soviet Russia, its origins lie in structures of belief and practice that identify modernity with a rational understanding of social order and the ability, consequently, to tell its "story" accurately.

Like the now discarded twelve-volume *History of the USSR from Ancient Times to the Present Day*, published by the Academy of Sciences in 1980, authoritative history tells the story "scientifically." It fits seamlessly into its archival foundations, its arguments verified by authoritative citations. It authenticates understanding of the past in ways that are persuasive not only because they explain the present but also because they legitimate efforts to use scientific pasts to construct rational futures.

Embedded in this fusing of archives and history is both a modern optimism about human capacities to understand the past, once the impediments to scientific research are removed, and the roots of belief in the teleologies of "modernity," in which history can follow its rational course if the structures and beliefs that stand in its way are removed. Indeed, while the Soviet Union collapsed for many reasons, one of the most trenchant was that Soviet historical understanding itself became increasingly unconvincing, the future written into the official Soviet past was increasingly beyond any reasonable hope of achievement. It is not too much to say that official history thus delegitimized the late Soviet regime every bit as much as the "historical necessity" of revolutionary change had initially underlain the Bolsheviks' claim to power.

The degree to which history mattered in Soviet Russia only strengthened the commitment of serious historians after 1991 to work in a modern, scientific way. Many archives were now wide open. Hundreds of thousands of Soviet-era documents were declassified. Historians could finally allow these documents to freely "speak for themselves," providing new understanding of the Russian and Soviet pasts. Indeed, it was precisely these commitments to knowing "how things really were" that formed the crux of a much broader and deeply affective understanding of world and self. What possible value would a new curriculum have for new historians if it distanced historical understanding from its archival foundations?

History as Science

Paradoxically, given the distortions of Soviet historiography and the horrific price many scholars had paid for "misinterpreting" Soviet historical truth, the force with which the Russian faculty traditionalists resisted the innovations of cultural studies and historical anthropology reflected their own deep connections to the leading currents of nineteenth-century European historical thought. The idea that historians could actually know "how things really were" was, of course, partly the legacy of Leopold von Ranke, the phrase itself (*wie es eigentlich gewesen*), one of the most celebrated in all of European historiography. Ranke understood "scientific" precisely in terms of the "strict presentation of the facts, conditional and unattractive as they may be."[1] Authentic history scratched at the archival sources until an assemblage of facts revealed the forms and contours of events that could then be woven into narratives about change. The particular was the only path to the general. Interpretation flowed logically and convincingly from the assemblage of information. The meaning of history itself emerged naturally from the authority of facts, which spoke for themselves.

The archives were the authority for those "facts." Archives fused historical description and interpretation with what the repositories themselves inscribed as authentic documentation. Beginning in the 1820s with his *History of the Latin and Teutonic Peoples*, and throughout an astonishing career that spanned more than six decades and culminated with his nine-volume *World History* (begun when he was 82!), Ranke pursued scientific history with amazing energy and what our senior Russian historians might have called Stakhanovite productivity. The collected edition of his works comprised fifty-four volumes, one shy of Lenin's.

This Rankean "canon" of scientific history, as Leonard Krieger has aptly called it,[2] centered on the notion of objective truth, located first and foremost in the authenticity of historical documents and other artifacts. The task of the historian was not so much to interpret the object "object-ively," whether it was an archival document, manuscript, or physical artifact, but to give it its own voice. Scientific history privileged the object's own historical "statement" over any inclination scholars might have to use it for purposes of their own. This was not simply an argument about the relationship between facts and concepts. It was a construction of historical authenticity fixed to the documentary residues of the past. The logic of history, familiar to students in first-year graduate seminars ever since, was embedded in the relationships these objects formed with each other.

Historical rigor for Ranke thus meant above all a critical reading of the sources, especially texts. Weaving their stories into history could be properly done only by deciphering their specific meaning. Specificity had to be fit into the larger patterns this meaning reflected—the greater "chains of being," to use a conceptualization of the time. When Ranke taught his students about the "objectivity" of truth, he meant, literally, that *the truth was in the object*. The historian in this respect was also an archaeologist, digging with great care to reveal the buried actualities of the past. The historian's own subjective biases could no more change these actualities than the archeologist's predilections could make Greek vases into Roman. The self-scrutiny demanded by critical enquiry was only a means of avoiding mistakes.

This was the stuff of Ranke's famous seminars, that had as much to do with the establishment of history as a modern professional discipline as his prodigious writings. Ranke's authority as a master historian rested not only on the range and depth of his studies and the skills of his narration but on his own supposed detachment from the meaning they conveyed: it was what it was. This apparent "distancing" from the sources emerged through Ranke and others as the most important element in modern historical scholarship. It separated the works of serious academic historians from an older and persistent tradition of commissioned court histories every bit as much as contemporary academic historians distance themselves from "popular" history. As the German university itself became the model for both American and Russian higher education, Ranke's seminars became known in New York and Boston, as well as in Moscow and

St. Petersburg, as paragons of critical historical enquiry and training. Students found themselves immersed in paleography and sphragistics. They studied papyrology and numismatics. They learned the importance of linguistic nuances, as well as the need to set discourse into context. They found themselves absorbed by documents and virtually possessed by the excitement of deciphering. Veracity for many became an obsession. Facts—reality—uncovered with detachment emerged as the central element of all historical understanding.[3]

Ranke's empiricism is commonly traced to central currents of eighteenth-century Enlightenment thought and contrasted with the practice of history as the heroic telling of tales, a genre associated with the great medieval and early modern chronicles as well as Thucydides and the Greeks. In fact, an essential difference between Thucydides and Ranke was not their treatment of evidence, which the ancient Greek historian took very seriously indeed, but in the way Ranke and the new scientific historians seemed to allow the evidence to "speak for itself," as do the laws of physics.[4] The Enlightenment thus links Rankean history to Bacon and Newton in its emphasis on inductive reasoning and scientific objectivity, and to Descartes, Montesquieu, Voltaire, D'Alembert and the Encyclopedists, among others, in its critical thinking and concern for historical logic.

But it must also be traced to the concurrent emergence of a modern conception of archives. While one can hardly understate the importance of Bacon's *Novum Organum* and Newton's *Principia* in resetting seventeenth- and eighteenth-century mentalities toward an understanding of factual neutrality in its effect on historical imagination, the notion that facts were purely objective also underlay the idea that great documentary repositories could be organized and administered to serve historical truth. Every historical moment was capable of being understood if sufficient factual material was available in the archives. History could thus be more than art and literature in the same way science was more than hypothesis and theory. Uncovering its patterns and logics required first and foremost a skeptical attitude to unsubstantiated claims and rigorous attention to verifiable data. By the time D'Alembert's *Encyclopedie* appeared in 1764, history could be presented as "le récit des faits donnés pour vrais, ou contraire de la fable" (the reciting of facts given as true, in contrast to fables). Historical understanding transmitted orally from generation to generation created only "probabilities," the degree of which declined with each successive generation. History as it had traditionally been practiced was thus little more than "annales des opinions." To "penetrate the shadows," historians had to seek "le sécours des archives" (the help of the archives).[5]

Archives as Authentic Records

Until this eighteenth-century turn toward archives as sources of authoritative history, archives generally referred to records relating to governing and administration and the places in which they were stored. The word itself derives from the

Greek *arkhe* (government, rule), where *arkheion* also means a government building, but the notion of archives as records of various transactions is as old as civilization itself. The earliest known archives around Ur and other towns in the
Tigris–Euphrates valley recorded official decisions and transactions of various
sorts between and among rulers and ruled, first on clay tablets, later on papyrus
and parchment. Archives and the process of archiving itself connoted authenticity
and officialization. Both were at the foundation of an ordered society. As such,
both records and their repositories had to be ordered to facilitate the safekeeping
of certain social and political facts.[6]

The nature and scale of what was considered essential documentation naturally
evolved with societies themselves. Grants, decrees, benefices, privileges, judicial
decisions, land transactions, tax payments, and the recording of births, mar-
riages, and deaths became part of how most societies defined social organization
and conceptualized property. Their records signified "essential" social transactions. From *arkhe* and *arkheion* to the Latin *archivum*, archives in Europe joined
those in China and elsewhere in strengthening the governing institutions that
created them, constructing and reproducing social structures, political institutions, and values.

With the beginning of the Christian era in the West, the idea of "vital"
records took on an additional sacramental importance. Archives now gave
structure and social purpose to the church as the epicenter of community in
the ways it officially recognized birth, marriage, and death. The process of recording these life moments provided additional links between church and
state. From the late Middle Ages onward, chanceries and other centralized institutions were organized in Europe to prepare and retain these records in an
orderly way, and to adjudicate disputes, especially over properties and boundaries. In particular, documents were required to verify benefices and grants
from royal households or the Pope. Because of the pervasive influence of the
papacy, the papal chancery increasingly served as the model for documentary
form and retention.[7]

The modern idea of "record" as an object derives from these age-old activities
of forming a document as a "memorial" of transactions or social events. Hence,
too, the contemporary notion of archives as places that permanently memorialize
what societies and institutions regard as essential transactions. From these conceptions derive yet another common idea: that archives and their records somehow engage a society's "memory" by preserving the authentic records of its past.
We can see in this conceptual and institutional evolution an important broadening of the meanings of "authority" and "authenticity." The accuracy of the
records as transactions migrates to the legitimacy of the institutions that preserve them, and from there to the sacralization of its "authentic" values and "authoritative" beliefs. Even as particular forms of government changed, archives
endured as repositories of basic transactions, a symbol of historical continuity,
order, and truth.[8]

This focus on the authenticity of the transactional record was not without problems. Transactional records became so authoritative in Western Europe in defining ownership, property, privilege, and other matters that forgeries became a real problem. The same was undoubtedly true in China. Anthony Grafton estimates that perhaps half the legal documents remaining from Merovingian times and two-thirds of all documents issued to ecclesiastics before 1100 A.D. were fakes.[9] As records became the sole authentic source for information about social transactions, methods were required for verifying their authenticity. In Europe, analytical methodologies were developed most notably at the Abbey of Saint-Germain-des-Prés in Paris. By the seventeenth century, these had culminated in a set of principles known as "diplomatics," a term brought into usage by the Benedictine monk Jean Mabillon in his treatise *De re diplomatica* (Regarding the Study of Documents).[10]

Mabillon's interest was specifically in setting out procedures for establishing whether legal claims and charters were true or false. These norms tied the perceptual and intellectual attributes of documents to both their forms and their origins. They also implicitly expanded the archival role from one simply as "keeper" of the documents to one that included some degree of responsibility for their authenticity. Particularly in France, but soon throughout continental Europe, the archivist took on the difficult and often contested task of verification. Through a study of seals, handwriting, the context of its origin, and comparison with similar materials, the archivist would render a verdict on a document's authenticity.

Over time, archival documents (and archivists) increasingly became the primary sources of proof and verification in contested claims and disputes, commonly between royalty and the papacy, between lesser nobles, between communities and monasteries, and later among royal heads of state. In the process, conceptions of archives themselves evolved into places where careful research could resolve contested claims at the highest level, giving the idea of "judicious use" both literal and figurative meaning. As European fiefdoms gave way to more modern states, records were increasingly gathered in organized archival repositories. In 1542, the Castellan crown gathered together all records of local councils, courts, chanceries, secretaries, and treasuries. In 1610, James I gathered core documents of the English crown into what would subsequently become the Public Records Office. A year later, Pope Paul V established the Archivio Segreto in the Vatican, drawing in documents from the various newly established Curial offices and from those held in the Vatican Library.

All of these archives were, of course, private institutions in the sense that they were closed for any but official use, which added to their authoritative role. Since a decision based on the authentic archival record was implicitly authoritative, archives themselves gained further social and political position as places of reference, verification, and adjudication based on truth. In Hungary, for example, the mere fact that a document was kept in a town hall or other official repository was itself sufficient to consider it authentic. There was no such guarantee in France, but decisions or interpretations based on an archivist's careful review of its authorship and origins were also, by implication, practice, and linguistic construction, "author-itative." By the early sixteenth century, this process was greatly enhanced by the development of printing. The existence of multiple copies of an authoritative document meant that authenticity could be determined not only by intrinsic analysis but also by matching one printed copy with another.[11]

Expanding the Conception of an Authentic Record

The sixteenth- and seventeenth-century transformation of European powers into vast empires with transcontinental interests required new bureaucratic structures to facilitate connection and coordination through briefs, diplomatic or expedition reports, and other new forms of documentation. This transformation also expanded the nature of archives and archival documentation. Documents involving diplomatic reports and communication with imperial administrations related to a variety of nontransactional operations, interests, and events. In this developing milieu, the authenticity of documents could no longer be defined exclusively by the information they contained. They depended also on the importance of the institution, event, or process to which they were related, as well as their relationship to other, similar, documents.

As a result, documents were increasingly archived away in clusters (or "files" in current terminology). In turn, this meant that archival documents were no longer purely "transactional," that is, evidence simply of particular transactions. Instead, they came to relate in the aggregate to complex social and political processes, and included materials that were evaluative, descriptive, prescriptive, or advisory, depending on the intent and function of the officials (or others) who generated them. When printed materials began to be added to the unique manuscripts held in archives, the task of archival verification expanded as well, along with a significant growth in the quantity of documentation.[12] The expansion of European state administrations soon overwhelmed the scope and scale of these processes. Already by the eighteenth century and perhaps even before, archivists could no longer analyze or verify every document with the care and diligence that gave authority to the documents under their supervision.

All of this had important implications for the authority of the archive itself. Clusters of documents had to be catalogued, registered, and identified according to some form of protocol. A protocol system had to be developed that linked documents to the specific bureaucratic process responsible for their generation. Variations of this kind of system can be still seen throughout Europe, in the archives of tsarist Russia, papal Rome, and Spanish, Italian, and German states, among others. If a document could be verified by the assignment of a protocol number, its authenticity could rest simply on its being in the archives. It no longer warranted the scrutiny of "diplomatics." In a similar way, files of documents generated in the course of regularized and well-defined bureaucratic processes also became "true" representations of these processes rather than documents whose verifiable content authenticated particular transactions.

"Authority" in the archives thus migrated toward the politics of administration, rather than toward accuracy. The intrinsic truth of such materials derived from their authentic role within the administration of various kinds of political systems. Within the Archivio Segreto Vaticano, for example, some of the documents of the Apostolic Datary were designated as "processus" and stored in a series of bundles or "buste." These were essentially comprised of dossiers prepared to recommend candidates for various positions. The "protocolli" of the Congregation for the Index of Forbidden Books began to document the procedures by which printed books were reviewed. While the extensive files of the Vatican's Secretariat of State included a growing variety of reports, exchanges, drafts, and background documents, these diverse materials became authentic records of important Vatican administrative processes by virtue of their agency, even though the truth of their content now depended on how they were read and by whom.[13] Moreover, because veracity of the content of a bureaucratic record lay in the eyes of the beholder more than in an intrinsic analysis of its content, documents were stored in repositories with far less individual analysis. This led to the perception of the archivist as a custodian—an inactive participant in the process of records generation and retention.

From the seventeenth century onward, consequently, as European monarchical states blended the idea of personal and state power, their archives became, in effect, private documentary preserves that were both a sign and source of authority and power. The records of decisions, diplomatic negotiations, and state administrative processes stored in royal repositories and vaults were bound directly to the sovereignty defining the state. Access also defined the limits of this sovereignty, and in most of Europe, the power of divine right. What was public in the sense of pertaining to the commonweal was private in terms of access and use. Throughout most of Europe before the French revolution, entry into the archives and the right to consult official archival holdings was a well-controlled privilege. Indeed, to this day the Vatican Archives are still termed "segreto," reaffirming the jurisdiction of their control and access.

The Transformation of Historical Records

As with so much else, the "Age of Revolutions" changed basic assumptions about the relationships between knowledge and power, institutionalizing new understandings of history and historical purpose. Effected in the name of reason and the possibilities of social betterment, the French and American revolutions both made progress a core political value. Modernity suddenly seemed to have literal meaning. History and its human struggles were progressive, the ineluctable movement toward the relations and institutions of civil liberty and individual freedom.

In the process, archives gained dramatic new purchase as places whose authoritative holdings now had to serve a public good, especially in France. As the protections of private holdings changed along with understandings of privacy, especially with respect to the state, documents and materials considered the property of ruling political and social elites fell subject to the public's claims. In the flick of a revolutionary moment, many of the official records and documents of the ancien régime lost their contemporary authoritative value. Property rights, tax obligations, royal charters, and the like ceased to be the foundations of privilege and obligation. New records had to be created on the basis of radical changes in the law and the ways it was enforced.

Major changes took place immediately in France with the creation of the Archives Nationales in 1790. Legislation creating the archives specifically designated the records of the previous regime as historical documents, separating them from contemporary and future records. A wide variety of historical materials were soon brought under its care, including documents previously the private holdings of the royal family and the church. These and other records were brought into the archives as the vestiges of defunct institutions, not as inactive administrative records of ongoing functioning agencies. In terms of archival administration, they no longer held any authority in the transactional life of contemporary France. Their importance was specifically historical, and more important for our purposes, their very authority as historical records was reinforced by their coming under this new jurisdiction. A special archival staff well trained in French history became the keepers of French historical patrimony. Their colleagues in the archives who managed current documents and materials became, more modestly, guardians of France's public record.[14]

Similar changes soon occurred elsewhere in Europe as well, although notably not in Russia until the Russian State Historical Archive was created in Petrograd (St. Petersburg) after the fall of the tsarist regime, nor in the United States, where the National Archives was not created as a national historical repository until 1934. In Austria and Belgium records were soon gathered on the basis of their presumed historical importance. The English Public Records Office was created in 1838. By the mid-nineteenth century, the National Historical Archive in Madrid and the Archives of the Indies in Seville had also been organized to preserve a "national heritage." The former was devoted exclusively to the records of institutions no longer in existence and excluded all contemporary materials. The Archives of the Indies celebrated Spain's imperial past by assembling historical documents from Spanish dominions. In England, the Public Records Act of 1877 noted that all records prior to 1715 were to be considered of historical importance and could not be discarded. The date was soon extended backwards to 1680. While the shift toward historical record keeping was more gradual and less consistent elsewhere, especially in North America, by the end of the nineteenth century virtually all major archives had taken on the dual function of historical repository, as well as holder of current agency records.

In the process, the physical space of the archive also consolidated the notion of archival records themselves as "historical," ascribing additional layers of meaning to records that had hitherto been considered simply transactional or bureaucratic. "Historical records" thus came to connote value, tradition, and a usable past. By providing authentic documentary links to long and embedded national traditions, they also enhanced conceptions of power and political legitimacy. At the same time, particularly important moments of that past made relevant historical documents "particularly valuable," a designation which in Soviet Russia also came to serve as a broad basis for more restrictive systems of archival classification. "Transactional" and "bureaucratic" designations still remained for police reports, wills, deeds, court transactions, and other kinds of routine records, but for the most part, this also left them outside the purview of professional historians. Scholars went to a historical archive to research the true history of the nation as embedded in records of those individuals and offices with power and influence in state processes.

All of this activity represented a quantum leap forward for historical study, to use an appropriate scientific metaphor for the time. Implicit here was a new concept of access in which archival research, as Michel Duchein has noted, was increasingly recognized as a civic right.[15] In France, the attitude was more radical. In their concern for the public nature of state archives, French archivists began to work systematically to teach and apply republican concepts to archival administration. In 1821, L'École Nationale des Chartes was established as a new training academy specifically for archivists. By mid-century, graduates of that school were widely recognized as the best-trained and most historically educated archivists in the world.

Thus, the concept of popular sovereignty had not only shifted the notion of privacy in the archives from the state to the public, validating secrecy only if it could be justified as in the public interest, but also expanded the legitimating role of the archives into one that embraced accountability. Archivists trained at L'École des Chartes were not simply expected to be able administrators. Although they were trained primarily in the analysis of medieval records, their more important task was now to assure that France's national heritage was preserved and accessible to historians.

This was still a complicated matter, however, and became more so as the century progressed. As Lara Moore has shown, even within France the admirable goal of restoring order in the archives led to significant variations in archival policies that did not always serve the goal of accessibility. Subject categories varied widely; historians lacked systematic inventories; and the question of who should see what materials depended in practice not only on the independent judgment of the archivist but on varied systems of classification, which protected sets of documents on the basis of their subject or other, sometimes unspecified, criteria.[16]

Meanwhile, in the large part of Europe that remained monarchical, the private "royal model" persevered, although here new classification schemes also emerged that resulted in the redistribution of many kinds of papers into new legislative, administrative, juridical, or historical divisions.

Control over archival materials was not substantially different outside of Europe at this time. In China, for example, it was long common practice for the documents of a particular reign to be destroyed with the death of the emperor (sometimes along with those who kept the records). In the eighteenth and nineteenth centuries, the Qing dynasty introduced new methods for how records were held and preserved. Still, all materials were considered official secrets unless they fit into a specific category of matter that the Emperor wanted known.[17] Even in the wilds of Massachusetts, colonial and early national materials were reordered in the early nineteenth century into a set of what seemed to be sensible and common public or subject categories, rather than on the basis of any formal or uniform archival standard.

Despite new emphasis on the archives' public function, access for historians thus continued to be problematic even though the records of vanished institutions posed no obvious threats to political interests. While attitudes toward record keeping changed markedly throughout Europe in the early part of the nineteenth century, it took some time for archival administrations to reconceptualize their roles toward furthering historical understanding. In contrast to archiving contemporary documents, processing the past required a new sensitivity to materials that might be historically significant. Moreover, as records shifted from a private preserve of the autocratic state to the public preserve of a democratic one, the obligation to provide effective access for the public required new attention to retrieval and classification systems appropriate to a public trust.

The Growing Authority of Archives-Based History

These problems did not in the least diminish the ardor with which nineteenth-century Rankean scholars plunged into newly accessible materials. The very conceptualization of historical archives encouraged the Enlightenment notion that history could and should be explored scientifically, while the conceptual shift toward archives as public repositories opened vast new possibilities for research, along with new arguments for access to previously restricted holdings. Along with these openings came a delight in testing historical hypotheses, reporting scientific discovery, and pursuing rational analysis in history every bit as ebullient as in other realms of the nineteenth-century scientific imagination. The archives were in effect the laboratory stocked with authentic records that enabled the process of searching for the truth of the past in a rigorous, scientific way.[18]

What was obscured in this enthusiasm was how the historical imagination actually worked. While Ranke and others, steeped in scientific methodologies of the time, insisted that their critical reading of archival materials allowed the documents to "speak for themselves," a point still fiercely defended by our traditionalists in St. Petersburg, the authenticity of Rankean historical truths was embedded as much in the logical connections historians made between the facts that archival documents seemed to reveal as in their content itself. These linkages made logical order out of an endless welter of factual information, which is to say, created historical understanding. And this, in turn, opens the question of how Ranke (or any scientific historian) creates and understands this logic, how the archival scholar moves from historical archeologist to historical craftsman. It hardly diminishes Ranke's achievement to say that the authority of his interpretative logic, like that of Thucydides, was only partly related to the veracity of his evidence. It was also very much a function of the ways his form of argumentation reflected (and helped create) the increasingly popular nineteenth-century languages that tied science and scientific explanation to "natural" evolutionary patterns and historical teleologies.

It was through the grander notions of human progress that the emerging scientific historical imagination also engaged current philosophical issues concerning reality and historical purpose, argued especially by Kant and Hegel, as well as the subjectivities of discovery, enthusiasm, and devotion to the historical cause. Facts written out as an argument of historical logic obviously implied the existence of (ideal) meanings greater than the sum of the (real) facts themselves, whether that logic revealed "freedom" in its Enlightenment or Romantic orderings, or more simply the historical preeminence of sociopolitical institutions, as Ranke's studies themselves maintained. In one of his most Hegelian formulations, Ranke represented states as "ideas of God," manifested in the ways that everyday occurrences and broader events were intrinsically connected. They constituted a particular kind of historical force, one that might be seen as analytically autonomous from the events their actions constituted. States thus encompassed collective historical destinies. Their evidentiary traces could be read and studied as a reflection of collective historical experience.[19]

What is interesting about this for our purposes is not so much that it situates scientific history within both the currents of post-Enlightenment romanticism and the scientific mindset of the Enlightenment itself. It is, rather, that the new opening of the archives also began to entwine the romantic with the archival in what has proved to be an enduring element of scientific historicism. For many, there was the sheer romantic pleasure of opening new historical treasures, engaging the authentic if fragmentary shards of a really lived past. Research in the archives produced (and still produces!) a strong sensation of being transported back in time.

Most archival historians are quite familiar with the near magical qualities of this experience, however solid their scientific commitments. Boxes containing fragile and faded remnants of long ago events and transactions have the capacity to bring one into literal forms of contact with the past, stimulating even the most resistant imaginations. Uncovering new materials relieves the arduousness of research by opening new avenues of attachment. The authenticity of this historic world is affirmed as much by the historian's imagined sense of "being there" as it is by the contents of the documents themselves, even if only the latter constitute the scientific content of evidence. In the process, the archival experience itself can override more detached concerns about the nature or meaning of documentary authenticity: whether, for example, a document is true in the sense of not being a forgery or in the sense of truly representing "real" past life; whether it is authentic simply to the transaction that produced it or a "living" artifact of essential structures of the nation and state. A sense of historical authenticity, in other words, can be *felt* in the archive in the very experience of encountering real fragments of a really lived past.

There is ample evidence that Ranke had just such transportive experiences. Certainly, he engendered these pleasures in his students. Ranke loved archival work with something resembling real passion. He reported that materials in the Prussian archives that had been

> strictly closed but opened willingly to me . . . were the chief joy of my curiosity and were otherwise close to my heart. . . . To look at the world, past and present, to absorb it into my being as far as my powers will enable me; to draw out and appropriate all that is beautiful and great, to see with unbiased eyes the progress of universal history, and in this spirit to produce beautiful and noble works; imagine what happiness it would be for me if I could realize this ideal, even in a small degree.[20]

These subjectivities of archival engagement, as we might call them, were also famously reflected by Ranke's renowned contemporary, the great French historian Jules Michelet, whose writing of history was also cast within the discourse of scientific plausibility. Michelet's romance of uncovering was more than simply the passion of discovery. As every French historian knows, his excitement lay in the fantasy that dust-covered archival boxes were a point of entry to actual French lives, the ghostly remains, to use a Micheletian metaphor, of those whose traces were entombed in the archival sepulcher. This symbolic rebirth came for Michelet when he unfolded the documents, made the ink speak, and wrote dead authors into being. As he described it in a famous passage:

> I was not slow to discern in the midst of the apparent silence of the galleries, a movement and murmur which were not those of death. The papers and parchments, so long deserted, desired no better than to be restored to the light of day. . . . Softly my dear friends, let us proceed in order if you please . . . as I breathed their dust, I saw them rise up. They rose from the sepulcher . . . as in the Last Judgment of Michelangelo or in the Dance of Death.[21]

The magical qualities of archival work were thus rooted for Michelet not only in the excitement of scientific discovery but in resurrecting the dead, translating and articulating their voices, and saying "what they 'really' meant and 'really' wanted, since they themselves 'did not understand.'" From then on, as Benedict Anderson has suggested, the silence of the dead was no longer an obstacle for historians. Archives could now reveal their long buried feelings and desires as if they too were facts.[22]

It was something of a paradox, of course, that the emergence of scientific history in the nineteenth century clearly rested in some measure on subjective engagement with the authority of newly opened archives. The influence of historians like Ranke and Michelet on growing numbers of students was almost certainly as much an effect of the excitement they generated in exploring the archival *sanctum* as it was of their extraordinary scholarship. The authoritative archive thus stimulated a positivist history with broadly celebratory possibilities, creating a scientific foundation in an understanding of past reality for what were, in fact, ideal conceptions of historical change.

What matters most about these subjectivities, therefore, is not their exaggerated sentimentality. It is that the archives themselves, the objects of what Ranke in other places described as his "lust," were almost entirely repositories created for and around the purposes of new national histories, centered on the politics and policies of what was increasingly understood as a natural organic state. The overwhelming bulk of documentation housed in European archives—those newly designated in some places as historical, as well as those simply held in places of record—reinforced this notion. The new scientific history was thus driven "naturally" by the archives to an emphasis on politics and the nation. In other words, the archives themselves constructed a particular kind of social and historical knowledge. The documents they contained were not direct links to any random elements of the past, but to the functions and actions of the dominant political authorities whose transactions they reflected and whose interests and needs were served by their preservation. These logically became the agents to which scientific history assigned primary historical purpose.

Here was the clearest example of the convergence of archival and historical authority. To understand those institutions was, in effect, to view both the internal and external histories of the nation through the structural lenses of the archives. Historical conceptions rooted in the primary importance of political institutions were the central concern both of historians in their work to uncover the past and of archivists in their work to order and represent the extant historical record. For historians and archivists both, the subjective pleasures of uncovering and ordering history "as it really was" were linked as well to deepening commitments to particular kinds of states and their historical importance. In effect, the authoritative archival histories that Ranke, Michelet, Burckhardt, and others came to narrate in the course of the nineteenth century constructed in imaginative ways the great national histories their scientific scholarship itself supposedly had revealed. For Michelet, moreover, as well as others, the process of exhumation gave life and voice not only to the agencies of politics and the powerful, as with Ranke, but to the organic nation itself.

In 1869, for example, the British government funded Lord Acton to travel throughout Europe to consult continental archives concerning British history. In recounting the history of Renaissance Florence, Burckhardt sought to move beyond the positivist concern for a history of facts and to isolate the particular characteristics and genius of the Italian spirit. Burckhardt drew instead on the Romantic historiographical tradition represented by Goethe and Herder that stressed the organic nature of national cultures. While his work required "a total immersion in the primary sources of the period," as a historian of the problem has observed, Burckhardt was "not concerned with either the historical veracity of the data they contained or the need to write a political history of facts but with their status as historical expressions of the prevailing national spirit."[23]

German and Italian scholars were also now scouring archival materials in efforts to conceptualize the historical context of national ambition, a process that inevitably brought them to the still closed doors of the Archivio Segreto Vaticano, still administered as the private repository of a royal court. That these histories themselves played a central role in creating the nations they described is by now generally recognized by those who study nineteenth-century national development. At its core, the "invention of tradition" is about the logical connections between historicism and the perceptions of continuities between a succession of archivally verified events. The causes and consequences of events and the people who made them emerge as the essential agents of the nation as well as of history itself.[24]

From this perspective, what is especially striking about works like Ranke's and Michelet's magisterial histories of Germany and France, about *Die Osmanen und die spanische Monarchie im 16 und 17 Jahrhundert, Die römischen Päpste in den Letzten vier Jahrhunderten, Legends democratique du nord, Jeanne D'Arc, Histoire de la révolution française*, and other writings of comparable scope and sweep, is the order they imposed on the still disorganized welter of materials—one might even say documentary chaos—on which they were based. While scientific history was part of a broader nineteenth-century search for order and regularity, these qualities were more commonly imposed on the materials than drawn scientifically from them. The great syntheses that Fourier, Proudhon, Comte, and especially Marx distilled from their materials clearly derived from the same cultural mentalities that produced Darwin, Pasteur, Edison, and Freud. At the same time, history seminars evolved in the description of Herbert Baxter Adams "from a nursery of dogma into a laboratory of scientific truth."[25] Faculty and students became engaged with the notion that a search for the underlying "laws" of history, not simply its causal logic, might be related to the stunning new discoveries of order and regularity in the physical and natural sciences.

The study of history consequently emerged as a professional academic discipline by the end of the nineteenth century in large part because its enquiries and methodologies themselves became increasingly disciplined, that is, ordered and practiced according to accepted standards of evidence and proof. At the same time, the authority of these syntheses also rested on the ways their master practitioners tamed the documents themselves, and thus the historical chaos their disorder might otherwise have reflected. Gaining control over the documents was gaining control over history itself. Authentic archival documents were linked to discretely constructed notions of how history "unfolded." In the process, randomness was not simply reduced to the logical patterns of historical change; the patterns themselves acted to efface from the reader's understanding a sense of what the archives and documents themselves were really like.

In these circumstances, it is not surprising that the increasing enthusiasm for writing national histories in informed and orderly ways was also increasingly balanced by a concern that the story be "accurately" told. Even at the Vatican, Pope Pius IX came to feel in reading the work of contemporary German and Italian historians that the church's own contributions to the new national histories was greatly unappreciated and required its own scientific verification. In 1881 the door to the Vatican Archives began to crack open by order of Pius's successor, Leo XIII. The historian Theodor von Sickel, head of the Austrian Institute in Rome and educated at L'École des Chartes, was among the first outsiders to be given the extraordinary privilege of access. Because Sickel was a Protestant, there was every assumption among Vatican figures resistant to opening the archives that the results of his work would be biased against the Holy See.

Sickel himself, however, was most interested in demonstrating from a position of undisputed objectivity the authenticity of a particular tenth-century document, the *Privilegium Ottonis*, through which the first German emperor, Otto I, was reported to have pledged loyalty to Rome in return for an array of privileges and gifts. The document was long thought to be a forgery. Dispute over its authenticity was a thorn in relations between the Vatican and the emerging German state. Using scientific methods of verification, von Sickel was indeed able to show the document was authentic, allowing the Pope to confront the growing offensive against the Vatican's reach and power.[26]

That a Protestant could use the archives to prove a long-held claim of the papacy so inspired Leo XIII that in 1883 he published an order opening the Archivio Segreto. Despite opposition, the Pope justified his decision by arguing that history written scientifically could overcome inherent biases against religion and the church. Leo argued for the need for a "true" history that would, among other benefits, "show the Italian people what they owe to the popes of past centuries." Let scholars "work at the sources, use prudence and not rashness in judgment.... Go to the sources. That is why I have opened the archives to you."[27] Even the Archivio Segreto itself was now positioned as an authentic arbiter of historical truth. Using the Vatican's long closeted materials and well versed in Ranke's own skeptical history of the papacy, another German historian, Ludwig von Pastor, was able in 1886 to publish the first of his monumental forty-volume *Geschichte der Päpste*, which indeed, as Pope Leo had hoped, combined detailed archival scholarship with zealous Catholic sympathies.[28] Von Pastor's work was in essence a scientifically argued counter narrative to German and Italian national histories.

Modernizing Bureaucracies and New Developments in Archival Administration

By the latter part of the nineteenth century, the authoritative archive had thus set modern European historiography firmly on positivist feet. The passion for discovery displayed by Rankean scholars like von Pastor stirred extraordinary energy, easily rivaling that displayed by those in the natural and physical sciences. Like the authority of Darwin's fossils or Pasteur's laboratory, the authority of the archive lent credence to the notion that the history of social organisms also followed natural laws. New access to their prized holdings endowed the subjectivities of historical engagement with the rigors of objective research. The authority of "primary sources" assured historical studies a key place in the emerging disciplines of social science. Ambitious archival publishing projects like that initiated in France by Francois Guizot were designed to bring out the most "important unpublished materials on the history of our fatherland."[29]

As this occurred, the practices of archival administration also came under new scrutiny, partly to make them more scientific in their own right, partly because the nineteenth century also saw an explosion of new kinds of records and materials for archives to handle. Urbanization, industrialization, and the concurrent expansion of state and commercial activity all produced new streams of documentation. This occurred within still centralized monarchies like Russia, as well as more democratic and decentralized systems. In the private sector, as Alfred Chandler has shown, the growing national and international business firms that fueled the imperial ambitions of modernizing states generated their own prodigious amounts of documentation as they produced, extracted, and distributed goods over larger and larger areas of the globe.[30] The dull underside of both industrialization and empire was a vast quantity and variety of new records and record types.

These changes in the quantity and type of documentation held momentous implications for archives, just as they would again with the electronic revolution beginning in the 1990s. New approaches designed to preserve and strengthen the authority of the archive had to be developed. The most significant of these emerged with the publication in 1898 of the *Dutch Manual*, authored by three prominent state archivists, Samuel Muller, J. A. Feith, and R. Fruin.[31] The volume was a work of seminal importance. Muller, Feith, and Fruin engaged archives intellectually, as a set of theoretical as well as practical problems. They had little tolerance for the subject-based classification schemes so in vogue in the late nineteenth century. Rather, they concentrated their attention on what they thought constituted the authorities derived from the context of the record itself. In contrast to the principles of diplomatics, their solution was to focus archivists away from the documents themselves to an analysis of the processes by which they were generated. Records in the bureaucratic environment, they argued, were organically related to the processes that generated them. If these processes were authentic, the documents they produced had to be considered authentic as well, regardless of their content. This principle would form the basis for both an understanding and a description of archival holdings.

As the contemporary Dutch archivist Eric Ketelaar has suggested about his predecessors, the authors of the *Dutch Manual* were not wholly original in their thinking.[32] Muller in particular developed his ideas while attending lectures at L'École des Chartes in Paris. Similar approaches were being developed in Italy and especially Prussia, where German archivists were now addressing the problems of their repositories with vigor. But the *Dutch Manual* addressed the issues at hand with a new and compelling clarity. In opposition to the ways European archives had been defined and structured by officeholders rather than by their offices, the *Manual* asserted an organic link between the documentation and the office that produced it, superseding the claims of its authors. In effect, the *Dutch Manual* was insisting that the great family archives of Western Europe were full of what we now would recognize as "official" rather than "governmental" records that belonged to society, as well as the state. If this was the case, the *Dutch Manual* argued that archivists were professionally obligated to respect the organic link between the documents and the activity that produced them. The idea was called *réspect des fonds*. The administrative linkages and the original order of the documentation had to be identified as much as possible and preserved in the ways it was arranged and described in the archives. In addition to challenging prevailing notions of what constituted an authentic record, these new methods and frameworks pushed the role of the archivist toward records management, both within and beyond the dominant archives of the state.

These new conceptions of archival management were no longer limited to the records of government. Private corporate organizations of various sorts also had layers of organizational accountability for which archives were essential. Complex organizational structures depended on information flow through records production in order to function efficiently.[33] Both within and outside the state sector, therefore, organizational processes also had to be evaluated in terms of the ways records could and should be generated and preserved. For this to be done properly, archivists had to acquire knowledge about the institutions whose documents they would archive in order to assure the records "authentically" reflected an institution's essential administrative practices. Only on this basis could an archive show "respect" for *fonds*, preserving the organic linkage between agency and record group, as well as the original internal order of the records that comprised the specific group.[34]

By the early twentieth century, all of this had further expanded the archivist's professional role in Europe and North America. Even in archives that were not designated as historical, archivists increasingly acquired important new responsibilities within the institutions they served, and they had to be trained to assure consistencies between archival and institutional organization. Records of individual ministries had to reflect ministerial practices. Corporate documents had to authenticate the processes by which corporate policies were made, implemented, and were accountable. Catalogues and finding aids had to facilitate retrieval but now also had to serve as blueprints of institutional administration in order to assure the authority of their materials.[35] Archival "science," too, in other words, was developing rapidly as a distinct disciplinary field, along with the professional role of the archivist.

In the process, historians and others came to see archives not so much as repositories or compilations of past records, however much they housed court reports, birth and death certificates, and the increasing body of materials that modernizing states thought necessary to keep track of their citizens. Instead, archives were increasingly regarded as an integrated, systematic, and authoritative set of sources for processing the past of the nation-state. For historians and archivists both, historical science and the legitimacy an authoritative past conferred on contemporary institutions were thus secured directly to the authenticity of the archival record. The work of the historian and the work of the archivist converged on a conception of the authentic document as source and evidence: the "basic data" for disciplined historical research based on progressive scientific methodologies. Especially in Europe but elsewhere as well, historians and archivists both found themselves in new positions of importance. Archival history now constituted the foundation of all verifiable historical knowledge and the keystone of national historical understanding.

2

The Turn Away from Historical
Authority in the Archives

Although the United States came late to the process of creating a national archive, the close association between historians and archivists, between authentic history and archival documentation, developed and flourished here in other ways. By the time the U.S. National Archives opened in 1934, most American states had their own archival repositories. Most were also closely allied with local historical societies, a particularly American institution. Indeed, the first organized collecting of institutional records and personal papers deemed historical began in America as early as 1791 with the founding of the Massachusetts Historical Society. In subsequent years a number of like societies were organized to collect and preserve particular kinds of valued documents, confirming a local sense of what was historically important.

If big events like dynastic change and revolution largely defined the "historical" in Europe, Russia, China, and elsewhere, "great" events like the Civil War had a similar effect in the United States. Particularly after the 1860s, extensive efforts were made to assemble the historical documentation of the old South into state historical societies and archives so as not to "forget." Many states like Minnesota and Wisconsin also began to invest public funds in collecting their own historical materials, a process that greatly expanded the range of collections. Ideas about which particular stories deserved to be documented varied greatly in different localities. Nevertheless, the American collecting tradition strengthened the conceptual convergence between the authenticity of the archives and the idea of what was historically important, that is, between archives and history.

Most of these historical societies were privately established and funded, although many later became partly or fully supported by the states. It may well be, as Walter Whitehill has argued, that precisely because they were initially unfettered by government, they shaped a sense of the American past in the nineteenth century that was more removed from the state interests dominating European archives.[1] Be this as it may, local and state historical collections in the United States were no less devoted to creating a national historical hagiography, celebrating great men and interweaving their families with the events that their members and collection managers thought should define an American national consciousness.[2] Although their practices contrasted with the much more centralized processes structuring European archives in the nineteenth century, they were no less significant in identifying the importance of archives with historical understanding. Even without the demarcation between current and historical archives that underlay the creation of the Archives Nationales in Paris after the French revolution, American collecting practices nourished the Rankean romance between historians and their archives.[3]

The problem was that the particularly local focus of American collecting institutions created major gaps in the broader historical record. This was most notably the case with documents generated by governments themselves at both the state and national level. By now the European style of seminar teaching had introduced Rankean notions of structured, document-based research in all major American universities. This formalism required much more careful documentation of historical argument in the pursuit of American historical truth.[4] While some of this material could be found in local archives and historical societies where archivists were ready and eager to serve the new scholarly needs of their patrons, historians increasingly sought access to the broadly scattered records of state and national political institutions, emulating their colleagues in Europe. How could American historians write their own national story without the systematic preservation of documents of state? How could the United States stand with other modern nations without a National Archives? The interdependence between scientific history and authoritative archives had become an essential matter of professional historical interest.

History as Archival "Authority"

For archivists engaged in preserving a historical record, there was a fundamental reliance on historical "authority" in the appraisal and acquisition of documents. Although the term has centered much of our discussion so far, we put it in quotation marks here because it has both a general and specific meaning for archival practices. The general meaning connotes the reliance of collectors on the views of historians themselves to determine what constituted a proper documentary record of the past. Within archives, its more specific and technical meaning relates to practices of description. "Authority" in this context is a technical term. It pertains to the source for particular descriptive identifiers used to catalogue a collection of documents. The larger the collection, the more important the categories by which the material is arranged and described. The authorities used to determine these categories consequently create (or recreate) the conceptual framework in which an archival collection is set and known.

In European archival practices one line of authority derived naturally from a shared appreciation of the historical and institutional context or agency in which records or documents were produced. If we use records to mean a series of documents related to a specific state or social activity (births, deaths, court decisions, taxes, wills, property records, and the like), the organic connections between, say, birth certificates or baptismal records and social service or church agencies are obvious. Once they are verified as accurate, the value of these records, as well as the terms used to describe them, gain their authority from the transactional role of the generating agency. The process is similar for documents that are not specifically transactional in nature. The authorities used to describe correspondence, orders or decrees, individual diaries, architectural plans, and the like derive from an understanding of their context within organizational processes: the agency, function, or in certain cases, the particular importance of the person who generated the documents or files.

Archival authorities in this sense create the repository's organizational scaffolding. "Authority"-based descriptive terminologies derive from a specific archival conception of provenance, a term signifying that the agency of origin of a record or record group is its fundamental characteristic. Provenance thus describes an axiomatic and organic relationship between records and the processes that generated them. Although focused primarily on specific provenance-based agencies, the concepts underlying archival description also reflect an assumed relationship between documents and their sociopolitical contexts. Through the language of finding aids, these authorities associate the importance of records and documents with an understanding of the social, cultural, or political importance of the individuals, events, or institutions that prevailed at the time of their accession. The description of records thus embeds these authorities in the archive. Both explicitly and inadvertently, these associations create the elements of continuity between the dominant authorities involved in the creation of the documents and the ways the documents are understood and processed by those who are subsequently responsible for their care.

As historical exploration gained scientific credibility in the nineteenth century, the interdependence of disciplined historical enquiry and archives of all sorts made these matters relatively simple. On the European continent, as well as in China, Japan, Russia, and other parts of what was understood as the modernizing world, what historians regarded as important for an understanding of the past corresponded neatly with the institutions, events, or transactions that produced documents and records, and hence the authorities by which they were acquisitioned and catalogued. The passage of dynasties, reigns, or administrations separated materials into "historical" and "current" designations almost as readily as great events like the French revolution, even if access to much of this material was restricted. Current records receded into historical designations with the passage of time, if sometimes less systematically.

In the United States, historical societies and early state archives played a similar role. Both used historical authorities in determining which materials were to be preserved, how they were to be catalogued, and hence how the nation's past and purpose were to be understood. Their historical documentation was assembled to authenticate historical narration. Like more institutionalized European archives, American repositories also developed widely in the course of the nineteenth century on the basis of the now commonplace positivist ideal that a single historical truth could be discovered through a careful reading of documentary vestiges of the past. As we know, the American story of progress joined a belief in the centrality of individuals to the European emphasis on institutions in the formation of historical understanding. This extended something like the attributes of royalty onto America's great families, a perspective that found (and still finds) particular resonance in the veneration of sons and daughters of the American revolution, war veterans, and the political biographies of American presidents and other important political figures.

Especially after the Civil War, institutions of U.S. national government were also increasingly considered to be the bedrock of historical understanding. A democratic society structured by representative institutions, whatever their limitations, seemed a true reflection of American greatness—its own special claim laid out in a century increasingly marked by competitive imperial positioning in an increasingly conflicted world. As the geographical boundaries of the country expanded westward, a physically larger state meshed nicely with these conceptions: America's great men and great institutions became the common core of the great American national adventure, shaped and validated by authentic local documentation. In the process, the contextual authorities for American archival material increasingly derived from a convergence between the archivists' understanding of how materials were generated and their understanding of why and how that activity was historically significant.

In much of the western world, moreover, the demographic and economic changes that resulted from urban and industrial transformations also led to a great increase in records production, prompting new interest in the capacity of documentation to inform and guide government decisions and policies. New forms of documentation sustained the burgeoning governmental bureaucracies required to administer increasingly complex urban environments. The emergence of mass production and mass distribution also led to the development of more complex records systems within the private sector.[5]

To the extent that records were housed in archival repositories in both Europe and North America, and were organized and catalogued on the basis of generally recognizable historical authorities, archivists could easily assume the mantle of history's custodians. In the literal sense, they safeguarded important documents whose historical value they not only helped create but which increased over time by virtue of their very preservation. More figuratively, archivists became the custodians of particular understandings of national histories, since the authorities they deployed in processing these pasts structured an understanding of the agencies involved in defining the contours of a historical present and its possible futures.

Historical Authority and Custodial Management in Practice: The American Paradigm

Well into the nineteenth century and even beyond, it was common practice for tsars, mandarin emperors, and other leading state figures to appoint official historians to describe their accomplishments and assure their self-defined place in history. Russian and Chinese rulers developed this practice into an art form both before and after their respective revolutions, but it was and remains a familiar practice in less autocratic societies as well. Indeed, one of the great archival scandals of the nineteenth century occurred during the French second empire when a prominent historian and admirer of Napoleon Bonaparte attacked Louis Napoleon's official edition of his putative uncle's complete *Correspondence*, which Louis hoped would strengthen his own claim to power. In what came to be known as *l'affaire d'Haussonville*, a French baron showed the publication was not, in fact, complete, and detailed the obstructions he himself had experienced in accessing supposedly open materials. Stressing that his own arguments were firmly based on authoritative archival materials, d'Haussonville used his critique to challenge the second empire's larger claim to historical legitimacy. He also laid bare the politically biased practices of the Archives Nationales itself.[6]

The d'Haussonville affair was a salutary experience for the growing corps of professional historians in the United States, especially those who were cloistered by this time in new academic departments of history. Many were playing an active role in managing local or regional historical collections. Their students were engaged in the rigors of documentary analysis and preservation. Training in the new social science of history was becoming the most common route to an archival career. At the ninth annual meeting of the American Historical Association in 1893, held in Chicago in conjunction with the World's Columbian Exhibition, great attention was focused on presentations such as "The Value of a National Archives to a Nation's Life." According to Ellen Hardin Walworth from New York, "what the Bible is to the theologian, and what statute law is to the lawyer, the state archive is to the historian."[7] Shortly afterwards, J. Franklin Jameson, a prominent historian from Brown University and editor of the new *American Historical Review*, submitted a proposal to the AHA Executive Council for the "systematic collection, organization, and selective publication of source materials in American history."[8] As a result of these efforts, the AHA established a Public Archives Commission, instructing its members to report annually to the association on "the extent and conditions of public records in the country."[9]

It quickly became known that in contrast to Europe, the condition of public records in the United States was in great disarray. Documents and records of the federal government were often stored haphazardly by departments. Fires and mismanagement took their toll, especially as collections expanded. In 1877 and 1881, fires devastated important collections housed at the Interior and War

Departments. On investigation, it turned out that more than 250 separate fires had destroyed federal records since Congress first authorized the preservation of state papers.

The AHA also gained support in Congress. After the Association passed a resolution drawing the attention of Congress "to the importance for American history that . . . a hall of records would possess," Senator Henry Cabot Lodge of Massachusetts, himself a historian, began work on bill to establish a national American archive modeled on the British Public Record Office Act of 1833. Lodge praised the PRO as the institution that "established the magnificent glory of historical scholarship in London," and with J. Franklin Jameson, helped secure the support of Presidents Theodore Roosevelt and William Howard Taft for a U.S. National Archives.[10]

The AHA's Archival Commission urged systematic responses within records-producing agencies of government to the scholarly need for historical documentation. The quest for a National Archives in the United States was thus substantially based on the established authorities of American historical understanding, as well as on a perceived need to spread this understanding broadly. Accessioning records into a centralized National Archives was to be a source of validation for the authentic history of the nation, the ultimate authority over the past. While the thrust of these reports and early legislative initiatives was for a more systematic and safe way to present the essential historical records of the nation, Jameson himself was particularly mindful of the practical arguments for records retention. Using the progressive rhetoric of the time, the Association president stressed that good records retention policies would also make the government more efficient.

Like other leading historians of the time, Jameson was also well versed in European archival practices. In assessing the condition of government records in the United States, he and others looked to replicate European models for archival institutions that sustained scholarly exploration of the history of the nation. In 1906, he traveled abroad to meet with the heads of major European archives and returned home further determined to make all possible documentary sources available to America's scholars as "the first requisites for a 'scientific' history of the country."[11] While America's various historical societies were ready and eager to serve research needs, Jameson viewed their selection and acquisition of manuscripts as parochial, "feeble and myopic."[12] He found unacceptable that venerable institutions like the New York Historical Society, one of the country's oldest and most distinguished private repositories, had by now become a membership-based institution whose library seemed largely devoted to the genealogical validation of the old aristocratic families.

By contrast, archivists in Germany, France, and elsewhere in Europe, placed a new emphasis on retaining government records for their possible use by historians, rather than taking the risk of destroying them for short-term practical gain. By the first decades of the twentieth century, the process of codifying professional archival practice had integrated the notion that "the scholarly archivist had to be consulted at an early stage and to be given a decisive influence, both in order to save the valuable and to discard the worthless."[13] German manuals began to note the importance of age, content, and placement of bodies of documentation within administrative hierarchies in the processes of appraising their historical value.

Jameson's thinking also reflected the emerging European conception of a "custodial" archivist, a concept that soon became fully elaborated in the writings of the English archivist Hilary Jenkinson. Jenkinson argued forcefully that professional archivists had to adopt a passive, noninterventionist position when it came to transferring and archiving active bureaucratic records. The archivists' role was to assure the records under their care had emerged from an authentic process of creation and to act simply as their custodian, overseeing for the state the needs of accurate records production and retention. What documents were created and what records were to survive was not the archivist's business, but a matter for the originating agency to determine. Sometime Keeper of Records in the British Public Records Office, sometime lecturer at Cambridge and the University of London, Jenkinson eventually drew his ideas about the archivist's custodial role together in a new *Manual of Archival Administration*, one that quickly rivaled its Dutch predecessor in importance.[14]

Jenkinson's influential volume was, however, more than a simple administrative manual. It defended a specific, unique, and in Jenkinson's view, highly moral position of archival neutrality, assigning a professional identity independent of persuasion and historical judgment. The archivist "ought not to be an historian." His [or her] role was to be "the servant of his archive first."[15] Rather than becoming skilled in diplomatics-based evaluations in the pursuit of documentary authenticity, archivists in the state's expanding bureaucratic milieu were simply to be receivers of records whose authenticity lay in their organic relationship to the bureaucratic processes that generated them. As these conceptions became broadly accepted, the passive custodial position of archivists as "keepers of the record" emerged as the hallmark of archival professionalism, even within historical archives.

While these transformations began to distance professional archivists from historical analysis, they still remained focused on the evolution and influence of government institutions and state officials, and hence on the central historical questions of the day. They stemmed not from new understandings of history, but from a recognition that the production of administrative documents was increasing rapidly and the professionalization of their archiving required more sophisticated methods for arrangement, description, and especially retrieval. The development of the modern finding aid thus gave further authority to the documents by clarifying their linkages to the originating agency's purpose and function. (More developed front matter with extensive "agency histories" and scope and content analysis is a largely American contribution of the mid-twentieth century.) A "series description" was soon devised that divided the records according to their physical arrangement in the offices where they were generated, while the "file folder" structure, with its specific file and folder headings, came to mirror the structure of the materials themselves as they were produced. A key advantage of Jenkinson's "passive" approach was that it discouraged any rearranging of these structures, preserving the seemingly clear historical picture they reflected. Established forms of organization and retrieval could simply be expanded to accommodate new materials.[16]

In this way, archivists were also discouraged from destroying records or restricting their access. Ideally, all files generated by a state agency or private organization were simply to be transferred from their creators to the archive. While the growing scale of documentation meant that selections increasingly had to be made about what records should be retained and who should be permitted to see them, these again were not to be decisions for the archives but the responsibility of the institutions generating the records. Historians could expect to find all available materials in an archive that initiating agencies themselves had not restricted.

The Jenkinsonian conception of the archivists' custodial role was soon universally recognized in the United States as the foundation of modern archival administration, although it was seen not so much as a question of archival theory as efficient archival practice.[17] Indeed, archival administration was still largely a task for historians in the United States. So many historians were engaged in archival administration that the American Historical Association began to convene a separate annual conference for its archivist members. a gathering that soon developed into the independent Society of American Archivists (SAA). At the same time, when the cornerstone of the National Archives was finally laid in 1933, a model of archival management had essentially emerged in the United States, in which the archivist and the historian were seen as pursuing tasks that were professionally distinct but entirely consonant in purpose, each working closely with the other in the use and preservation of essential historical documentation. Herbert Hoover celebrated this mutuality with exuberance at the 1933 dedication:

> The romance of history will have living habitation here in the writings of statesmen, soldiers, and all the others, both men and women, who have built the great structure of our national life. This temple of our history will appropriately be one of the most beautiful buildings in America, an expression of the American soul. It will be one of the most durable, an expression of the American character.[18]

In this heady atmosphere, it is hardly surprising that the Executive Committee of the AHA assumed that the new position of Archivist of the United States would have to be occupied by a distinguished historian. Acting on the AHA's recommendation, President Franklin Roosevelt appointed R. D. W. Connor, professor of history at the University of North Carolina and secretary of the North Carolina State Historical Commission, to the position. Among the staff of 300 that Connor chose to assist him in managing and appraising documents for their historical value, seventy-four had MAs and thirty-two held PhDs. One hundred and sixty additional staff members were college graduates with at least some training in history.[19]

Challenges to the Custodial Model

To see how solidly archival practice in the United States was oriented around custodial practices in the service of history and historians by the mid-1930s, one need only look at the façades of the grand neoclassical National Archives building in Washington, D.C. There chiseled in limestone were reminders that "The Glory and Romance of Our History are Here Preserved in the Chronicles of Those who Conceived and Builded [sic] the Structure of Our Nation"; "What is Past is Prologue"; "Study the Past"; "The Heritage of the Past is the Seed [of the Future]." When the two most sacred documents of American history, the Constitution and the Declaration of Independence, were moved to the building from the Library of Congress, they came with a full military escort and were housed in what was designed as an altar of repose.[20]

From the very moment the U.S. National Archives opened its doors however, the archivist-historians responsible for its administration encountered serious challenges to the ambitions they brought to the capital. The new Archivist of the United States, R. D. W. Connor and his colleagues were well aware that the majestic "Temple to Clio" on Constitution Avenue would house the prosaic records of state administration, as well as serve as the "permanent repository of American historical source material," as FDR put it in congratulating Connor.[21] But like other monumental projects that take too long in the making, the tasks for which the Archives was originally designed had now become much more extensive and problematic. The sheer weight of organizing and accounting for what had become a large and rapidly increasing output of bureaucratic processes was daunting. The burden of these responsibilities quickly affected the day-to-day work of identifying, selecting, ordering, arranging, and housing even most routine materials.

Unlike their European colleagues, moreover, the Americans had no standardized manuals to guide them. Instead, Jameson and others had long emphasized that "the authority of history" itself would inform the archival processes of selection and retention.[22] Yet it was no longer an easy matter to translate the functions of custodian of the historical record into the orderly management of tons of material that government departments at all levels were now transferring to the archivists' custody. There was also the problem of assuring that records thought to have historical value were properly retained by individual agencies, as well as the need to persuade some of the government's most important bureaus to relinquish materials that some officials regarded as too sensitive.

At the same time, the very opening of the National Archives strengthened the authority of history itself in U.S. repositories during the 1930s as well as new national and local interest in documenting "the great American story." Among the other undertakings of FDR's Work Projects Administration (WPA) were the Historical Records Surveys, a massive effort to survey historical records all over the nation wherever they might be housed. In turn, the large number of reports that emerged from the canvas of materials held by churches, town halls, libraries, historical societies, and prominent individuals, among other sources, stimulated awareness of American historical documentation more broadly. At the new National Archives, Connor and his staff began to supervise the preparation of detailed indices for records series on cemetery interments, military service, newspapers, and the like, as well as the U.S. national censuses, whose data was still locally held.

The transformation of the archives from a storehouse to an accessible repository was thus a complex matter requiring substantial new work in arrangement and description. There were other challenges as well. It was soon apparent that the sheer bulk of material now coming under the National Archives administration presented problems as monumental as the new building itself. When Solon J. Buck succeeded Connor in 1941, his greatest concern was with "this elephantine records management problem."[23] By 1943 there were more than 16 million cubic feet of government records, only half of which were in Washington.

The Second World War increased this volume exponentially, even with the passage of the Records Disposal Act. By 1945, Buck felt it was becoming impossible under these conditions for the National Archives to manage an adequate program of records administration.[24] In David Lowenthal's felicitous phrase, archivists were becoming adrift in the "chaos of accumulation."[25] In the view of Buck's assistant Philip C. Brooks, the problem of records administration "was to the archivist of today what the study of diplomatics was to the archivist of earlier times—and more . . . The complexities of modern administrative documentation have so multiplied the technical facets of filing that many persons regard it as a mysterious cult."[26]

By what criteria, then, should a document be judged worthy of retention? What set of questions should govern the retention of whole series of records? And what, in particular, was the role of historical understanding itself in shaping the appraisal criteria? Could new archival authorities be usefully derived from historical study—new authorities to guide the processes of selection and retention when the production of documents was increasing so rapidly? The historical authorities that gave most collections their categorical identities were localized and unsystematic. They could not provide the conceptual framework for ordering the scope and content of the vast array of records that now came under National Archives control. The technical concept of "authorities" had to be given a more refined and effective content.

The pages of the *American Archivist* during these years show how the growing archival profession was working on a number of conceptual fronts. In 1944 Hilary Jenkinson himself focused on the value of archives as "sanctuaries" for "evidence" in the hope that in the turmoil of the postwar world there would be ample resources for both reconstruction of archives and an appreciation of them as a "means of knowledge."[27] The April issue of that year also contained a model act for individual American states for the creation of Departments of Archives and History whose language identified among their objectives "the stimulation of research, study, and activity in the field of [name of state] history."[28] In the 1950s archivists began to probe the nature of documentation for emerging subfields of historical study. Paul Lewinson of the National Archives, for example, provided an analysis of records relating to the modern labor movement.[29] Fritz Epstein delivered an overview of research resources in the Washington area relating to the Second World War.[30] Oliver W. Holmes wrote on developments in the formation of historical collections by U.S. businesses and Eldon S. Cohen and Seymour V. Connor wrote on French archives in Indochina and American legal materials as new historical sources.[31] The pages of the journal were becoming a bridge between those exploring new topics in historical study and those who had some understanding of the sources that were most likely to be useful.

At the same time, new ideas were emerging about how to define the role of the archive bureaucratically within the structures of government. Influenced by European emphasis on *fonds* and *provenance* as categories of bureaucratic structure and behavior, archivists such as Margaret Cross Norton, of the State Archives in Illinois, and Theodore Schellenberg of the National Archives, began to argue that archival structures in the United States also had to reflect in a uniform and systematic way their relation to the institutions that created their materials.[32] Although their views of the archival profession varied in important respects, they both echoed the English and French by emphasizing national archives as a bureaucratic function of government obligated to serve the state and its institutions. They existed primarily as holders of the evidence of governmental transactions and decisions, as well as a repository for information gleaned in the process of governmental operations.

Appraisal in this perspective was not so much a question of determining the historical importance of the records themselves. It concerned instead the presumed importance of the creating agency or the completeness of the accumulated information. In other words, documents were to be archived because of their importance in understanding the institutional context of the record group itself. In effect, the archive was to privilege the institutional over the historical. History would be served only by implication insofar as the institutions whose materials were archived remained seminal actors in producing knowledge of the past.

This model also suggested the need for an independent archival profession, one that needed its own language and procedures in response to the complexities of contemporary state records production. Historical authorities were not explicitly dismissed in these circumstances but their value was now largely based on the fact that the records of government remained central to current historiographical concerns. Most historians could therefore assume that good archival practice would assure the preservation of records critical to what they needed to know. At least to archivists like Norton and Schellenberg, the key here was to develop the most sophisticated system for administering agency materials either by placing employees of the National Archives themselves in the most important government offices or assuring these offices hired their own trained archivists to manage their papers. In essence, the administration of archives was to become a function of American government.

The Advance of Records Management

These ideas took increasing hold. By the end of the 1940s, the National Archives itself had become part of a new National Archives and Records Administration within the government's General Services Administration, losing its institutional independence if not its administrative autonomy to an agency whose mission and concerns were storage and administrative infrastructure. To the dismay of most archivists and historians, this placement diminished the scholarly profile of the archives in the name of government efficiency. Although rhetorically still a "temple of history" and a "sacred place of historical memory," the Archives was increasingly challenged by the comparatively mundane bureaucratic necessities of records management.

As debates about these approaches soon revealed, the very notion of "records management" carried a logic far removed from the premises of historical preservation. Discussion also took place in venues rarely frequented by historians, and while it touched directly the practices that affected how they could do their work, it had little if any resonance in the historical community. None of the principal manuals of historical method published by historians in the 1950s concerned themselves with the relationship between systems of record keeping and the historical value of the records they preserved. Jacques Barzun, Louis Gottschalk, Marc Bloch, and other distinguished scholars seemed to take archives as a given for historians, unproblematic in either their practices or their relationship to the construction of historical understanding. On one hand, the presumptive relationship between archives, archival administrative practices, and historical understanding remained unquestioned and unexplored.[33] On the other, the profession of history dedicated to the study and interpretation of the past was moving away from professional archivists increasingly dedicated to the maintenance of institutional archives.

In these circumstances, the Society of American Archivists (SAA) rapidly developed into a robust professional association after splitting from the American Historical Association, organized to promote sound principles of archival administration and to facilitate cooperation between archivists and archiving agencies. Increasingly in the 1960s, its journal, the *American Archivist*, focused on developing new professional standards for managing complex records. As the association's membership grew, the journal's pages also began to air very different points of view about how records should be managed. The questions inherent in these problems were also seen as "archival" ones, to be handled by those who had committed to the identity and practices of a professional archivist despite their training as historians.[34]

This concern for the management of archives also continued to develop well under the radar of historians, as the "Loewenheim case" came to demonstrate. In 1968, the historian Francis Loewenheim charged that a staff member at the Franklin D. Roosevelt Library had withheld six letters crucial to his research in order to advance the staff member's own project. In response, the Organization of American Historians (OAH) and the American Historical Association formed a joint investigative committee, ignoring the Society of American Archivists (SAA). Even though the historians subsequently found in favor of the Library, the SAA membership was outraged at being left out of a matter they felt should have been looked into first and foremost by the archival profession itself.[35]

While the archivists' umbrage measured the degree of their own professional distancing from historians, the pressures for professional independence only strengthened after this incident. With characteristic understatement, the secretary of the SAA, Robert Warner, noted in his 1972 report that "there were many unfortunate aspects of this case, but from the archival standpoint one of the most serious aspects was the virtual exclusions of archivists from [its] adjudication. . . . In all fairness to the historians, I do not see this in any way as a studied insult to our profession. I see it merely as an oversight. For the most part they simply were not aware that we had a professional society, and those that were did not think it important enough to be involved."[36] With Philip Mason, a historian and archivist serving as director of the labor archives at Wayne State University and the historian Herman Kahn, director of the department of archives and manuscripts at Yale University's Sterling Library, Warner began discussions with the OAH and the AHA in an effort to redefine their joint committee structure and to assure the SAA was included in all matters pertaining to historical archives.

Along with others in the SAA, Warner hoped to establish a strong presence for archivists as an independent profession. He believed strongly that the archivist was not a historian, and decidedly not a librarian or curator. Archivists were professionally distinguished by particular values, methodologies, theory, and especially training. The SAA had to be a visible, active, and effective force in developing the archivists' unique identity.

Both the Loewenheim case and a new Joint SAA-AHA-OAH Committee on Historians and Archivists thus underscored the extent to which the world of the professional historian and that of the professional archivist had separated institutionally. Yet the outrage and the nature of the solution also underscored that despite the acrimony, the SAA, AHA, and OAH shared a mutual sense that archives also existed to serve historical understanding. As Warner insisted, while archivists and historians now had different professional roles and identities, they also commonly recognized the centrality of archives to the historian's craft.[37]

New Archival Thinking

Subsequent discussions in the 1970s moved archivists even further beyond a sense of professional exclusivity. At their annual meetings and in the pages of their journals, archivists began to occupy a new position of conceptual independence in which the fundamental nature and purpose of archival work was more and more removed from the work of professional historians. This increasingly independent mindset not only gave archivists an even more distinct professional identity but also led them to further redefine their professional roles. For example, F. Gerald Ham, the State Archivist of Wisconsin who also held a Ph.D. in history from the University of Kentucky, began to argue that the sheer bulk of the records coming under the purview of state and national archives was pressing archives well beyond their history-serving custodial roles. The exponential increase in the quantity of materials required archival processes that focused on *eliminating* records rather than preserving them. Bulk, in other words, meant archivists had to make preserve-or-destroy decisions.

Ham consequently called on archivists to investigate new technologies for the storage of information, to think through more complex approaches to the appraisal of materials, to identify new systems for records scheduling and for the routine transfer of records, and to address the new complexities that derived from "right to know" and other new privacy legislation. In effect, he argued for a new and radical interventionism. The archivists' tasks would have to be governed not by anything resembling historical concerns but by an agenda that was archival in conception and designed to serve the archivists' managerial needs.[38]

Understandably, Ham's views generated controversy within the archival community. Arguing against them, Frank G. Burke, an information retrieval specialist at the National Archives and former head of the Manuscript Division of the Library of Congress who like Ham also held a history Ph.D., urged that archivists preserve a historically oriented approach. Archives and their records still had to be understood in terms of the societies that created them, despite the exponential increase in the production of documents. Although Burke was one of the first National Archives administrators to advocate the use of new technologies to store and retrieve archival materials, he did so, in contrast to Ham, from a clear historical and sociological perspective. "What is it within the nature of society that makes it create the records that it does?" he wanted archivists to ask. "What are the sociological aspects of records management?" "What is the nature of history, historical fact, and historical thought?" And how should these questions affect the ways documents are assessed?[39]

Burke maintained that archivists needed to focus on these theoretical and analytical issues in order to formulate collections that would illuminate the past. His point of departure was the now challenged perspective that at its core, archival management was part of the same vital set of social interests and needs as history itself. In effect, Burke's views pointed in the direction of a new archival historicism. He insisted archivists incorporate a sense of historical understanding into the core of any new archival theory. In contrast, Ham was now positing that archives had entered what he called the "post-custodial era." Rather than be concerned about history, archivists needed to focus on the increasingly complex technical questions of records management, storage, selection, and description—concerns for which historiographical understandings seemed marginal.

These discussions were further complicated by sharp exchanges over policies relating to the papers of public officials prompted by the Pentagon Papers and the Watergate affair, both of which touched issues at the core of the archival management debate. What kinds of materials should archives collect and retain, and when (and to whom) should access be provided? And how, in fact, should these decisions be made, and by whom? For most historians, the central issue in both cases was one of access to the "complete" historical record and the relationship between archival secrecy and the integrity of a democratic state. For most archivists, and especially those persuaded by Ham's new approach to the problem of records management, this focus on broader policy debates seemed naïve. The issue instead was to develop creative responses to the increasingly intractable problems of quantity.

Not surprisingly, given the growing distance between the archival and historical professions, the views of Ham and Burke and the intensive discussion in archival journals received little if any attention from historians, who still assumed that the relationship between archives and historical knowledge was and had to be "history driven." Historians continued to embrace what archivists were now regarding as the outdated custodial model, itself in their view rather quaint. Insofar as historians were interested in understanding the new problems confronting archivists, these seemed largely technical, organizational, and even rather boring—very much outside the boundaries of historical scholarship and the historians' academic concerns.

Perhaps for this reason, the voice of one prominent historian acquired inordinate influence among archivists. In a scathing review of the question in the *American Archivist*, Lester J. Cappon, editor of the Adams–Jefferson letters and a distinguished research fellow at Chicago's Newberry Library, openly ridiculed Burke's historicist position. In a haughty tone that could not have endeared him to his archivist readers, Cappon insisted instead that Burke's theoretical concerns were solely the "province of the historian," not the business of archivists. History was and is "what historians do," not something for archivists to be concerned about. Reaching back to Hilary Jenkinson, the classic defender of the custodial approach to archives, Cappon posited that "archives were not drawn up in the interest of, or for the information, of posterity." They simply kept the records that institutions and individuals wanted them to keep and had to do so "impartially" and in ways that preserved their "authenticity." These were the two common qualities of supreme importance to archivists. Records had to "tell the truth." Historical concerns could only "compromise the status of archives as a separate discipline, maintaining the *integrity* of the records as its first principle."[40] Here, in other words, was a contemporary version of the now well-worn Jenkinsonian vision of the scientific historian being aided by passive archivists charged simply with preserving "authentic" documentation.

The "Cappon effect," however, was not to restore the preeminence of Hilary Jenkinson, whose notions of archival impartiality had rested on an unquestioned acceptance by historians that curators would receive, catalogue, and take good care of all the materials "history" sent their way. Cappon's rear guard reaction ignored the critically changed context to which Ham and Burke were reacting.[41] Although the need for some level of historical understanding still remained part of the thinking within the archival community as a whole, archivists in the main increasingly agreed with Ham that their urgent priority was defining new usable principles and processes to guide what had become of necessity an interventionist, rather than custodial approach, one that could only marginalize historiographically derived authorities even further.[42]

As the growing literature on the question increasingly made clear, the archivists' sense of urgency came from three areas: the increasingly intractable problem of "bulk," the growth of multiple archival constituencies, and changes in the private archival environment.

The Insurmountable Problem of "Bulk"

By the end of the 1970s, American archivists along with their colleagues in other nations recognized the sheer practical impossibility of retaining the vast majority of diverse materials that societies were now generating about themselves. There was simply not enough space to properly house the records. Public officials with growing staffs were producing more documentation. Everett Dirksen in his eighteen years in the U.S. Senate generated more than 280 linear feet of records. The presidency of Ronald Reagan generated 13,470 linear feet. The very short term of Gerald R. Ford generated more records than the entire presidency of Franklin D. Roosevelt. These numbers only hint at the total volume of records that were now being produced by public officials and their associated offices in the United States and elsewhere. Even relatively small institutions like universities and corporations were becoming more bureaucratic in the production of documents, generating hundreds or more feet of records per year.

What to save? What to discard? And by what criteria should these decisions be made, even assuming some new funding and space could be found? What was needed to solve these questions was not simply an awareness of potential historical value but some new set of authorities that could guide archivists in selecting, from the growing mountain of material, the documents that held the most social and historical value. And once these difficult decisions were made, it was necessary to construct more adequate structures and processes for their retention, organization, and retrieval—the essential elements, in other words, of a new, post-custodial "interventionism."

Factors governing the selection of material thus became dependent on the practicalities of space, budget, and institutional politics, usually in some slippery combination. When public agencies transferred material to the archives without themselves making the decisions about what should be retained or destroyed, archivists had no choice but to use their best judgment in determining what social or institutional needs the material might serve. In the process, established historical authorities were necessarily subordinated to what might be regarded as the mundane considerations of practicality. What was left of the historic partnership between historians and archivists was reduced to the archivists' assumption that what they managed to preserve would somehow prove useful to historians in the future.

"Multiple Constituencies" and the Changing Private Environment

The further subordination of historical authorities in the definition of archival collections also came from pressures on archives to serve a broader public, as well as from the changing environment of private archives. Who were archives intended to serve? Those in the archival agencies of government could possibly gain a greater edge in seeking funding if they were perceived to serve a broader range of users. The focus of many public archives consequently shifted further from the needs of academic history and historians toward those of a broader public, as well as various contemporary organizations and social groups.

The move in this direction was signaled in part by a change in archival terminology. Records deemed of long-term significance began to be thought of as having not "historical" but "enduring" value, a term coined by Larry Hackman, the entrepreneurial Archivist of the State of New York.[43] Archivists quickly adopted this new word as a way of neatly expressing their broader mission to a wide range of constituencies. The idea of the "historical" was further pushed to the margins as this linguistic shift strengthened the alliance between records retention and the current political, administrative, and cultural needs of their supporting institutions or agencies, rather than between archives and their scholarly users.

It also reflected the growing influence of Margaret Cross Norton and Theodore Schellenberg, who maintained in somewhat different ways that archives were in essence a function of government, thus validating the view of public archivists as professionals working in agencies closely tied to the state's procedures and legal requirements of information flow—a sociocultural justification for archives, in Terry Cook's view, that is grounded in wider public policy and public use, rather than broad historical visions and scholarly constituencies.[44] Indeed, the re-publication of Norton's collected essays in 1975 and again in 2003 signaled that these notions were now directly relevant to the archivists' contemporary dilemmas.

The conception of archives as having an institutional, rather than historical, responsibility was also strengthened by the fact that scholars and the research community more broadly were not in any formal way the "sponsors" of archival activity. As Ann Morgan Campbell, the first paid executive director of the SAA, repeatedly pointed out, if archives and the archival profession were to thrive, archives had to be most directly responsible to those large number of users from outside the scholarly community who now constituted the great majority of their patrons and directly or indirectly paid their bills.

Thus, the interests of these users also had to be respected among the authorities guiding the processes of acquisition and preservation. In the United States, for example, genealogy was rapidly moving beyond its historically validating connections to the early American republic to a broader movement interested in tracing social roots and recovering "identity." The historic preservation and restoration movements encouraged the use of archives in restoring old homes and buildings. Civil War and other "re-enactors" popularized local historical collections and placed new demands on state records. In some places, the large number of new users these and other activities brought to the archives were now overwhelming domains that were long thought to be the preserves of academic scholars.

At the same time, within large private organizations—the corporate environment in particular—increasing competition, concerns about trade secrets, a more aggressive and contentious legal environment, and complex processes of government oversight also raised new problems of how materials should be used. Among other consequences, these developments increasingly inclined keepers of private and corporate records to affiliate with the Association of Records Managers and Administrators (ARMA), a group formed in 1955. By the end of the 1980s it had grown to include more than 10,000 public and private archivists and records managers in some thirty countries. The professional identity of ARMA members was strictly as managers who served institutional interests exclusively in terms of the management of information flow. ARMA's bimonthly *Information Management Journal* became a principal venue for the development of international records management standards, as well as for discussing new trends in technology. Historical considerations were nowhere to be seen.

3

Archival Authorities and New Technologies

As is usually the case with revolutions, the full-blown revolution in information technologies carried with it a host of unanticipated consequences. Beginning rather quietly in the 1960s with the increasing use of "machine-readable data," and then expanding rapidly into the complex environment of digitization, radical changes in the technologies of managing information soon began to overwhelm the document-producing world. They also affected almost every aspect of the ways archivists processed and understood their materials.

By the 1990s, nearly all new state and institutional records originated in digital form. Yet the extraordinary pace with which electronic processes enveloped document production was paralleled not by a reduction in paper records and documents but by their even more explosive growth. The greater ease with which documents were generated and produced only fed a burgeoning business in copiers and printers. The ever-increasing volume of records in various formats significantly complicated every aspect of appraisal and retention.

Did historical authorities have any relevance at all in this challenging new world of digitally generated records production, or did they have to be complemented or displaced by new principles? Did archivists need only to steep themselves in the mechanics of the new technology to manage new archival material, or did these radically different materials require a radical transformation in their managerial or custodial roles as well? The emerging electronic world was for the most part ahistorical, technical, and very engineered. Clearly archivists had to think differently about their training, their practices, and the very nature of their repositories, as well as about themselves and their profession.

First Steps

Ironically, the earliest changes in archival technologies, those related to archiving machine-readable data, were firmly rooted in the scholarship of social historians interested in the creation and analysis of statistical compilations. The challenges here were also occupying a small group of archivists well before the processes of digitization developed in earnest. As the remarkable capacity of large mainframe computers to store and analyze vast amounts of data became clear, it was also obvious that governments and other large institutions would soon be holding huge data banks of great importance to the core work of their respective archives, as well as, of course, to an understanding of how they functioned.

In the United States, Meyer Fishbein and others at the National Archives and Records Administration were soon working to develop systems for maintaining these records in what they called "archives in machine readable form."[1] Major research universities were also becoming increasingly interested in permanently archiving the data their researchers were now accumulating in this way. Creating data archives would assure that the time-consuming steps of acquiring and coding quantitative information would not have to be replicated. If the technology was right, new data sets could also be electronically "read" against others. The initial work of constructing these data archives was consequently still based on authorities derived from historical study, particularly those used in quantitative history. How historians were reading the data formed the authoritative coding practices, which in turn created the categories under which the data could be archived and retrieved.

One exemplary effort of this sort resulted in the establishment of the Inter-University Consortium for Political and Social Research (ICPSR) located at the University of Michigan. Founded in 1962 "to assure that data resources are available to future generations of scholars," the Consortium developed what became, in essence, a large archive of electronic materials intended for use by current and future social scientists. Member universities contributed the data generated by their own research projects. In return, their scholars were granted broad access.[2] The result was an archive of historical collections in which nothing was on paper. Its holdings were entirely digital objects housed on machines and read only by those machines. At the time the ICPSR archive seemed quite esoteric, entirely separated from the ubiquitous worlds of texts and visual documents that dominated the archival profession. How to archive and administer large statistical databases was not most archivists' concern. Many even considered these materials to be "nonrecords" in the sense that they were unrelated to institutional transactions and therefore not the archives' business.[3]

The first significant steps toward digitization soon changed this perspective. Archivists were now pressed to consider what their repositories might be like if these computational devices could be as efficient with text as they were with numbers. At precisely the moment many historians were starting to wrestle with the implications in terms of archival evidence of social and cultural history, gender, race, ethnicity, discourse, colonial studies, and other new analytic approaches, archivists were beginning to ask a very different set of questions. Should they now contemplate the systematic organization of archives that were entirely digital in form? If so, what would be their nature? How would they fit with traditional archives and archival practices? What would likely be their strengths and limitations? And most important for scholars, what were the implications of all of this for current and future historical collections and the continued preservation of nondigital materials? In other words, what would the consequences be for historians in the future if archivists saw their tasks in terms of managing records systems that needed to be regularly purged of most of their documentation rather than in terms of evaluating and preserving materials that had possible historical value?

New Computer-Based Access Systems: The "Library Model"

The stunning possibilities that new technology had to offer were apparent with the first arrivals of complex text-processing programs, and then, more broadly, with the development of the now ubiquitous desktop computer. All of the challenges of contemporary archives and records management suddenly seemed linked to digital technologies. At first it was reasonable to think that the very nature of the archival record itself would be transformed, along with the ways it was described and accessed. It also seemed likely that the amount or kinds of electronic records that computer-based archives could store were questions only of hardware capacity and clever metadata management programs.

Pushed by these technological possibilities, archivists soon produced a spate of new writing on archival theory and practice "in the electronic age," reevaluating and redefining their work. Thinking on these issues moved in two directions. One focused on how the power of computation might be used to construct archival access systems that could be searched across institutions, breaking down the insularity in conceptual and descriptive methodologies that had historically structured archives as individualized and unique collections. A second thrust focused on the idea of fully digital archives. This perspective recognized that digital records would themselves require digital solutions for arrangement, description, and long-term preservation. The work of Margaret Hedstrom and David Bearman was particularly stimulating at this juncture.[4]

For archivists interested in computer-based access systems, the early efforts of several major libraries to take advantage of the new technology offered something of a model. Well before their users could even dream of carrying PCs in their backpacks, librarians were shifting from retrieval and cataloging systems based on individual index cards to machine-readable identifiers. In the late nineteenth century, librarians had begun to formulate fixed formats using controlled vocabularies for their card systems, an approach that was later codified by the Library of Congress. A century later, this work provided the conceptual basis for the formation of integrated on-line catalogs.

As every library user knows, in the 1980s and 1990s, millions of individual library cards prepared over the course of a century were read into these catalogs in digital form. Although the technical challenges of constructing a machine-based program that would accept these various cataloging "fields" of information were complex, a uniform and controlled structure and language made its implementation possible. Controlled terminologies also made it easy for users to move from library to library through integrated cataloguing structures like the Research Libraries database (RLIN) and the Online Computer Library Center (OCLC).

The archival community was understandably intrigued by the possibility of providing a similarly integrated system of access to information in archives and records collections. Many regarded this as an important initiative, although by their very nature, archives, manuscripts, and records are unique and disparate collections in which access depends on finding aids or indices specific to particular institutions. In contrast to libraries, where the same publication can be found in many places and where electronic cataloguing was now being centralized through the Library of Congress, archivists with their unique holdings needed to test the applicability of the bibliographic principles of cataloging and classification to the archive's tasks of arrangement and description. For a database application archival practices would need to be codified and thus be predictable in format and presentation. They had to be able to serve a variety of retrieval and cataloging needs over time and geographic space. Could archivists create a uniform set of categories covering huge numbers of different documents and records? Unlike books that were already filed and arranged on the basis of established and well-defined subject categories, a whole new set of concepts, cataloguing structures, and even vocabularies would be required if similar kinds of archival documents in different kinds of repositories were to be integrated and accessed by common practices and procedures.

In other words, the key to shared archival access was standardization.[5] Initially, the only models for this were systems based on the essential features governing access to printed materials: author, title, date, and subject classification. However, archivists and records managers commonly relied on provenance-based concepts of arrangement and description. Collections of archival documents were described not by standardized tags but in ways that reflected the unique organizational structures and activities that generated them. In contrast to library systems, the dominant concept was the record group: a "unit of convenient size and character for the work of arrangement and description."[6] Standard library categories were essentially irrelevant to archivists.

In tackling the challenges of constructing electronically shared access systems, archivists consequently looked first to the finding aid, the basic document of archival description. As Frank Burke, one of the principal contributors to this discussion, emphasized, the descriptive "forematter" in the registers and inventories that historians and others found so useful commonly outlined the context (but not the details) of the collection:

The context is the life and times of the individual, or the provenance of papers, or the administrative controls such as physical dimension or material form, and is introductory to an actual analysis of the contents of the body of material. It is in this fore matter that the documentation is put in its natural context, and where the researcher should be able to search for functional statements, authorities for action, inter-organizational or interpersonal relationships, structure, mass, chronology, and statements of policy.[7]

The basic principle of "subject access" to archival material thus had to be derived from the function of the office or institution. If one knows the function of office X, then one can safely say that the correspondence in the papers of office X will relate to that function. [8]

The development of uniform access categories consequently required archivists to shift their traditional focus on record groups, and their unique characteristics, to a more structured system of description that would represent all holdings in a uniform way. But how could this approach be standardized to the point where a machine-usable system could be applicable across hundreds of different and often quite unique repositories and countless numbers of different kinds of records?

Machine-Compatible Standardization: The Development of "Essential" Cataloguing Categories for Archives and Manuscripts

This was the challenge that the Society of American Archivists handed in 1977 to a National Information Systems Task Force. Initially, even the idea of machine-compatible standardization was met with great skepticism. Most archival institutions had their own idiosyncratic methods for description and access, based on the uniqueness of their collections, their history, and their resources. Still, fueled in part by the growing energy that the new technologies stimulated, the task force produced what came to be called the Machine Reading Cataloging format (MARC) for Archives and Manuscript Control (AMC). Essentially, its members designed a template to accommodate the various categories of materials that were generally found in finding aids.[9]

In effect, MARC-AMC was a variation on library cataloguing. The "author" became the "generating agency"; "title" became "series title"; dates could span a long but defined time frame; and other machine-readable fields could be added to identify the size of the collection in linear feet, and the availability of new or existing finding aids. Subject language would be controlled by Library of Congress structures. Institutions that signed on to the concept would be required to review the cataloging data for all their manuscript and archival holdings, bringing them into conformity with the MARC-AMC field structure. The system clearly depended on the ability and willingness of archivists to relabel descriptive information according to a series of strict, standardized authorities, since it could function properly only if all participants conformed to the same set of rules and linguistic structures.[10]

What was most important in this early initiative was its reliance on what we would call "essentializing" identifiers. These were the names, places, agencies, dates of creation and the like that seemed to be essential qualities of the record: enduring, applicable to past records, and both uniform and acceptable across different kinds of institutions. As the system was advanced, the Library of Congress thesaurus of subject headings became the authority for tags that could permit searching a variety of archival materials covering many specific topics.

Essential identifiers, in other words, were reductionist. They simplified the complexities of subjects that many documents reflected into a rigid set of subject constructions, reducing the range of descriptive tags. This simplification was not necessarily a bad thing for most archivists, since it facilitated cataloguing in the same way the Library of Congress "cataloguing in publication" system eliminated the need for librarians to physically review most new acquisitions and decide where they belonged. For historians and other scholars, however, it was a very rigid construction, ill fitted to the range of issues many wanted to explore. Archives and records categories for any repository that joined the system would effectively be subsumed within the concepts and categories of historical knowledge that determined the Library of Congress's own subject categories.

Although this move toward imitating library systems in defining new archival authorities was developed before the full onslaught of computers (and when many scholars still quaintly resisted the idea of even composing on a PC, much less surfing the internet for their sources), it soon proved important to archivists themselves as a means of accessing collections through just these kinds of linkages. Indeed, one of its very strengths was that it was systematic in its construction and based on essentialized categories that were adaptable to computer and internet connections. At the same time, and somewhat paradoxically considering the archival community's quest for professional independence, this new preoccupation with essentialist criteria reflected in the MARC-AMC standards moved archivists headlong toward library and information science, with its notions of bibliographic authorities, and away from their long established independence in training, work, professional organizations, and identity, as well as their collaborations with historians and others engaged in computer-based social science. "Archival authorities" would now govern the elements that allowed the electronic exchange of collection-level information between and among archives, institutions, and individual users, rather than anything like the documents' own possible layers of historical meaning.

Encoded Archival Description (EAD) and Standard Markup Language (SGML)

Once these shared access categories were in place and functioning, the next step was to move finding aids themselves into the overall architecture of access systems. Again, this required new uniform standards, although ones that now allowed the incorporation of the nuances of document collections while also enabling some level of cross searching within and across institutions.

The system that emerged to do this sought to standardize the basic relationships between records and their agencies of origin. Called Encoded Archival Description or EAD, it came out of a project begun at the University of California, Berkeley, in 1993, "to investigate the desirability and feasibility of developing nonproprietary encoding standards for machine-readable finding aids such as inventories, registers, indexes, and other documents created by archives, libraries, museums, and manuscript repositories to support the use of their holdings."[11] After reviewing a variety of possibilities, its originators opted for the use of a Standard Generalized Markup Language (SGML) that would make encoded archival descriptions compatible with electronic communication while also reflecting the documents' logical structure, "thereby enabling software products to control the searching retrieval, and structured display of those documents." SGML also encouraged consistency by introducing the concept of a "document type definition" (DTD). This prescribed the set of SGML markup tags available for encoding the parts of documents in a similar class.[12]

The need for such precision in the EAD system further refocused discussion within the archives field. The technical requirements for such systems and their adaptation to individual repositories and document series became (and remain) a source of concern and debate. The notion of "shared" bases of documentary data is not a simple concept. Neither is EAD. Both require many difficult and time-consuming decisions on how to "fit" a collection into a preexisting conceptual structure.

Some of the most interesting discussion about these matters took place in Ann Arbor in 1995 under the auspices of the Bentley Library Research Fellowship Program for the Study of Modern Archives.[13] The "Bentley team," led by Daniel Pitti, the principal investigator for the Berkeley EAD project, struggled to develop a set of principles that would encompass those essential characteristics of archival documents and thus provide consistent information for finding aids that also linked the document to its records group. The Bentley group drew its expertise from leading figures in the Network Development Office of the Library of Congress, the Research Libraries Group, the Online Computer Library Center, and the UK Public Records Offices, as well as major Information Science departments around the country.[14]

Combining these descriptive and generic elements of archival records and documents became the conceptual foundation for all further work on Encoded

Archival Description. It also further amplified the importance of standardization, now being elevated to something like a new life form by the transforming impact of distributed computing. The potential benefit of all of this for users of archives were, of course, obvious and enormous: the possibilities of searching across institutional holdings; integrating holdings of the smallest and most remote repositories with the great collections; and integrating separated collections were all opened by these efforts. Searching through integrated finding aids also opened the possibility of uncovering file names and other pointers, presenting the user with research possibilities that were not likely to be found through traditional search practices. In sum, EAD opened the possibility of a whole new level of integrated searching that was not directly related to the essential descriptive categories of a collection or record series as a whole.

But the new technology was (and is) also dependent on word searching and thus on particular linguistic structures. By their nature, these are not amenable to conceptual shifts from, say, "women" to "gender," "governing institutions" to "relations of power," or "identity" into issues of culture, social relations, group psychology, or "diversity." Rather, the EAD system depends on the terms and language used in the file structures of originating agencies. Archivists now correctly argued, however, as many had already been doing since the "Cappon effect" debates in the 1970s, that it was no longer practical to try to comprehend all the current historiographical possibilities of any given collection, let alone predict its future use. Their focus remained on the essential relationships between records and activity that generated them. The necessary emphasis on technical precision and system construction took precedence over any extensive analysis of how collections or record groups might be used by historians and other scholars immediately or in the future.

Defining the Attributes of Electronic Records

The emergence of new information technologies also held the possibility that archivists could be relieved of most of the physical work involved in managing paper records and other artifacts, replacing it with seamless, electronically driven processes that would move the record electronically from the point of creation to the point of archival disposition. By the mid-1990s, archives composed of enormous quantities of digital texts were already becoming a reality. Archival methodologies seemed about to become a subfunction of the paperless office. Digitization thus brought similar challenges to archival thinking as the notion of electronic books and journals were soon bringing to libraries. For archivists, however, these centered not only on the processes of acquisition and description but on complex matters concerning the intrinsic and contextual attributes of new electronic records themselves. These issues soon preoccupied two groups of archivists with differing perspectives.

The first emerged around the work of archivists David Bearman and somewhat later, Adrian Cunningham, who put forward the idea of "context control" rather than that of traditional archival authorities in defining the attributes of electronic records.[15] Bearman approached this challenge from the traditional framework of provenance but with a significant difference in terms of individual documents and records series. At the time he was deputy director of the Office of Information Resources Management at the Smithsonian Institution and editor of the journal *Archives and Museum Informatics*. (He would soon yield to the demand for his services by starting his own consulting firm.) His innovation was to approach electronic materials in terms of the ways they were themselves embedded in a variety of systems—a digital-era version, in a sense, of the ways traditional documents were embedded in administrative structures and systems and had to be understood in terms of their institutional contexts.

Bearman's focus was on the retention of evidence of administrative processes or transactions apart from its possible historical significance. The system was now a new mediating factor between the actors and the information that they produced. As such, its key components were not the traditional elements of institutional transactions, including their importance according to established historical authorities, but the electronic and administrative elements that made the system work: its hardware, software, explicit policies and procedures, and not least, the training and expertise required to maintain it and keep all of its elements working together to retrieve information (evidence). The archivists' first task, therefore, was to understand the administrative contexts that produced the system and "work with" it to appraise the value of the documentation it produced. Archivists could then decide which systems themselves should be preserved and maintained in their archives—the only way, in effect, in Bearman's view, to retain and access their documentation.[16]

Bearman also argued that large-scale organizations had always required a certain amount of institutionally structured communication through their written documents, emphasizing the relationship between these documents and institutionalized processes of decision making. These forms and structures would have to transfer somehow to the digital world if the nature of key institutional processes was to be preserved. In other words, the function of electronic documentation within institutions was the same as that of paper communications, even as the form of the document moved from paper to digital. While archivists had long emphasized the relationship between an organization and the documents it produces, Bearman suggested that this basic element of the modern archival process had not actually been developed to its full potential, since the systematic presentation of the full context in which a set of materials was processed was rarely evident in a typical modern finding aid.[17] One great advantage of the new digital environment was that it forced a need for full and comprehensive description, since understanding the contexts of records construction was essential in assuring access and preservation.

Bearman's insights soon led to new attempts at standardizing contextual information itself. With the support of the International Council on Archives, an International Standard Archival Authority Record for Corporate Bodies, Persons and Families [ISAAR(CPF)] was developed that deliberately separated descriptive information from information on provenance, providing a richer conceptualization of context. Work also began on developing a system for Encoded Archival Context (EAC), as distinct from the attributes of Encoded Archival Description (EAD); and to develop new international standards to describe the activities and functions of corporate bodies (ISAF).[18] Work continued under the auspices of the International Organization for Standards (ISO) to codify standards for the administration of records, particularly of digital origin. Still, the development of comprehensive descriptive categories that would in a practical way assign organizational contextual attributes to specific records and records series remain a difficult challenge. The available models come from organizational theory, administrative history, and structural analyses of the purpose, functions, and political "realities" of organizational behavior, elements that were difficult enough to identify in any practical way across different kinds of organizations, much less to codify across different kinds of archives.[19]

A second group of archivists focused more intensively on the characteristics of the document itself, reflected in the work of Luciana Duranti at the University of British Columbia. Classically trained in archivistics (the study of archives), paleography, and diplomatics at the University of Rome, Duranti sought to link the structures of information contained in large-scale digital documentary systems to basic documentary categories derived from these fields. Rather than pulling archivists back to traditional practices and understandings, however, her effort sought to explore the applications of these categories as a way to better understanding the nature of the digital environment.

Duranti's work stemmed from a 1990 U.N. study that tried to alert its members to the problems of ensuring the preservation of electronic records and systems for the long term. Among its other observations, the report emphasized that unlike paper materials, electronic information was often created by computers themselves. Since electronic documents and their meanings could not be extracted in any case without computers, only the designers of electronic records systems themselves could determine the kind of records their systems would produce. Moreover, because electronic documents and records were managed by electronic records information *systems*, rather than by archivists, and were inseparable from those systems except by means of programs integral to the system itself, archivists and records managers had to be involved in the system's design. So did the creators of the documentation. Only their active participation would allow the records passing electronically through record systems to be accountable in terms of the ways they served an institution's needs.[20]

Here, in effect, was a new "digital" version of the concept of provenance. Digital document systems had to be transferred to archives not as collections of discrete, individual documents authenticated by the places and processes of origin, but as a single digital "object" containing what could amount to vast numbers of discrete files. Because digital material would be accessioned in mass, the meaning (and sense) of any individual document was dependent on the structure of the system it was in. Individual digital documents could also be retrieved only by going actively into the system by means of specific technical protocols and pulling them out, but these protocols were necessarily linked to the procedures and policies, technical and otherwise, of the agencies that created the record. They were thus intrinsic to the record itself. In matters of acquisition and appraisal, therefore, archives had to accession and evaluate digital record-keeping systems in their entirety, not by individual documents or document groups, since only the systems themselves actively and intrinsically determined the ways organizations created and used information. To process digital records effectively, archivists needed access to the technical information that determined each system's requirements and parameters, something over which they had no independent control.[21]

Duranti and her colleagues fixed particularly on the problem of assuring that digital records were authentic. In what sounded like a nod to tradition, they suggested that if archivists focused on the purposes for which digital records were created, as well as how these records reflected the transactional or administrative processes of their creating institutions, they could identify the essential components and functions of the documents. This approach essentially applied traditional European archival concepts derived from diplomatics to the new tasks archivists were confronting. A digital record, like the paper documents of traditional historical archives, would be considered reliable when it could be authenticated not by its relationship to any broader historical processes, but "when it is the document it claims to be":

> Genuineness is the closest concept. It is generally accepted by all literate civilizations that documents that are trustworthy (that is *reliable*) because of their completeness and controlled procedure of creation, and which are (that is guaranteed to be intact and what they purport to be (that is *authentic*). Here, though, authenticity is strictly juridical in its definition. By controlled procedures of transmission and preservation, documents can be *presumed* to be truthful (that is *genuine*) as to their content. Thus, for those who make and preserve records, the two key concepts remain reliability and authenticity, as genuineness is embedded in them.[22]

For Duranti and others, the fundamental concern of archivists thus had to center on the essential and unchanging relationships between a document and its creator, the linkage that determined its "enduring value" as a transactional record, and thus, eventually, as a possible historical source. The key effort here, in other words, was to find a predictable and systemic set of authorities that were not time-bound, but built on axiomatic relationships determined as in the past by the importance of the transaction itself.

These ideas most strongly influenced archivists in the public sector, who were challenged by their burgeoning responsibilities as agents of digital information flows within governmental agencies. Not surprisingly, archivists here embraced these new archival conceptions in part because they had somehow to accommodate the new technologies through which governments were producing their documents, and in part because these technologies also promised to help address the demands and costs of meeting the needs of their broadening public constituencies. In fact, state archivists in the United States soon broke from the SAA to form their own National Association of Government Archives and Records Administrators (NAGARA), dedicated "solely to helping government archivists and records managers," and to the improvement of federal, state, and local government records and information management. The concern of its members was on efficiency, "the effective use and management of government information . . . [and] improving the quality of records and information management at all levels of government."[23] NAGARA's "core purpose" was "to promote the availability of our documentary legacy by improving the quality of records and information management at all levels of government."[24]

Underlying the creation of this new organization was not so much its members' desire to distance themselves from the SAA but their efforts to gain strength and support in navigating the complex politics, requirements, technologies, and legal questions that were affecting the nature and creation of government records and the tasks of state records management. In language that was strikingly "contemporary corporate" rather than "traditional scholarly," NAGARA listed as one of its primary values "delivering practical, specific and cost-effective products that are responsive to our members' needs."[25]

The Appraisal Debates: Rethinking Archival Authorities

These new theoretical and conceptual perspectives also centered the question of archival authorities—the criteria as we have described to be used in selecting that portion of documentation considered to be of "enduring value"—directly on organizational structures and behaviors. The value of records was now increasingly seen to be a reflection of the importance of the office producing them within a contributing or sponsoring institution. Some in this discussion also engaged the methodologies of social science sampling, in which the authorities guiding the retention of documents were also to be derived from the validating parameters of statistical research.[26] Others focused on the contexts of generation and use.[27]

What was particularly striking in these new debates was practical problems archivists were now facing in terms of the huge quantity of materials arriving at their doors. The contributions of Frank Boles and Julia Young, archivists who tried to couple appraisal as a theoretical concern with these practical issues, were especially important here. Boles and Young stressed the importance of such factors as the costs of preservation, the condition of the material, and the possible degree of user interest in reaching appraisal decisions. Using elaborate diagrams, they identified nearly fifty different factors they thought archivists and records managers now had to consider in developing a consistent set of new archival authorities. On one hand, they suggested, the problems of managing vast new quantities of material were simply beyond the capabilities of established archival thinking. On the other, the interventionist necessities of the post-custodial digital era required even more radical changes in managerial practices and standards.[28]

Within the archival profession there was now a near universal tendency to see the issue of archival authorities on the basis exclusively of archival needs and concerns. Of necessity, archivists struggled to establish the new conceptual frameworks and methodologies needed to inform and resolve the complex issues brought on by the new technologies. Pressing practical needs, far removed from the historical values that were once at the center of the appraisal process, now structured archivists' thinking about the authorities needed to guide their work. Traditional history-based authorities were even further marginalized, since the interests of historians and historical understanding added little to the types of authorities now required by the sheer volume of documentation and the emerging new technologies. The explosion of both paper and computer-based documentation, the rapid growth of nonacademic constituencies, complex new technological programs and systems, the increasing demands of organizational and institutional politics—all of this combined to pull archivists further away from their onetime historian colleagues in deciding what was of value. The appraisal debates situated this issue exclusively as a problem for archivists alone, a matter that had to be addressed solely by what was now called archival theory and in terms that were now entirely "archival."

4

The Turn Away from Archival Authority in History

At the time the archival community began to confront the problems of acquisition and retention created by the exponential growth of documentation in all of its forms, historians still assumed their craft required the archiving of everything that was conceivably of historical value. Many still do. When the issue came up in 2008 at yet another contentious meeting of historians in St. Petersburg, a leading scholar responded to the question "what should be saved?" with a loud and resounding "everything!" His colleagues all nodded in agreement. How this could possibly be done was simply not his or their concern. The very thought that archivists might be even more engaged in discarding material than in its acquisition was (and remains) far from the historians' mindset.

Indeed, as archivists were starting to consider the need for new "post-custodial" paradigms after the Second World War, the authority of the archive and archival history were actually being strengthened within the academic community by the standardization of scholarly research protocols embodied in the formal historical monograph. Although rooted as we have seen in the nineteenth-century methodologies of scientific history, these practices had now become the common currency of academic scholarship. The way these standards were used by scholars affected university appointments, promotions, and history's broader reception within the social science community at large.

As with archivists, however, the world of the historian was also changing, challenged by the devastations of the Second World War. Many now felt bound to reconsider well-established assumptions about how and why societies developed, and in what ways "progress" itself might still be an appropriate description of broader historical trajectories. New questions and concerns began to press at the boundaries of their discipline. While increasing numbers of historians were now able to visit the archives, aided by easier transportation and stimulated to extend the informational and explanatory power of historical scholarship, the traditional authorities embedded in the historical record were themselves being redefined by new areas and subjects of enquiry. Some of these questions began to tear at the very notion of historical authority itself.

Archival Access, Research Protocols, and the Laws of History

The standardization of research protocols within the academic community had to do with the practices of archival access, a crucial issue for historians as every archival scholar will attest. Although the principle of open access was now broadly recognized in Europe and North America as matter of civic right, the actual practice varied widely in terms of the nature of the materials, how they were catalogued, and certainly not least with respect to historical archives, the prerogatives of the archivist. Many contemporary historians' sojourn to the archives still resembled Leopold von Ranke's nineteenth-century reliance on cultivated personal relationships, contacts also essential to his students. "By the kindness of . . . I was given access to . . ." Ranke often wrote in a style familiar to those who read the dutiful acknowledgments of contemporary archival historians. Despite the conceptual repositioning of archives as institutions reflecting a public trust, most still required users to present some form of status, reference, credentialing, or other indicator of competence and probity. Even in the open repositories of the National Archives and Records Service in the United States or the Archives Nationales in France, archivists still had the power to protect certain kinds of historical materials simply by virtue of their custodial roles. In more restricted private repositories or those like Soviet historical collections where access was not legally assured, the archivist's word was law.

Access thus continued to connote status and legitimacy for historians and their work, just as it had a century earlier. It provided a recognizable credential of scholarly promise or achievement. Here, too, readers will sense the familiar claims to authority that phrases like "based on access to newly opened archives" or "hitherto unstudied materials" often ascribe to historical scholarship. Since public archives even in the United States were now consolidated as well around the dominant sociopolitical institutions of government and the state, access also signified for the historian some degree of trustworthiness in the eyes of the archivist.

Access also strengthened the authority of archival history through the increasingly stylized language of footnotes and citations. As Anthony Grafton has shown in a fascinating exploration, citations themselves have a very long pedigree, but until sometime early in the eighteenth century they served as references to authorities themselves, rather than to sources on which particular arguments were based.[1] In its modern form, however, the citation is not simply to authority (as we have just used it here in citing Grafton) but more commonly in archival scholarship to the source on which the authority of the text itself is grounded: that is, to the original documents that serve as verifiable evidence that the historical narrative is based on authentic and identifiable sources.

Grafton places the transformation in the eighteenth century. Under the reciprocal and compounding weight of Bacon, Descartes, Bayle, and other progenitors of the Enlightenment, the citation moved to a position of critical reflection in which doubts and criticisms could be expressed about alternative descriptions or explanations as a way of empowering new texts, and hence new understandings.[2] By the time Rankean practices and the university seminar became foundational elements of the science of history, and archival documents themselves something of a scholarly fetish, the protocols of citation had come to signify an authenticating "truth" even if there was no evidence that truth itself had been critically examined.

Integral to this shift was the emergence of what might be called a particular "grammar of objectivity" with which histories based on archival sources increasingly came to be written: a style of representing evidence that itself further positioned the archive as the source of modern historical authority. By grammar of objectivity, we have in mind the structural form of archival reference in which any potentially contested fact or any presentation of new data is "objectively" validated by its citation to a specific archival source. In response to the reader's implicit question "how do you know?" the scholar's language of citation implicitly answers that the story presented is "verifiable" if readers care to pack their bags, secure the necessary credentials, and journey to the archive where the documents can be examined.

Although the scientistic assumption here is that historical truth itself is objective, it is actually not the source that is certified by the citation but the historian's text. The certification of the source has been left to the archivist, and to the presumption that the scholar has read it critically, can detect any fraud or forgery the archivist may have missed, and has cited it with accuracy. In the mid-twentieth century the prevalent notion was that a topic was "covered" or "done" once the relevant archives had been explored. Graduate students were encouraged to pursue "new" topics based on unexplored archival materials. Hence the proliferation, especially in the United States but elsewhere as well, of state and regional studies of particular aspects of political institutions or policy.

Every historian now knows, of course, the limits of these presumptions. Accusations about the misuse or incorrect citation of sources have always been one of the liveliest forms of scholarly exchange. In spite of this (or perhaps even because of it), the archival citation also came to connote research as an objective (scientific) process of uncovering truths whose very collection and preservation in the archive also represented them as authentic, again barring forgery or fraud. By inviting verification, the citation in and of itself thus indicated both objectivity and accuracy. Since how much of what historians thought to be true depended on how much of the truth had been collected in the archives, one can also agree with the historian Steven Shapin that what is assumed to be true in archival scholarship has also been determined by what was collected, preserved, and "discovered" through archival research.[3]

By the time records production began to overwhelm archives and archivists in the 1940s and 1950s, standardized research protocols and their authenticating grammars were not only universal elements of historical scholarship; they had also come to underlie contemporary historical understandings of the nature and causes of modernity. These were firmly consolidated in the aftermath of the Second World War around two very different kinds of broad historical narrative, each of which served to define the modern quest for historical truth. Although they scarcely resembled each other in their historical descriptions, each emerged from ways accessible archives and the kinds of materials they collected encouraged an emphasis on the importance of institutional politics and political actors.

One linked the historical future of the postwar world with the longer term agencies, ideologies, institutions, and social formations of Western European and North American liberalism. The second was the powerful and opposing narrative of progressive socialist achievement, now convincingly demonstrated for some by the Red Army's triumphant arrival in Berlin, and for much of the non-western world, now the interpretive core of conceptions of modernity. Here it was not the institutions of liberal capitalism that charted the future but the rationalities of planning and the democratic allocation of social resources. In both cases, however, scientific history continued to mean the deduction from archival sources of broad historical laws. In the more extreme Marxian version that underlay official Soviet historiography, the dynamic patterns of social evolution contained by necessity the same elements of regularity and order as the natural and physical universes, however more difficult they were to discern. These were presented as theoretical in the same way Newton's *Principia* was regarded as theory: careful (scientific) examination of the historical universe would provide the same kinds of verification as experimental physics. The western historical canon was far more contingent in its understanding of historical order, but no less deterministically a history of rational progress toward brighter futures, a chart of what was to come as well as of the past.

At their core, both of these broad narratives were thus partly a quest for historical meaning. What was narrated in addition to the events and politics themselves was the direction and purpose history seemed to reflect. Modernity emerged in this process as a scientifically determined temporal location, the place toward which history was naturally and demonstrably moving. Archive-based narratives thus implicitly became histories of the future as well as the past, even if the interpretations of an emancipatory political modernization were grander stories of human progress and development than the archives themselves could demonstrate.

Together, these dominant quests for historical meaning held virtually exclusive hold on historical imaginations, explaining why and how some nations had "gone wrong," as well as why others had gotten things "right." Despite their interpretive differences, moreover, modernity in both was also more than historical direction or temporality. It was the achievement of a positivist mindset, the very recognition that the natural laws of historical change were there to be discovered and demonstrated by careful archival research. However different in content and methodology, both narratives consequently relied in almost all of their many forms on a grammar that assured the possibility of authentication through archival reference. Indeed, Soviet texts were almost always more thoroughly drenched with archival citations than western ones, since the scientific truths of history this grammar connoted were also the foundation of Soviet political legitimacy. It mattered little in this respect that restrictions on archival access made their verification virtually impossible, even if scholars were inclined to try. Paradoxically, Soviet readers had to take the veracity of their scientific histories on faith.

The *Annales* Critique

Strong challenges to these two competing understandings of historical progress were also emerging at this time, however, as scholars questioned the political uses to which their teleologies were being put. New historical thinking began to question the "authenticity" of history centered solely on great events, political institutions, and (male) human agency, whether or not it was archivally based. Part of the impetus for this came from what some saw as the catastrophes of modernity itself, reflected in the recent histories of Germany, Italy, Stalinist Russia, Imperial Japan, and even the "western" world as a whole. The distinguished French medievalist Marc Bloch, for example, experienced the cataclysm of war directly as a member of the French resistance when he drafted his magisterial (and unfinished) *The Historian's Craft*, which caused something of a sensation when it was published posthumously in 1953. (Bloch was captured and, tragically, executed in 1944.) The "modernity" of institutions and institutional abstractions divorced from the everyday realities of human existence compromised for Bloch the essential relationship between the meanings of history and the human condition. The historian's craft had to focus on what affected the lives of ordinary men and women in its careful pursuit of historical truth, and how these influences could be understood in nonlinear human terms.[4]

Not surprisingly, given the impact of Bloch's writing and the way he died, an early set of challenges to the modernist historical vision emerged in postwar France from Bloch's colleague Fernand Braudel and others involved with the journal *Annales*.[5] While the approach they reflected was partly rooted in Bloch's work, it also echoed the broader concerns of Claude Lévi-Strauss, Jean Paul Sartre, Lucien Febvre, and other postwar scholars and public intellectuals in its attention to the broader dynamics of human development reflected in sociocultural and socioeconomic terms. *Annales* projected the broadest kind of historical vision. Its full title, *Annales. Economiques, Sociétés, Civilisations*, signified an approach that situated specific events and historical actors, the traditional subjects of historical enquiry, within a much vaster and controlling sweep of historical motion and time. The seminal works here were Braudel's own magisterial studies *The Mediterranean and the Mediterranean World in the Age of Philip II*, first published in 1949 and reworked in a second edition in 1966, and a piece he wrote for *Annales* in

1959 on "History and the Social Sciences: The *Longue Durée*," a trenchant essay that had a particularly strong impact in terms of challenging traditional modes of historical thought and research.[6]

Braudel declared here a "general crisis in the human sciences." The crisis stemmed from excessive disciplinary and scholarly narrowness, reflected in obsession with the most detailed descriptions of events, as if this focus somehow explained how societies developed. Braudel did not challenge archival history for its reliance on archival materials, but implicitly undermined the fundamental premise on which this traditional work was grounded: that authoritative archives housed the most important materials that were necessary for fundamental historical explanation.

Like Bloch before him, Braudel instead urged new connections between "economists, ethnographers, anthropologists, sociologists, psychologists, linguists, demographers, geographers, even social mathematicians or statisticians" whose work complemented and informed history. He directly confronted the assumptions of "traditional history, with its concern for the short time span, for the individual and the event," which has "long accustomed us to the headlong, dramatic, breathless rush of its narrative." This *l'histoire événementielle* consisted of a distorting fixation on the moment, whose "delusive smoke" obscures "the flames that produced it."[7] The break with traditional forms of history did not mean ignoring short time spans, but embedding them in the broader foundational currents of historical change. Politics, political history, the history of individual people and events—precisely the primary subjects of collection and preservation of all historical archives—could only be understood in their conjunctural relationship to slower, deeper patterns of societal evolution: humanity in relation to its surroundings.

The reach of the *Annalistes* was most powerfully to psychology, economic and cultural anthropology, and the problem of language (or communication, as Braudel referred to it), as well as to the task of uncovering the broader historical patterns of human experience with which these related sets of enquiries were concerned. Psychological mindedness was important to historical understanding not so much in terms of individual mindsets or behaviors, however important these might be as determinants of personal actions, but in order to situate the specificity of thinking and action into broad cultural mentalities and processes of change. The issue was not that men made their own history but not as they pleased, as Marx famously argued, but to explain much more comprehensively the range of processes and structures that Marxian historiography had essentially restricted to the social and political economies of class.

The issue here was not whether material (economic) base and political, cultural, or social superstructure were related. It was how the relationships between patterns of commodity exchange, social values, and forms of political control variously and complexly developed over time. Claude Lévi-Strauss was particularly influential in this regard in terms of the ways these patterns also involved critical elements of communication. For him and others, the crucial set of problems revolved around how meanings were derived and transmitted through linguistic, as well as phonemic structures, or as Braudel put it, "the whole underlying *unconscious* reality of language" and its relationship to historical time.[8]

Initially, this discussion did not seem to relate directly to the kinds of materials collected in archives. Braudel's understanding of the *longue durée* was also highly political. Yet his reconceptualization of the nature of history and historical change was centered on the complex relationship between events and historical time. Deeper patterns and structures did not obviate the devastation that Hitlers or Stalins could precipitate, but embedded their roles into broader causalities. These needed to be understood first and foremost if catastrophes of the sort the world had recently experienced were to be avoided. "More than one of our contemporaries would be happy to believe that everything is the result of the agreements at Yalta or Potsdam, the incidents at Dien Bien Phu or Sakhiet-Sidi-Youseff. . . . Unconscious history proceeds beyond the reach of these illuminations and their brief flashes."[9]

"Decentering" the event as historical subject (to use a jargony term in this growing discussion) was a way of recognizing the limitations of traditional understandings of politics and traditional political narratives. Power, too, flowed more deeply: in the cohesions of social formations, the impositions of geography and climate, in mentalities and political cultures, as well as instruments of force themselves. Here, Braudel and others were going well beyond the archives in an effort to understand "what happened," looking past the central institutions and processes so critical for earlier generations. The relations of control and subordination that these patterns reflected were not readily accessible, if at all, in traditional archival collections.

This did not mean that the *Annalistes* were dismissing the importance of the "event" in historical change. The centrality of archival research was also still quite clear, both in scrutinizing its broader contours and in determining as accurately as possible its specific components and forms. The *Annalistes* saw the relationship between history as *longue durée* and history as political event as moments of "conjuncture": points in historical time when immediate and longer term processes came together and interacted to alter historical "directions." Understanding these moments required detailed archival exploration, since institutional or personal documents had to be closely read to uncover the underlying conflicts they reflected. The historian's task here was thus to understand what the documents left unsaid, as well as what they voiced in their manifest content.

At the same time, these views were also bound to have implications for what archives acquired and appraised as materials of "historical" value. Some elements of this new understanding had to come from a rigorous (scientific) scrutiny of data, often held in private collections and libraries rather than state archives, especially that relating to new questions of social history: trade and commerce, the effects of climate, processes of urbanization, and especially in the late 1960s and early 1970s, the nature and forms of social protest. Paris soon became the center of new kinds of quantitative analysis for historians, with strong ties to the United States through historical sociologists such as Charles Tilly, who worked extensively in both places, and also with links to the Soviet east through Boris Anan'ch, Ivan Kovalchenko, and a small cohort of quantitative historians, who also managed at times to travel to Paris to use private bank materials and access other kinds of data. In Moscow and Leningrad, rigorous statistical study and quantitative analysis facilitated new criticism of the existing historiography on the basis of a politically irrefutable methodology, especially work relating to finance, the development of market relations, demography, and the changing nature of the Russian countryside. Some of the imaginative changes in historical research that the *Annalistes* stimulated in the late 1960s and 1970s were thus still quite scientifically oriented. As Georges Lefebvre told his acolytes, "if you want to become a historian you have to learn to count."[10]

The specific challenges that the *Annalistes* leveled against traditional historical thinking also very much complemented a broader area of critical enquiry that virtually exploded during the 1960s and 1970s on issues like the conceptualization of western "progress," whose values for many now seemed shattered by the terrors, wars, and other devastations of the "modern" world. The question of power in particular was already a principal concern of those in Paris like Michel Foucault, whose essays and critical reviews began to appear regularly in the late 1950s. In 1963 Foucault took up the question of language and representation in *Tel Quel*, joining Jacques Derrida and others probing relations of power within structures of thinking and "mentalities" from the perspectives of psycholinguistics. With the publication in 1966 of Foucault's seminal *Les Mots et les choses: Une archéologie des sciences humaines*,[11] the question of how history and the social sciences were themselves part of the very technologies of social control that they purported to study objectively became itself the subject of growing debate.

The *Annalistes'* questions thus linked directly to new understandings of culture and the political roles of language and symbolic representation being explored by Theodor Adorno, Clifford Geertz, Jürgen Habermas, and Hayden White, among others. Adorno's work critiqued directly the positivist claims inherent in sociology and the "jargon of authenticity" [*jargon der eigentlichkeit*], building on a broad critical rethinking of Marx. Geertz took up the issues of ritual, social change, and relationship between symbols, symbolic communication, and worldviews. Adding the notion of "thick description" to a rapidly growing lexicon of new concepts and ideas demonstrated the importance of highly focused points of entry into otherwise larger and more opaque social and historical realities and processes. In quite different ways, the explorations of Habermas and the first essays by White also confronted the question of "description," Habermas in terms of the political uses of language, White more directly in historiographic terms, as a textual element of narration. By the early 1970s, Adorno's *The Jargon of Authenticity*, Geertz's *The Interpretation of Cultures*, and Habermas's long essays on

technology, science, and the concept of "modernity" itself as ideology[12] constituted essential elements of a "turn" toward social history, language, and linguistics as fundamental aspects of how presents and pasts now needed to be
understood.

Archives and the New Social History

For many historians of Europe, the central issues of social history raised by the
Annalistes were brought into the clearest kind of focus in 1963 by E. P. Thompson's
The Making of the English Working Class, arguably the most influential new history
in English to appear in the postwar period. For Russianists, shortly afterwards, it
was the appearance of what many still regard as one of the most important analytical pieces on the late imperial period, the two-part article by Leopold Haimson
in the *Slavic Review* on "Social Stability in Russia on the Eve of the First World
War."[13] In different but complementary ways, both historians offered radically
new historical explanations about issues long assumed to be solved. In the process,
they also further challenged the two "grand" or "master" narratives of the time,
that of emancipatory liberalism and progressive socialism—each neatly plotted
with clear beginnings and ends, centered on the nation-state, and peopled by
heroes and villains with discrete ideological perspectives, the "winners" and
"losers" in their interpretations of historical progress.

By the 1960s, of course, the grand narrative of liberal capitalism was now
locked in bitter Cold War struggle with the teleologies of Soviet socialism. The
heroic logic of the first was premised on what Francis Fukuyama would later
describe as the "end of history" in the sense that the world's struggle for stability
and order would eventually come to a successful and triumphant (liberal) end.[14]
Closely related was a powerful and complementary narrative of ongoing conflict
as a result of Soviet global ambitions and communist conspiracy. In its broadest
form, this story was written in terms of historically regressive reactions against
liberalism, rationality, and democratic governance. It was especially appealing for
many because it linked the individual and collective sufferings of millions of
people to a particular and carefully formulated plot, figuratively, but also literally,
sketching out a Soviet drive to extend power, expand its totalitarian hegemony,
and realize the end of history in its own utopian terms.

The contest between these narratives was soon in full play in many different
arenas: new struggles over civil rights and citizenship, the tensions of decolonialization, conflict over social inequalities, and especially the bloody struggle over
which narrative would shape the future of Africa, the Middle East, and of course
Vietnam and Southeast Asia. The ways each story processed history defined the
future trajectories of citizenship, nationhood, social order, and "modernity" itself.
At the same time, the powerful military weapons that both the liberal and Soviet
socialist narratives could bring to bear also exposed the world as a whole to what

some regarded as the ultimate "modern" moment: the possibility that scientific creativity would result in total nuclear destruction. Historical understanding in these circumstances was not simply a matter of intellectual or academic conceit. It held real clues to the possibilities of political mediation based on comprehension of how and why the potential for global conflict had reached such a perilous point.

In this context, the seminal challenge to the basic plot lines of both these narratives situated revolutionary movements not as the historical consequence of political will or communist conspiracy, but in terms of real dislocations between broad-based sociocultural values, mentalities, and relations, and the political systems that controlled them. The keys to understanding the past accurately lay in the obscured and neglected realm of popular mind-sets and social behaviors, and the ways these were "out of joint" with how politically dominant groups related and thought about themselves and each other, especially within unstable societies. In other words, historical explanation even in terms of large-scale events like the Vietnamese "struggle for liberation" was best located in the neglected realms of human behaviors and relations that occurred at some remove from the formal and familiar institutions of high politics. They were thus not readily given to representation in grand narrative form. Instead, they constituted the complex patterns of largely unarchived behaviors and relations that were soon commonly labeled with the vague and troublemaking identifier of "the social."

If Haimson encouraged a fundamental rethinking of late imperial Russian and early Soviet history in these terms, stimulating "revisionist" looks at both late Imperial and Soviet Russia as systemic phenomenon of sociocultural relations, as well as locations of power, it took E. P. Thompson's magisterial work to restore both historical presence and agency to those excluded from the condescending gaze of the grand narrators, to paraphrase his famous aphorism. Thompson brought two different but complementary challenges to the discussion. One was substantive and clearly debatable. It focused on how social groups come to understand and represent themselves within broader sociocultural milieus and how these understandings and representations affected (and were affected by) politics and political institutions. The other was analytical and much harder to debate. It centered on the distorting tendencies of grand national narratives and stories of national identity themselves—the very narratives that were foundational in the establishment and definition of state archives and provided the authorities that structured their holdings. The traditional archival approach to "telling the story," to doing history, was thus directly challenged.

Thompson, Haimson, and others in the United States and Europe thus encouraged a new generation of social historians to probe "interior" social spaces and cultural relations: the ways men and women; peasants and landowners; managers, foremen, and workers; officers and soldiers; merchants and manufacturers; state officials and state subjects; hegemons and subalterns—all of these social formations and others—related to each other, thought about and represented themselves and others, and imagined their futures through the ways they processed their pasts.

This new social-historical approach was a significant departure from the *Annalistes'* earlier focus on deeper social structures. It challenged bright graduate students to explore a greatly expanded range of historical subjects, experiences, processes, and meanings.[15] The new social history was thus also about how histories "from below" related to more familiar fields of politics, ideology, and the structural aspects of "modernization," where it was traditionally understood that history was "made." These realms of enquiry pushed the boundaries of what constituted historical meaning and knowledge. Work in these new areas clearly required archival research, but the kinds of sources needed were not always readily discernable in politically and institutionally generated collections. Equally important, these new questions and approaches affected conceptions of the archive itself and the kinds of materials these "temples" of history needed to preserve.

The Problem of Historical Narration

The broader issues of historical narration itself were also central here. As they emerged with new clarity in the work especially of Hayden White, questions about how scholars and nations both used types of historical narration were not seen by historians as those primarily of social purpose, factual distortion, concealment, the limitations of sources, or the restricted possibilities of archival verification. Rather, they centered on how what White came to describe as the "deep structures of historical imagination" affected the ways histories are written and told.[16]

While the literature concerning the "metahistorical" role of narrative techniques is now quite extensive, little thought has been given to its relation to archives. Most important here is the ways in which the work of first-rate archival scholars also demonstrates that a well-crafted telling of their stories can be authoritative in and of itself, simply through the persuasive power of its voice: that, as White has argued, the style of narration itself in its various forms can evoke a convincing resonance in readers. This resonance may derive from the commonalities of language, from the reader's sympathy to the narrative's logic, from a broader understanding of the context that the narrative is attempting to shape, or from some other empathic point of connection between historian and reader. In each case it is the resonance itself, rather than the narrative's sources, that affects the degree to which the history being told seems true. A heroic or tragic ordering of a historical narrative tends to touch readers sensibilities in especially powerful ways. Empathy (or antipathy, or sympathy) becomes a basis for presumptions of historical authority and understanding, however problematically or ahistorically these are projected onto different cultures and historical times.

So, too, with the grander forms of historical explanation. As White suggests in his penetrating discussions of Ranke, Michelet, Burckhardt, and other nineteenth-century historians, the explanatory grammars of plot lines, ideological disposi-tions, or formal logic itself can convey notions of historical truth as forcefully as archival citations, especially to readers unaccustomed to reading authoritative history critically. The grand syntheses of the nineteenth-century masters nar-rated the linkages that they perceived between events around convincing claims about political progress and decline, tropes that reflected familiar life cycles and experience. Their historicism was expressed in grand and persuasive literary styles that transported their readers into historical space with the same sense of cer-tainty as Melville, de Maupassant, and Tolstoy transported theirs.

Processing the past through a skillfully told story, in other words, can tran-scend the objective principles of archival verification. In the process, the archives may be reduced figuratively, as well as literally, to a footnote. The most rigorous archival scholarship always leaves room for imagination in the historian's craft. In place of the footnote, or more precisely, in addition to the verifying role of the authoritative archival citation, is the authority skillful narratives convey simply because their stories "ring true."

Archival Implications of the Linguistic and Cultural Turns

As these new challenges to "authoritative" history continued to develop in the 1970s, the various currents of critical thinking and enquiry that soon came to be grouped as "postmodernism" were also taking root in widespread assaults against established authorities of all kinds: political, social, cultural, patriarchal, and (not least) academic. University communities in particular became centers of intellec-tual challenge, social activism, and political confrontation with "the authorities." Institutions then seemed to be sites of wrongheaded or outmoded ("traditional") thinking about how and why societies changed and, especially in France and the United States, how and why "wars of liberation" were actually fought.

In the Braudelian vocabulary of conjuncture, 1968 was obviously a critical moment. The unexpected force of the Tet offensive in Vietnam, the Soviet sup-pression of "socialism with a human face" in Prague, as well as at home, the blunt-ing of liberal politics and the American civil rights campaign with the assassinations of Martin Luther King, Jr., and Robert Kennedy, the election of Richard Nixon instead of Hubert Humphrey after the bloody Chicago protests at the Democratic National Convention, the effective end of the "war on poverty" by the return of Republicans to power in the United States, the consequent extension of the Viet-nam war into Laos and Cambodia, and worldwide demonstrations of protest—all of these sharp moments were easily situated within a commonly understood his-tory événementielle, riveting attention on what the two hegemonic world powers were doing and why. In various ways and with varying degrees of intensity, they all focused on the connections between knowledge and power, between what is known and knowable about the past inside the archives and out, how this knowledge is concealed or revealed, and especially how it is used. Yet these various strands of new thinking were not for the most part "political" in origin, in the sense that term had traditionally been used and understood by historians and archivists. They emerged from the new focus on how and why social relations, cultural forms, everyday experience, and the various forms, locations, and uses of power shaped the historical process.

In this changing analytical milieu, it is not surprising that the elaboration of critical linguistic theory and "deconstruction" became suddenly attractive to historians, although this additional set of perspectives also had its own intellectual genealogy. The same can be said for the concurrent scholarly elaborations of social movements and *mentalités* among historians and historical sociologists like Eric Hobsbawm, Michelle Perrot, and others, as well as the new interest in the "constructions" of ethnicity and the "inventions" of tradition reflected by Benedict Anderson and Fredric Jameson.[17] Each of these currents further fueled a desire, intellectual and otherwise, to turn away from established historical interpretations, sources, and ways of thinking. An effort to understand minds and hearts is a qualitatively different historical exercise than the construction of national histories through an exploration of their institutional archives. It is an effort instead to rescue the telling of history itself from the exclusionary teleologies of modernity embedded in dominant political, institutional, and personal narratives, grand and small.

Throughout the 1970s, this was especially the case with how political authorities and historical texts in both the Soviet Union and the United States processed the past. Both linked power to transcendent beliefs, institutions, and the modernizing efforts of great individuals and powerful social elites. Both also insisted their stories reflected the steady historical march of reason and truth. What mattered most at the time in terms of new historical thinking, however, was not that the political implementations of these arguments stood in such antagonistic relationship to each other, but that the representations themselves in both instances were in such transparent opposition to broad understandings of what had "really taken place." For a new generation of scholars, in other words, both stories were increasingly unconvincing.

Few serious historians now believed, for example, that the U.S. effort to "roll back communism" in Southeast Asia was in any way related to the progress of liberal democracy, any more than they believed that the forceful spread of Soviet hegemony in Czechoslovakia and Eastern Europe advanced anything resembling democratic socialism. While both narratives continued to dominate state policy and popular understanding, each was increasingly out of joint with the ways that new modes of enquiry now argued the past had to be studied. Both lost much of their authority and representational integrity. The categories of social, political, and national identity that they each produced and reproduced thus became the objects of analytic scrutiny rather than simply the subjects or agents of social modernization. Reaching backward to deploy these approaches in historical scholarship consequently required an expanded or alternative range of sources—new "authorities" to make new interpretations convincing.

The growing emphasis among historians on language and culture—the now familiar and well-rehearsed linguistic and cultural turns—thus emerged as part of a range of efforts to understand more precisely how various ways of processing historical "realities" did or did not relate to the subjects, practices, or experiences being described. In turning to language and culture, areas of exploration that were well developed in other disciplines but which historians had tended to neglect, the question was how cultural and linguistic practices might themselves constitute determining elements of historical change. Among other consequences, this broadening of interests strongly challenged any attempt to define a singular comprehensive and archivally grounded past. A unified "history of the nation" became plural pasts, in contrast to assumptions about a common or "shared" national experience. In the process, as Robert Berkhofer has nicely argued, the interpretative unity that pursuit of the "great story" tried to construct was subjected to increasing critique.[18] Historians "de-constructed" the once commonplace notion that a singular authoritative framework, formulated within national boundaries and based on well-organized fonds in national archives and official state collections, could embrace a singular shared national past. Although no one yet considered the issue, this "turn" implicitly undermined the traditional kindred relationship between archives and history, gendered as "sister" professions and founded on similar notions of how authoritative history had to be written.

The notion of "deconstruction" is, of course, most famously associated with Jacques Derrida's provocative aphorism *il n'y a pas de hors-texte* [there is nothing outside the text], even if only a small number of a growing new cohort of postmodern thinkers regarded this assertion as literally true. For most it has meant instead that the language of representation has a powerful actuality of its own. It creates its own categories in ways that both presumes their existence and facilitates their coming into being. It consequently obscures the timeless Platonic distinction between subject and object, conflating the idealist duality between material and mental worlds with stories about "progress" and "liberation" that allegedly have "real" content. The concern for understanding text, in other words, was an equally strong concern for understanding context. Although Derrida and others took one strand of postmodernism to the point where context—historical actuality—seemed to dissolve, for most this simply meant, more prosaically, "getting the story right." Both perspectives, however, held profound implications for the established ways history was researched, used and understood. Even if very few moved to the radical position that history had "ended," that the past just "was," and all coherences ordering its infinite welter of experiences were essentially fictive (however real life was actually lived), history was now to be understood, researched, and told, in different ways.

One of the most broadly attractive of these ways picked up the concerns of Clifford Geertz, Mary Douglas, Victor Turner, and others for thick social and cultural description.[19] For some, it seemed transparently obvious that the "facts" underlying the dominant western and Soviet narratives were belied by sociocultural processes and formations of quite different sorts. Cultural linkages in Indochina and elsewhere which provided the politically weak with powerful weapons, acts, and "hidden transcripts of resistance" were increasingly more convincing explanations of why and how "history" in that region and elsewhere was moving than those based on formal politics and political institutions.[20]

Analytically, there was an important difference between the emerging efforts to explore cultural locations and forms for their own sake, a tendency that soon became generally identified as the "cultural turn," and the broader effort among historians to look more closely at the effects of cultural forms and relations on the development of political institutions and other elements of social order and change. Both of these moves toward an understanding of culture and power in their broader senses, however, further "decentered" familiar conceptions of history as a social science, since both challenged traditional conceptions of the autonomy of political institutions and of power itself. Here, new arguments about the ways that power, culture, and culturally embedded economic and social relations were and could be linked to each other had a growing resonance.[21] In an additional twist to this remarkable intellectual and political conjuncture, these new approaches also connected directly in American historical and social thought to the powerful attention the civil rights movement had generated about race and racial identities, and stimulated new thinking about another pivotal but hitherto neglected substantive and analytical category, that of gender.

Race and gender were analytically related not only by their obvious implications for political mobilization and activism, but by an understanding of the terms "race" and "gender" themselves as categories constructed from social and political needs, rather than genetic difference, and highly reified in the languages that both created and reproduced their specific cultural meanings. In effect, the concepts of race and gender joined the linguistic turn with identity politics, and both to the importance methodologically of "doing social history from below," divorced from the state- and society-centered teleologies of modernization and progress. Narratives could now be seen as *creating* race and gender, effectively subordinating as historical determinants the archived actualities of lived experience to the ways this experience was written out as a linked chain of events by what purported to be historical "description." As Robert Berkhofer neatly put it, race, gender, and soon ethnicity more broadly were "denaturalized," removed that is from the category of observable, real world objects capable of detached scientific study.[22]

What constituted the past now embraced all of human experience: from the lofty issues of international politics to the most common of everyday interactions.

Research in these newer areas of history "from below" required sources that were not in any reliable or systematic form among the holdings of research-oriented archival repositories. The documents as assembled in some cases also seemed in conflict with the historian's own set of memories and experiences about particular facets of the human story. Particularly in the areas of race, gender, first nations, and ethnic minorities, the authorities that guided archival processes proved counterintuitive in their substance and obscure if not absent entirely in traditional finding aids.

The Challenges of Postmodernism to the Authority of the Archive

Traditional narrative history and the historical archives whose holdings both derived from and inspired that approach were thus increasingly suspect among many academic historians for reasons going far beyond the epistemological issues of how the past could or could not be represented and evidenced, issues which could be reasonably well confined to academic concerns about the truth claims of archival scholarship. While these shifts in historical thinking were mainly centered in France and the United States, they had wide resonance everywhere in the historians' scholarly world. The curricular debates that roiled Russian history departments after the collapse of the Soviet Union, for example, and which we referred to at the beginning of this volume, were not simply about creating new kinds of courses. For many Russian historians with international reputations for careful scholarship on a variety of topics in European and prerevolutionary Russian history, what was now to be taught was the least of the matter. At issue instead was how to preserve the authority of archival scholarship and the conviction that accurate history could only be written on the basis of scientific archival research, especially Russia's own. The corrupted narratives of Soviet historical representation only reinforced these scholars' sense that archives remained the only authoritative way to process real pasts.

These passionate arguments were more than matched in western history faculties at the time, especially in the United States. As the Princeton historian Lawrence Stone put it in the journal *Past and Present* in 1991, the "subject-matter of history—that is, events and behavior"—had now been brought seriously into question. So had traditional understandings about sources and the central problem of historical analysis, the "explanation of change over time."[23] In Stone's view, postmodernism held a threefold threat: from linguistics ("building up from Saussure to Derrida and climaxing in deconstruction according to which there is nothing besides text"); from the "influence of cultural and symbolic anthropology" (whose practitioners say "the real is as imagined as the imaginary"); and from a "new historicism" (in which "language is 'the medium in which the real is constructed and apprehended'"). Stone concluded his provocative note by wondering whether "history might be on the way to becoming an endangered species," unselfconsciously evoking a key scientific concept of the nineteenth century.[24]

Whether Stone deliberately referenced Darwin, his attack on "postmodernism" was above all a defense of the received truths and practices of scientific history. We put "postmodernism" in quotation marks here partly to indicate that the term itself was a target of fierce opposition from historians. The term in its unqualified form reduces a variety of related tendencies and approaches to a convenient and easily misunderstood commonality: that what the western world has generally valued as modernity is seriously limited in its reflection of historical processes and progress. Modern here means the set of assumptions rooted in the individualistic rationality of the Enlightenment project, whether they relate to the emancipatory power of science and reason or the creation of progressive and liberating sociopolitical systems. As such, it embraces the technological and scientific advances that the Enlightenment helped to stimulate.

In a variety of complex and interesting ways, what might be best thought of as the postmodern syndrome challenges these assumptions. It does so, however, not in terms of their intrinsic values, but in terms of how these values have functioned within the complex dynamics of human welfare and social change. What links all varieties of postmodernism together is their challenge to understandings about how a complex human world was, is, and even should be developing since the teleologies of reason became an integral part of the educated western mindset. In other words, postmodernism in all of its variants critiques the values, technologies, and logics of modernization that have come almost everywhere to be regarded as the natural and universal course of human progress that situated the grand western and Soviet narratives of the Cold War.

For some, this has meant a direct confrontation with the assumptions of science itself. Central here is a doubt about the neutrality of scientific enquiry and the progressive nature of much scientific discovery, especially in terms of the destructive inventions of nuclear physics. These doubts have led to additional questions about cultural determinism and the intrinsic nature of scientific objectivity, focusing on the claims that are made in its name for how social resources should be distributed and the corresponding definitions of social goals.[25] A complementary approach has involved a deeper rooted challenge to the nature of reason itself in philosophical terms, particularly in the work of Nietzsche and Heidegger. Among the seminal critics here are Foucault and Derrida, whose analytical fault lines run along the explosive power of feeling and will and what Foucault has described as the microphysics of power. For Foucault, essential structures of social control can be found in the commonplace realms of everyday life, as well as in the more obvious institutions of the state. They include the disciplinary systems of "good" and "bad" language, as well as the elevation of reason and science to superordinate systems of value and the controlling institutions and institutionalized technologies of social "progress."[26]

All of these elements of postmodernism critique the authority of scientific history and traditional sources of historical knowledge, and hence the ways many historians have traditionally thought about their subjects and their sources. In other words, the postmodern move away from historical and archival "science" has been problematic not because it has undermined the advantages of reason, objectivity, verification, and "modernization"—something the postmodern syndrome has actually affected rather little—but because it has altered in fundamental ways the kinds of sources many historians now need to tell their stories, and hence the authority of the archive itself. Our point of entry into the problem is not therefore the nature of the "modern" so much as its understandings of the meanings and uses of historical authority that archives have traditionally reflected.

The concept of authority itself, moreover, has itself been a controversial issue in these discussions. The cultural historian Bruce Lincoln, one of the more sophisticated participants in this extended debate, has differentiated what he sardonically calls the three "ruts" of analytic and descriptive authority: the concern for social order and control that neoliberal and especially neoconservative observers see as fundamental to maintaining the natural course of modernization and progress in its Enlightenment and post-Enlightenment forms; the related concern for the consequences of dehumanizing (and antihuman) "authoritarianism" in its various horrific twentieth-century forms; and the more academic (but equally political) emphasis on assuring the progressive development of Weberian forms of legal authority embedded in the structures of modern bureaucratic states.[27] For our purposes, Lincoln shifts the discussion in a very useful direction. He translates each of these approaches into a series of interrelated questions about who, and under what conditions, individuals, groups, or states are able to speak with authority, that is, in ways regarded as right.

In this sense, archives have always "spoken with authority" in the different ways we have described. Historical narratives drawn from their documentation have always linked the authority of their descriptions and interpretations with the authenticity of their archival sources. In the process, understandings of contemporary circumstances and events have also been situated in longer kinds of authentic archival narrations, lending authority to (or discrediting) the institutions and practices they reflect in these terms. This perspective also situates the authority of the archives historically, dramatizing their social and political importance to understandings of historical change. It also historicizes the postmodern challenges to traditional historiography in the particular circumstances of the "long 1960s" when the turn away from authority in history began in earnest. If these challenges have led in several postmodern directions, some more fruitful than others, all have simultaneously challenged established assumptions about archives as authoritative sources of historical understanding. And all have produced similar resistances to those articulated by Stone.

In the mid-1990s, for example, Eugene Genovese, Gertrude Himmelfarb, and other prominent historians went so far as to break from what they regarded as the hopelessly postmodern American Historical Association and attempted to form a new professional group to save historians from themselves and history from the dustbin of irrelevancy. They and others joined Stone in his fear that the historical profession as a whole was in a steep decline, along with long-established norms of scholarly research. Politically liberal or left-leaning social historians like Bryan Palmer and Elizabeth Fox Genovese saw the new historical approaches as diminishing the significance of real life struggles by really oppressed social groups, not to mention their anguish. Palmer deployed E. P. Thompson's own polemic against abstract theorizing in rejecting from a Marxist perspective "the *ideological* project of rationalizing and legitimating this postmodern order as something above and beyond the social relations of a capitalist political economy."[28] Fox-Genovese passionately insisted that "history consists in something more than 'just one damn thing after another' . . . even in something more than what happened in the past . . . [It] must also be recognized as what did happen in the past—of the social relations and, yes, 'events,' of which our records offer only imperfect clues."[29] It also galvanized more conservative "traditionalists" like Gertrude Himmelfarb, who began in a series of quite public statements to assail these and other postmodern "distortions" as politicized "flight from fact." Feminist history was

> consciously and profoundly subversive, not only of traditional history but of earlier varieties of women's history. . . . Thus it is that the 'poetics' of history become the 'politics' of history. Postmodernism, even more overtly than Marxism, makes of history—the writing of history rather than the 'praxis' of history—an instrument in the struggle for power. The new historian, like the proletariat of old, is the bearer of the race/class/gender 'war'—or rather 'wars'. . . . If 'Everyman his own historian' must now be rendered 'Everyman/woman his/her own historian' . . . why not 'Every black/white/Hispanic/Asian/Native-American . . . ?' Or 'Every Christian/ Jew/Catholic/Protestant/Muslim/Hindu/agnostic/atheist . . . ?' Or 'Every heterosexual/homosexual/bisexual/androgynous/polymorphous/misogamist/misogynous . . . ?' And so on, through all the ethnic, racial, religious, sexual, national, ideological, and other characteristics that distinguish people?[30]

Here was a vision of the archival historian—the detached, circumspect recorder and objective interpreter of the past—under widespread attack. The intensity of this concern, however, was only partly because of the serious inroads the varieties of new history were making in scholarship and teaching. By the 1980s, ethnicity was firmly joined with race and gender as a "useful category" of historical, social, and cultural analysis, to paraphrase Joan Scott.[31] Postmodernism in history had ushered in a broad reorientation away from the traditional positivist assumptions that good historians could somehow recover the past from the archives as it "actually was," breathing as Michelet imagined the dead back to life. Challenges to the authority of traditional history were also challenges to institutional authority itself and the traditional ways academic power and resources were allocated. As programs in women's, ethnic, and African/African-American studies were created in many universities with full faculty lines, they encroached on the relationships between established knowledge and the powers of appointment and promotion tightly held by traditional academic departments. In the process, the role and power of those whose positivist understandings of scholarship had long structured social science disciplines was weakened or displaced.

So was the meaning of authoritative scholarship itself. No single template could now be used to validate historical description or interpretation or, more prosaically, to determine what work deserved an academic appointment or promotion. The very authorities of traditional political and institutional history, the foundational elements of modern archival science, had now become the subject of multiple and contentious points of view, each seeking validity in the scholarly depth and persuasiveness of its contending presentations and representations.

New Histories and Traditional Archives

To what extent, then, could history exert conceptual authority over the archive or derive its own authority from archival boxes and folders? The categories of race and gender, for example, that had no reference in traditional archival finding aids, were essentially morphing into the authorities that gave historical meaning to identity, memory, and experience. In the process, they challenged the traditional institutional and political authorities on which archives acquired and preserved materials, and on which they were still traditionally ordered.[32]

Even this brief review should thus suggest that the turn away from authority in history has not been a uniform or consistent process. Its contradictions, as for example between the ultimate need for historians to write in some comprehensible (narrative) prose even as they struggled to get away from its constraints, has roiled the profession from within even as assaults increased from without. Lawrence Stone insisted that the historical profession was in a "crisis of self-confidence about what it is doing and how it is doing it." Patrick Joyce's rejoinder was that historians simply had to register the major advance of postmodernism, "namely, that the events, structures and processes of the past are indistinguishable from the forms of documentary representation, the conceptual and political appropriations, and the historical discourses that construct them."[33]

What joined even Joyce and Stone together, however, was an understanding that the hitherto dominant understanding of the authority of archival evidence and its relation to historical logic were now open to serious question. Actually, it would be better to say these certainties were open to questions, since all of the contentious strands of thinking here have focused not on one issue but several larger ones. What is the proper unit of historical analysis? What is the relationship of historical texts to historical actualities? What, if any, are the embedded logics underlining historical change and how do they function? And what, finally, is the nature and role of archivally based authority in history itself—that is, for whom and how does history based on authentic documentation function in the production of social, cultural, and especially political certainties?

The first question has embraced the structural positivism of the *Annalistes*, as well as the subjectivism and poststructuralism of many who explore race, ethnicity, gender, and the identities invented by national institutions and traditions. The second question has not only engaged Derridean deconstructionists but those like Stone, Moses Finley, and even Carlo Ginzburg, who have argued in different ways for the representational virtues of a self-consciously drawn historical narrative. As Richard Vann has pointed out in *History and Theory*, the question of the historian's language itself may have come to supersede the broader issue of the relationship between historical and scientific knowledge, but the Platonic elements of linguistic representation have been almost universally recognized as historiographically relevant, regardless of where one stands on textuality.[34]

The issues raised by the question of embedded historical logics and the role of authority in history itself have absorbed the broadest kind of scrutiny and argumentation. The more esoteric elements of the poststructuralist critique of social science theory have been written more largely into post-Marxist reevaluations and a thorough (and sometimes intellectually brutal) reexamination of social history. Post-Marxism itself has fruitfully queried established Marxist understandings of the historical relationship between "base" and "superstructure." It has also assailed the teleology of progressive class conflict, especially in terms of the differences between historical representations and lived experience, and introduced new arguments about cultural as well as socioeconomic determinants of change. At the same time, the discussion has touched the question of how what has been represented as lived experience in archive-based historical narratives has correlated with what memory and other kinds of nonarchival evidence suggested might have occurred. In the process, the authority of memory and identity have been further placed in opposition to the institutional and political authorities structuring archival acquisition and description.

Finally, with the collapse of the Soviet Union itself and the radical transformation of state systems in Eastern Europe, the whole question of for whom and how authoritative history functions to create sociocultural and political certainties has come into focus even for historians who disdained the earlier scholarly debates. Despite its patent distortions, falsifications, and erasures, history continued to the Soviet Union's very end to hold broad authority as a legitimizing set of explanations for communist power by linking a scientific historical past to a radiant future. The actual collapse of this future could not therefore help but accelerate the almost literally explosive reexamination of the political uses of history by the state in this and other parts of the scholarly world, a process which has only become more contentious.

At the same time, regardless of where historians stood on the value of ethnicity or gender as historical categories, the end of the Soviet empire also strengthened examinations of "orientalism" and the conditions of "postcoloniality," focusing additional attention on the ways authoritative archives helped write particular mind-sets into what were in large measure historical prescriptions, rather than objective descriptive narratives as they purported to be. In Thomas Richards' view, the archive actually gave an artificial structure, clarity, and system to imperial/colonial relations, rather than the possibility of historical understanding.[35] As Appleby, Hunt, and Jacob have pointed out in *Telling the Truth about History*, the "end of history" that Francis Fukuyama and others celebrated when the historical alternatives to western neoliberalism seemed to collapse was true only in the sense that the pervasive authority of traditional political history had in large measure been eclipsed, at least among academic historians.[36]

In this eclipse, the extraordinarily productive intellectual revolution of the long 1960s had also largely run its course. Its many twists and turns, however, continued to have crucial implications for the archives. Social history "from below," as well as histories centering on the categories of race, ethnicity, and gender, required a kind of documentation either absent or almost entirely irretrievable in any direct and systematic way. Problems like race and gender had to be teased obliquely from sources collected, catalogued, and preserved as other kinds of testimony. In these and other areas, oral histories, photographs, judicial records, physical artifacts, and other less "traditional" kinds of sources took on new significance. Still, archives themselves received scant attention from historians, almost as if they were irrelevant to the issues roiling their profession. Indeed, it was not until the publication of Derrida's *Archive Fever* in 1994 that the nature and role of an archive in the process of historical recovery began to get any serious notice outside the professional circles and journals of archivists themselves.

Taken as a whole, the long 1960s was thus a period of intense critical thinking and intellectual innovation as important to the emergence of new kinds of historical understanding as the spread of scientific thinking a century earlier. Still, and most importantly, the turn away from traditional authority in history did not diminish the urge of most historians to get to the archives. The new ranges of subjects and approaches required authenticating evidence no less than the traditional subjects they displaced, however difficult it was to find. Even for many postmodernists, the transporting lure of archival dust was still every bit as intoxicating as it had been to Ranke and Michelet, however self-conscious and conceptually antitraditionalist they had become.

5

Archival Essentialism and the Archival Divide

While historians were actively exploring an increasing variety of questions during these years, archivists were equally active in addressing issues arising from the changing nature of documentation. In these discussions among archivists, historians representing new historiographical or methodological concerns were simply not in evidence. Concepts drawn from the changing disciplines of archival administration and information sciences informed the expertise needed to meet the challenges archives now faced. For archivists, documents had enduring value in the post-custodial and increasingly digital world not in terms of shared notions of their historical importance, but primarily as a result of a functional, institutionally focused definition of what constituted a record and its position within the system in which it was generated.

As the thoughtful archivist Preben Mortensen pointed out, these perspectives were grounded on a particular, ahistorical view of archival fundamentals. Archival science here has a "foundational," rather than historical character. Repositories have a "distinct nature," a "specific essence" with universally valid features "that can be found in all or almost all human cultures."[1] As Mortensen further suggested, this view also defined the three features of contemporary archival theory that would allow it to still be considered scientific in the post-custodial, digital age: universality, autonomy, internal consistency and logic.[2] None had anything to do with history or historians.

The Embrace of Essentialism by Archivists

The emphasis on the "essence" of archives, the scientific nature of archival processes, and the question of what constitutes the essential characteristics of their materials soon came to center archivists' responses to the rapidly increasing volume of records production and the new and fast-growing challenges of technology. At Monash University in Australia, the Records Continuum Research Group took up the problem of inconsistencies or gaps in metadata syntax and semantics, and their effect on systematic data applications and retention. Elizabeth Yakel at the University of Michigan focused on the contextualities in the recording of digital data, especially health-related information. At Indiana University, Philip Bantin concentrated on defining the information categories required for generating documents as evidence and analyzing the extent to which existing information systems satisfied those requirements. In the United Kingdom, efforts focused on defining the functional requirements of records management systems with an eye, again, to assuring consistency in access and strengthening a common archival understanding of "enduring value." Fundamental questions continued to revolve around the elements or attributes that need to be considered in working through the ways digital systems had to be designed.[3]

Archivists were consequently drawn increasingly toward the process of records generation and the institutional values, priorities, uses, practices, and needs that shape records creation—the central processes touching the design and circulation of information within specific institutions and organizations. Paradoxically, the new technologies were actually adding to rather than reducing the complexities of managing vast quantities of records, the challenge that initially pulled the archival profession out of its traditional custodial mode.

Moreover, as their professional interests and concerns were increasingly dominated by the problems of utilizing digital technology for description and access, as well as to manage what seemed to be an almost limitless number of digital records, these issues also further shaped a new professional identity for contemporary archivists, one far removed from the historical orientation of their custodial predecessors. Of necessity, the professional archivist now had to focus on technical and conceptual issues around the essential nature of a record and the consequent problems of arrangement, description, access, and technology associated with archiving records in a permanent way. As a result, archives as document-processing institutions have become increasingly self-contained.

In sum, contemporary archivists have come to think quite differently than their custodial predecessors about the theoretical parameters of archival practice itself. Refocused on the fundamental and organic connection between records and the agencies that produced them, an essential nexus considered foundational to the understanding of large records series, as well as to the constructions of digital archival systems, conceptions of archival authorities derived by the much more fluid process of historical analysis—the "changing winds of historiography," as the archivist F. Gerald Ham put it—could simply not be applied with any consistency or stability.[4] The approach of Luciana Duranti and others marginalized historical understanding even further. The role of history (and historians) in determining the value of a document now lay entirely outside the archival system and hence the archivists' concern. Duranti herself put it most forcefully: making archival decisions based on some notion of what the historical value of documents might be in the future was to "renounce impartiality, endorse ideology, and consciously and arbitrarily alter the societal record."[5]

Thus, while historians were broadening the range of their explorations and largely acknowledging the postmodern view that no historical story was without some merit, no document without value, no one conception of change deserving of a privileged metanarrative position, they were also losing their capacity to influence archival decisions that could identify documents as historically significant. From the new archival perspective, these broadened understandings of the past simply could not provide the kinds of authoritative structures and taxonomies of relative significance that archivists now needed to guide them in determining records of "enduring" value. More importantly, with purely digital materials, neither could they provide the kind of structured, consistent, and enduring vocabulary essential to electronic information system design, implementation, and retrieval.

In these terms, postmodernism in history can be thought of from an archival perspective as the emergence of a set of "counter authorities": unstable and contested evaluations of history's central and determining elements with no consistent practical use in determining what sorts of materials archives should acquire and preserve. Moreover, historians mindful of the range of interests now preoccupying their colleagues, themselves became reluctant to take on responsibility in the processes of appraisal or of electronic system design, even if they had some notion of what this required. To choose one descriptor is to diminish the possibilities of others. To privilege one conceptual framework is inconsistent with the notion that the past must be understood in multiple ways, that indeed, social groups, societies, and nations have multiple pasts rather than singular ones. It has not only been the question of technological competence that has precluded engagement in the construction of archival descriptive systems but the changes in the nature of historical study itself.

This is also the case with the even more problematic question of document destruction, the dark side for historians of the issue of "enduring value." Given the new breadth of historical enquiry, how can historians assume responsibility for disposing of materials that might conceivably be of interest to their colleagues in the future? Indeed, one of the most distinguished Latin American historians in the United States recently demonstrated how important a simple receipt for the sale of a mule was in understanding the nature of slavery and indenture in nineteenth-century Cuba.[6] In important ways, all documents are of at least some historical value if historians themselves have some say about the matter. When every story is of some historical merit, every voice of some historical value, then every document has the potential to contain some important historical meaning.

For archivists, meanwhile, even those familiar with the new breadth of historical interests, the practical difficulties of the appraisal process have affirmed the view that archives cannot embrace the idea of providing all documents for answering all questions. Difficult disposition decisions simply could not be avoided even, and in some respects especially, with digital systems that were now producing documents in seemingly unlimited amounts. In these circumstances, archivists further embraced the effort to identify "essential" qualities both of the record itself and the context of its creation, and in these terms alone form the strategies they need for retention and destruction.

What then is a document of enduring value in these terms? What are the essential elements that will determine whether or not it becomes part of the future historical record? And how, again in practical terms, are archivists and records keepers actually to appraise the truly gigantic body of material under their care on this basis, digital or otherwise? If the interventionist necessities of the post-custodial era required radically new strategies and standards, and if these were now questions for archival theory and information science alone, is it not still the case that the determination of "enduring value" still somehow needed to take the interests of future historians into account?

Echoing Ham and Duranti, some of the most imaginative thinkers about archives have answered with an emphatic "no!" Helen Willa Samuels, for example, who gained prominence among archivists with the 1992 publication of a study of university archives, has stressed that archivists could no longer rely on subjective guesses about what the future interests of historians might be like. Even less could archivists determine what bodies of records had significance for historical as opposed to contemporary understanding: descriptive analyses of future "pasts" rather than descriptive studies of the present. Samuels offered instead the application of "functional analysis" to the problem of selection. Rather than gazing into crystal balls, archivists had to make their decisions in terms of the phenomenon or institution the records documented. Since archivists could not predict future research, they had to document the processes or institutions that produced their records as adequately as possible.[7]

Recognizing that no selection process could be entirely objective, Samuels proposed that if documents were set in a functional rather than historical context, they would best preserve an understanding of the institution's structure and procedures themselves, rather than "tell its story." In other words, the organizational complexities of the institution itself formed the analytic construct for the selection of records. While Samuels focused specifically on university archives, what made her work so influential in the archival community was the way she laid out for those institutions the functional activities, structures, layers, purposes, and aspirations that reflected and defined the documents they produced in ways entirely independent of any historical periodization.

The question of designating records of enduring value thus became a question of understanding which documents and records were likely to reflect the essential features of an institution in all of its administrative and procedural complexity. In creating a historical record, in other words, Samuels argued that the selection process should begin not by reading "historical works" or focusing on "the specific history, people, events, structures or records of an institution," but on an understanding of the function of the documentation. On this basis, archivists and other records keepers could formulate an appraisal strategy that identified documentation essential to the functions at hand and therefore worth preserving for the future.[8] Here was a further, even for some a definitive embrace of archival "essentialism," the central element of which remained its focus on the primary organizational relationship—the essential relationship—between the record and the agency that produced it.

Given the extraordinary new challenges facing the archives and records management community, the logic, rationality, and efficiencies of this essentialist approach have had enormous appeal. Among its other attractions, it dovetails neatly with the ways archivists have approached the most difficult of these challenges: the archiving of electronic records and the creation of digital archives. Since all digital systems rely on certain essential elements of linguistic fixity and structural order, digital records of enduring value emerge in this perspective as a necessary and essential part of the archival process itself, providing only that archivists and records managers fully understand the "particular organizational, business, technological, and cultural environments that they are trying to influence," as Margaret Hedstrom has put it, and apply appropriate and enduring standards, system designs, and mechanisms for retrieval.[9]

These essentialist views have also led to new and contending understandings of the digitally structured archive itself. For some, the embrace of essentialism challenges the traditional place of archival administration and practice. As archival decision making increasingly takes place at the time records are created, rather than at the end of the cycle of use, there is understandable concern about how distant archivists themselves are from this process, and hence any useful perspective on the integrity of the record and the reasons for its preservation. Without this understanding, "enduring value" can simply become an unintended consequence of the act of preservation. In these circumstances, digital records are not likely to be part of any future historical archives unless the processes of their origination can be fully documented, as with their paper predecessors, and unless they can be moved to the custody of formal archival institutions separate and independent of their agencies of origin and professionally devoted to serving a variety of publics, including not least the current and future generations of historians.[10]

For others, however, archives have again become thought of as full and appropriate partners in the corporate and institutional mission, just as they were during their rapid earlier development in relation to political institutions and the state. Indeed, many newly trained archivists and professional records managers now see themselves in a critical position at the very center of information flows, indispensible to the functioning of all contemporary organizations that communicate and transact electronically. This view has strengthened the notions of Bearman and others of archives positioned basically as modern information systems in terms of the ways their materials are embedded in administrative structures and continually generate usable documentation (or "evidence") for the agencies that produce them. From this perspective, the very nature of these archives allows its documentary evidence be used for all kinds of arguments including historical ones even if not designed to do so, providing only that it can be accessed.

The Rejection of Essentialism by Historians

As we have seen, the turn away from authority in history was a complex and multidimensional process. At its core, however, was a view of historical processes that was increasingly suspicious of the ways historians had traditionally understood the nature and role of institutions, especially those associated with the state. While the celebrated innovations in history "from below" echoed in some ways the long-established conventions of historical Marxism, especially in Europe, these and other new initiatives focusing on gender and reconsidering the concept of class also challenged established thinking about how institutions functioned and exercised their power.

Guided by a remarkable eruption of new social theory, historians became increasingly aware of the ways the structures and processes of political institutions were themselves affected by sociocultural factors like gender, while social institutions like the family also reflected overarching relations of institutionalized power. The new interest in ethnicity, identity formation, and the authority of experience also intersected with a reexamination of how and why various social and political institutions functioned as they did.[11] If race became the primary focus for many American scholars, and new courses on race and ethnicity became required parts of college curricula, the nature and claims of nationality dominated thinking elsewhere. The breakup of the Soviet Union, one of the most remarkable and unanticipated events in all of European political history, further stimulated explorations already underway on the complex institutional relationships between hegemonic and subaltern cultures, the cultural and social, as well as the political components of institutionalized imperialism, and what James Scott had identified as the arts of resistance to institutionalized domination.

It is thus somewhat ironic that as archivists and records managers have essentialized relationships between documents and institutions as the only viable way to create effective new classification authorities for retrievable records of enduring value, historians have developed radically different ways of understanding institutions themselves. To be sure, historical work still focuses on great men, great events, and powerful institutions, more the stuff of popular as opposed to academic history. In any event, an important understanding produced by the innovations in historical analysis over the last two decades is that there are no essential and universally recognized determinants of the historical process. The nature of each historical event, each element of social change, and each historical actor large or small must be analyzed and understood within the complexities of discrete historical contexts, circumstances, and representations. Even among sophisticated comparative historians, essential commonalities are now to be found only in the kinds of questions historians formulate and explore, not in their essentialized answers.

Moreover, at a time when archival description is focused on controlled vocabularies and fixed linguistic structures, many historians have come to find language itself a culturally based and politically charged instrument. Even an understanding of the nation-state, perhaps the most venerable subject of historical description, has been expanded to embrace the ways it has been an effect of discourse, the creation of rhetorics designed in part as political claims. The role and value of language are themselves evidence of highly contextualized relationships. As Gabrielle Spiegel has proposed, one of the features of the linguistic turn in historical study has been to "undermine our faith in the instrumental capacity of language to convey information about the world."[12]

For many contemporary historians, perhaps especially those in the academic world, it therefore goes without saying that institutions of the type that generate records are both more and less than what they represent themselves to be. More, in the sense that the transactions within and between government agencies or corporations encompass a range of processes and actions quite different from those that find reflection in what the archivist regards as authentic transactions. Less, because while the offices and institutions within an Enron Corporation or Department of Defense may appear to be entirely about making money or fighting wars, the ways these purposes are pursued is also conditioned fundamentally by the greater socioeconomic, cultural, and political environments in which they function. From a historian's point of view, unless these larger patterns become part of the appraisal and descriptive processes of archival institutions, the records of enduring value now being accessioned by archivists may well be perceived to have little historical importance.

The Archival Divide

One of the more surprising aspects of this sea change in the conception and administration of archives is that historians themselves have scarcely seemed to notice. In 1999, John Carlin, Archivist of the United States and a man skilled in management as a former governor of Kansas but without training either as an archivist or as a historian, spoke at the annual meeting of the American Historical Association. He reported that the approximately 90,000 files of electronic records already received by the archives was less than 10 percent of the annual production of digital materials being generated by agencies like the Departments of State and Treasury that "we are likely to need to preserve." While the many important projects then underway around the world to digitize historical documents obviously held incredible opportunities for scholarly access, Carlin focused on the real dangers to the historical record that the "unprecedented challenge" electronic records now posed, both because of their quantity and form. "They can be easily erased; they degenerate relatively quickly; and they can be rendered unreadable by the obsolescence of the hardware and software on which they were created." For assistance, the National Archives and Records Administration (NARA) had just formed a new partnership with the San Diego Supercomputer Center. There was no mention of how the historians in his audience might themselves possibly assist in assuring these challenges were met in ways that, as the National Archives building itself proclaimed, "the Glory and Romance of Our History are Here Preserved."[13] Indeed, even if Carlin had asked for help, it was unlikely that anyone in his audience of historians would have had a clue about what to do.

Whether or not historians understand these matters, there is no doubt they have very significant implications for how the past will be processed by future historians and archivists in both conceptual and practical terms. While historians continue to beat down archival doors in their admirable pursuit of all kinds of history, new and traditional, the intellectual and administrative challenges of identifying selecting, organizing, and conceptualizing the archive as a historical source have become too complex, and historical study has become too unstable, for historians to have much notion of what the historical archives of the future will be like.

The distance that has emerged between the historian and archivist is thus much more than a separation of professional interaction and activity. It is, instead, symptomatic of a much deeper divide: between divergent conceptual frameworks for understanding and using contemporary and historical documentation; between the evolving conceptual frameworks for historical understanding and those related to the efficient and practical retention of records; between the ways archivists and historians now and in the future will process the past.

For a time, this growing separation seemed largely the result of the lack of common interest: a disconnect of professional circles, in which each group was informed by separate associations, separate preparations, separate journals. Career paths simply seemed not to cross. Methodological issues associated with archival processes were rarely a part of the offerings of history departments; historians were scarcely interested in the type of education archivists were receiving. However, as we have reflected on issues of the use of authority in historical understanding and the role of authorities in archival systems, on attention to language as a contested historical construction and the importance of rigidity in language as an access tool, and on the evaluation of the research potential of documentation and the relation of documentation and the importance of documentation in organizational information flow, we have come to realize that the divide is more than a case of newly separate professional paths. Perhaps to the surprise of historians, archival administration has evolved in the digital age into a complex discipline based on its own set of practices, principles, and assumptions. At the leading edges of historical thinking, how the past is technologically processed by archival professionals who were once their disciplinary colleagues is now virtually incomprehensible. Perhaps to the surprise of archivists, history has become a fluid and rapidly changing discipline that has moved beyond the categories that conform to standardized descriptive terminologies and needs. At the leading edges of archival thinking, there is little use and even less time for the needs and complexities of innovative history. The categories of knowledge most important to the training of archivists now derive from organizational theory, complex systems, information science, communications, and computer technology situated in emerging programs in Schools of Information. For archivists, history has yielded in the post-custodial digital age to the importance of bureaucratic behavior and the imperatives of technology.

The archival divide between historians and archivists is thus a deeply conceptual separation based on different readings of the relation between past and present, on how pasts can and should be literally and figuratively processed. Yet it is precisely these expanding conceptual parameters that should give both archivists and historians pause. Contestation over the nature of sources, over the complex problem of "social memory," over new historical understandings of culture and power, and over the ways even passive archivists are active in the production of specific kinds of knowledge are all questions of pressing concern to historians and archivists alike. It is therefore possible that attending to these issues, as we attempt to do in the following chapters, may also provide some better understanding for each of how the past is now being processed by the other, and hence offer at least some possibilities for bridging the divide.

PART TWO

PROCESSING THE PAST

6

The Social Memory Problem

As we have seen, the turn away from archival authority in history during the "long 1960s" was propelled in part by a rejection of traditional historical authorities in forming an understanding of the past. The possibilities of what encompassed the past, and affected historical development, involved quite different questions than those traditional archives were organized to answer. New lines of enquiry required a more creative sense of what constituted a historical source. In the process, archival documents became only one set of a variety of authoritative sources that could give credence to historical interpretation. Increasing attention to social processes, cultural encounters, gender, the formation of social identities, and the various neglected forms of power relations moved historians and other scholars beyond the capacity of the archives to inform their work in traditionally satisfactory ways.

Pursuing new kinds of history also involved an explosion of interest in something identified as "social memory." Despite the imprecision of this concept, it soon took on the role of validating a variety of new historical descriptions and interpretations, a powerful public good whose authority stood in varying degrees of opposition to more formal and traditional understandings of the past. By the late 1980s, as one historian put it, the postmodern age seemed "obsessed" with memory.[1] A whole new "memory industry" was springing up, fixed on the capacity of memory to achieve a sensitive and affective relationship to a variety of newly discovered pasts.[2] Several leading scholarly journals devoted whole issues to the subject. In Europe the concept itself was recognized as an important new element in the history of concepts [begriffgeschichte]. A decade or more later, memory was still a leading term in cultural history.[3]

What was increasingly described as social memory was understood as the collective formation of individual recollections and identities. Its creation and re-creation in a variety of social practices came to validate historical understanding. Together with the related concept of "social identity," social memory also became a way of ascribing meaning to the past in ways often unrelated to any representations in the archives. Charles Dickens's introduction to *Great Expectations*, expresses the view succinctly: "I will tell the story not as it actually happened, but as I remember

it." Lived "experience" thus emerged as an authoritative source for historical validation, despite the complexities of how it was remembered. The experience of
alienation from a dominant culture, the experience of changing class and gender
affiliations, the perceptions formed by personal experience, experience learned
"first hand" from others—all of these were now being read back into affective
pasts, making them "usable" in a variety of new ways.

As "memory work" challenged traditional historical understanding, it engaged
an understanding of traditional archives as well. Its approach to the past as social
process and the arguments of some of its new practitioners concerning the validity of multiple pasts challenged established archival assumptions of a shared and
unified past. The archival practices underlying these assumptions also came into
question. In this broader memory framework, archives themselves became a part
of the historical problem in the ways they served and reinforced traditional historiographies and authorities.[4] Like postmodernism, social memory created its own
set of "counter authorities." In the process, the very purpose of historical archives
past and future became a contested subject, along with their practices of appraisal,
acquisition, and preservation. Long-held views about the archive as a formal place
of historical memory also came under challenge. So did the role of archivists
themselves as its custodians. Upon being sworn in as the ninth Archivist of the
United States and head of the National Archives and Records Administration
(NARA) in 2005, Allen Weinstein felt compelled to allude to these challenges by
reaffirming that "all who work for NARA are [still] the designated custodians of
America's national memory."[5]

The social memory problem thus requires attention here in these terms. The
concept itself needs interrogation if archivists are to understand more fully what
the historians' interest in memory has been about, and how it has affected the
archival aspects of new research. At the same time, historians and others need to
understand the problems it has raised for archives.

The Reemergence of Memory through "Memory Studies"

The problem of memory, of course, has never been very far from questions of historical understanding. When the U.S. National Archives proclaimed on its façade
that "The Glory and Romance of Our History are Here Preserved," it spoke directly
to the subjectivities of nostalgia, remembrance, and commemoration, all ways in
which memory had long connected history to the archives. The common notion of
remembering history has long found routine expression in the concepts of historical memory and historical consciousness. For nineteenth-century thinkers like
Hegel and Marx, these notions held power for political reasons: the "tradition of
dead generations" that weighed for Marx "like a nightmare on the minds of the
living" or carried for Hegel the cumulative strivings for freedom.[6] "Historical

memory" designated those elements of the past that were brought to mind only through historical exploration, rather than individual recall.

When social memory displaced traditional notions of historical memory in the 1970s and 1980s, it did so as a "nonparadigmatic, transdisciplinary, centerless enterprise," as the sociologists Jeffrey Olick and Joyce Robbins have rather critically described it.[7] Social memory became a focal point of discussions about identity, multiculturalism, orientalism, and imperial domination. Among postmodernists, it was relevant to issues of objectivity, evidence, truth, and narrativity, all of which intersect the complex boundaries between mentality and physical reality.[8] Sociologists rediscovered Maurice Halbwachs' 1925 work *Les Cadres sociaux de la mémoire* (Social Frameworks of Memory), and his *La Mémoire collective*.[9] Scholars in cultural studies, literature, and literary criticism saw social memory as an important set of practices by which representations of the past could create new sets of contemporary meaning. A revitalized heritage industry, meanwhile, moved memory studies forcefully into public spaces. "Je me souviens" [I will remember] began to adorn Quebec's license plates. New commercial interests developed around sites like the Gettysburg battlefield and "history themed" amusement parks.[10] As cable television extended its reach, the History Channel emerged as one of its most popular (and profitable) ventures. More important, the opening of Holocaust museums in Washington, D.C., Berlin, and elsewhere, as well as the stunning film productions *Shoah* and *Shindler's List*, forcefully reminded visitors and viewers of the moral dimensions of social memory and the imperative not to forget.[11]

All of this complicated the issue of memory for historians and archivists alike, particularly around the issue of the authority of the archive. While memory had commonly served to amplify historical understanding or raise doubts about the accuracy of historical narratives, the whole thrust of scientific scholarship was to move away from its distortions and imprecisions. Archives claimed their role as places of memory because the authenticity of their documents validated or invalidated the various ways the past was recalled.

Among historians, the surge of interest in social memory came largely from the same places as other new critiques of traditionally authoritative history. Prominent again were members of the *Annales* group such as Philippe Aries, whose *Centuries of Childhood* charted memory and recollection rather than social experience;[12] and in European history the work again of E. P. Thompson, who set out to "rescue the poor stockinger, the Luddite cropper, the 'obsolete' hand-loom weaver," and other socially marginal groups from the "enormous condescension of posterity." Both within and outside academic communities, Thompson brought wide attention to the varieties of lived experience that were obscured or lost in traditional archival collections and in the ways they were described.[13]

New work in this area had a particular impact because authoritative history and authoritative archives were still largely about formal institutions of power, as we have seen. Archival historians largely focused on the historical concepts and structures that underlay archival description. This encouraged the histories of "winners" and "losers," and the corresponding roles of rising and falling institutions and the sources of their fate. Imaginative approaches were needed to document the stories of those whose place in history did not warrant archival attention.

This was especially the case in repressive societies with highly developed archival systems like the Soviet Union, the largest employer of professional archivists in the world. The new prominence of social history in Western Europe and the United States was paralleled here by a new clandestine memory history, circulated as *samizdat*. The Russian word signified materials that were typed and "self-published" in carbon copies or by mimeograph, but the idea of *samizdat* also empowered the veracity of individual and collective memories themselves in countering the hegemonic narrative of triumphal Soviet progress.

A seminal event here was the publication of *Let History Judge* in 1971 by the dissident Russian historian Roy Medvedev. In more than 500 detailed pages, Medvedev managed to explore the origins and consequences of Stalinism largely through the complex and painful memories of hundreds of its victims, whose secret letters, diaries, and personal stories had somehow made their way into his study. Smuggled out of the Soviet Union and soon translated into every major language, *Let History Judge* held readers in thrall not only because of the richness and poignancy of its memory material but also the ways in which the lived histories Medvedev depicted stood in such stark odds with virtually the entire body of published Soviet history. In a society where it was literally quite dangerous to remember, Medvedev, in effect, presented memory as an alternative and far more credible form of truth telling.[14] His work also testified to the ways in which the social memory of lived experience could capture and deploy alternative (and hence multiple) pasts, whether recently lived or recreated in some way for more distant events and experiences.

For a broad American public, these concerns were strengthened with the appearance in 1976 of Alex Haley's *Roots*, a controversial look at black Americans' African heritage. For scholars, they gained new analytical sophistication with the publication of work by Eric Hobsbawm and others on the "invention of tradition" and especially with Benedict Anderson's masterful *Imagined Communities* in 1983.[15] Thereafter, the connections between social memory and collective identity developed along several complementary trajectories. In the identity-conscious United States but elsewhere as well, particularly in former colonial areas, this linkage quickly became a foundational element of new understandings of race and ethnicity. In Western Europe it underlay new struggles over the fraught questions of social responsibility for the Holocaust, as well as new explorations into the role of the Vichy government and other collaborationist regimes. By the late 1980s in Mikhail Gorbachev's rapidly changing Soviet Union, invented traditions and collectively remembered pasts became a key element in the breakup of the world's second most powerful state. Everywhere in the region, social groups began to make claims based on identities shaped by the memory of common historical experience, however doubtful the possibilities that these rediscovered pasts were actually experienced in common or uniform ways, and however distant their evidence was from any archival holding.

What, then, *is* social memory? How should we understand this overworked and often clichéd concept? How, indeed, can we recover any memories outside of the experience of those who actually remembered? If social memory exists as more than an analytical concept, where and how can we see it as having authority in processing the past? And central to our purpose here, how in particular did the emergence of an "obsession" with memory in the 1980s and 1990s affect archival practices and authorities and find reflection in the archival divide?

Individual and Social Memory in the Creation of "Usable" Pasts

Answers to these questions are rooted in the complex relationship between individual memory and the very different nature of "collective" remembering, which means in the simplest terms how social groups represent themselves and their pasts. Individual memory is, of course, about the physiology and neurology of the brain, the subject of a voluminous literature. Most of this focuses on the physiology of brain recall and the central role memory plays in structuring thought and behavior. These are important to historians and archivists insofar as they touch on the differences between active and passive recall, the effects on memory of physical or emotional trauma, and the layered nature of active and suppressed consciousness. Each of these areas of enquiry has helped historians understand and explain why and how individuals act as they do.

We also know from the physiological literature that individual memory works by assembling various bits of information stored in different parts of the brain. These are produced by learning and experience, and are constantly recalled as memory in ways that make the past constantly relevant to the present.[16] This rather simple notion has interesting historical implications concerning the accessibility of the past, and hence about the reality of lived experience. It also raises basic questions about how individual memories link information together, which is to say, about time and narration. Since these are also principal points of linkage between individuals and their social milieus, they also frame the relationships between individuals and the practices of "social remembering."[17]

While time, experience, and narration are common concepts, they are also more complex and problematic in terms of the way individuals and societies process their pasts than everyday usage might suggest. Time is the trickiest. Individuals are constantly aware of its passage, but in ways that reinforce cultural notions of cyclical or lineal change. Individual memory "proves" that the past really existed in lineal or cyclical relation to the present in ways that are both irrefutable and, if one forgets, unprovable without some external reference. As Michael

Lambek has pointed out, to remember is never solely to report on the past (much less to report the past). It functions as a way of establishing one's *relationship* to the past, to access in pragmatic as well as moral ways what past experience can "teach." Individual remembering authenticates these social positions because memory insists what one remembers about the past was real.[18]

Experience therefore frames an individual's relation to the past by turning it into history. What individuals retrieve are representations mediated by the concepts and processes that give them narrative form and historical meaning. Experience is therefore an extremely difficult area of historical enquiry. The popular tendency to essentialize it as the rock-bottom foundation of historical reality largely ignores the role of narrative as a mediating practice, and indeed, the ways all experience gains meaning through narrative expression as the subjectivities of experience are objectivized into a describable story of some sort.[19] As Iuri Lotman put it, the event itself may seem to those who lived through it as something "disorganized, chaotic, or without any broader meaning or historical logic. But when an event is told and retold through language, it inevitably acquires a structural unity."[20] In other words, by ordering experience into narrative, individuals remember "their" history. Memory narratives make lived history capable of being told, understood, documented, repeated, and hence available for a variety of uses.

The problems of memory that are associated with trauma also engage problems of telling and documenting the past. Comprehensive narratives have to be found (or "uncovered") to give traumatic experiences comprehensible meaning and allow them to be told. Traumatic events are precisely those rare episodes that are distinguishable by their location outside the ordinary realms of discourse. Those who experience them are often literally struck dumb. They cannot integrate their experiences into any comprehensible narrative, at least not without substantial therapeutic help.[21] When narratives are accessed or created to situate these kinds of experiences into meaningful stories, they tend to be particularly powerful ones. The experiences they reflect often constitute elemental turning points in individual life histories.

In rare instances, one can also use trauma fruitfully to reference collective experiences whose meaning is also not easily understood or rendered into narrative. Much of the literature about trauma in this sense refers to the Jewish Holocaust, whose comprehension and meaning may always remain difficult to grasp. Certainly the effects of this horrific trauma are still being played out in the histories of contemporary Europe and the Middle East.[22] In a similar way, the traumatic events of September 11 were initially both unimaginable and indescribable in these terms as well. It was only after they were spun out as an attack on America and the "Pearl Harbor of the war against terrorism" that they became broadly comprehensible. Narrating the events of 9/11 into the real and imagined meanings of America's entry into its "last great war against tyranny" was the form through which the dismembered incoherencies of this awful moment were historically put together, or in Lara Moore's felicitous phrase, "re-membered."[23]

It was also the process through which the events of 9/11 could be used to reproduce and strengthen the traditional authorities of the American historical past. Remembering Pearl Harbor as a way of understanding 9/11 not only framed the ways in which this event entered the American national narrative but also constituted hierarchies of comparative historical importance. In contrast to the ways the first attack on the World Trade Center in 1994 was processed as a criminal event, and whose documents were relegated to routine police and court archives, those pertaining to 9/11 acquired the importance of primary historical artifacts. Some thought they required their own distinct archive.

Here one can begin to see an important point of linkage between individual memories and something we can usefully call social or collective memory, however unreflectively this term is commonly used. Maurice Halbwachs suggested many years ago that individual memory is not really possible outside the frameworks used by people living in society to determine and retrieve their recollections. In his view, individuals require social interactions to give meaning to their memories. They therefore recall, recognize, and localize their memories in social contexts.[24] These views have drawn extensive criticism, but one can agree with Halbwachs and others that individual memory is also a social practice insofar as the knowledge it creates is refracted through social discourses and institutions.[25] Since the complex set of subjectivities that individuals feel when living through a particular event are essentially impressionistic (i.e., prediscursive), coherent narratives about them only emerge through interactions with the discourses, individuals, and institutions that surround them. These interactions also give them meaning in both individual and social terms by setting them in established logics, understandings, and value systems.

Although there is substantial disagreement among historians, archivists, and others about the nature and conceptual value of social memory, not to say its meaning, the concept can be quite useful analytically. This is especially so when it is used in careful ways to describe common understandings about the past that are formed when shared narratives, institutions, and broader sociocultural practices define and give meaning to what members of the group recognize as constitutive experiences.

As Derrida has explored in *Archive Fever*, making the past usable in this way has much to do with the complex ways in which individuals feel the need to "know" or "uncover" their pasts as a way of defining their presents. Derrida's fever is the drive to understand one's origins and "roots," and to situate oneself and one's community in ways that create a necessary sense (ego) of who one is and is not, which is to say one's individual and social identities.[26] "Know" and "uncover" require quotation marks here, however, to signify that what is known and uncovered is not necessarily an accurate reflection of the past, however much it comes to be represented in these terms. The historical authority of memory relies on a powerful set of subjective understandings that exist independently of scholarly analysis or archival verification. "Shared" pasts of this sort take on their own moral, social, cultural, and even political complexions in ways that carry the weight of contemporary political and cultural struggles. They then serve as evidence of how history has determined or denied the ways things should have been, should be, or should become in the future.

Social Memory, Social Identity, and the Ascription of Historical Meaning

The relationship between history and memory, between how written history remembers or forgets, has been a central question in the expansive literature on history and memory. As Francis Yates and Jacques LeGoff developed the history of social memory, drawing on the work of the British anthropologist Jack Goody and others, the role of memory as history developed in five distinct stages: from its key position in societies without writing, to some reduction in its role with the rise of memory writing and a medieval equilibrium between the oral and the written, to its extensive devaluation after the printing press displaced it from a moralizing oral discourse to the moral neutrality of new scientific knowledge. This later stage reached a point of fulfillment during the Enlightenment with the publications of the French *Encyclopédie*. In LeGoff's interpretation, it was only with the French revolution that the importance of memory was reasserted in France and elsewhere in Europe, since this cataclysm demanded a legitimizing explanation in moral terms. The subsequent overflowing of memory in the ways societies constituted themselves drew fundamentally from their need to justify and legitimize their institutions and power in the moralities of social welfare and virtue. The truth of the past lay in the moralizing and legitimizing connections that its memory and commemoration made to the values and institutions of the present, in contrast to the ways "scientific" history drew its authority from an objectively verifiable understanding of "truth."[27]

Whether historians can actually be objective is another matter. (It is also, of course, the subject of a large literature in its own right.) Obviously, even the most morally neutral historians make choices about what is worthy of study and ascribe meaning to the past by connoting through emphasizing or omitting what they think needs to be known. Verification can also inscribe particular values of right and wrong, as for example in the case of histories of religion that show how faith-based institutions derive from particular historical and social circumstances. Most good historians would agree with Paul Ricoeur that history cannot, in fact, be objective in the ways many would like, and even at its most scientific is inherently inexact, like memory. Both practices can only reconstruct the past through narrative structures that make it comprehensible.[28]

For many engaged in this discussion, however, the problem is not the inexactness of history or memory. It is the ways objectivizing history is destructive to the needs of societies to preserve and strengthen their faiths and identities. Yosef

Yerushalmi set the discussion most sharply in these terms in his 1982 volume *Zakhor: Jewish History and Jewish Memory*, where he contrasted the sacred roles of collective Jewish memory with the desacralizing effects of a secular modern Jewish historiography. At stake was not the accuracy of Jewish historiography but the spiritual integrity of Jewish history itself. The Hebrew word *zakhor* (remember) in Yerushalmi's title was itself an injunction of Jewish religious and cultural tradition: to prevent the destruction of a people long bound together by memory's "mystic chords," as Abraham Lincoln described it in his first inaugural address, and whose identity was now inextricably linked to an endangered political state. For Jews especially, history of the sort Yerushalmi himself was practicing in *Zakhor* desacralized a chosen people, not to mention the role of God in determining their fate.[29]

The threat to Jewish cultural and political identity posed by secular historiography signals the ways in which the ascription of meaning into history reflects a tension about morality for historians that is commonly a core element of the symbolic and narrative structures of social memory. When Yerushalmi, Jacques LeGoff, Pierre Nora, and others worry about history usurping the function of memory, they have in mind the ways serious historical scholarship attempts to approach the past with a dispassion and objectivity that tries to avoid moralization. Good historians recognize that their task is both descriptive and interpretive, and that interpretation and analysis will always stir discussion and controversy. They are also aware, as Michel de Certeau has argued, that the credibility of their narratives is partly the reflection of their skills as writers, that their narratives themselves process and synthesize the complex past "realities" they reflect, obscuring in its very writing the analytic and narrative practices which create it. At the same time, even the most careful of historians cannot avoid approaching the past from a value-laden present. Historical analysis necessarily reflects a way of thinking, a means of processing the past that implicitly inscribes judgments. For good historians, this requires a self-conscious effort not to read the past back through contemporary value systems. The intellectual struggle for historians is to allow whatever moral lessons the past might offer to flow directly from its objective rendering, not from his or her own convictions.

The common notion that history is itself a kind of social memory is thus a misnomer. Historical writing might contribute strongly to a shared or collective understanding of the past; and court historians of various kinds sometimes with privileged access to restricted documents, are constantly at work to reinforce particular historical views. Not surprisingly, what academic historians sometimes scorn as "popular" histories, books like Tom Brokaw's *The Greatest Generation* for example, are also eagerly read by those who prefer historians to reinforce their own memories and values, strengthening their feelings of social identification and affiliation.[30] Popular history engages, as well as creates, social memory because it conforms to well-established and widely memorialized social and cultural narratives, which is largely what makes it popular.

Critical history, however, stirs discussion and debate not only about historical actualities but about their meaning. Few areas have been more rife with argument, for example, than investigations into everyday Stalinism and Nazism, even though few would accuse the participants in these contentious debates of being disinterested in getting these histories right. The idea that Stalinism might have had any grounding in social opportunities, cultural predilections, individual strivings, or popular support is as jarring to many contemporary sensibilities as the argument that Hitler ruled a country of willing executioners.[31] In contrast to the dominant narratives of social memory, which almost always are cast in one way or the other to ascribe meaning in morally positive terms, one can hardly describe the scholarship or its authors here of being moral or immoral. Serious historians may ascribe meanings to their material that serve a moral purpose and may hope to cultivate in individual readers an understanding, say, of good and evil, or of complexity, nuance, doubt, ambition, or indifference—a range of matters that their readers might regard in morally judgmental terms. Still these historical explorations can prove a challenge to the valorized narratives of social memory rather than a source of confirmation or reproduction.

A serious biography of "Bomber Harris," for example, the leader of the allied firebombing of Dresden and other German cities, whose heroic statue stands in the heart of London, can reveal the level of wartime indifference to the desperation of noncombatants, rather than strengthen notices of courage and sacrifice. The deaths of Native Americans at Wounded Knee can emerge as an intended consequence of American "manifest destiny." A careful exploration of the "rape of Nanking" can startle social memories of several societies out of varied degrees of amnesia.[32] And an effort to represent the aircraft Enola Gay as a symbol of horrific devastation, as well as American heroism, in the "right and proper" atomic bombing of Japan can jolt a broad-based sense of social rectitude. Since the various practices of collective or social remembering typically serve to legitimize and strengthen sociocultural and political orders, serious history at odds with broader memory narratives is often read in a facile way as subversive, especially (but not only) in more authoritarian orders.

Social Memory and Social Identity

These problems are particularly acute as they pertain to "identity narratives": those practices of social memory that serve to give particular kinds of meaning to one's affiliation with a larger group and the representations of its past. As the connections between identity and memory necessarily tie individuals to larger groups, they also structure the relationships between different groups themselves. Who and what a social group has become, how it developed historically, and why, is learned in large part through the representations of collective memory that ascribe its character in historical terms. In this way, social memory also legitimizes individual and collective claims for recognition. In their telling and retelling, its practices and representations affirm broader notions of self and collective realization. What is affirmed as the true history of the social collective becomes by necessity a foundational element of its identity, just as individual memory serves to constitute and define the self. Indeed, as Hobsbawm, Anderson, and others began to clarify the dimensions of invented or imagined communities in the 1970s and 1980s, the links between social memory and social claims also became increasingly clear. Jonathan Boyarin has gone so far as to suggest that social identity and collective memory are virtually the same concept, since the "life" of a collective, like its "memory," are both anthropomorphic metaphors of an organic collective "self."[33] In any case, collective representations of historical myths and realities are clearly constitutive elements of the politics of identity, as Hobsbawm and others have pointed out. Historical narratives that construct collectively remembered pasts are key elements in all collective political representations. They allow a "unitary" past to be usefully deployed for a variety of presentist claims.[34]

Here, too, is the latent historical power of identity politics, whose full-blown emergence in the 1970s and 1980s further marked the transition away from traditional understandings of historical authority, and hence the authorities archivists traditionally used to construct hierarchies of meanings for the documents in their collections. As social memory constructed new notions of likeness, it also created demands for loyalty and allegiance, and from the archives, usable evidence. The more strongly collective identities could be rooted in the archived memory of historical "truths," the stronger the collective's demand for allegiance and its collective claims for entitlement, whether among the subjugated nationalities in the collapsing states of Eastern Europe, disadvantaged ethnic or racial groups, or those marginalized and discriminated against elsewhere on the basis of skin color, religion, language, or sexual orientation. In these cases the archives played a supporting role since they were but one possible source of evidence or validation. However, the absence of archival evidence could be as powerful a verification as the presence of some sort of record. The affirmative struggle for rights engaged not only what a group needed to remember but what those opposing its claims had socially and archivally "forgotten."[35]

Commemoration and Social Amnesia

How societies "forget" is also closely linked to the means collectives use to assure particular aspects of the past are properly remembered. The creation and internalization of dominant narratives is the most obvious and pervasive of these methods, but ceremonies, monuments, celebrations, and other semiotic practices also produce and reproduce social memory, sometimes in ways more subtle, and hence more powerful, than formal narratives.[36] Particular "places of memory," as Pierre Nora has termed them, create social identifications based on quite selective understandings of the past. Unlike narratives, they rarely acknowledge even the possibility of alternative understandings, much less ones at variance with interpretations held by those maintaining the site. Cemeteries, pageants, capitols, monuments, even empty battlefields act to create individual linkages to particular pasts in ways that often brook no argument. The specific power of particular places of memory relates in large measure to the ways one's experience with them helps shape or reshape one's own memories into experiences compatible with those "remembered" by societies as a whole. What is not commemorated is thus socially "forgotten." What is deliberately or inadvertently neglected in the representations that constitute social memory can thus "change" the past as forcefully as what is collectively "remembered." Like Halbwachs, Nora has been a seminal thinker about these issues. His "Places of Memory" project was both literally and figuratively monumental: an effort to locate the specific places in which the meaning of the French past was symbolically inscribed and to chart in this way the meanings of the present and the trajectories of the future. It was thus specifically about the French nation, an organic collectivity not only with the capacity to remember but whose very constitution depended on what was remembered and why.

Nora's own term is "memory nation." His *Les Lieux de la mémoire* sought to identify the monuments and artifacts in which the nation was embedded, including places like the monumental Archives Nationales, and whose preservation was consequently urgent to its future. On one hand, Nora's massive project was intended to give memory itself a history in France: to chart the ways memory practices had initially grounded *La République* and subsequently worked to consolidate and preserve *La Nation*. Here he worked as a cultural historian fully within the scholarly traditions that he also recognized were working against the important historical role that he believed memory practices played in France. On the other hand, as a public intellectual, Nora also strove to preserve the memory culture that constituted the essence of being French and which formal history undermined. "History is perpetually suspicious of memory," he wrote, "and its true mission is to suppress and destroy it."[37] The processes of modernization pointed to a "permanent secularization" of society, *La France* replaced by *Les France*, fragmented and without a common sense of itself and its past.

Strikingly, the fundamental problem with history was its objectivized relation to sources:

> Modern memory is, above all, archival. It relies entirely on the materiality of the trace, the immediacy of the recording, the visibility of the image. What began as writing ends up as high fidelity and tape recording. The less memory is experienced from the inside the more it exists only through its external scaffolding and outward signs—hence the obsession with the archive that marks our age.[38]

In contrast to archival "memory" and scholarship, Nora counterpoised the importance for *"La France"*—its very Frenchness—of the subjectivities of "re-experiencing" what the quintessential sites of French national patrimony reflected. In his view, France has "no reality *but* a memorial one," since France existed as a nation only if collective memory validated its claims. In a well known aphorism, Nora insisted that memory was of vital importance to France precisely because there was so little of it left. The predations of modernity reflected in archival memory jeopardized France's national cohesion and its future:

> Have we not sufficiently regretted and deployed the loss or destruction, by our predecessors, of potentially informative sources to avoid opening ourselves to the same reproach from our successors? Memory has been wholly absorbed by its meticulous reconstitution. Its new vocation is to record; delegating to the archive the responsibility of remembering, it sheds its signs upon depositing them there as a snake sheds its skin.[39]

As Nora himself demonstrated, the role of commemorations in creating socially cohesive nations was formally recognized in the French constitution as long ago as 1791. It decreed that national celebrations would be established to preserve the revolution's "memory." In the United States, an official day of commemoration was first established shortly after the Civil War and named Memorial Day in 1882. By the end of the nineteenth century, commemorative practices were an important component of modern state building everywhere, in addition to the role that they played in sustaining religious and other basic social practices.

Still, the widespread effort to memorialize and commemorate "shared" events of the past as a deliberate way of creating and sustaining social and cultural unity is a relatively recent extension of these practices, engendered particularly by the enormous social traumas created by the First World War.[40] And here, unlike religious commemorations, there is an obvious and some would say banal nostalgia in the ways memory creates particular kinds of communities linked by presumptively shared experience.

Commemoration and memorialization in this sense is almost always an effort to keep memory "alive" by emplotting the past in a romantic mode, to use Hayden White's typology, where virtue triumphs over evil, all deaths need to be respected and remembered, and shared experience suppresses individual divergence.[41] With rare exceptions like the Vietnam War Memorial in Washington, they resolve ambiguity into unifying reverence and belief.[42] They also contextualize socially what David Lowenthal has nicely termed the "heritage industry": that astounding profusion of nostalgia-creating commodities, businesses, and practices that produce and reproduce a remembered past through the commercialization of artifacts and places, and especially in the United States, by "reenacting" past experiences like the Civil War.[43]

So-called historical films are also quite important here, since photography seems to recreate the past in all of its stunning detail. As Jay Winter has discussed in *Sites of Memory*, the 1919 Abel Gance film *J'Accuse* summoned up the war's dead to return home and see if their sacrifice had been in vain. Steven Spielberg's *Saving Private Ryan* makes a similar point, if somewhat more subtly. In these and other ways, the products of this very successful memory industry both create and respond to these desires to connect with the past by creating and ascribing very particular kinds of historical meaning.

If social remembering is thus fraught with epistemological, as well as moral issues, so is social amnesia. If memory can be constituted through identity politics as a moral practice that empowers political, cultural, and social action, as Michael Lambek and others have proposed, resistance to remembering is an equally powerful determinant of its moral, political, and social uses, especially if this resistance is abetted by the archives.[44] Some cultural anthropologists see collective forgetting as a pivotal stage in what they have identified as an ethnography of memory, in which closed archives and other aspects of collective forgetting constitute an essential part of social efforts to valorize the past in order to make it usable. In ethnographic terms, social constitution is facilitated by the ways in which the pasts of others become a reality for those who did not actually have comparable experiences. "Forgetting" works nicely here, since individual memories offer no countervailing evidence and none is available in the archives.[45]

Social amnesia in this sense can be politically benign, since its function is social cohesion rather than claims making or other forms of political action. By mis-remembering the past, mild forms of social forgetting can also serve as the basis for nostalgic complaints about the present. Far more problematic, however, are collective reconstitutions of the past that deliberately and aggressively "forget" and destroy countervailing evidence. Quite typically, this involves classifying victims as enemies in order for social memory practices to do their legitimizing work. What might be called the "enemy syndrome" in social memory was brutally clear in the 1990s Balkan wars, when politically inspired ethnic cleansing found its social and cultural legitimization in the allegedly remembered abuses and conflicts of the past, and where contrary documentation was deliberately destroyed.[46]

Less radical if at times no less murderous examples can be found in most other societies and cultures where social memories invent the identities and traditions of particular nationhoods: the positioning of Native Americans as "Indians" and "savages"; the pervasive European demonization of Jews and Turks; Japanese attitudes toward Koreans and Chinese; and in the Soviet Union, the representations and fates of kulaks, "bourgeois" classes, and other "enemies of the people." Among their other awful consequences, the public denunciations of the 1930s gave powerful support to changing the past by reconstituting lived relationships into necessarily antagonistic social conflicts, even between children and their parents.[47]

Social Memory and the Archive

As individual "telling" becomes the social "told," and particular lived (or "historical") experiences are written large, the subjects of individual memory become, in effect, social objects. They acquire categorical meaning and hence are expected to be historical authority for the archives as recognized elements of important pasts. Whether these subjects are represented in established archival institutions or not, there is an expectation and a yearning for an archive as a way to validate "shared" history.

In simplest terms one can say that social memory has thus become centrally important to contemporary archives and the ways that they assemble and present their holdings. Archival practices obviously vary by institution but in general there is a greater sense of multiple pasts as collections are defined and identified. In these processes the categories that emerge can reflect the needs of identity, victimization, triumph, heroism and defeat, as well as political strategy. However, what is "remembered" or "forgotten" in society at large may have little connection to what is archivally accessed and described, especially in those archives whose documentation reflections dominant institutions of power.[48] The diaries and similar memory materials found in newly opened archives of the former Soviet Union did not "find themselves" in these repositories but were uncovered by scholars seeking them for reasons other than those that led to their preservation.

American historians have had similar experiences in discovering material on Native Americans, collected and preserved by the Bureau of Indian Affairs because of the importance attributed to military operations or the administration of reservations. In terms of the role of archives in this process, the question of the purposes of preservation, as well as the ways documents are arranged and described, has to be distinguished from the simple fact of preservation itself. Archival practices affect memory projects through the use of prevailing authorities that determine whether and how materials will be acquired. Here, the needs or tasks of social memory may be subordinated in fixed descriptive systems that come to have little value as contextualities shift. In many Soviet archives, for example, "enemies of the people" was an authoritative category of document classification. In other repositories, so were (and are) "heretics," "subversives," "counterrevolutionaries," and more recently, one suspects, "terrorist organizations."[49]

Social memory also affects "amnesia" in the archives. In its more benign forms, this might be seen as something analogous to amnesia in individuals: as a way social bodies may struggle to adjust to experiences too horribly jarring to gain meaning, and hence incapable of being rendered into familiar social narratives. Amnesia in these circumstances might be thought of a sociopsychological adaptation that allows the societies to cope, just as individual amnesia sometimes allows individuals to escape the devastating and debilitating consequences of trauma. Again, however, the role of the archives in processing the materials of social trauma directly affects how the processes of adaptation might work. In the case of German concentration camp documents, one argument defending their conceal-ment for more than fifty years was that German society was simply not ready to process the implications of what they revealed.

In somewhat different ways, social amnesia in the archives can also resemble the processes by which individuals "un-remember" the agonies, fears, and tor-ments of traumatic moments in favor of sanitized heroics. Un-remembering in this sense is different from amnesia, since what is experienced is not actually forgotten or incapable of being told but displaced onto other more acceptable nar-ratives. Among combat veterans, cowardly feelings often turn into manly engage-ment. Handsome military photographs sanitize the soiled clothing of real war experience.[50] In societies like the United States, this form of social amnesia has served very well to preserve notions of racial difference and formal institutions of discrimination. Collective memory of lynchings, for example, is denied its moral ground. The elements of carnival mask individual or social conflict for those who might feel disturbed by participating or even observing its brutal horrors, while those identified with the victim mask the real agony of their experience in favor of social survival.

The role of Soviet and other archives in the processes of social amnesia also suggests how collective social representations and their archival categories are also linked to actual tasks of governance. It is not too much to argue that in the Soviet Union, collective un-remembering constituted a key element in the tech-nologies of communist rule. Almost from the moment the Bolsheviks took power, individual memories were socially dangerous. They became universally so with the consolidation of Stalinist power in the late 1920s. In Louisa Passerini's phrase, Soviet society was "forced into amnesia," since Stalinist claims to legitimacy depended fundamentally on individuals un-remembering what really was in favor of what should have been and, especially, the radiant future that official historical narratives indicated in their logic and substance was about to be. The past could only structure and legitimize the future insofar as the official constructs of Soviet social memory, if not universally internalized, were quiescently accepted. Enor-mous institutional resources and vast amounts of energy were devoted to this effort. In the process, Stalinist social memory literally turned individual remem-bering, for many, into a crime, especially if someone dared to bring archival evi-dence to bear.[51]

In its various practices, social memory is thus not some magically constructed body of ideas or images, but a sociocultural artifact in and of itself, an imagined "reality" of the past that is socially and culturally articulated and maintained.[52] As such, the case has been made that its elements are archivable and should be archived, along with other socially important materials. Since social memory is, at best, the product only of imperfectly recorded pasts, however, and reflects the ways social collectives assume (or are given) anthropomorphic qualities in the ways they are represented, its essential qualities are not archivally verifiable.

Aside from individual feelings of attachment or social affiliation, social memory obviously has no physiological constitution. It involves the construction of shared memory artifacts through prescriptive practices that link in Bakhtinian terms the internally persuasive with the socially authoritative.[53]

But can these authorities possibly serve to guide archival practices? As an organic metaphor, social memory projects on individuals and collectives a unifying and authoritative set of sociohistorical meanings. In doing so, it validates and legitimizes the social structures and institutions that reflect and articulate its meanings. Archives can be central to this validation if the processes of acquisition and representation of holdings authenticate in some way the dominant tropes of memory narratives.

This has occurred, for example, with long-established archives like those of the Soviet Union, as well as very recently organized repositories like the ANC archives in South Africa, created in part to assure the new South African state could remember its own legitimizing past.[54] In these and other cases, it can be extremely difficult for individual memories to compete openly with those that have been fixed literally and symbolically in the archives. If individual testimony written large in the archives shapes collective meaning and understanding, collective meaning written small without archival "verification" requires individuals to "know" what their experiences "meant." Historical truth through collective memory, whether individual or collective and whether archivally grounded or not, is therefore founded on belief, on feeling, and (not least) on the act itself of belonging. For individuals to insist that their remembered pasts refract a reality different from what the collective memory has archivally constructed as true not only undermines the collective itself but further isolates distrusting individuals psychologically, socially, and often politically, sometimes with grave consequences.

Indeed, especially in authoritarian societies and regimes but in more open societies as well, this conflict means that competing recollections are often repressed, but not simply to protect the regime. Individuals cannot easily navigate their own social institutions and systems if their memories of "what really happened" are fundamentally at odds with established social beliefs that the archives seem to verify.[55] Yet actually verifying social memory in the archives is inherently problematic. The "shared" experiences of invented traditions constitute core elements of social memory practices whether or not they are true. "History" is mobilized in social memory archives for presentist objectives and scholarship that is politically sensitive.

The "truths" of social memory thus carry heavy archival freight. They can influence social and historical authorities in ways that are often at odds with established hierarchies of archival description, contesting how archives have processed their documentation. If the representations of collective memory tap a usable past and are then uncovered in existing documentation in the archives, those representations may well be one that is historically suspect based on other points of view. At the same time, socially remembered identities that reinforce the authorities used in acquisition and description of archival materials can be readily forgotten if they do not gain a firm foothold in these archival processes. It is in this way that the archives has agency in assisting individuals and groups in forgetting as well as remembering.

In contrast to the ways that individuals forget, however, the process of "forgetting" in the archive is obviously not something that occurs because of a memory lapse. Archives have no senior moments. They do have procedures that restrict access that in the worst cases can be designed to obscure aspects of the past or conceal them indirectly.[56] Remarkably detailed material on the horrors of Nazi concentration camps for example, was "forgotten" in the postwar German archives by being long kept from public view in an effort to mediate postwar social conflict and facilitate reconstruction.

A closely related issue, consequently, is how representations of social memories themselves can be affected by archival access. As an old (and clandestine) Soviet joke used to express it, the problem with the past in this social sense is that it is always so unpredictable. The role of archives in these aspects of the social memory problem are among the most difficult to untangle because memory itself is such a powerful claim to truth. For the historian and archivist both, confronting social amnesia itself enjoins broad issues of social identity and political legitimacy, as well as more basic issues of historical evidence and meaning.

Here is an additional component of the social memory problem for archives and archivists: their relation to the formation of dominant myths and collective understandings as they are being created and publicly signified. All archives exist to support the needs of those who create them, whether these needs are public or private. At the same time, however, despite the dependency this creates in terms of funding and other kinds of material support, the relationship does not discharge the archivist from the responsibility of making significant decisions on these matters. Even in authoritarian societies, the processes of appraisal and acquisition necessarily leave a significant degree of discretion in the archivists' hands. Materials of all sorts can still be gathered, catalogued, given restricted access, squirreled away, or even destroyed unless there are specific instructions to the contrary. The documents of political dissidents or opposition movements might be sought initially for reasons of surveillance, but decisions about their subsequent preservation will necessarily engage the possibility of alternative narratives eventually being told. In more democratic regimes, where state archives also formally serve a loosely defined public interest, archivists face an even sharper question: whether the public is best served by assuring the possibility through multiple archives of multiple understandings in competition with those of the state.

Here, too, is where the close linkages between social memory and the politics of identity become so problematic for the archive, especially historical repositories that purport to have a broader, less self-interested political role. Archives can be formed and developed for reasons that have little or nothing to do with the uses and forms of social memory. How documentary or other collections are compiled must obviously be separated from how they come to be read and by whom. While historians have been enjoined to "stand aside from the passions of identity politics, even if [they] feel them also," so as to preserve as fully as possible the objectivity serious historical scholarship requires, good historians can also understand better than others the historically reductive nature of national or ethnic myths or the mobilizing role of mythmaking itself, even in the midst of conflicts over social, ethnic, or national identity.[57]

The new historical paradigms on matters like race, ethnicity, gender, and empire, for example, that emerged as historians turned away from traditional notions of authority in history implicitly contested these reductions and did so quite explicitly when good historians wove their own archival evidence into persuasive alternative stories. Unfortunately, even the best of these efforts are sometimes trumped by the authenticating power of memory, whether recollections are accurate or not. "I was there, and I know" is almost always a more powerful claim to truth than the thickest oppositional grammar of archival reference.

Archives and archivists, then, are situated at a central and contested point of connection between history and memory. Their sites reinforce the very abstractions of social memory, while their processes affirm and validate particular kinds of collective understanding. Whether they serve public, state, or private interests, their acquisition and descriptive practices necessarily affect the concepts and categories that the sponsors of these archives deploy in collectively remembering and narrating their pasts. These practices literally create, as well as recreate, these pasts, both through the choices that are made and through the contents of the documents themselves. This obviously—and necessarily—involves selective "forgetting" as much as selective "remembering," since the choices archivists have to make determine what specifically about the past may or may not be documented. When memory's "mystic chords" challenge master narratives and new interpretations turn away from consensual understandings about the nature of the past and what has historical meaning for the present, the value of archival sources themselves comes under challenge.

With respect to the practices of social memory, archives in all of these ways are no more inert, and no less selective, than the memories of individuals. In both, as Derrida has elaborated, the fever to uncover is in continual struggle with the tendency to suppress. That archives, like individual memories, often contain evidence in sharp contradiction with dominant historical beliefs only strengthens their importance in determining the ways societies collectively understand their pasts, validate their presents, and (not least) imagine their futures. It is hardly surprising, therefore, that the contested narratives of memory and history also lead naturally to contested sources, as well as to the contested authority of archives themselves.

7

Contested Archives, Contested Sources

In early 1993, the Smithsonian Institution's National Air and Space Museum in Washington, D.C., began planning for the exhibition in 1995 of the Enola Gay, the first aircraft to drop the atomic bomb on Japan. In initiating what was soon to become a fierce and well-known controversy, the director of the museum Martin Harwit and his colleagues sought to use a range of archival documents to describe the impact of the bombing on the end of the war, its aftermath, and the onset of the Cold War. Within months, *Air Force* magazine, the journal of the U.S. Air Force Association, received an appeal from a number of B-29 veterans concerned about how the bombing might be represented. A petition with more than 5,000 signatures was soon forwarded to the museum requesting that the airplane be displayed "proudly."[1]

At one level, the Enola Gay controversy unfolded over the descriptive and analytical scripts that the Smithsonian was preparing to use in presenting the exhibition. These sought interpretative balance by including materials on the devastating consequences of the bombing on Japanese civilians, as well as its broader effects on the history of the postwar world. Congressional staffers soon requested copies of the scripts. Copies were also made available to the press. A number of scathing denunciations soon followed from powerful groups including the Air Force Association itself and the American Legion. Twenty-four members of Congress expressed their "concern and dismay" that the exhibit would portray Japan "more as an innocent victim than a ruthless aggressor." For their part, a number of American historians rallied to the museum's defense, but this only broadened the controversy. The scholarly efforts of the exhibit's curators to document a "full" and "impartial" version of the past ran headlong into a broad-based and politically energetic disdain.

For some, the curators' attempts to "decenter" a dominant understanding of the bombing by representing its disastrous human consequences placed it outside of the bounds of contemporary and historical morality, the country's duty to honor the memory of its veterans. In September 1994, a Sense of the Senate resolution that passed unanimously described the exhibition script as "revisionist and offensive." Respected Scholars like Barton Bernstein, Robert Jay Lifton, Martin J. Sherwin, and others were accused of being "revisionists," dishonoring the memory of American sacrifice. Gar Alperovitz of the University of Maryland was condemned at the "father of revisionist theory." Shortly afterwards, in January 1995, eighty-one members of Congress demanded Martin Harwit resign. One week later the exhibit was cancelled.[2]

The storm of recriminations centered for the most part on the morality of "evenhandedness" in the Smithsonian's presentation. The public arguments in favor of heroic remembrance were countered by equally strong views from scholars on the importance of historical objectivity and the presentation of different understandings and interpretations. For our purposes, what is equally important about the episode is that it brought clearly into focus the ways representations of social memory affirmed dominant narratives and their power to resist the very notion of multiple pasts. Especially for veterans' organizations and their congressional supporters, the exhibition pulled archivally based interpretations of the historical significance of the bombing from the ethical and political certainties of 1945 to the immoralities and instabilities of the 1990s.

The Smithsonian exhibition thus raised basic issues of archival conceptualization. It directly engaged what some insisted were the degradations of postmodernism and brought out in the most heated of forms the ways historical artifacts themselves could become highly contested objects along with the repositories that held them.[3] Indeed, one of the permanent legacies of the controversy was the creation of a new digital Enola Gay Archive, sponsored and maintained by the Air Force Association, and designed to show the real heroism embedded in the Air Force's own narrative of the bombing and allow the "true" story to be properly told.[4] In these ways, the exhibition reflected the deeper and more complicated questions about sources and archives that were now coming to characterize the archival divide. How "neutral," for example, are *any* archival sources in terms of the ways knowledge is created? How inert is the archive itself in this sense? Most important, to what extent is knowledge about the past produced by the very "uncovering" of documents themselves? To what extent, in other words, is the meaning and value of sources created by the engaged historian and active archivist, rather than simply interpreted?

These and other problematic questions are associated particularly with the rapidly growing number of what we would call "identity archives," organized around the particular histories of specific social groups. Like the Enola Gay Archive, these new repositories reconstitute, in effect, the very conception of an archive from an inert institution of documentary preservation into a contested and even contentious space. Across the deepening archival divide, the nature of documentation and its meaning has itself become a growing point of difference between and among historians and archivists. So has the very meaning of the archive itself as an institution built on a specific history of policies and actions that resulted in a particular collection of records. Although good historians and archivists have always recognized that struggles over how the past should be described are also struggles over the nature and meaning of sources, a new element in the Enola Gay discussion now concerned the ways that historical study could challenge the conception of archives and archivists as historically "neutral."

In the case of identity archives, the Enola Gay case focused attention as well on a central issue of these new repositories: the kinds of authorities archivists had traditionally used in the processes of appraisal and classification, and whether new or multiple histories now deserved their own new set of authorities and sources. Contested archives thus also meant contested sources and raised related questions about archives themselves as "agents" of their sources and even as "authors." It also generated additional controversy about how archival sources themselves should and could be used, an issue that was also being engaged at the time by a rancorous argument over archival usage by the Princeton historian David Abraham, as we will see. Underlying these questions, and in some ways most consequential in terms of the archival divide, lay the issue of whether archival institutions themselves might need to be "read" in terms of how and why they collected their materials, and whether this reading might have to focus on their institutional as well as documentary forms.

Reading the Archives: The Archival Grain

As we have seen, the opening of the archival divide has left historians and archivists on separate planes of understanding. While both communities are diverse, and while occasional voices still try to be heard across the separation, the discourse on records management has little in common with such interpretative frames as those of postcolonialism, gender, everyday life, social identity, or "new political history," where the locations of power can sometimes carry as much interpretative weight as its uses. The divide has thus left many historians and archivists with different understandings of archives, as well as at odds over the meaning and nature of archival sources: as institutions and evidence, as a set of practices, and as sources of historical meaning. In the post-custodial era, consequently, when the professional needs and interests of archivists and historians have gone in significantly different directions, research into any historical subject requires that scholars make some effort to discern how and why their sources have been assembled, what they evidence indirectly as well as directly, what sociocultural and sociopolitical conventions lie behind their formation, and what their silences may mean.

As we know, historians usually come to the archive intending to tell a story or substantiate an interpretation. Their research is designed to place the documents they seek within some broader narrative and conceptual frame, even if the conceptualizations are often implicit rather than fully thought through. Careful historians expect the full contours of their stories to emerge from their examination of the materials rather than their preconceptions, that is, from the primacy of their archival research. It is in this sense that many historians would agree with the historian Carolyn Steedman's notion of archives themselves as essentially inert until the historian weaves their documents into a historical narrative. In her view, what the documents reveal about the past "is not *part of* the events that are narrated. The telling is always something different from *what happened* (whatever it was)."[5]

In our view, however, what Steedman and others ignore is that access to sources opens the possibility of teasing out their historical meaning only if a scholar understands what the archivists and their archives have been up to, and the historical contexts in which their sources were formed.[6] In state or organizational archives especially, but in collecting institutions as well, good historians may understand that archival genres and conventions will affect the kinds of sources they can use, as well as the kinds of information they produce. Understanding the archival practices that have created these conventions, the "dynamics" of the archive, however, is another matter altogether.

Most historians well understand, for example, that absences in the archives can have as great an effect on the kinds of knowledge that can come from an archive as the actual sources its contains. Yet these absences are themselves part of a broader set of processes and institutional orientations that constitute the ways the archive has been formed. The very nature of the archival repository is constituted as much from the mediation of its policies and processes, in other words, as from its forms of documentation, its access practices, and the particular kinds of collections it houses. As a result, scholars not only need to use archival sources critically in terms of their content; they must also incorporate an understanding about the processes by which sources were assembled, appraised, and described if they hope to reach conclusions other than those the documents may have been retained to provide.

Archives in all of these ways are no more inert, and no less selective, than individual memories or the dispositions of individual scholars. In both realms, the Derridian "fever to uncover" is in continual struggle with both the inclinations and institutional practices of making the past "orderly." Archives do this by framing the way the past can be understood every bit as much as individual scholars do, although archival "narratives" themselves are far more difficult to read. How documents are appraised and arranged by archivists frames certain kinds of questions and particular kinds of answers. In the process, appraisal, arrangement, and description also ascribe particular kinds of historical meaning.

The anthropologist Ann Stoler has deftly identified this process as the formation of an "archival grain": the "text," as it were, of archival processes that has to be read as carefully as the documents themselves. Reading carefully "with this grain," as Stoler puts it, is the only way scholars can fully understand the broader meanings archives and archivists may have contributed to their sources, the kinds of knowledge archival processes produce. By the same token, reading against it is the point of entry into what kinds of knowledge archival processes have obscured or suppressed.[7]

Stoler's elaboration and exploration of the idea of an archival grain has been in the area of colonial and postcolonial studies, where she and others have tried to discern and interpret the analytical categories that imperial powers imposed on their colonial subjects, and hence on colonial archival administrations. Thomas Richards and Nicholas Dirks have joined her in using the concept to show how "orientalist" perceptions have molded the categories underlying both the production and arrangement of documents.[8] One of their further contributions has been to show the political and cultural environments in which the creation of certain kinds of colonial records are set. In archival holdings on colonial administration, collection is seldom random, however much it may appear so when repositories or collections themselves are disorderly. The form of communication, justification, explanation, presentation, evaluation, compilation, categorization, and summarization—all attributes of bureaucratic record keeping everywhere— stem from conventions and expectations that are part of the cultures of institutions and individuals who create the records, as well as those who process and preserve them.

In other words, archival records, as well as archives themselves, are produced from culturally embedded expectations and conventions. When those who use the documents share these underlying conventions, this "grain" of the archive can be read most comfortably.[9] When scholars look at archival records to answer questions that run counter to these conventions and assumptions, the process is more complex. Here the researcher has to have more clearly in mind the ways he or she may have different assumptions and analytical conventions from those underlying the archive, how and through what kinds of processes the archive reflects different or contesting historical or current conventions. Reading "against the grain" in this way is especially difficult when the scholar's goal is to uncover insights or voices that run counter to the archives' conceptual assumptions.

Nicholas Dirks shows the virtues of this effort very well in his study *Castes of Mind*, an exploration of the changing culture of record keeping in British India. Dirks is able to demonstrate how the first phase of this process reflected the culture of the East India Company, whose interests and practices impressed a set of corporate conventions on the production and organization of information. These were then supplanted by those of the colonial state, first established as a source for authority for mercantilist trading monopolies, but which soon needed kinds and forms of knowledge that fit its own ambitions, and which was pressured to set public standards for the empire "that subjected history to the scrutiny of metropolitan moral codes."[10] In the process, a particular kind of bureaucracy developed in support of a particular set of conceptions about colonial sovereignty, along, of course, with its archives. The archives themselves deployed these conceptions and categories as their archivists assessed whether records fit the categories of information that were thought to be needed and which therefore pertained to matters of "importance." Dirks labels this process one of colonial "governmentality in the archive."[11]

Dirks goes on to explore the ways imperial Britain then came to understand its Indian colony through the category of hierarchies it produced, and which were then reflected and reproduced in its archival collections. In the process, the descriptive categories imposed on the archives actually muted the voices they were supposed to record, since they superimposed the colonizers' concepts of social differentiation and order rather than using those constituted by local histories and social systems. Dirks focused on the collection of "oriental manuscripts on the life and literature of the south of India" assembled by Colin MacKenzie now housed in London's Public Records Office. In his analysis of the collection, he observed that when local documents were collected and archived, they were not only affected by the interests and values of local agents "but transferred from local to colonial contexts. The different voices, agencies, and modes of authorization that were implicated in the production of the archive became muffled and then lost, once they inhabited the new colonial archive."[12]

Although a particular kind of institutional repository, the archives Dirks used reflect the tendency of all archives to prefigure both the present and the future. The assumptions and conceptualizations through which they process their materials create the categories through which their sources gain historical meaning. Michel de Certeau has made a similar argument about historical narration. In his view, historical discourse gives itself credibility in the name of the past realities it tries to represent, but its "authorized appearance of the 'real'" only camouflages the narrative conventions, assumptions, and practices that determine how it is produced and understood.[13] By adding the role of the archival grain to this process, we can further understand that the narrative structures deployed by the historian also reflect those created at least in part by the way archives process and present their sources. It is clear, for example, that state archives tend to privilege the historical role of institutions, politics, power relations, and the agency of political actors by the very act of assembling and preserving what state officials themselves regard as important, yet collecting institutions and identity archives are no different. They, too, serve to create (or occlude) conceptual categories that inscribe significance and meaning, and hence condition the ways the pasts they evidence are understood. They, too, consequently, have to be read as critically as the documents they house and the narratives they encourage their users to produce.

Does this place any special burdens on the archivist, like the injunctions of scholarly objectivity ostensibly place on historians? Should archivists then assure the possibility of multiple ways of remembering and understanding through acquisition policies that are themselves "against the grain"? Should the whole concept of provenance be rethought as a barrier to preserving the diversity of ways the past can be processed? And if the authenticating practices of state archives serve to make certain kinds of historical understanding seem like the "natural" course of a society's development, should not state archivists confront this reduction, and systematically work to minimize its effects?

Our answer would be: not necessarily. What we think might be needed instead is for historians and other scholars themselves to come to the archive capable of "reading" it well. Those engaged along with Stoler and Dirks in colonial and subaltern studies, for example, and who have been particularly challenged by the problem of the archival grain, have proved themselves quite adept at working their way through the obstacles it presents. Florencia Mallon, for example, whose work has been on the development of the postcolonial state in Mexico and Peru, has stressed that understanding these processes requires "digging them out from under the dominant discourses that suppressed them" often by concentrating on local municipal archives or other regional repositories rather than those closest to central administrations.[14] Historians probing the history of Native Americans using Record Group 75 of the Bureau of Indian Affairs have also uncovered suppressed voices in official reports.[15] In a similar way, Latin American historians like James Sanders and Rebecca Scott have used seemingly conventional archival sources but read them carefully against the grain of their repositories to discover meaningful information they were never processed to reveal. For these historians and others, documentation that is less "processed," and hence is still somewhat removed from an archives' categorical conventions even if they are more difficult to use, can often prove more valuable than materials that are fully ordered.[16]

In many cases, of course, historically important voices cannot be heard at all in the archive, sometimes, of course, as the result of deliberate concealment. In the former Soviet Union, Western historians were also used to seeing sources carefully selected for them by archivists who usually checked first to be sure they had already been used by authorized Soviet scholars. Documents delivered in special reading rooms for foreigners were almost always read with an understanding of their selectivity, their texts carefully parsed to assure their use as evidence was credible. While the difficulties in such authoritarian systems are quite obvious, they are in some ways even more consequential in open societies where classification principles themselves are often less than fully transparent. Documents or files that subvert national myths or dominant elements of collective memory may well be restricted by processes and rules of classification that have nothing to do with individual privacy or national security. In Soviet archives, files were labeled and restricted as "especially valuable" if they had any references at all to Lenin or Stalin or if they contained any sort of controversial material. Huge collections like those on oppositional parties like the Mensheviks or purged Bolshevik leaders like Trotsky or Bukharin were simply locked away. In the United States, blanket security classifications and the associated labor costs of sorting out genuinely sensitive materials, have in some cases produced similar voids, leaving established interpretations unruffled by documentation. Vast amounts of government records from security agencies as well as major institutions like the State Department are often withheld for these reasons, even if their content may no longer be at all sensitive to security concerns. At NARA, the recently issued

"National Declassification Center Prioritization Plan" (2010) lists a number of record groups that are awaiting declassification, including those of the CIA, U.S. Army, and National Security Council. The motto of this effort is: "Releasing all we can, protecting all we must."[17]

As many historians have discovered when they sought assistance through various Freedom of Information Acts, (FOIA) seeking out sources that challenge the validity of dominant national narratives can be more subversive to the credibility of governments than to the security of the state. The National Security Archive in Washington, D.C., is an example of one institution whose mission is specifically to uncover these kinds of counternarratives.[18] With the collapse of the Soviet Union, similar freedom of information legislation was enacted in Russia, Ukraine, and several other successor Soviet republics along with new legislation on archival access. (Paradoxically, this not only opened vast amounts of hitherto closed materials, at least for a while, but also suggested that these materials would likely have been destroyed, if Soviet officials had ever imagined they might become broadly accessible.)

At the same time, the opening of these archives and the dramatic expansion of access elsewhere through freedom of information legislation did not solve one of the principal concerns that some historians had already raised more generally about sources: many of the most interesting new explorations into the areas of social and cultural history were still about subjects whose sources had traditionally been ignored and were largely or entirely absent from traditional cataloguing systems. Historians have generally been inclined to read these silences as reflecting the practices of social, cultural, and especially political marginalization. While careful analysis of this sort can be very fruitful, a more productive (if more difficult) approach would be to understand the contexts and processes through which archives and their documentation were assembled, and to ascertain as Ann Stoler has suggested "which categories were privileged and resilient, and which were demoted or ignored," or as Patricia Galloway has put it, the principles of exclusion as well as inclusion not only in the formation of archival holdings but also in the formation of the record itself, "the context of [its] creation."[19] In sum, the archival "grain" that emerges from all of these processes establishes and reproduces particular categories of historical and contemporary understanding. The processes of formation of an archive, whether its documentation is in paper or digital form, produce and reproduce their own conceptualizations, as well as those of the institutions that it supports and is supported by, reifying the categories through which its materials are identified. However obscure these categories may be for historians and other users, they push scholars toward the kinds of narratives embedded in the archives' own processes and purposes. These are not determined simply by the nature of the sources themselves, by deliberate erasures, or by restrictive classifications, but by the presumptions, values, and predispositions underlying the archives own formation, practices, and processes in its development.

"Monumental" Archives: Contested by Purpose

The way an archive is formed—the essence of its "grain"—is also often reflected in its physical appearance. Like the processes by which it acquires particular kinds of sources, appearances reflect particular sets of values; and both affirm particular social, cultural, and political formations. As Nick Dirks has put the matter in writing about state archives, "the archive, that primary site of state monumentality, is the very institution that canonizes, crystallizes, and classifies the knowledge required by the state even as it makes this knowledge available to subsequent generations in the cultural form of a neutral repository of the past."[20]

The representational meanings of monumental state archives are thus a particularly contested terrain, since the acquisition and preservation of particular kinds of documents at specific moments in time can substantially strengthen particular sets of sociocultural or political values. When the State Archive of the Russian Federation sent trucks to the burning parliament building after Boris Yeltsin's tanks shelled it in 1993, for instance, the Russian Archival Administration publicly positioned itself in defense of post-Soviet democratization, even though the documents were rescued primarily because the government thought they might be useful in prosecuting rebellious deputies. In the United States, the acquisition by presidential libraries formally under the administrative control of the National Archives and Records Administration of documents that members of the presidential administrations themselves deem worthy of retention helps create the notion that all American presidents are equally worthy of being memorialized in their own buildings, however selective the documents they may offer to prove it.[21]

From the middle of the nineteenth century onward, the most important of the conceptual frames structuring the organization and reorganization of archival collections was provenance, which connects documents with the processes of the modern nation-state. Before this time, historical archives were essentially warehouses of various kinds of documents whose material was largely known only to its curators. What University of Michigan archivist Nancy Bartlett has thoughtfully described as the "*ur* text" of the modern use of provenance was the 1841 French ministerial decree, which formally assigned archival record keeping to all state administrative agencies and developed a template for organizing and cataloging materials "pour la mise en ordre et le classement des archives départementales."[22] The French intent was to create standardizing practices that would make a rapidly growing state bureaucracy more orderly and efficient, and also, perhaps, more accountable. Standards developed for the curatorial care of existing records (whose administration was seized from French provincial repositories) also required a new generation of professional archivists trained to manage the records of the new state order. The burgeoning French national archive not only helped regularize state administration but also fixed more solidly the modern concept of the nation itself.[23]

French practices became the model for state archives elsewhere. Archivists across Europe and eventually in North American increasingly emphasized documents themselves as the primary sources of national understanding, as the "raw material" that would consolidate a common national narrative.[24] Following the French lead, efforts to "publish the national record" also became a widespread ambition, as state archives standardized their practices and consolidated their hold on materials. In Germany, France, and later the Soviet Union, the publication of annotated collections of documents developed into a principal function of archival and historical scholarship, one that undergirded an increasingly dominant national narrative with genuine erudition. The same kind of scholarship gained even more prominence in Russia after the Soviet Union's collapse in 1991, when a new spate of carefully prepared documentary publications that were assumed to "speak for themselves" laid the foundations for alternative national narratives.[25] Rich in content and of exceptional value to a wide range of scholars, these volumes still reflected the institutional effects of diplomatics and provenance in terms of their social and political subject categories.

Physically detaching U.S. presidential libraries from the U.S. National Archives has also created hagiographic archival monuments. The myths or "legacies" that presidents and their staffs have quite consciously tried to create are strengthened not simply by carefully displayed documentation but by the relationship between the grandeur of space and the documentation's implicit significance: the ways the building itself valorizes the importance of its holdings.[26] In Soviet Russia, the Central State Archive of the October Revolution obviously sanctified the founding moment of the state in ways that had little to do with lived experience, lending scholarly authority to the party's massive efforts to position the narrative of historical inevitability at the center of Soviet collective understanding. Within this archive, special collections of documents on the History of the Factories helped create a narrative of heroic struggle and social emancipation. That Soviet historiography and social memory formed around these and other distortions served among other consequences to suppress very different kinds of memories and understandings, testifying both to the archive's importance as an element of Soviet rule and to the virtual irrelevance in this regard of historical actualities.

Post-Soviet Russia has also witnessed a remarkable example of archival monumentalism connecting the physicality of the archive to political legitimacy. For many years the archives of the tsarist regime were housed in the historic former building of the old Imperial State Senate and the Holy Synod of the Orthodox Church, on the Neva River embankment. The building was already in some disrepair before the collapse of the Soviet Union. Its priceless collection of historic materials was stored on tinder dry wooden shelves. Although historians throughout the world worried that the repository was in perilous condition, a fact supported by a comprehensive UNESCO investigation, the Yeltsin government insisted it did not have the funding to rebuild the archive after the collapse of the Soviet Union and preferred to move it elsewhere. Many suspected this had more to do with the rapidly growing property value of the archives' historic buildings (a fine site on the Neva for a luxury hotel), rather than any real concern of the regime for the value of the collection.

Vladimir Putin, however, seems to have fully understood the relationship between monumental archives and their legitimizing effects. Under his direction, the original plan to move the archives to an abandoned bank building near the end of the metro line was ramped into a total transformation of the site into a state of the art repository. The old bank building was completely transformed and incorporated into a complex of three gleaming new structures, all connected at various levels and at some places more than seven stories high. No expense was spared in its construction, or apparently in the care with which the millions of documents themselves were packed in special crates and transferred. Each truck came under police escort. The new building was also lavishly equipped. The document preservation laboratory, for example, was designed to maintain a sterile air quality equivalent to that of hospital operating rooms and provided with the most advanced equipment available anywhere in the world. The air quality of the buildings themselves is controlled by special heating and cooling equipment, requiring its own specialized staff. And the spacious reading rooms, library, and meeting rooms create a visually stunning as well as exceptionally functional workspace. The structures themselves were set back from the street, surrounded by gates, and adorned with large gold lettering identifying the complex as the Russian State Historical Archive.

In several ways, however, this was the least important of its significations, a mere marking of what the buildings were. As President Putin himself stressed at the building's dedication, far more important was the linkage the new building created between contemporary Russia and its historic (prerevolutionary) past. The building connoted fundamental continuities. It physically demonstrated a reverence for Russian history. It clearly signified that the new state would spare no expense to construct the physical and symbolic space for that history, and treat it as reverently as the rebuilt cathedral of Christ the Savior in Moscow, the site of former President Yeltsin's funeral and the Russian president's annual blessing by the Patriarch. Indeed, the only thing initially missing from the magnificent new archives when these lines were written was users. Nothing in the state budget provided for the salaries required to lure people back into the woefully underpaid archival profession. Two years after its completion, until it finally opened its doors in 2008, the complex functioned as a spectacular repository maintained by a handful of administrative staff, some quite pleased no doubt that the archives' marvelous order was not yet being disturbed by the actual use of its materials!

Archives constituted in this way are not only a privileged space for historical sources whose nature and meaning may be contested but also a part of a contested story itself. As the historian Frederick Cooper has shown, archival institutions have played a particular role in this regard not only in established states like Russia and the United States but in the new states of postcolonial Africa as well.[27]

In their physical representation, as well as their ordering of documents, archives most readily illuminate the history of the institutions they were designed to memorialize and whose documents physically attest to their importance. In this sense, we can agree with Jacques LeGoff that "the document is not objective, innocent raw material, but expresses past society's power over memory and the future."[28]

We would add, however, that this is so not only because of the ways archives position sources as links to particular pasts but also because of the monumentality of the structures in which the documents are often stored. Especially in state archives, but in other repositories as well, the monumental archive passes elements of historical fixity onto its documents, assuring that certain kinds of documentation become a privileged base for a "common" historical record.

Forms, Stability, and Contests over Usage of Archival Documentation: The Abraham Case

Even before the turn away from authority in history and the onset of digital records, the meaning and value of certain kinds of sources was itself contested ground. The question of preserving documentation that best testified to "historical experience" raised issues about what forms of documentation archives should preserve. Should photographs, films, oral testimony, and other artifacts be sought, arranged, preserved, and described by archives as assiduously as written documents? Questions about the kinds of sources archives should seek to acquire and retain are not simply ones about archival administration, although there is plenty of conflict on that score. More complicated conflicts here concern the stability of the source, and also the degree to which traditional archival records are less suitable points of entry into certain kinds of historical understanding than nonwritten documents, like photographs or oral testimony.

One advantage of provenance as testimony to the authenticity of a document was that the question of authorship was subordinated to that of its place of origin. While it was obviously desirable to identify the authors of documents if this was possible, the authority of a source was affirmed by the authority of its institutional identity. With oral testimonies, however, authorship itself is the sole test of authenticity. With photographs and films, authenticity depends on the process of composition. If an archive is to preserve oral or visual testimony, it has to make a series of judgments about the importance of the subject being evidenced, and how it meets the archive's social and scholarly purpose. Related here are complex issues concerning the social, cultural, or political standing of the person providing the testimony or the subject being photographed, and the process by which the material was recorded. None of these decisions can be made on the basis of principles that have traditionally governed archival administration.

Questions about the authenticity of photographs and films present particular archival issues. On the surface, photographs and films would seem to need no authentication, since they capture visually some part of actual pasts. Identifying the photographer or film maker is also unimportant to the value of the images themselves, however much it might matter for other reasons. Yet the very "actuality" of the image obscures the artifactual issues that are central to archiving. Was the scene staged or natural? Did the photographer or film maker set the equipment to capture some particular dimensions of a scene, to communicate a mood as well as a setting, or to make a particular argument in a creative way, or simply run the camera as if it were an open and unbiased historical recorder?

Written documentation can validate specific claims, as well as general recollections, but visual representations communicate instantly, directly, and often sensationally. The infamous photographs of Abu-Graib prisoner abuse constructed elements of American and Iraqi identity in ways more immediate and powerful than any written document could possibly have done, regardless of questions concerning their authenticity. They stirred (or recreated?) past Arab memories of "imperial subjugation" as sharply as they confronted nostalgic American recollections of good democratic people again fighting a totally just war. As Bonnie Shawn Smith has detailed, the distribution of the photographs over the Internet also created a powerful "counter archive" to official American sources on the conduct of the war, one which quickly spun completely out of American control. In the view of Donald Rumsfeld, George W. Bush, and other U.S. officials who displaced the reality of abuse onto its artifactual evidence, it was the photographs that "did the damage." In one sense they were right, since it was the images, not the actual events, which were the most powerful elements in condensing American and Iraqi (or Arab) identities around the moralized positions of oppressor and oppressed, and challenging the well-documented traditional alternative representations of liberator and liberated.[29]

Archivists and others who have worked on these problems understand that there is no neutral or univocal visible world, as W. J. T. Mitchell has put it, "no vision without purpose . . . no naked reality [not] clothed in our systems of representation."[30] In this respect, photographs and films are the most misleading of artifacts. What seems to recreate a live, three-dimensional past is in fact a two-dimensional compression that condenses past experience and reduces the complexity of historical narratives every bit as much as a written document, and equally excludes the subjectivities so important to history and memory, like outlooks, attitudes, feelings, and mentalities. As with written artifacts, these need to be deduced by the scholarly user. They also need to be argued more convincingly than a casual look at the image might suggest.

For these reasons, film and photographic archives have traditionally been set apart from other repositories and administered according to different protocols and standards. Typically, they house large and often undifferentiated collections, commonly ordered by subject or date. Visuality, meanwhile, has emerged as a complicated (and still poorly defined) area of historical enquiry in relation in particular to textuality, since the various meanings of visual images are analytically more complicated than those for texts.[31] From an archival perspective, their sheer bulk deprives archivists of the type of attention and scrutiny normally given to written records, especially with respect to a contextual understanding of their provenance and use. Thus, in the view of Joan Schwartz, a leading photographic archivist, the importance and prevalence of photographs and films obligates the archival community to think more carefully about the nature, production, and purpose of photographs, especially in terms of the ways they, too, convey government policy, communicate ideology, construct identity, shape collective memory, and in a variety of contested ways, define concepts of self and the cultural other.[32] The same can be said for the methodological obligations photographs and film place on archival scholars.[33]

Making the issue of sources even more conflicted are the shifting views of some historians themselves about the meanings of documentary authorship and authenticity. Among their other qualities, historical archives, whether state or private, can be thought of as institutionalized efforts to detach the present from the past, insofar as their documents are commonly authenticated as in terms of their historical provenance, and protected from use for some discrete period of time. For some scholars, especially those involved with questions of social memory, the more archivists are self-consciously active in producing and reproducing "traditional" historical understandings, the more they reinforce the very notions that the turn away from authority in history was meant to unsettle, including that of social memory itself. Even acquisition policies designed to assure the preservation of certain kinds of knowledge or intended to protect the multiplicity and diversity of social memories are necessarily dependent on the selective biases of the archivist and the institutional affiliations of the archive. Indeed, the turn away from authority in history has raised questions not about the value of documentation but about its very nature.

For some, this has included an effort to examine more closely traditional conceptualizations of historical time itself, and the idea that historical pasts are susceptible to being recaptured in any but the most romantic notions of individual and social memory. Here, history is instead, at best, a contestable field of representations. It reflects in the concept of multiple pasts the entwined nature of many different kinds of experience, rather than any single "authentic" past. From this perspective, the archive's documents can also remain authoritative sources while not constituting in any sense the authentic "memory of the nation." The archive, too, becomes a representational field.

An example of this new set of concerns is reflected in Jonathan Boyarin's collective volume *Remapping Memory: The Politics of Timespace*, where the very stability of archival documentation comes into question.[34] Rather than assume that archives are fixed institutions, and that the documents they hold are authentic as a result of this stability, an alternative posed here is to regard the authority of the document as an effect of its being archived, that is, to recognize the archive as an active agent in the creation of historically specific conceptions of lineal time. Boyarin himself argues that traditional notions of historical time are also related to how social and individual memory are socially understood, that is, as a linkage to actual pasts rather than an ordering of the present or a prescription about historically appropriate futures. In his view, the fact that Einsteinian changes in the understanding of space and time have not been incorporated into historical or archival thinking has left both "stuck" in an eighteenth-century positivist mode of thinking and interpretation. An archival effort to authenticate even nondominant social memories would only reinforce the close connections between modern notions of absolute (lineal) time and the authority of the modern nation-state.[35] Reinhart Koselleck, a noted historian of theory, has formulated the same problem somewhat differently. In his view, historical reality had to be understood as a central element of present-time social reality: "an internally differentiated structure of functional relationships in which the rights and interests of one group collide with those of other groups, and lead to conflicts." The contest here is fundamentally about sources. Defeat on the part of one or another group about which sources archives make available is experienced as a perversion of historical truth. It is also often presented as a moral failure, since sources are not being deployed to illustrate properly "what went wrong." The past is pulled "out of time," obscuring its proper relation to the present.[36]

Here we can see an additional dimension of the Enola Gay controversy: its relation to questions about the nature and stability of evidence. As we have seen, the exhibition was offensive for many not simply in terms of what it visually depicted, but because the curators appeared to be using archival evidence to destabilize historical certainties. In return, many regarded this use of documentation itself to be "unstable," in the sense that it wrongly and falsely eclipsed the social and individual heroism that gave the bombing its "real" historical meaning. Even some scholars intellectually sympathetic to postmodernism accused their colleagues of precipitating the crisis themselves by moving beyond the sureties of modernity to the newly fashionable paradigms of multiple pasts and a jargony language that was neither popularly recognized nor easily understood outside (or even, at times, within) the academic community.

The Derridian notion that "there was nothing outside the text" seemed especially at fault here. For many, this idea seemed to dissolve any importance in the real sensations, heroics, tragedies, and pains of really lived experience, especially really fought wars. As a result, efforts to "decenter" authority and replace black and white heroics with more nuanced and subtle historical understanding became an affront to the meanings that historical experience had socially acquired. In this sense, the Enola Gay controversy was a reflection of the broader struggles in the United States over how that country's past should be remembered and evidenced, swirling bitterly around the muted Vietnam War Memorial and the decision of

Congress to build a new, militarily graphic monument commemorating American losses (and American losses alone) in the Second World War.[37]

In fact, the argument that there was nothing outside the text hardly diminished the importance of archival documentation in textual form. Rather, it brought the question of historical authority to its authorial root, displacing the issue of content—what the document said—with a focus on who wrote it and how. Ranke himself, of course, had badgered his seminar students with precisely this question, but as a way of making content itself intelligible and assuring it was trustworthy. The new concern for the textuality of documents, like "new historicism" more generally in literary criticism, held them as artifacts of their creators rather than evidence of actual pasts.

Perhaps nothing in the broad intellectual revolt against the teleologies of modernism exercised scholars more than this move against sources as evidence of really lived pasts. Even sophisticated explorations like Steven Shapin's *A Social History of Truth* and Mary Poovey's carefully researched *A History of the Modern Fact* were pushed aside (unread?) by many who, with Gertrude Himmelfarb, regarded even thoughtful studies of the concept of truth as evidence of an unrestrained intellectual nihilism. As Shapin acknowledges, "truth is not supposed to change over time—to have a history—neither is it supposed to have a sociology. Whatever bears the marks of collective production cannot be truth."[38] Yet the sensible interrogation of history's "truth claims" in a burst of reactive articles and books did not deter some historians, on one hand, from rejecting archival research altogether as the best way to trace the residues of the past, or many others from a new skepticism about how archival sources were actually used and deployed. The archive, after all, is clearly just such a "collective production" if not of truth, certainly of particular kinds of knowledge and truth claims. Between 1991 and 1995, the journal *Critical Theory* devoted more than forty articles to questions relating to the question of evidence in historical understanding.

The troubling case of David Abraham fueled this contention. A young, untenured historian at Princeton, Abraham published in 1981 a well-documented study on the relationship between German industrialists in the 1920s and the nascent Nazi movement.[39] On the basis of almost universally positive reviews which complemented its own reading, the Princeton department recommended him for tenure, but the promotion was denied by the university administration after accusations from the Germanist Gordon Turner at Yale that Abraham had used his sources improperly. In a petulant letter, a version of which was published in the *American Historical Review*, Turner essentially accused Abraham of fraud.

Turner and Gerald Feldman at Berkeley undertook a vituperative campaign to discredit the work—Turner at one point called it "the Brink's robbery of German history." Feldman argued he "invented" documents and carried on "a systematic effort to cover up the truth."[40] Princeton then cancelled a planned revision of the volume, and Abraham himself, despite a spirited and broadly persuasive defense by many distinguished historians, left the field.

According to the front page *New York Times* account of the Abraham case, this disturbing episode forced historians and others to wonder whether the ways sources were being used by contemporary historians did not flaw "countless modern works of history."[41] A more accurate and less provocative way of describing the effects of this episode would be to say that it reinforced a general sense among historians concerning the relativity of archival sources as necessarily selective materials, and made very public what most archival scholars had always known: that the selection and use of archival documentation is far from the scientific exploration that the objectivizing grammar of archival citation suggests. Abraham himself admitted that in an eighteen-month stint in the German archives as a graduate student he "committed the embarrassing and elementary error of hasty and niggardly note taking. The consequence was that my transcriptions sometimes yielded quotations that were elided or not precise."[42] His Princeton colleague Lawrence Stone, who had himself helped fueled the cultural wars when he warned in *Past and Present* that "deconstruction" was a dire threat to history, put the matter very well: "When you work in the archives you're far from home, you're bored, you're in a hurry, you're scribbling like crazy. You're bound to make mistakes. I don't believe any scholar in the Western world has impeccable footnotes. Archival research is a special case of the general messiness of life."[43]

As Stone suggests, and as Appleby, Hunt, and Jacob later properly insisted in their *Telling the Truth about History*, the "truth claims" of archival documentation, to put the issue in its epistemological terms, was not the principal issue for most historians. The question instead centered on the care with which historians and other scholars—but not archivists—used these materials. Appleby, Hunt, and Jacob made a useful distinction in this regard between truth and meaning. However difficult it may be to access past experience, to seek history through its documentary and other traces, most historians digested the important controversies here by ratcheting up their thresholds of demonstration and certainty, rather than abandoning the effort.[44] At the same time, it is fair to say that understandings of the historians' enterprise itself had substantially changed. As the great teleologies of reason and modernization gave way to new approaches and levels of understanding at least among academic historians, so did the scientific assumption that archival sources in and of themselves gave authority to their writing.

The Solutions of "Identity Archives": Authorship, Agency, and New Archival Authorities

Already by the 1970s, well-known archivists like F. Gerald Ham, the State Archivist of Wisconsin and President of the Society of American Archivists, began to lament that new historical approaches seemed unable to inform archival practice. The divide that was opening between the ways many archivists and historians were now processing the past was not only weakening relationships that had long made authoritative archives close partners in the writing of authoritative history; it was opening troublesome questions about how archives acquired historical material, their purported historical objectivity, and the relation of both to new subjects of archival enquiry. Coming at a moment when issues of identity were also emerging as a potent political force, these growing divisions served to encourage a new kind of "identity archive," one organized around new conceptualizations of what constituted historical importance based on the primacy of identity.

In a world of increasingly fluid communications, the new emphasis on identity extended in turn the question of the archives' relation to established national narratives well beyond the borders of existing national states. Black history in the United States engaged African, Caribbean, and Latin American materials; Ukrainian and other East European national histories encompassed a range of diaspora archives, as well as the disengaging of national materials from their subordination to Soviet archival categories; Jewish and gender studies essentially had no national boundaries at all.

At the same time, the ostensibly objective or disinterested role of the archive in maintaining certain kinds of national narratives was also brought into question, along with the historical authorities that had traditionally guided the appraisal and preservation of documentation. As we have seen, the authority of the archive and the professional objectivity of the archivist derived in the Jenkinsonian tradition from a consensual understanding of the past that privileged certain processes and institutions, including archives themselves, on the basis of their perceived dominance in the production and maintenance of normative social and political systems. The professional capabilities of the archivist centered on the ability to authenticate sources by determining and identifying how they were created, and by assuring a system of arrangement and description that allowed users to understand their contextual origins. Judgments on the relationship between kinds of sources and their potential value to historians were essentially inappropriate to the tasks of preservation.

More complex understandings of identity and of accompanying politics directly challenged these long-held assumptions and practices. The "imagined communities" linked to subordinated ethnicities and nationalities along with the presumed commonalities of race and gender created their own hierarchies of historical authorities, radically at odds with those underlying the established practices at historical archives. Where was the authority of gender in understanding relations of power? If existing national archives reified dominant social and political groups, subordinated ethnicities and nationalities were entitled at the very least to assemble their "own" historical materials in their own archives, if not within their own discrete states.

Like other kinds of repositories, the assembling of identity archives thus constructed its own kinds of knowledge, based like traditional archives on the assumptions regarding historical authority implicit in their appraisal and acquisition practices, as well as their new structures of organization and cataloguing. The archival problem with such repositories as the Schomburg Center at the New York Public Library, the Leo Baeck Institute, or the Lesbian and Gay Archives in San Francisco was not, therefore, that they were organized by groups that had a particular interest in their subjects. Nor was it that these new repositories selectively inscribed meaning on to certain kinds of documentation. Instead, the problem lay in two areas: the unsystematic nature of the conceptual authorities that structured identity collections; and the transparent shift of the archive's role as the formally neutral receiver of documentation generated by the institutions, individuals, or agencies to which it was responsible.

The question of identity "authorities" was (and remains) particularly vexing. Conceptually, identity issues necessarily imply the existence of multiple pasts: contending narratives about who one was (and is) and according to which set of narrative representations. But can archives be matched in any effective way to these multiple pasts? By what set of principles were "identity" materials to be appraised? Was everything related to women appropriate for the women's history archive, or everything relating to the lives of particular ethnic groups worthy of perpetual preservation? Did the qualities of ethnicity, nationality, or race determine in and of themselves the value of material to be collected and preserved?

And what about different kinds of artifactual documentation? Were the kinds of documentation around which historical archives have traditionally been organized now inadequate for historical representations of national pasts? Should archivists simply let collecting institutions solve whatever problems the changing nature of sources may present? Was it appropriate for identity archives to assemble any kinds of testimony, or only materials whose provenance and authenticity could be determined in certain ways, and whose forms of production met certain methodological thresholds?

An important effect of the turn away from traditional approaches to politics and institutions among historians was that it simultaneously involved a turn toward what some now called "new history" on the part of the other human sciences. Narrativity, culture, and causality took on new interest to sociologists. The "anthropological experience" in historical contexts prompted new explorations into how traditional field research in anthropology attempted to "read" historic pasts out of observable presents. The "stabilizing and destabilizing" functions of historical study itself received new attention in terms of how law was conceived and legal arguments constructed. Politics for some political scientists became "non-science," while explorations of the uses and misuses of historicization spread easily through literature studies and widespread discussions of the western canon.

If new understandings of discursive forms, locations of power, and cultural practices further freed historians from E. P. Thompson's condescensions of "tradition," "historicity" equally liberated their colleagues from the disciplinary isolation social science had traditionally modeled. The reasons why new thinking insisted on an exploration of the context of the historian, as well as of his or her particular scholarship, were not rooted in the peculiarities of historical as opposed to anthropological or sociological enquiry, but in its scientistic claims. The self-reflection this had encouraged among historians not only spread across the social sciences as a whole, but stimulated new interest in the "problem" of history in fields like historical sociology, which for a time had seemed likely to be displaced by the technologists of numbers crunching.

All of this work also created demands for new kinds of sources, especially those that could help create "proper" memories and reproduce the experiences of people "without history" or whom history "had forgotten." As Eric Wolf demonstrated in his seminal *Europe and the People without History*, published in 1982, new histories "from below" required a kind of documentation either absent or almost entirely irretrievable in any direct and systematic way from state historical archives at all levels.[45] This was also increasingly apparent to historians now working on problems of nationality, race, and gender. While virtually any institutional history or biography could be explored with relative ease in existing collections, providing only that relevant materials had been preserved, the sources for new kinds of history had to be teased obliquely from sources that had been collected, catalogued, and preserved as other kinds of testimony. Present day Serbs, Lithuanians, or Ukrainians could only "share" the lived experience of their forbearers by remembering its forms and imagining its subjective content, something historians and archivists were called upon to provide. The same was true for Black or Native Americans, and other groups whose ways of remembering served to mobilize against real or imagined wrongs.

A further problem with identity archives involved the way many were deliberately engaged in creating new or alternative historical narratives. If the neutrality of more traditional historical archives was already compromised by the arrangement and description processes that constituted their grain and which reproduced their underlying narratives, and if local repositories of various sorts often accumulated certain types of "neglected" materials, identity archives left the question of neutrality entirely behind. Their goal was precisely to encourage the kinds of exploration that would produce new understandings of their subjects, past and present. In effect, they authored their own stories, albeit in general and often contested ways.

Archives as Authors

The issue of archives as "authors" is not a new one. Patrick Geary, for example, has examined in some detail the process of selecting and assembling medieval charters and texts into cartularies, invoking in a provocative way a Foucauldian challenge to contemporary notions of authorship more generally.[46] The fact that archivist monks of the ninth and tenth centuries actively selected the charters they transcribed focuses attention on the ways in which many of the documents held by modern archives are also the products of complex processes of assembly and creation, rather than authored in the commonplace sense of the term. One does not have to be a Foucauldian to understand that many archival documents are "authorless" in the figurative sense of being solely attributable to a particular, identifiable writer. The value of the document to the scholar depends not simply on its text, compiled in various ways, but to the role of the archive in rendering it into some usable form. The archives' placement of a text within an archival fond effectively gives additional "authorship" to the document in ways as important to scholarship as its initial composition.

A good example of an authored archive occurred after the Soviet archives were opened in the late 1980s. Historians found a trove of hitherto secret materials reporting on the "mood" of ordinary citizens as early as 1919 and 1920, at the height of the Russian civil war. These were collected and archived as part of a developing system of comprehensive surveillance, subsequently expanded by the NKVD and its secret police successors into a central component of social control. Initially, the materials seemed to be evidence of what ordinary people were thinking and feeling, authored by a legion of informants. They seemed unusually good sources for how the actualities of individual experience contradicted the ways it was recorded in Soviet historiography. On further exploration, however, scholars realized that many of these descriptions were written and rewritten both initially and as they traveled upwards in the system to provide the authorities with the descriptions they wanted to receive. When they got to the archives, archivists themselves catalogued them as authentic descriptions of popular feeling. What the archives were actually creating, however, was not an alternative narrative about popular mood but an account of the surveillance network itself.

The case of imperial interests in China provides another example of authorial archives, one that reflects a desire to write a "rational" history of Chinese history and culture in western terms, what James Hevia has called the decoding and recoding of Asia. Hevia argues that comprehending even mundane archival and administrative processes are essential for "understanding the relation between the real and the fictional, between the archives and imaginings of empire." In nineteenth-century China, British administrators and archivists worked to assemble documentation in centralized sites—nodal points of archival accumulation that, in Hevia's view also "allowed authority to collect." In effect, however, these archives, like those studied by Stoler and Dirks, not only "authored" the narratives of British imperial adventure in China; they produced essential elements of British imperial identity.[47] As Thomas Richards suggests, the archive here was less a specific institution than an entire epistemological complex for representing knowledge within the context of empire, "a fantasy of knowledge collected and united in the service of state and Empire."[48]

These sources also engaged other kinds of narratives, what Hevia cleverly calls the "imperial" knowledge of China.[49] As he shows, for example, in 1913 Hosea B. Morse's *Trade and Administration of the Chinese Empire* combined statistical tables and documents into a narrative of economic progress using documents he helped assemble in his position in the Imperial Maritime Customs. Morse's most thorough compilations were his five-volume *The Chronicles of the East India Company Trading to China, 1615–1834*, and his three-volume *International Relations of the Chinese Empire 1834–1911*.[50] These volumes became, in effect, the standard archival window into western understanding of China, one that was framed by indexing and cataloguing practices that authored a taxonomy of historical significance. As with Geary's medieval cartularies, and Dirks' South Asian materials, archivists and cataloguers like Morse not only constructed particular categories of understanding, as Stoler has shown was the case in other colonial archives; they were actively involved in creating many of the documents that produced particular narratives of engagement, transformation, and progress.

As in China, how archivists and archives select specific kinds of documentation from a multiplicity of bureaucratic interactions on the basis of their own self-conscious sense of administrative authority is a process that is always set within larger issues of power and administrative direction. Archival processes reflect these relationships in all repositories, but especially in the various kinds of identity archives where these relationships are often quite explicit. Archival processes here can then author material in similar ways.

For good historians, documents may therefore "speak for themselves" but archivists actively create their "voice," since the representations of historical truth constantly circle around prefigured archival categories of selection and retention. In the hands of good scholars, documents can consequently be quite destabilizing to the historical narratives the archive itself helps author. Implicit here is the contentious notion that the historical meanings of sources are not inherent. For scholars trained within the conceptual frameworks of postmodernism, and perhaps especially those now engaged in research in identity archives, this idea would seem axiomatic. One of the scholarly needs underlying the organization of these repositories was that of disengaging the "fixed" meanings that identity materials in traditional historical archives seemed to have acquired.

Contesting Discourses: Archives and History across the Divide

New challenges to the ways historians have understood and processed the past have thus been challenges as well to archives and their sources. Historicizing the nature of historical narration demands a corresponding historicizing of the essentialism of documents, as well as archival practices. Perhaps most important, the opening of the archival divide has made the question of how and why sources should be regarded as historical—in the sense of carrying interpretative weight about the past, rather than simply being old—one that must be increasingly addressed by the historical community itself, rather than the archivists. Indeed, attributing historical qualities to particular kinds of documentation is no longer an essential part of most archival practices. In an earlier time, when historians and archivists constituted a single professional community and largely focused their attention on great men and political institutions, the words "historical" and "old" were used interchangeably. In contrast, contemporary archivists are no longer prepared to unravel the many layers of historical meaning that might lie within the materials they administer. Away from historians, on the other side of the divide, the archivist can no longer incorporate the multiple, interdisciplinary, conceptually broad, and ever-shifting historiographical categories in any archivally useful way.

Should the traditional juridical-administrative justification for archives, grounded in conceptualizations of the state and nation, therefore be replaced by sociocultural justifications grounded in wider public policies and uses, as the Canadian archivist Terry Cook has suggested?[52] And if so, what is the responsibility of the state or public archive, like that of the public library, to assure that alternative historical voices be archived and heard? Should archives in any respect be obligated, in other words, to discourage the selective remembering that selective archiving engenders? Are the national archives of multiethnic states bound by their very obligations to the state to acquire and preserve materials that themselves define contending identities and construct conflicting social memories?

One common position on this issue is that initiative in these matters is best left to identity archives organized by different social interest groups, rather than the state. This solution may facilitate new kinds of understanding, as we have suggested, but it also encourages a selective forgetting. And what about even stronger forms of social amnesia? Should professional and ethical responsibilities obligate identity archives to preserve access to materials that document alternative understandings or explanations, providing like the Abu-Graib photographs "counter-archives" for counter-narratives?[53] If historians are held to ethical norms that assure they do not distort their sources, do archivists have a responsibility to preserve materials that may be destructive to identity myths or that contest social memories that are prefigured in the archive's mission or objective? Must there be a place in private Jewish collections, for example, or Israeli state archives, for anti-Zionist materials, those that attest to powerful secular traditions, or even in the case of the Holocaust to the roles of Jewish (and other) collaborators? These questions can (and have) been posed as well in the case of Vichy France, the Quisling movement in Norway, and with regard to collaborationists elsewhere. How must we understand the archive and its processes to be confident that historians will be able to extract alternative narratives from documentation already embedded in the archive's own institutional formation and contingent descriptive categories? Where are the sources for alternative possibilities? Counter-meanings can be clearly inscribed in these archives only if archivists question the authority their repositories reflect, and engage in the discourses, dominant and marginal, that have conceptualized their formation and structured their practices.

Here we circle back to the difficult issues we started with: how the past is differently processed by archivists and historians; and what the roles are of archivists themselves, in addition to archival institutions, in giving the sources specific kinds of meaning. To understand its implications for both contemporary archives and the new digitized archives of the present and future, we need now to take a much closer look at what archivists actually do.

8

The Archivist as Activist in the Production of (Historical) Knowledge

Among its other effects, the appearance in 1995 of Jacques Derrida's *Mal d'Archive* signaled a burst of new interest in archives as cultural and social artifacts.[1] A number of interdisciplinary explorations soon followed, some in the form of seminars and conferences, some in print. Two issues of the British journal *History of the Human Sciences* were devoted entirely to the archive in its various forms and representations.[2] A major conference on "Archiving Modernism" focused on the question "What is an 'Archive'?" A gathering at the Radcliffe Institute devoted to "Opening Up the Archives" focused on access to and understanding of complex archives worldwide. In 2001, Carolyn Steedman published *Dust: The Archive and Cultural History.*[3]

Each of these explorations regarded the archive as central to the ways historians and other scholars understand the past. In the jargon of our times, the archive was problematized as part of broader historiographical and epistemological issues: how historical knowledge is formed and processed. Aside from the substance of these explorations, what is most interesting about them is the almost total absence of archivists themselves from the discussion. The understanding of those who work in the repositories, who are trained in the complex processes of records creation, retention, and accessibility, and whose knowledge of how archives actually function were relegated to the margins, mirroring the marginalization of historians in the archivists' own appraisal debates that were occurring at the same time. We doubt that this slight was intentional. But it signals an additional aspect of the separation between the professional interests of historians and archivists—the cultural and disciplinary elements of the archival divide.

These contemporary forays into the idea of the archive reflect two quite different readings about the activities of archivists and their roles in the production of historical knowledge: the documentation in any form that over time becomes, de facto, a foundation for future historical understanding. The first reading engages the abstract idea that the archives is a place for "uncovering," reflecting as Jacques Derrida suggested, user practices of articulation and repression. Michel Foucault has elaborated on this notion by regarding the archive as sets of processes through which scholars and other users relate statements to "events" and "things." In his *Archaeology of Knowledge*, he theorizes archives as elements of social organizational hierarchy, with their own languages and systems. As with Derrida, the archive here becomes a "construction" of, and surrogate for, the processes of individual memory, as well as a manifestation of deeper psychological processes of personal and social recollection.[4]

Absent here again is any significant role for the archivist. He or she serves simply as a (sometimes officious) keeper of the record. Although Carolyn Steedman has strong words for Derrida about what "archive fever" is really all about—in her view, it is a matter of bacteriology, not psychology—she goes even further in diminishing any notion of the archivist as active in knowledge production. The archive is a stable, static, dusty enterprise full of what she calls "stuff" and watched over by its keepers.[5]

Steedman's *Dust* nicely articulates this first reading: the common and enduring sense that the archives are "catacombs" of manuscripts in Michelet's terms: an eternal tomb of long corridors neatly arranged years ago and scarcely disturbed since. Upon these accumulations of neatly tied bundles, files, and dossiers are the layers of very real (and sometime physically infectious) dust that the historian, not the archivist, must literally blow away, uncovering the equally physical realities of the past.[6] Indeed, how often are dust and archives associated in the public imagination? And how often is the dusty archive associated with the passive clerks who preserve it? For Steedman and Michelet, as well as, we daresay, most historians, the archive and archivist are both static and quiet, a warehouse and watchman for the often random documentary residue of the past. Both wait patiently (and sometimes forever) for readers "unintended" by those who produced the documents, as Steedman puts it, to transform the texts of registers, memoranda, reports, and the like into coherent narratives of some imagined past.

While archives and archivists are usually acknowledged in prefatory statements to historical studies, it is the historian and the historian alone who is seen as active in processing historical knowledge. Historians, not archivists, engage archival materials with the dynamism of individual or "national imagining," to use the terminology of scholars of identity. Historians, not archivists, infuse ideas, imagination, and interpretation into the archives. The writing of history processes the past through engagement with vestigial, dust-laden archival scraps, a process that is ideally dynamic, thoughtful, and full of decisions that the historian alone must make. In contrast, as Steedman puts it, the stuff of the archive just "sits there" until it is seen.[7]

A second quite different reading sees the archive and archivist as direct products of changing cultures, each in their own ways. Here, archives and archivists are thought of as representations and representatives of dynamic social, cultural, and political processes. What intrigues the historical anthropologist Ann Stoler about the archives, for example, is "an emotional economy manifest in disparate understandings of what was imagined, what was feared, what was witnessed, and what was overheard."[8]

This reading emphasizes what we might call the "cultural determinant" approach to archives. It has the advantage, in our view, of recognizing the role of archivists themselves. Here it is the archive that creates the structures of contemporary and historical understanding. This approach abstracts an archive of a different sort, one that is important and useful especially to contemporary scholars engaged in studies of empire, subalterns, colonization, or "postcoloniality." But while we are sympathetic to the understanding of archives it engages, it is again a perspective that places archivists themselves in the position of the agents of action, rather than its initiators. And like the conceptions of archival passivity, it is also one that remains at some distance from the work professional archivists actually do.

In fact, as even Derrida and Steedman would admit, the archive has its own dynamic, as do even the most static of cultural or political institutions. The issue in attempting to understand this dynamic from a perspective outside the archive is not one of "static" archives or of "passive" archivists. Nor is it a question of the lack of agency on the part of archivists. Rather, it is the lack of transparency about what actually occurs in the archive for anyone not directly engaged in its processes. Indeed, far from being a site of passive curation, archives seen from the inside out are places of constant decision making, where archivists themselves, like historians and others scholars, are constantly involved in processes that shape the "stuff" from which history is made.

Thoughtful archivists are themselves not unmindful of the implications for scholars of how archival records are selected, assembled, represented, and distributed. More than twenty years ago, the Australian archivist Ann Pederson wrote that the activism of archivists in assembling the record "may even be said to be orchestrating the quantity and quality of documentation and thus intervening to produce resources for future history which would not otherwise be available."[9] Like other archivists, however, Pederson was not emphasizing the activism of her colleagues in this regard so much as worrying that that "this type of intrusion into the natural course of events does not harmonize well with traditional archival principles which advocate a much more neutral and objective stance for the archivist."[10] The issue for her and others was to hold on to professional representations of neutrality rather than to confront the issues that activism involves.

Is it also therefore the case that the archivist is active in creating historical knowledge? In other words, do archivists function through their practices, placements, and self-conceptions to create particular kinds of historical universes? Do their everyday practices help define the parameters by which the historical knowledge latent in their materials is produced? And if so, is this an aspect of archiving that yesterday's curators and today's technologically trained records managers are themselves generally aware?

The answers lie in two areas. The first is an explicit and clearly articulated set of practices and procedures that hone documentary records directly within specific frameworks of archival time and space. The second is a broader less explicit cultural dimension outside the literal boundaries of the archives that implicitly shapes archivists' decisions on what ultimately comes to the stacks.

Assembling the Record: The Essentialist Foundations of Agency in the Archive and the Mediations of Archival Practice

As archival administration turned toward essentialism, the specific historical authorities that had long guided the processes of document evaluation yielded as we have seen to a reemphasis on authorities derived from the activity that generated the record itself, its essential foundation. These contextual authorities freed the archivist from having to wrestle with changing historiographies and notions of what might be "historically important" in determining the significance of documents that had largely guided their custodial predecessors. But while the new essentialism has shifted both archival authorities and professional activists toward institutional contexts in the generation of records, it has hardly diminished their active role in assembling these materials. In thousands of archival institutions across the globe, decisions are made every day on the selection, retention, and description of records that will eventually become the historian's sources. These are explicit actions, clearly set in broader local and national cultures of records creation and disposition. In the conduct of their professional responsibilities, archivists preside over what ultimately forms the archive.

The first step in acquisition is to determine the relationship of a body of documents to the collecting responsibilities and interests of the archival institution that will ultimately administer and house the records. The first task of the archivist is consequently to determine which materials of a sponsoring agency it should receive and why. The process is similar in collecting or identity archives, since even a broad collecting mandate has to be applied to specific kinds of materials.

In the United States, for example, the National Archives and Records Administration must take into consideration a very broad mandate to preserve the "records of American democracy" as generated through the governmental process. In France, where the Archives Nationales is supposed to hold the "records of the nation," the Department of Defense and other government agencies have their own separate repositories, and hence their own mandates for archivists to apply. In some cases the acquisition may be based on a legal mandate or requirement such as a data set from a weather satellite.

The tensions and difficulties in determining the parameters of these mandates have been evident in the changing ways national archivists make their selections for inclusion. In the early years of the National Archives, U.S. archivists concentrated on acquiring government materials in terms of their current and potential historic value. Over time, they began to assume an increasingly broad sense of the archives' potential service to a broader public rather than to scholars alone. Genealogical material came to play an increasingly important role here, corresponding to a developing public interest in these materials. At Library and Archives Canada, the mandate to preserve the documentary foundation of Canadian history has been subordinated over time to a broader cultural mission focused on social memory.[11]

Acquisition decisions must also engage what might be called the "ownership" issue, although the actual ownership of materials to be archived is rarely in question. What archivists confront here is really the claims of originating agencies or other donors to control the transfer process. Government agencies may have a legal obligation to transfer their materials because their documents officially belong to the government, but which materials agencies actually prepare for transfer, how they prepare them, and when transfers occur are still under their control. Even within specific institutional settings, archivists can assemble the record only by knowing how and when to intervene: for example, by relying on persuasion or scheduling records for transfer according to a set schedule.

In collecting institutions, the process of acquisition is made more complex by a focus on donor relations. It is not uncommon for private donors to overvalue the materials they think an archive should retain, especially when these touch on their own experiences or careers. Sometime private donors want to insist that archives accept their donation in its entirety. Obviously, many sponsoring agencies and donors also pay the bills, or are otherwise in a position to influence an archival accession. Negotiating the transfer, gift, or purchase can thus be a particularly difficult part of the acquisition process. Testing the sensitivities of donor tolerance often requires an archivist to have skills attuned to personalities as much as to the assembling of materials. In the final analysis, the archivist has as much ability to resist, encourage, or even compel transfers from resistant donors as he or she has time, knowledge of the materials, and negotiating skill, as well as in some cases a familiarity with the law.

Once archivists actually manage to get their hands on the documents they have identified for inclusion in the archives, the next step usually involves a careful review or "survey" of the records.[12] The archival survey is the archivist's first explicit mediation in the content of acquired records. It begins with a quick review of the corpus of records, assesses their quantity and form, and distinguishes what the archivist may regard as routine records from those related to policy or other broader issues, including possibly their importance to scholars if the archivist is so inclined. Additional aspects of the survey include determining whether records can be sampled as illustrative, rather than retained in their entirety; whether they adequately reflect the practices of the originating agency if they are institutional records; and how the records as a whole meet the archival needs and objectives of the donor. With digital records, surveys also require attention to questions of technical systems, formats, the fixity of text or data, and the utility especially of metadata sets, such as undifferentiated e-mail files. Here archivists can appraise only large categories of data, not individual files or documents. In all of these areas, a seemingly routine survey process involves quite active archival intervention.

While the kinds of decisions archivists must make at this stage are similar in institutional and collecting archives, the scale of mediation is often quite different. So are the kinds of negotiations a survey might prompt. In the late 1970s, for example, a consortium of archives in the northeastern United States was called in to survey a whole warehouse of historical records from the long defunct New York Central System and the Pennsylvania Railroad, stored by the Conrail Corporation. These consisted of some 360,000 linear feet of materials housed in seven contiguous warehouses. After two years work only some 20,000 linear feet were retained. The remainder, judged by the process to be of secondary and even marginal value, was destroyed.[13]

Archivists now make similar kinds of decisions even with records that were once thought to be permanent. In the early 1980s, to take another example, archivists surveyed 150 years of Massachusetts Superior Court records running to hundreds of linear feet. They soon found themselves unable to tell whether all cases should be regarded as having equal value, whether thick files represented more significant or simply more complicated cases, or which cases might be thought to be samples of the court's policies and behaviors over time. In this case, local historians were brought in to help. While scholarly input seemed important to the process, even this unusual intervention did not relieve the archivists of their difficult tasks, since the scholars' views could not be assumed to reflect the interests that their colleagues in the future might bring to the collection.[14]

Once the survey identifies those records that archivists think are most appropriate for the archive, the next step is to accession them into the repository. Those that are not accessioned are either returned to the donor or, more commonly, destroyed. Sometimes paper documents are accessioned gradually, sometimes all at once. For practical reasons archivists may prefer the originating agency or donor to determine when the desired records are to be transferred over time, and even which future records fit what the survey has determined was accessionable material. The archivist essentially delegates to the originator of the record the authority to dispose of what the archivists think they do not want.

Archival Appraisal: Assigning Value to Records

It may come as a surprise to many historians, but accessioning materials into an archive once they have been surveyed does not necessarily mean they will be preserved. With paper records, the next step in the process involves the archivist's appraisal of individual files or record sets to determine which ones specifically reflect what the survey initially deemed important about the collection as a whole. With smaller acquisitions, as well as in smaller digital or paper archives, appraisal may be part of the initial survey. In major repositories and with large groups of records, appraisal is more complicated and may require archivists who are familiar and experienced with similar kinds of materials. On occasion, and depending on the nature of the materials, archivists may also seek counsel from historians or other outside experts.

It is at this point that archivists—and almost always archivists alone—decide which documents to save and which to destroy. Most often there is an effort to eliminate duplicates and "routine" materials, so that a researcher is not buried in repetitive minutia. Where surveys have designated records of considerable importance, appraisal is often made file by file, by reviewing individual documents and documentary sets. For experienced archivists, this process is often a well informed, even intuitive activity: what seems "inconsequential" or "repetitive" in the record can appear obvious and self-evident to an archivist familiar with similar sets of material.

There can also be cases where whole sections of documents are removed, often because archivists assume rightly or wrongly that similar and better material can be found elsewhere. Again, the rationale for these kinds of separations is derived from essentialist archival policies and particular institutional definitions. As the Canadian scholar archivist Tom Nesmith has observed, however, destruction can privilege some records in the process of destroying others by repositioning or reframing materials that survive, indirectly adding to their importance.[15]

In appraising individual documents and files, the archivist's professional responsibility is still largely grounded on the categories of evidence and information laid out in classical form by Theodore Schellenberg. "Evidence" covers qualities in the record that testify to the specifics of administrative policies, finances, or law. "Information" covers materials that include data considered central to administrative functions, such as census schedules. The U.S. National Archives and Records Administration, for example, still uses the word "evidence" to underscore its broader mission, although in recent years archivists have been developing new criteria for appraisal that move well beyond these traditional ones.[16]

It is at this point that the eclipse of specific historical authorities as guideposts in the process of document evaluation becomes strikingly evident. All the literature that now guides the appraisal process rests on the importance of authorities derived from the record-producing activities themselves, its essential foundation. As we have seen, this essentialist approach has also helped archivists address the problem of bulk in both paper and digital form. Here again there is studied neutrality with respect to various historical issues, schools, and interpretations. During the 1980s, for example, the U.S. government annually generated close to 100 million cubic feet of various kinds of records; by 2002, its employees were estimated to be handling more than 37 billion e-mails alone each year, let alone the equally exponential growth of other state transactions. From an archival perspective, there has simply been no practical way for these documents to appraised and retained in terms other than the ways they mattered to their generating institutions. Moreover, there has been little investment by archivists in the analysis of actual nodes of power within governmental institutions, or historical shifts in power relations among agencies themselves over time. As a result, archivists have necessarily relied on enduring perceptions concerning importance or the position of a particular agency in the broader administrative hierarchy of an institution.

Thus, the particular structure of an institution or organization can also inform the appraisal process, sometimes in subtle ways. For example, archivists may be more interested in documenting high-level interactions "of consequence" and tend to dismiss the activities of lesser staff as "routine." Similar choices may be made in judgments that particular records are more likely to be needed in the future than others, and appraise them positively on this basis rather than on notions of enduring values. Intuitively or not, however, it is at this point in the processing of archival materials that the future historical record is created.

Archivists make decisions constantly. While international professional standards still require that the archivist not intentionally appraise the record from a particular bias or point of view, the sheer quantity of contemporary records, especially digital documents, requires a fairly draconian policy of weeding out materials regardless of the archivists' best intentions. Although future scholarly users may not know it, this might well be the most important contextual reality that determines what materials they can use.[17]

The Interventions of Arrangement and Description

The practices of archival arrangement and description are a further moment of activism for the archivist, one which also has significant implications for the ways historical knowledge is formed. While appraisal is a discipline of discrimination (it removes material), arrangement and description is a discipline of representation and is additive.[18] Archivists have traditionally arranged and described records to convey a general and accurate sense of their content. As with other elements of processing, professional archivists have long regarded this as another neutral act, based on objective concepts of original order and *respect des fonds*.[19] Yet the preparation of descriptions is also a deliberate and creative act of representation. However professionally it is done, and however detached the archivist might be from the inherent qualities of the records, it is thus a further point of significant mediation.

Depending on the repository, this can be a source of user complaint. Description is a multilayered activity. Ideally it is meant to convey accurately the content and structure of a holding, but it is always contingent on the capacities and interests of the archivist, as well as the values reflected in the archive.[20] At the very least, it is a challenging and often contested task, the point of access where users sometimes throw up their hands in despair. In some archives, descriptions have traditionally been signed by their authors. In principle, this allows a user at least the possibility of seeking additional information from the archivist most familiar with the collection. In actual practice, and especially over time, the user has to rely on whoever is available for help, including that of other scholars using the archives.

The Vatican Archives provide a good example of the challenges of description. Scholars have often complained that descriptions here are impenetrable and difficult to use. They mistakenly imagine this means the holdings themselves are disorganized. What is actually at issue is the inadequacy of the descriptive structure. Although scholars almost never see them, the stacks of the Vatican archives are very neatly arranged. Similar holdings are shelved together in neat chronologies and grouped by their originating agencies, just as they were initially shelved in the offices that created them. Some material has been on the shelves in this way for more than 400 years, added to or not depending on the nature of the record series. Using language, terminology, and protocols established at the time the records were created, and which have served as indices to their contents, it is possible for very knowledgeable scholars to retrieve a file with some precision (although some registers, unfortunately, refer to material that was lost during the Napoleonic wars and no longer exists). Not all users, however, understand the particular descriptive language that arises from the nature of the Vatican bureaucracy and has consequently been used in the preparation of finding aids and indexes. More commonly, scholars have to rely on knowledgeable archivists, if they can be found, or laboriously trace the footnotes of previous users to find clues about documents they might want. While archivists at the Archivio Segreto have been responding to this problem by preparing more comprehensive and accurate listings, the new aids have little contextual information. The nature of the work of the agency of origin of the record is not explained. Nor do they offer any insights on the possibilities for the use of the material. For example what records series may contain information on works of art or on artists.

The separate Archives for the Congregation of the Doctrine of the Faith (CDF) at the Vatican is a notable exception. Under the direction of a historian at the University of Padova, Ugo Baldini, a comprehensive effort has been undertaken to analyze the nature and range of holdings of the records of the Congregation of the Index of Forbidden Books that are housed in the CDF Archives. Though these records date back to the sixteenth century, they were only opened for research in 1998. The project is designed to provide a comprehensive understanding of the varied record types, institutional processes, and organizational structures used by the congregation. These records can then be used more effectively as a source for understanding intellectual life in Europe over the past centuries. In many ways the Baldini project is the exception that proves the rule, in the Vatican archives as well as elsewhere. The magnitude of the task of description, as well as the time and knowledge it requires, preclude the kinds of finding aids most scholars want and need.[21]

Elsewhere, in Soviet-era archives, for example, historians and others encounter a different problem. Here the very categories of archival classification often structure the kinds of materials scholars can find. As the former head of the Russian State Historical Archive has written, Soviet archival catalogs were often as much a hindrance to scholars in these terms as a help, since their descriptions were not comprehensive listings of records holdings but rather attempted to construct in advance the types of historical subjects their users were to research.[22] For most western scholars working in Soviet archives, moreover, descriptive materials were entirely unavailable. Scholars described their topics to archivists, indicated the fonds and files they knew from other work were likely to contain materials they wanted, and hoped for the best.

Archival description is also closely tied to another task: the physical placement of the records in particular boxes in a particular order. Most modern archivists have given priority to the original order of the records, physically arranging records as they were in the originating office. Files arranged chronologically at their points of origin have remained so in the archives; those organized by topics are kept according to those rubrics. Again, the archivist's professional objectivity with respect to the files ostensibly precludes their reordering. Yet his or her reliance on original arrangements in preparing archival descriptions can sometimes camouflage their contents and obscure their possible relevance to the kinds of topics scholars are researching.

While arrangement in many cases is a similar reflection of original order, materials often arrive at repositories in no recognizable order whatsoever. Here the archivist must try to arrange the records in ways that highlight what is most germane to the archives' own mission. The emphasis in these cases is to point to how and why a collection or record series was chosen for accession. The resulting descriptive materials may be a reflection of the archivist's own predilections with regard to a particular understanding of the purpose of the archival institution. Even the most objective descriptions and physical placements are also to some degree culture bound. Placing the records of political opponents in "special collections" in Soviet archives, or hiding FBI investigations of "subversives" in separate repositories is a way of producing and reproducing cultural values and prescribing what was historically significant.

Insightful archivists like Elizabeth Yakel have struggled with the implications of these mediations, insisting to sometimes resistant colleagues that finding aids are best thought of as "representational systems that are both manifestations of a culture as well as the infrastructure to support that culture." Preparing even the most useful of finding aids is thus "not always a routine matter. Information is moved around, assumptions are made about administrative as well as descriptive information, and other liberties are taken with the original text and structure of the finding aid."[23] Yet finding aids are gateways to the past. How they are prepared is thus as important as what they say.

Finally in the area of appraisal and arrangement is the ubiquitous problem of capacity: there are simply not enough professional archivists capable of addressing what have long been monumental tasks. In recent years some archivists have tried to address this problem with what are known as "scope and content" notes: abstracts based on the processing archivists' particular knowledge of a collection that do not provide comprehensive descriptions or subject analysis. Scope and content notes can usefully indicate, for example, whether records mirror the structure of the originating agency, or contain significant gaps in the total scope of the generating agency's activities and records, injecting some transparency into the descriptive process. Still, such notes cannot link past and contemporary research to the possibilities of the records being described, let alone meet other possible needs of future users.

Mediations in the Reading Room: Access and Reference

Once the record group has been arranged and described, the final stage of accession should make the collection available to users. Here again, however, the archivist must act to assure a repository's particular rules concerning access are put into effect. Questions of access in their most familiar forms involve any conditions that restrict material. In some cases these are determined by archival laws and other kinds of proscriptions, and cover such matters as individual privacy, specific codes of classification, or more elastic matters concerning corporate secrets, organizational integrity, or national security. Particularly in government archives there are rigidly defined systems of classification that generally cover whole bodies of material, especially those designated rightly or wrongly as relating to issues of security. There are also legal restrictions on access to records, such as the U.S. Family Educational Rights and Privacy Act.[24] The archives of tobacco companies have included highly sensitive material about the cultivation of addiction, some of which has only been pried loose by court order in civil suits.

This kind of intrusion into record-keeping practices of classification can only be applied with some degree of caution. To lean too heavily on an individual's or agency's own interests in the administration of records risks encouraging a secretive records environment. At one time, for example, the Walter Reuther Library of Labor and Urban Affairs at Wayne State University in Detroit limited access to anyone working for the government in order to reduce the possibility that its holdings on strikes and other labor protests might lead to prosecutions. In these and other matters of access, the archivist effectively functions as a mediator between the interests of the document's creator and the user.[25]

For years following the Soviet government's confiscation of archives in occupied Eastern Europe, Russian collections at Columbia and Stanford were also very closely guarded lest their materials be used by the "wrong" people or otherwise fall into "hostile" hands. Such environments can be tolerated in private corporate settings, but in public settings, restrictions commonly appear as violations of user rights. On the other hand, if donors or agencies feel that either public or private archives are too liberal in granting access, the archive risks losing their trust, and hence their deposits. Important and sought after records may then find their way into other forms of storage, be destroyed, or not be created at all. In highly charged cases like that of the extraordinarily detailed archives of the International Tracing Service in Bad Arolsen, Germany (a vast collection of documentation on victims of Nazi persecution, opened only in 2007), institutional values and politics invariably trumped public demands for access.[26] The same is true for other sensitive collections. Court appeals may produce specific remedies in individual cases, but the archivist's activism even here can be directed toward protecting institutional values and what he or she may believe is the integrity of the record.

Moreover, in the digital environment there are new kinds of pressure on archival access. A whole new industry of data mining and harvesting has grown up around even the most unstructured digital data banks, and which may remain active even after the material has been archived. In the paper environment, by contrast, the challenge of culling large records collections or administrative files has always been somewhat discouraging to all but the most determined and systematic researchers. Different kinds of information have existed in all traditional archives in what Justice John Paul Stevens once called a state of "practical obscurity."[27] While professional historians may have the time and patience to sift through vast amounts of documentation, other users like journalists, legislators, and Supreme Court clerks usually have little of either. Here too, consequently, there is pressure to make materials more accessible, effectively leaving the task of choosing relevant documents to the archivist.

Private for-profit companies have consequently developed programs capable of mining huge data repositories and aggregates of digital storage sites for information specifically tailored to their clients' needs. On one hand, these commercial services expose the content of various archives to broader publics. On the other, the possibilities of misuse, identity theft, or just unwarranted intrusion push the digital repositories themselves against the standards that bar inappropriate personal or institutional disclosure. Policies that discourage unwarranted disclosure will also have an impact on scholarly access. Institutions will be under pressure to withhold access to their digital holdings if they fear the legal consequences of misuse.

Finally in the long process of creating an archival record is the mediation between the archivist and the user at the archives' points of reference. This may occur at formal "Information" or "Research Assistance" desks in large and heavily used repositories or simply through conversations between users and curators. As every archival scholar knows, the quality of reference assistance depends on an archivist's background, knowledge, experience, and personal disposition. Few researchers in Soviet archives were unaware that small tokens of esteem were always culturally appreciated, even if they were not in any sense an obligation;

and as we have seen, historians from Ranke's time forward have benefited from other kinds of personal associations that opened otherwise locked doors.

Of all the mediating practices of the archivist, it is perhaps archival reference that is most in jeopardy from the archival divide. Archivists newly trained in the technologies of records management cannot always act in ways that effectively consider the implications of new historiographies or other kinds of scholarship. The subject interests of users in contemporary archival materials are already filtered through the necessary processes of appraisal, arrangement, and description. Future encounters between historians and archivists are not likely to see the kind of convergence between an archivist's expertise, the usefulness of description, and the substantive quality of documentation that has traditionally sustained historical scholarship.[28]

The Active Archivist and Cultures of Records Production

The work of the archivist is thus one of an active professional who is required to manage accumulations of documents and records within the constraints of their resources. In this role the archivist actively interacts with documentation in ways that shape what future generations will know as the record of the past. Clearly the archivist has substantial agency here in shaping and defining what constitutes the archive itself—the explicit activist interventions that shape historical knowledge.

There is also another kind of influence at work here, however, one that is less explicit but still of importance in how we understand how the archival record has been constituted more broadly. No matter how active, archivists must work within a particular universe of documentation, and make selections only from these materials. How that universe is constituted depends on the social, political, and cultural forces that encouraged the creation of records in the first place.

The idea of a culture of record keeping is hardly new, and certainly one that historians and other scholars of record-conscious societies like Russia, France, and China know very well.[29] The conceptual, as well as practical, missions of state archives in democratic and authoritarian regimes alike validate social and political processes, as well as record them. As we have seen, the explicit mission statement of the National Archives in the United States is that all Americans will understand the vital role records play in a democracy.[30] This positions the culture of documentation as part of a political and social heritage, with its own implications for social and cultural understandings of openness and accountability. Reflecting on the history of the Archives Nationales in France, Lucie Favier comparably saw its task as one of preserving *la mémoire de l'état*—a broader mission linking archivists and archives to cultural notions of France as a nation.[31] And in both Soviet and post-Soviet Russia, historical archives have been structured and represented quite consciously to legitimize political and social values, as we have shown, reflecting cultures of party and personality, as well as historical teleologies.[32]

At a more fundamental level, the predominance of text in archives has itself reflected a discrete cultural understanding of records production, at least until recently. Authority has rested with texts composed of words that can be quoted and analyzed with other words. Among other consequences, this has long marginalized visual and oral materials as archival records, as we have suggested, even if, as Joan Schwartz has argued, visual materials can no longer be considered simply "illustrative" and, along with recordings and other oral materials, might be considered for some purposes as important if not more so than their textual counterparts. Photographs, once assumed to be "truthful representations, reliable facts, and authentic evidence of some external reality" are themselves, in fact, the "product of social practices which, through the containment and ordering of facts, offer the promise of knowledge and control."[33] The same can be said for oral materials.[34]

Assembling records that will eventually become "historical" thus engages the archivist from the start in mediating competitive and shifting cultural notions of value. In both democratic and more authoritarian societies, it often requires negotiating as well between the cultures of the archive and those of the records-generating group or organization. The familiar story of the Nixon tapes is instructive in this regard. Until its sudden termination, the Nixon presidency was the most fully documented administration in U.S. history. As we know, almost every official Oval Office conversation was recorded, including those whose importance to scholars turned out to be that the people involved thought they were literally "off the record." On one hand, presidential archivists struggled almost immediately to secure these materials as part of their formal "national heritage" mission. On the other, they served at the discretion of the presidential office and quickly found themselves in the midst of a bitter conflict over which of these presidential records belonged in the national archives.

The eventual triumph of openness in this struggle ultimately situated the tapes in the archives, but the clash of cultures it reflected had an unexpected consequence. No American president since Nixon (and we dare say no national executive in any country since) has allowed a similar real-space, real-time recording system to be installed, as far as we know. Almost all Oval Office conversations, on or off the record, have no direct transcripts for future scholars to examine. In a similar way, a court determination that the diaries of former U.S. Senator Packwood were public rather than private documents has also chilled a long culture of diary production.[35] Even memoirs and other personally sensitive materials that find their way into paper or electronic form have become points of cultural, as well as legal and political conflict, further changing the culture of records production itself.

Similar situations can be found in other contexts. The Dutch archivist Peter Horsman has studied the city archives of Dordrecht in the Netherlands. From the thirteenth through the nineteenth century, the city underwent a variety of changes in the conduct of record-keeping processes. Throughout this time he found that archives did indeed reflect the organizations that generated those records, namely those of Dordrecht's city government. But over time there a difference in "quality and completeness" of the record emerged as a result of changing cultural behaviour of the recordkeeping system." Horsman concludes that how the records keepers approached their tasks and how those cultural practices changed over time necessarily affected what was included and what was excluded in the corpus of documentation that resulted. [36]

His colleague, Dutch professor, Theo Thomassen goes further in his examination of the archives of the Dutch States-General from 1576 to 1796. He finds that over a period of four centuries the archives "have constantly been adapted to changing ideas and needs." Clerks and archivists frequently rearranged the archive, removing and adding as the politics of the times dictated. The archives proved to be both "representations and instruments of power, not only of political power, the power to manage and control developments in society, but also of memory power, the power to determine how that society is memorized [sic]."[37]

We thus need to recognize that the archive is a complex social, political, and cultural construction, the product of culturally determined policies and procedures that may well be forgotten over time as its records sit on shelves, or now with digital materials, lie hidden someplace in large machines. The activism of the archivist in this broader milieu is thus one of struggling, sometimes quite courageously, to assure records creation, retention, and release, and thus fulfilling their professional responsibilities in the face of cultural resistances. But we also have to recognize that there are real limitations here. Even the most active of archivists often cannot compel the process without the risk of compromising their appointments and positions, especially where archives are the specific creations of sponsoring institutions with different institutional cultures. As we know, the heads of national archival administrations in most countries are appointed by the heads of state, even if they may report to relatively independent legislatures, as in the United States. In industry, archivists like those who manage the records of Ford Motor, JP Morgan Chase, and Coca Cola have specific reporting lines. The Coca Cola archivist, for example, reports to the Vice President for Public Relations, which directly affects any conception of what the company's archive should be like. The Presidential Libraries in the United States are an even more dramatic example of this effect, as we have suggested, even if they are officially under what is supposed to be politically neutral supervision by the Archivist of the United States.

It is in observing government archives of this latter sort that we can get the clearest glimpse of the challenges presented in particular cultures of records production. In 2006 the office of the U.S. Archivist worked to prevent the Bush administration from reclassifying archived materials whose classified status had expired and which already had been available to users.[38] The new Clinton library has accessioned nearly 40 million e-mails that his administration's permanent staff created. One cannot be sure that archivists assembling these materials have had any way of knowing how selective these e-mails are or if they will ever be able to pass this knowledge on clearly to scholars. A study by Alasdair Roberts provides small comfort by pointing out that e-mail has become "too deeply entrenched in contemporary work life for self-censorship to be effective" and busy officials "struggling to manage an always expanding inbox, find it easier and faster to write candidly."[39] But candor is not always what public officials expect to appear in the archives. The ease and speed of e-mail and other messaging systems consequently prompts easy and quick deletions.

Paradoxically, the Freedom of Information Acts (FOIA) now in place in many countries have also affected the cultures of records production by creating in some cases precisely the opposite of what they intended. Within records-generating organizations, the very existence of the legislation has affected whether records will be generated, retained, or assembled, indeed, the very cultures of administration and communication. When records are retained within or outside the archive, it is often a "FOIA officer" who is responsible for redacting materials whose release has been ordered in accordance with the specific guidelines and categories set out in, or derived from, the law, and who therefore mediates between the cultures of access (some would say openness) and those of privacy (some would say concealment). Although there is great interest in the archival community about the problems of the adequacy of documentation, archivists have actually had very limited authority over the process of records creation in the paper world.

This is equally evident in the processes of digital records creation where archivists rarely can compel a record to be created or released. For example, as Alfred Chandler has described, the evolution of corporate records has moved from transactional data that covered such matters as procurements and sales to complex systems designed to measure, analyze, and compile elements of corporate behavior over time. In his view, the culture of records production in the modern industrial firm has become both an element that affected its administrative and organizational development and a consequence of the changes it helped produce.[40] JoAnne Yates takes this one step further and finds the role of the archivist in the process of corporate record keeping linked to a culture of corporate control, since documents are not simply informational sources but are specifically designed in many cases to shape particular elements of the strategy and structure of corporate activity. New forms of analytic documentation resulted that measured stock turn in retail, freight per mile for the railroads, hours per unit of production, all records designed to inform and rationalize. Records then are consequently generated and managed with deliberate and specific expectations in mind.[41] How much of this documentation becomes part of a public archive is thus very much in question. Closed archives affect historical understanding.

The activism of archivists is thus set within particular cultures of records production. These may affect the kinds of decisions archivists can make by structuring what records are available for preservation even before the archivist engages the processes of their management.

Archivists within the Cultures of "Collecting Institutions"

These cultural issues affect private and other "collecting institutions" every bit as much, as state archives, whose record production is only a fraction of the total record universe, and particularly those of identity and other local "collecting" repositories that gather materials on specific topics or themes. Such repositories abound in the United States but they can be found as well all over the world. In some ways these collecting archives even more clearly identify the cultural forces that shape the stuff of the archives. Those engaged in organizing local "historical" collections or identity archives, for example, act within a context of specific expectations about the kinds of stories their materials allow to be told. We put historical in quotes here to suggest that what the archivists, for example, of local Civil War repositories actively acquire in the United States, or those whose mission is to record certain historical processes like the "expansion of the American West," cannot in any practical way be conceptually neutral about the stories they want their archives to tell. In initiating the archival processes of collecting institutions, archivists are thus clearly directed by the repository's express mission and purpose. The same is true with highly professional archivists who administer university-based repositories like the Schlesinger Library of Women's History at Radcliffe or the Immigration History Center at the University of Minnesota.

Here as elsewhere, records and the historical archives they become are products of particular constructions of history and memory at particular moments in time. Decisions on what historical materials to bring into these institutions are more often than not determined by specific historiographical conceptions of the time or by particular interests of groups located in related communities. As we have seen, these collections have their own purposes, designs, and intentionalities, whether explicitly stated, or, as is more often the case, implicit in the cultural practices by which their records are assembled. Even in the case of university collecting institutions like the Schlesinger Library, particular academic milieus lead to both inclusions and exclusions in what becomes their enduring content, significantly affecting the broader nature of the historical record.

Often these missions are the result of past historical interests whose urgency for contemporary scholars may has faded. The Hagley Museum and Library in Wilmington, Delaware, for example, holds impressive archival collections of more than 1,000 American corporate firms, mostly records prior to 1950 and including the business records and personal papers of the du Pont family, materials on northeastern American railroads, and records of local iron, steel, coal, and oil production in Delaware, New Jersey, and Pennsylvania. Although the idea of business history in this institutional sense is of relatively low interest to contemporary academic historians, these collections have been rediscovered as historians have found new ways of using their content to probe issues relating to more contemporary topics such as technological change, gender, and environmental concerns. In the Vatican, a large amount of shelf space houses collections of Italian families that archivists long ago felt were particularly important. The distinguished Institute for Social History in Amsterdam was created to focus broadly on socialist parties and movements. While its holdings are now of immense historical value, scholarly interests in these topics have shifted to different kinds of subjects from those that formed the initial conception of the archival collection. Given these contemporary historical concerns, one might wish that the decisions about what to include in these major archives decades ago had been different. The historian Gary Nash has tackled this problem within the context of the shifting collecting cultures of private historical societies in Philadelphia. He shows in detail how various local interests among the city's elite defined "historical importance" and how this, in turn, strengthened and reproduced certain sociocultural patterns. Among his other insights is the degree to which those engaged in assembling materials in these repositories were rarely self-reflective about the specific cultural and conceptual influences that formed their collections and which designated the activities of one segment of local society as worthy of being considered "historical" while totally ignoring others.[42] One might dare say the same even for university-related collections like the virtual Hiphop Archive at Harvard, whose mission is "to facilitate and encourage the pursuit of knowledge, art, culture, and responsible leadership through Hiphop." Here too there is a specific cultural argument for historical importance.[43]

In some instances cultural politics play a direct role in the process of assembling records. Archivists at collections like the Bakhmeteff Archive at Columbia University or the Leo Baeck Institute for the Study of the History and Culture of German-speaking Jewry are obviously required to mediate what is included and what is excluded.[44] In other cases, particularly in institutions collecting older documents, potential collections also have high market value. What is bought and sold, and who pays the bills, will almost always affect what is included or not. All are elements of the dynamic by which historical collections are formed. They are also fundamental to how the grain of a collecting institution, which provides the raw materials for a variety of historical narratives, must be "read" and understood, and as Christopher Klemek points out, how materials that have been acquired under one set of assumptions may still have "unexpected utility" over time.[45]

Moreover, in collecting institutions of various sorts as well as state and institutional archives, activism in the archive is contingent on the cultural context out of which the archive itself arises. Archivists are necessarily agents of that culture insofar as they are situated within its practices and act in ways that are conditioned by its forces. Thus the new cultures of records creation and management have involved the emergence of the new essentialist foundation of archival processes, shifting both archival authorities and the concerns of professional archivists away from scholarship towards those of the institutional contexts generating the records.

At the same time, however, all of this has hardly diminished the active role of archivists in assembling these materials. Especially in the digital realm, archivists are directly involved in the often complex legal, administrative, and technological systems and procedures that determine both the final form of documents and records well before they reach the archives. The process of identifying what is socially, politically, or culturally "essential" in terms of institutional values is also full of subtle mediation. "Value neutral" is, in effect, a reflection of the archivists' dependence on broader cultural values and definitions in forming the content of their archives. In turn, this dependence creates a layer of meaning that specifically contextualizes the documents' importance: the archivist comes to "speak" as the organization's permanent "voice," and hence as the indirect spokesperson of its interests.

The Active Archivist and the Historical Record

At some level, the mediations we have outlined are all based on the archivist's implicit or explicit assumptions about what constitutes the "enduring value" of the record. "Appraisal debates" continue to engage archivists in discussions about the values and factors that should be brought to bear here.[46] "Enduring value" may be contingent on the importance of the functions or activities being documented, or dependent on the archives' collecting mission or constituencies. In any case both approaches create the documentation future historians will use to study a particular past.

The social and cultural underpinnings of this process are thus inescapable, since value systems of various kinds underlie all aspects of acquisition. Evaluations made within the context of specific national or nationalist frameworks carry obvious assumptions of hierarchy and importance. In states where consensus obscures underlying values and assumptions, the role of these assumptions may be less obvious than, say, in states like Russia that undergo revolutionary transformations, but they are no less influential in creating the archival foundations of historical knowledge. The archivist Shirley Spragge's call for archives to "document national identity" is a particularly clear example of the problems here. As Terry Cook and others have suggested, what exactly "national identity" consists of, and how exactly an archivist can actively pursue its documentation is quite unclear. In the Canadian case, Cook calls this finding the "Canadian voice," one that wrongly privileges the official narrations of the state over documented stories of individual groups.[47]

The slippery notions of social memory come back to play a role here as well. In an essay on "The Great War: Archives and Modern Memory," the archivist Robert McIntosh has described very well the ways that he and his colleagues can act as "creators of memory" in deciding what deserves to be retained in the archive and what is discarded. He writes:

> Throughout the gamut of professional activity archivists practice a politics of memory, a determination of what will be remembered. This influence can be exercised overtly, by the records we create, acquire, and destroy. But our politics can also be practiced more subtly, by the cues or prompts we give users of records. As the ultimate custodian of this archival record, the National Archives and Records Administration has written its own narrative of the war by its inclusive acquisition practices and the high profile it has given the archival record of the First World War.[48]

Terry Cook and Joan Schwartz put the matter even more bluntly when they argue that archives are "active sites where social power is negotiated, contested, confirmed."[49]

Yet the judgments of archivists that come into play "at every step of preserving, arranging, listing, publishing, and exhibiting" materials are also, as McIntosh points out, fundamentally judgments of value. This is essentially what the French historian Jacques LeGoff has in mind when he states that documents are not "innocent raw material," but express "past society's power over memory and over the future."[50] Because of increasing social complexity, the huge expansion of government as well as the processes of governance itself in the twentieth century, and especially the sheer bulk of modern records, a logical and inevitable consequence of technological change, decisions about what needs to be retained and how it should be represented effectively for future scholars secretes contemporary "memory" records behind very general descriptive structures.

Archivists can tread carefully in this area, hewing closely to the traditional mandates of provenance by preserving and describing only official transactions, or yield to the obvious attractions of preserving all sorts of "interesting" material that usually comes with these records. They can find themselves under considerable pressures to meet users' interests and demands. For example, a 2009 poster invited riders in the Washington D.C. Metro, among others, to share "the National Archives Experience" by visiting an exhibition of "Big Records, Big Events, Big Ideas in American History." Against a perfect blue sky it showed a globe, an upended Titanic, a bathtub, some odd canvas thing, and a strange looking animal all sticking out from the Archive's roof. The banner read, "What's all this doing in the National Archives? Ask the Question." The solution for at least some American archivists is clearly not to avoid appealing to their publics or otherwise constrain their roles in this regard, but as McIntosh put it, to be open and frank about their practices, and "acknowledge our authorship, our vital place in the creation of society's memory."[51]

This position is also not without real problems, however. When McIntosh and others write about the archivists' role in the "creation" of social memory, they are assuming that what they create has validity not only because it links social to individual memories, but also because it is verifiable in the documents. While archivists engaged in this work may be actively constructing some forms of historical knowledge, social memories themselves, as we have seen, are artifactual elements of a community's development, parts of history itself. Even if the role that collective memory plays at various moments of social development is in some way recognized as an archival category, it is quite doubtful that archivists could effectively exercise responsibility for assembling, cataloguing, and preserving its representational forms. Must archivists then stand aside from the subject their own practices serve to create?

Although history has been marginalized as a source for authority in most records processing, how archivists answer these questions in assembling archival materials clearly affects future historical understanding. Indeed, some historians might wonder what the National Archives people may have had in mind as an appropriate answer to their question. Our thoughtful colleague Nancy Bartlett is surely correct in maintaining that the mediating roles of archivist involve multiple interventions in what already is or someday will be historical evidence.[52] So is Ann Stoler when she observes that "the space of the archive resides in the disjuncture between prescription and practice, between state mandates and the maneuvers people made in response to them, between normative rules and how people actually lived their lives."[53] Far from a place of dust and stasis—although we agree there can be plenty of both—archives are thus very active sites of constant and multiple possibilities: acquisition and destruction, cultural determinism and challenge, social conformity and opposition, opportunities gained and lost for discovery and repression—a vibrant site of knowledge accumulation. How the archivist forms and presents the historical record is itself a historical problem, and future scholars are certain to face daunting tasks in understanding the institutional values and contexts embedded in their archives and archival descriptions. They will only have documents and descriptive materials in the quantity, form, and nature that archivists' have decided to give them, however these relate to the historical questions at hand. For archivists and historians alike, here perhaps is the most important meaning of Derrida's multilayered assertion that "archivization produces as much as it records the event."[54]

9

Rethinking Archival Politics

Trust, Truth, and the Law

In February 1994, the U.S. National Archives and Records Administration convened a conference on "Access to Archives" at the Conference Center in Bellagio, Italy. Hosted by the Acting Archivist of the United States, Trudy Huskamp Peterson, the meeting brought together leading archivists from Western and Eastern Europe, and the states of the former Soviet Union. The Vice President for Research of the American Historical Association (AHA) was invited to give a keynote address on "The Expectations of Historians Regarding Archival Access." At the time, the American Historical Association was involved in a series of legal actions against the U.S. National Archives and Records Administration (NARA) and Peterson's predecessor, former archivist of the United States, Don Wilson. The issue involved access to thousands of records generated by the President's National Security Council and withheld from scholars and the public as private presidential papers. The AHA itself soon became the lead plaintiff in a case, challenging the agreement made between President George H. W. Bush and Archivist Wilson concerning the transfer of these and other White House materials to the Bush Presidential Library. In its court brief, the AHA charged that as National Archivist, Wilson's actions in this matter were "arbitrary, capricious, an abuse of discretion, and contrary to law."[1]

Like the Loewenheim conflict with the curators of the Roosevelt papers at Hyde Park, the Bellagio conference reflected another pivotal moment in the opening of the archival divide, although it was not fully apparent at the time. The meetings were premised on traditional assumptions about the historical record and about the relationships between historians and archivists. The keynote presentation argued the crucial importance of archival repositories to the ways a nation's history and social memory are shaped. It stressed their connections to the formations of collective national identities, in all of their complexities and contradictions. It argued that the least important (as well as least interesting) conceptualization of archives was as the holding places for information alone. Their vital political and social role rested instead on the necessary connections between their collections and the formation of authenticated, if also contested and competitive, national narratives, essential to notions of political legitimacy and an understanding of social development. As such, all national archives represented a unique national trust. While legally the property of the state, the notion of legal ownership of archival materials falsely implied that the memories and identities they constituted also belonged in some way to the state, and that the state was therefore entitled to the same restrictive ownership rights as private individuals. The same was true with nonstate groups that maintained proprietary collections or identity archives. The presumption of a scholar's access to archives openly and impartially, without political hindrance, therefore had to be thought of as the first of a set of "fundamental principles" whose recognition, formally or informally, was essential to defend against the tendencies of those with power over the archives to safeguard their own historical representations, their own constructions of imagined pasts.

The other suggested principles elaborated this theme: that restrictions to archival access be accepted only when it could be clearly and legally demonstrated that the harm to public or personal interests warranted an exemption to the public's legally guaranteed right to know; that archival administrations, and especially national archival administrations, had to represent not simply the interests of the proprietors that appoint and support them, but those of the scholarly and research communities themselves, whose public interests they had a duty and responsibility to defend; and finally, that archivists were bound by the importance of their political, social, and professional roles to provide full and accurate representation of the general nature and content of their collections, including materials whose specific contents for appropriate reasons might be restricted from scholarly review for some fixed period of time.[2]

However pleased the keynote speaker may have been with his eloquence, his talk fell on totally deaf ears. Almost all of the conference participants were old enough to have been trained in the traditional way as historians, as well as archivists, many from Eastern Europe and the former Soviet Union at the prestigious Moscow State Historical Archival Institute (MGIAI). A number were scholars of real distinction. All listened sympathetically. The problem was that without exception, all of the Eastern European archivists were also in the midst of overwhelming changes in archival administration, precipitated not only by the explosive growth in the generation of records and new technologies, but also by the changing legal foundations for public access, by the problematic nature of public and private funding, and by the complex political challenges of maintaining open access. Most important, there was now a clear perception especially on the part of archivists from the former Soviet Union that archives now had to function on principles that were clearly archival, without privileging the state over the needs and concerns of scholars and other users or those of society at large. The question was how to establish the legal foundations that were strong enough to assure that the rights of all users were equally protected.

The Nature and Forms of Archival Politics

For historians, as well as for archivists, the issue of politics has never been far removed from any important question about the role and function of archives. The basic archival processes of appraisal, acquisition, preservation, and access all have important political as well as historical implications. Many forms of archival politics are both obvious and ubiquitous in democratic as well as authoritarian regimes. As the historian Thomas Osborne has observed, "the person who speaks from the archive is the person who mediates between the secrets or obscurities of the archive and some or other kind of public" (a condition that exists in all contemporary restricted archives, as well as archival processes historically, when archives were tied to sovereign rather than liberal forms of power).[3] Another historian, Patrick Joyce, further sees the role of the archive as a "political technology of liberal governmentality," arguing that here, too, the archive is not politically neutral and that historians' engagement with it is also therefore political.[4] We can certainly agree with Joyce in terms of the archive's political neutrality, at least with regard to state archives that are everywhere the creations of established political and administrative authorities, designed to serve state interests. Their funding comes from the state, their employees work for the state, their rules and regulations are in some way prescribed by state decrees or legislation.[5]

Yet, collecting archival institutions that are focused on identity issues also reflect political perspectives, and may not present a more open climate for the researcher. Unlike state archives, these repositories are not likely to restrict access to materials they have accessioned unless a donor has so stipulated, but neither are they commonly subject to Freedom of Information laws. Historical materials can be particularly problematic in this regard. As we have suggested, what collecting archival institutions invariably try to assure, subtly or more overtly, is that the narratives their materials encourage are consistent with their own social and political values, their particular institutional context, and their sense of what is or was historically important. Their presentation of materials may also be directed or derived from the set of historiographical references that was common at the time of their acquisition.

Of course, the interests at the time of the formulation of their collections and descriptive apparatuses of both private institutions and the state may also include providing for and protecting the public's right to know, at least in principle. The U.S. National Archives and Records Administration has itself presented this idea as the essence of a "true" public archives.[6] Even here, however, the rights and interests of the public have always had to be balanced against how representatives of the archives broker the interests of their administration or the intentions of their donors. In this respect, the archival politics of open (and opening) societies can sometimes differ from those of overtly authoritarian regimes only in the more subtle ways access is controlled. The founding decree for Soviet archives, for example, issued at Lenin's direction in 1918 in an effort to assure that the Bolshevik regime could control access to all historical and contemporary records, extended government control over all archives within the new Soviet state, abolishing the very possibility of independent or private collections.[7] Even here, however, the state's appropriation of the past was always subject to challenge by those involved in the creation of documents or by archivists who knew what their holdings contained.

Even in democracies, where state interests encompass the protection of objective scholarship and a citizen's reasonable right to information, questions concerning acquisition, access, preservation, and especially classification (secrecy) of public documents or government records are almost always decided in ways that privilege the state. As state agencies responsible to administrative and political authorities, state archives (and state archivists) have a functional responsibility to preserve and protect dominant political and bureaucratic values, ideologies, and interests. These may be formally reflected in enabling legislation like the U.S. Federal Records Act (FRA) or more crudely, as in the Soviet Union, through the bureaucratic processes of appointment and (especially) removal. Although it is not always apparent, a historian working in state archives, particularly on topics related to the recent past, is constantly engaged in some way in a struggle with the politics of state-protected knowledge. Those working in collecting archival institutions, meanwhile, also need to contend in some way with the political and social narratives these repositories are structured to reflect.

Perhaps paradoxically, however, the most obvious aspects of archival politics may sometimes be the least important for historians. When President Bill Clinton announced his intention to appoint John Carlin as the Archivist of the United States, representatives of the American Historical Association and the Society of American Archivists visited the White House to register the protests of sixteen national professional and scholarly organizations.[8] The appointment clearly violated the legal stipulation that position be held by a professionally trained archivist. It drew an editorial protest from the Washington Post, and critical pieces in the New York Times.[9] While these protests were duly noted by the White House, even responded to sympathetically, the appointment was announced three weeks later. It passed through Congress by unanimous consent at 8:30 P.M. as one of a long list of presidential nominations. There was no debate or roll call.

It was no secret why President Clinton paid attention to the appointment of the National Archivist. The question of presidential records and how they were to be archived was a contentious issue at the time, working its way through the courts. Like most politicians, President Clinton wanted to assure that his "place in history" met his own assumptions and expectations. He was hardly the first. Chester Arthur burned his papers in White House garbage cans. Calvin Coolidge systematically destroyed most of his during his final months in office, lest historians see clearly how his administration had actually performed. Richard Nixon's long effort to have the Watergate tapes sealed as "private property" found at least pale imitation in George H. W. Bush's insistence that all White House e-mail communications belonged personally to him, a position with significant consequences for the preservation of the record. Sixteen years later Vice President Richard Cheney was still insisting that only he could determine what of his records was government property.

These attempts to control historical understanding and interpretation are sometimes brazenly overt. If one examines closely Franklin Roosevelt's remarks at the dedication of his library in 1941, it is possible to hear the faint echoes of Pope Leo XIII words on the opening of the Vatican archives: the need for records to be preserved and used so that men and women can have a "true" understanding of their pasts. The George H. W. Bush Library documents his "distinguished public career" as a dedicated public servant in a succession of important government posts. Ronald Reagan's papers "provide physical evidence of his extraordinary life." The pasts and futures to be believed in here are consequently well scripted. When an alternative museum and archive of John F. Kennedy materials was opened by a private collector in Florida, organized around thousands of items left in the care of Kennedy's personal secretary, Evelyn Lincoln, the Kennedy Presidential Library in Boston began a concerted effort to regain control over materials it had long ignored. There was little question that a primary concern in this effort was to assure Kennedy his reputation was "properly" represented. From documents obtained only in response to FOIA requests, it became known that the Library's efforts to challenge the rights of the private collector had involved the FBI, been improperly coordinated with the National Archives, and according to the courts, were a "flagrant abuse" of delegated powers.[10]

These attempts to politicize historical understanding are so overt, however, as to warrant little analysis. Their purpose differs little from the kinds of restrictions placed on access to archives by the popes in Rome, the presidents of France, or by Soviet and Russian leaders in limiting access to what is now called the Presidential Archive and locked away near the Kremlin in Moscow. John Carlin, moreover, proved a very able U.S. National Archivist, despite his overtly political appointment by President Clinton. NARA thrived under his leadership.

The interesting issues of archival politics turn instead on three more complicated sets of questions. The first concerns the question of "public rights" as they relate to archives and archiving: whether there is a something that can be called a "public interest" that must be taken into account in the administration of archival materials, and if so, how it can be protected. The second, closely related, concerns what is worth preserving as part of the historical record, who should make this decision, and what principles should guide them? Both of these issues lead to a third set of questions about the role (and rule) of law. To what extent are the complex ways that archives and active archivists process the past actually amenable to legal controls?

The Question of Public Interest and "Freedom of Information"

The concept of a public interest in archives and archival administration was first advanced at the time of the French revolution. It has played a role in archival thinking ever since. Legislation establishing the Archives Nationale in 1790 set its purpose to include the benefit of the French citizenry at large. *Le Citoyen* rather than *le roi* were now *l'état*. The new archives soon assumed jurisdiction over university, hospital, church, local, and provincial government records, as well as those of the state, and were to be open to all, setting a standard that came to symbolize a basic relationship between access to information and democratic governance, protected by law.

How strong this connection remains as a core democratic value was clear in the series of events that led to the collapse of the Soviet Union and the liberation of Eastern Europe. *Glasnost'* [openness] was not only a key element of Mikhail Gorbachev's striking effort to democratize the Soviet Union; it found one of its sharpest expressions in the demand for open access to Soviet historical archives as a way to assure new transparency about the past, present, and future. It was of no small importance that the loudest voices to "re-process" the Soviet and Eastern European pasts in this way came from Moscow State Historical Archival Institute (MGIAI), headed by Iuri Afanasiev. Leading Soviet archivists clearly understood the centrality of their political role as guardians of historical orthodoxy, as well as its implications for their professional integrity as archivists and historians.

Between 1987 and 1991, Afanasiev wrote frequently on the subject in popular Soviet journals like *Literaturnaia Gazeta*. He spoke eloquently about it at the Woodrow Wilson Center in Washington, the University of Michigan, and other American and European institutions. Discussions about the cardinal role archives play in a society's ability to understand itself soon extended out from Eastern Europe to become a central theme in a range of international conferences, including the one held at Bellagio. In the Russian case in particular, the role of archivists themselves as figures wielding enormous power "over the past" became as newly evident to ordinary Russians (and many elsewhere) as it had always been to the users of Soviet archives themselves. Throughout the USSR and Eastern Europe even very loyal and distinguished scholars were often subjected to the crudest forms of archival administrative surveillance and censorship. It was not only western historians who had to gain special permission to enter the documentary "holy of holies," had their themes approved or modified by people with no real understanding of their topics, and waited anxiously for the archivists themselves to select the materials they were permitted to see.

Prominent Soviet historians and archivists like N. N. Bolkovitinov, B. S. Ilizarov, and S. V. Zhitomirskaia soon added their strong voices to the cause of archival reform. Within a number of repositories courageous archivists took the first steps on their own to "democratize" access to knowledge "from below" in ways that supported the transformatory needs of the late Soviet state itself. Writing for a western audience in the *American Archivist* in 1990, Bolkovitinov argued that a "catastrophic decline in the professional level" of Soviet archival administrators was a natural consequence of their subservience to the Soviet state, and remarked on the absence of outstanding historians among archive directors. To the same audience S. V. Zhitomirskaia emphasized the incompleteness of the Soviet record, a consequence not so much of the destruction of documents but of the principles that governed the selection of documents for long-term preservation. B. S. Ilizarov echoed the views of his colleagues in pointing out the ways in which a discourse of "enemies" caused archival documents to be made secret "on an unprecedented scale"[11]:

> This situation was used craftily by the most varied departments: from those who were supposed to adhere to the regime of secrecy and therefore increased their staffs or used archival documents to falsify legal matters, to those whose information was kept from scholars and society as a whole in the hopes of hiding their failures and crimes.[12]

Much of the public debate in Russia understandably centered on the need for a new archival law. Already in 1988, B. S. Ilizarov and others at MGIAI took a strong position against the efforts of the Soviet Archival Administration (Glavarkhiv) to rework archival legislation without broad public discussion. They and others opposed Glavarkhiv's intention to transfer archival administration to the Ministry of Justice, which might well have made access to increasingly sensitive historical materials even more restrictive, and affirmed state control rather than extending archival autonomy and independence. The degree to which Soviet archives "remained inaccessible, and had turned into a branch of the bureaucratic system, preserving only the memories which that system wanted to preserve," as Iuri Afanasiev wrote in the reformist weekly *Moskovskie Novosti*, required the complete reworking of all laws and regulations governing archival affairs.[13] The issue was not simply one of access to the archives, but of the control retained by various Soviet agencies over their documents; the political uses of classification; the secrecy, private holding, and inadequacy of finding aids; and especially the direct control archivists themselves retained over who might see what material— in sum, the politicized practices of all record keeping in Soviet and Soviet-style societies.

Immediately after the Soviet Union's collapse these concerns led to efforts in Russia at drafting one of the most democratic and comprehensive archival laws in the world.[14] Parallel efforts occurred elsewhere in the former USSR and Eastern Europe.[15] Historians and other archival scholars eagerly awaited these laws, even as new archive directors committed to democratic practices made vast amounts of new material available on their own. What was lost in the euphoria of the moment, however, especially for historians, was that it was not politics per se that distinguished Soviet archives and state record keeping from practices in other countries. However much the subservience of Soviet archival administrators to the state directly reflected the regime's own authoritarian ambitions, each of the areas in which the Soviet archival record was corrupted only exaggerated— however greatly—the problems of politics common to state archival systems everywhere and to many nonstate repositories as well.

First and foremost is the central issue of access. The question here is not simply whether one is allowed in the door, although this is hardly trivial, but the specific and complex problems of freedom of information, the right to privacy, and the relationship between the public interest and the protection of confidential information, that is, all matters of classification and declassification. Most archives in democratic societies do not require that researchers have special credentials to gain physical access to their documents. Yet access in other ways is everywhere restricted by the ways archival institutions broker between the interests of the generator of the records and the interests of various subsets of the public at large.

Obviously, there are the various and familiar restraints on access to recent materials, especially those classified as confidential or as state secrets or including confidential information on living persons. The thirty-year International Standard adopted in 1968 for assuring access to all archival materials, including classified information, has been a significant step forward for historians, considering that states like Italy protected many government records for a period of 100 years. Yet however good the intention of this principle, it can easily be breached by the sheer burden of administrative processing.

In Washington, it is not uncommon for huge amounts of outdated materials from agencies such as the CIA to sit well beyond the time limit for their release, ostensibly awaiting review.[16] Archives in Great Britain, moreover, and others as well, do not accept the thirty-year rule for many types of Foreign Office materials. Some U.K. materials pertaining to the American revolutionary war are still permanently closed. The International Standard also provides for exemptions, particularly for documents that contain personal information of various sorts about individual citizens, with no requirement that scholars be told what constitutes the nature of the records. In practice, this can mean the unannounced withholding of large amounts of important sociological (or labor camp) data. Although there are obviously good reasons for this in terms of public interest, access here is made dependent on policy and the interpretation (or mediation) of that policy by archivists and those with authority over their collections. In the most complicated cases of this kind that derive from records of the CIA, FBI, or KGB archives, for example, protecting the public interest in this way also strengthens the power of certain political interests.

The policies and practices of declassification also involve a heavy dose of politics in the archives. The interests of scholars often conflict with those of the state, and not only in the most obvious terms of protecting sensitive material. Under all regimes, and in nonstate as well as state archives, decisions about declassifying secret materials are ostensibly based on the familiar question of whether the documents contain information whose release would harm state, individual, or organizational interests. In state archives, the primary test for declassification is "irreparable harm," a term of continual contestation and one sometimes requiring court adjudication. In nonstate archives, however, the situation can be even more restrictive for scholars because their right to know is not legally protected. The private American corporation ChoicePoint, for example, which was purchased in 2008 by the parent corporation of LexisNexis and which allows users to "easily browse through billions of current and historical records on individuals and businesses" holds in its archive more than 20 billion records containing various kinds of personal information, none of which is subject to the U.S. Freedom of Information Act.[17] In May 2007, the Los Alamos National Laboratory announced it would no longer permit historians and other scholars to access its records because the private company that assumed management from the University of California was not a state agency.[18]

Questions of declassification, in other words, are usually seen as decisions about content though more often than not they relate to the authorities under which the records were prepared. Thus, materials for entire institutions or agencies like the Communist Party of the Soviet Union or the U.S. National Security Council are thought by definition to contain inherently protectable material. The evaluation of content or position, in turn, is necessarily a question of interpretation, one often made by archivists or records managers in ways that reflect institutional policy, authority, and procedure.[19] Occasionally, there are notable exceptions to this practice. The rapid declassification in Moscow, by 1993, of more than 250,000 of the 5 million classified files was facilitated by special commissions of historians and archivists. In the United States, a similar commission has worked to declassify a large number of foreign relations materials held by the State Department. Unfortunately, these cooperative efforts are the exception rather than the rule. They also depend on the agency and its archival component having a clear understanding of the meaning and importance of the public interests and a willingness to meet them.

A discussion of archival politics in this area could readily be expanded to other familiar and restrictive practices. Ministries of defense, foreign affairs, and intelligence are almost always politically strong enough to be exempt from national archival laws, or arrange to be governed by separate, more accommodating legislation. Specific transfer agreements between originating agencies and state archives are in essence a bureaucratic transaction where the interests of the agencies have great weight. The interests of scholars or the public at large may be subordinated in order simply to assure that the transfers take place. Whole categories of materials might be exempted for reasons rarely known to researchers, much less the broader public. Their very existence is often itself restricted information.

It is also the case that however successful efforts have been to declassify older documents, the classification of new materials continues to run at a much faster pace. In 2003, the U.S. government classified as secret more than 14.2 million documents, most in digital form.[20] Given the labor and costs of assuring documents do not, in fact, contain information that should be classified, state agencies everywhere have found it expedient simply to assign blanket classifications to specific categories of records that are based as much on the person or process creating the record as on what the record may actually contain. Future archivists, scholars, and the courts are left to worry about when and how the material might eventually become available.

This problem is compounded in many ways by the introduction of new information technologies. While we will discuss electronic records in detail in the following chapter, it is worth noting here that digitization has radically changed what might be called the political balance between the creator of documents, archivists, and historians. On one hand, of course, digitization has the potential to vastly improve archival access through comprehensive and even interactive finding aids and by facilitating document retrieval in various forms. On the other, however, it has also greatly complicated the problem of access as a result of continually changing electronic languages, the ease of concealment, the difficulties of migrating one set of electronic records into a newer format, and the ways digital records can be easily altered. The archival dimension of the retention of electronic records has been particularly challenging because of constantly changing technologies. At the University of Michigan in the 1990s, the first full set of digitized administrative records prepared during the technologically innovative presidency of James Duderstadt, an engineer, was dependent on outdated software when hegemonic programs like Microsoft Word put widely used early word processors like FinalWord and WordStar out of business. Each digital document had to be painstakingly reformatted at a great administrative cost and time.

In the United States and elsewhere, new state regulations and common public practices requiring digital records be backed up has lessened the impact on history and scholarship of the all-powerful delete key, a revolutionary paper shredder. Still, "mistakes" frequently happen. Early in January 2000, the U.S. National Archives and Records Administration, the agency responsible for issuing guidance to all other U.S. agencies on the preservation of their electronic records, reported that it had lost 43,000 digital messages of its own through accidental erasure. Although the National Archives was supposed to have a backup system, it was not working properly. There was no way to restore the lost material.[21]

What seems at first to be at issue in all of these cases is simply the need to develop adequate laws or administrative systems and regulations to govern archival practices. Indeed, the implicit assumption behind the strenuous efforts of most post-Soviet bloc countries after 1989 and 1991 to draft new comprehensive archival laws was the need to objectify these processes through carefully drawn laws and regulations. Subjective biases, personal interests, and overt politics were to give way to professionalism and professionally regulated practices that would defend in a nonpartisan way the needs of "person, society, and the state," to use the formula of the 1998 symposium celebrating the 80th anniversary of the Russian state archival service.[22] Efforts in Moscow to bring the 1993 Russian archival law into correspondence with more recent legislation on freedom of information and state secrets have been based on similar assumptions that "the organization of archival practices [must be] on the basis of democratization, depoliticization, the accessibility of state archives, and respect for the property rights of other [private] archives."[23]

Objectivizing and depoliticizing archival practices through laws and regulations is obviously of vital importance to protecting the public's "right to know" in all societies, however developed their democratic institutions. Moreover, unfettered archival access is the key to social self-scrutiny, the means through which scholars can most fully and convincingly interpret the past. Recognition of these values underlay the passage of the first U.S. Freedom of Information Act (FOIA) in 1966. There followed a rapid proliferation of similar legislation in Europe and elsewhere after the Eastern European revolutions of 1989. The Maastricht Treaty creating the European Union in 1992 included a conception of access to information that formally acknowledged "transparency . . . strengthens the democratic nature of institutions and the public's confidence in [state] administration."[24] By 2004, fifty-nine countries had FOI laws.[25]

Yet even the most comprehensive freedom of information legislation cannot guarantee full access to the documentary production of a given society. Nor can such legislation determine the ways archivists will interpret and implement these laws as they exercise their designated responsibilities. Most Freedom of Information Acts (FOIA) require that specific documents or files be requested. Unless a scholar knows exactly which files or documents contain the information he or she is requesting, there is little chance the request can be honored.[26] An important implication of this is that the FOIA processes are very much dependent on the construction and formulation of finding aids and indices to agency holdings that are publicly available in some usable form. In the case of the East German Stasi archives, which contain surveillance records of more than 170,000 informants, retrieval was entirely dependent on a single index. If it had been destroyed, the retrieval of specific information would have become virtually impossible.[27]

Again, the explosive use of digital media has created an additional set of problems. Large sets of government and other records are now commonly held as "structured" data in electronic data banks in highly standardized form. Access to this material often requires the use of the special programming that created it. In the United States, the Freedom of Information Act was amended in 1996 after government agencies resisted sharing access software. In principle, such large databases are now open to outsiders. In fact, however, access problems continue. In 2004, the U.S. Department of Justice responded to a FOIA request from the Center for Public Integrity for access to its database on foreign lobbyists by saying that the database had become so fragile than an attempt to process the request risked a program crash and a "major loss of data."[28]

For historians, then, the critical questions remain. Under whose authority were the documents prepared and who currently controls their content? Where was data stored, and how? And who holds the access keys that can retrieve it? Even in the most democratic of societies, the politics inherent in archival practice can only be effectively navigated by understanding how an archives' documentation is actually processed and authenticated, the hidden, as well as open, ways these processes influence the scholar's and public's right and ability to know. While the same questions were important to scholars when valuable paper documents were locked in archival closets, the sheer volume of contemporary records production has made the very universe of future historical documentation far more subject to political manipulation and exponentially more difficult for archivists themselves to order and control.[29]

The "Records" Problem

In the current post-custodial age of archives and records administration when archival institutions have a distinct professional identity and even the best archival training programs rarely involve comprehensive historical study, the issue of "what is historical?" has been eclipsed by what at first glance might seem to scholars an uninteresting, even esoteric issue: what actually constitutes a record? In fact, the "records" problem is a question of what will consequently become the body of historical documents for future scholars and has become an increasingly complex issue.

The current standardized archival definition of a record is straightforward: a document in whatever form that evidences a particular activity or transaction. The archivist David Wallace adds to the concept by describing records as composed of three elements: content, structure, and context, referring to text, documentary forms (like reports or letters), and the circumstances in which they were created and used.[30]

What constitutes a record is thus a question about documents whose preservation is essential to creating any archive. Since archives process and hold records that reflect the societies, organizations, or institutions that determined their collecting missions, how archivists now tend to subordinate the idea of the "historical" to more essentialist frameworks derived from purely archival principles obviously affects what records will endure as historical documents even if the archivists no longer regard the records as historical or not historical, only as archival.

In the United States, even a quick look at NARA's website will show the degree to which considerations of historical understanding are now at best a secondary part of the U.S. National Archives' overall presentation, despite what remains chiseled on its façade. As with contemporary archives elsewhere, it reaches out to a user public that includes genealogists, teachers at all levels, and the simply curious, as well as those who need the information in archived federal records. The most common enquiries are about military service records, the Declaration of Independence and the Constitution, World War II photos, genealogy, and materials related to "recovering from disaster."[31]

One need not rehearse the ways in which politics can intrude here in assuring certain records are preserved regardless of their potential historical importance. Years ago archivists had little difficulty identifying whether a document was worthy of retention. In the United States, the first comprehensive federal records legislation in 1853 assumed that every document generated by the federal government was worthy of preservation and made their destruction a felony. This ideal world for historians lasted only as long as the available warehouse space.

By the turn of the twentieth century, Congress itself had joined federal department heads in the United States in determining which records could be destroyed, a responsibility that passed to the Librarian of Congress in 1912 and then to the National Archives after its creation in 1934. Subsequent legislation refined the definition of a federal record in the United States by providing new rules regarding preservation and destruction. According to the Federal Records Disposal Act of 1943, federal records were "all books, papers, maps, photographs, or other documentary materials *regardless of physical form or characteristics* made or received by an agency of the U.S. government" (our italics).[32] Records "appropriate for preservation" were those that served "as evidence of the organization, functions, policies, decisions, procedures, operations, *or other activities of the government*, or because of the informational value of the data contained therein" (our italics).[33] The much amended U.S. Federal Records Act (FRA) of 1950 elaborated on these provisions but retained their essence. So did the Presidential Records Act (PRA) of 1978, which became effective with the inauguration of Ronald Reagan in January 1981. In both laws, the responsibility for preserving records was retained by the National Archives and Records Administration, which also assumed the right to their ownership in the government's name.[34]

Archival records here were conceived as documents serving broad public, as well as state needs; the archival record itself was assumed to transcend the politics of party division, as well as the changing forms and agencies of government administration. In the United States, both the Presidential Records Act and a number of amendments to the Federal Records Act stemmed from contentious disputes about the ownership and release of the Nixon tapes, as well as issues associated with the turmoil of the 1960s and 1970s. In a case brought by the American Friends Service Committee against FBI director William Webster to prevent the destruction of field office files assumed to contain information about civil rights violations, the court explicitly affirmed the responsibility of the National Archives through the Federal Records Act to determine whether the materials should be saved and expressed concern that the Archives was losing the confidence of professional historians.[35]

Within this context the seemingly mundane issue of what constituted a record became a source of portentous dispute. When Henry Kissinger left his position as U.S. Secretary of State, he took with him the official State Department transcripts of all his telephone conversations, over the protest of the National Archives and the General Accounting Office, claiming they were personal papers not agency records. Although both a federal district court and the Court of Appeals ruled against him, the Supreme Court reversed their judgments, affirming that only agency heads like Kissinger could determine what were or were not governmental records. In cases where such political officials deemed materials not to be records, neither the Archives' jurisdiction over preservation nor the Freedom of Information Act applied.

In sum, there is now no way of predicting what will endure in the archives as a historical record, or even how what constitutes a record in the future might be redefined. How a document ultimately comes to endure is the product of a variety of considerations and processes in which politics plays a role sometimes visible and other times subtle. The idea of a record then, as our Dutch colleagues have shown so strikingly in the past and as contemporary experience has reaffirmed, is a multifaceted concept driven by actions on the part of the activities that produced the record and by archival institutions over time that have contended with the push and pull of forces that determine what will endure.

The PROFS Case

The widespread introduction during the 1980s of digital documentation has greatly complicated these questions. In the United States, the Reagan presidency was the first to make extensive use of e-mails, and the first in which their form and disposition gained international attention in connection with the Iran-Contra affair. More than 7 million e-mails traveled within and between various Reagan White House agencies, as well as between the White House and other parts of the government. The software system that managed their use was an innovative program called the Professional Office System. Among its other virtues was its ability to preserve transactions on separate backup tapes.

As the new technologies of electronic communications developed, there was widespread confusion even as to how e-mails should be defined. At the University of Michigan, for example, the early view was that e-mail was not a record but a surrogate for a telephone conversation. The federal government considered e-mails to be records only if they were also printed out in hard copies. Whether an e-mail should or would become a record was thus made by anyone along the sometimes complex chain of communication who decided to hit the print key. These paper materials were then assembled, classified, and assessed as records in traditional ways, with responsibility for their destruction still vested in the National Archives and Records Administration. As late as 1989, as the White House shifted from Ronald Reagan to George H. W. Bush, leading NARA officials, including the archivist, Don Wilson and NARA's director of presidential libraries, continued to argue that documents not in paper form could not be considered official records.

These early attempts at a definition of digital "recordness" were soon overwhelmed by the phenomenal spread of e-mail communications, and the use of a software product developed by IBM called the Professional Office System, or PROFS. In addition to making copies of all messages, it allowed for the retention of digital attachments created by other kinds of software, giving the recipient the possibility of editing them directly before passing them forward or returning them to the sender.[36] In 1989, a private foundation in Washington seeking information on the Iran-Contra scandal discovered that the PROFS backup tapes pertaining to the case were scheduled to be erased and recycled apparently because their managers assumed that all of the records they contained were already in print form and incorporated into paper filing systems. Since the tapes themselves were not records, the National Archives and Records Administration had no rights over their disposal. Eighteen short hours before the end of the Reagan administration, a temporary restraining order preventing their destruction was issued by the Federal District Court in Washington. The first phase of the PROFS case had begun, in which the American Historical Association, the Society of American Archivists, and the U.S. National Archives and Records Administration itself would all play prominent roles.[37]

Through its various arguments and rulings, adjudicated at all levels of the U.S. federal judiciary up to the Supreme Court, the case touched several issues of importance here. For historians, it established that by their very nature, electronic communications in their original forms contained essential information not necessarily reproduced on paper printouts and were thus government records in their own right. As such, they were subject to all of the provisions of the laws governing federal and presidential records regardless of their physical form. In one court ruling, issued just two weeks before the end of the Bush presidency in January 1993, the D.C. District Court went so far as to rule that the record-keeping practices of the Executive Office of the President and the National Security Council were "arbitrary and capricious" because they allowed for the improper destruction of federal records. The Archivist of the United States was also chastised for failure to fulfill his statutory obligations under the Federal Records Act. Copies of electronic materials, including backup tapes, were ordered transferred immediately to the archives and placed under the control of the National Archives. The transfer occurred under police escort at 1:00 A.M. on January 20, 1993, the day of President Clinton's inauguration.[38]

The District Court's intentions here were partly thwarted, however, by three subsequent developments affecting what constituted historical federal records. First, the Federal Appeals Court ruled that along with most offices established to advise the president, the National Security Council (NSC) was not an agency within the definition of the Presidential and Federal Records Acts, and therefore not subject to its provisions. Nor, in fact, was the NSC or any comparable presidential office subject to the Freedom of Information Act, despite the fact, as Judge David Tatel pointed out in his strong dissent to the split opinion, that it had already applied FOIA to itself during the course of four separate administrations. Records produced by the NSC thus became the private papers of the president, subject to disposition in accordance with the liberal provisions of the Presidential Records Act.

Second, by agreement between Archivist Wilson and President Bush, the president himself was given "exclusive legal control of all presidential information and all derivative information in whatever form, contained in the materials."[39] When it was subsequently learned that the archivist had already accepted the position as executive director of the George Bush Presidential Center, the American Historical Association became the lead plaintiff in an additional lawsuit challenging the legality and propriety of the agreement under the terms of the Presidential Records Act, which, with Richard Nixon's White House tapes in mind, requires presidential papers to be owned, possessed, and controlled by the United States. In its brief, the AHA described Wilson's decision as archivist to be "arbitrary, capricious, an abuse of discretion, and contrary to law." Although Wilson argued that as an employee of the executive branch of government he owed specific responsibility to the chief executive, Federal District Court Judge Richey, the presiding judge throughout the whole PROFS episode, fully concurred with the other side.[40]

Acting Archivist Trudy Peterson, the convener of the Bellagio Conference on archival access and Don Wilson's temporary replacement as National Archivist, was ordered to refrain from implementing its requirements to assure that, in the words of the AHA's complaint, "presidential records of historical value [not] be alienated from the ownership of the United States, destroyed, and/or shielded from public access, to the injury of plaintiff's interests in historical and archival research."[41] Somewhat to its surprise, given the determinations that had occurred in the PROFS case, the AHA ultimately prevailed in having the Wilson–Bush agreement nullified, to the apparent distress of President Clinton's new appointment as Archivist of the United States, John Carlin. There was also the crucial matter of the nature of the electronic records themselves, now saved by court order from destruction and seemingly safe and sound in the archives. The 1:00 A.M. transfer on Inauguration Day 1993 brought some 1,850 tapes from the National Security Council to the National Archives, and 2,843 backup tapes from the Executive Office of the President. In addition, there were 32 tapes left over from the Reagan administration and 135 hard drives from NSC computers that had been stored in the White House Situation Room Systems Staff Office, and hastily thrown into boxes for the move without special packing.

Acting Archivist Trudy Peterson sent the materials to NARA's Center for Electronic Records to handle, but the Center had no software systems that were able to read or even copy the tapes. All the materials were dependent on specific hardware and software in violation of the Center's policy, and there was little or no documentation concerning either. No staff member also had anything close to the required security clearance to vet the materials even if they could be read![42] The historians had won the battle but the clever manipulators of technology had won the war. The public's interest was simultaneously served and defeated.

Archival Politics and Relations of Trust

The convolutions of the PROFS case and related lawsuits are a clear indication that however admirable efforts might be to depoliticize archival practices through laws and regulations, comprehensive legislation cannot fully regulate the ways archivists, and the agencies to which they report, hold and exercise power over the records that they control even in the most democratic regimes. Well-intentioned archivists are now working vigorously to assure that digital materials are free from dependence on particular software, and hence readable; and new provisions in Electronic FOIA legislation require in the United States and elsewhere that agencies subject to its provisions make "reasonable efforts to search" for records in electronic formats except, in the U.S. case at least, when such efforts "would significantly interfere with the operation of the agency's automated information system."[43] Sophisticated new search engines also hold the possibility that archival documents can be searched internally for material pertaining to a scholar's needs, opening the possibility for a whole new kind of finding aid. The costs of all of this can be significant, sometimes estimated as high as $1,000 for the work required to respond to an electronic FOIA request. The problem of overwhelming bulk also continues to affect how FOIA requests are processed as it did with paper document, if not more so. Still, politics in some form remains an inescapable part of archival practice in the post-custodial era.

This is not in any way to minimize the egregious ways in which archives in authoritarian societies like the U.S.S.R. were politically corrupt, to depreciate the effects of overtly politicized repositories on historical understanding, or to express any lack of support or appreciation for the important efforts at democratizing archival law. It is to suggest instead, first, that the task of addressing adequately the objective questions of archival law, and especially those about its effectiveness, necessarily requires an understanding of the actual locations of power in the archives, and the subjective as well as objective ways this power influences administrative practices; and second, that the inability of any law to fully regulate this power means that archival politics, which is to say the administration of a society's documentary past, are also fundamentally a matter of ethics and constant vigilance among interested parties. In other words, even with the protection of archival laws designed specifically with the public's interest in mind, an archival scholar's access to the past still depends essentially on relations of trust.

This dependency begins from the time a scholar initially enters an archival reading room—often a moment of some anxiety and concern. This nervousness is not simply because the archive itself is unfamiliar and scholars need to learn their way around. Instead it is because most researchers, and especially those who have come from some distance, have made important decisions about their time, resources, and research plan, only because the available general registers (or colleagues or archivists themselves) have suggested that particular archives hold records that will be useful for their research. The historian does not really know this yet, since few general registers in any archive inform users of all records that are archived, how comprehensive they are, whether similar or additional records may be housed elsewhere, or even whether they may be fully accessible. The scholar can only trust that he or she has been pointed in the right direction.

Even detailed lists of holdings and descriptions of particular archival fonds or record groups requires the scholar to understand the archival principles that have led to its design and content, and then to trust that archivists have fully applied these principles to the material in an arrangement schema that is appropriate and transparent. The user must also trust that material is represented accurately in the descriptions of individual files. There may also be the expectation that the archivist has achieved a certain level of historical understanding of the material and may have highlighted the contents of those files without distorting what they may contain. This expectation is, however, predicated on the user's own sense of what is historically significant. What may be considered a matter of competence and historical understanding on the part of the archivist can readily be seen by scholars as abject bias—implicit or explicit—in the processes that have come to structure the archivist's work. Relations of trust again underlie the historian's link to the archivist and the degree to which the historian and the archivist may at any point in time share a common understanding of the significance of the documents at hand. No archival legislation can assure transparency or create a particular set of historical categories in these matters. Even more important is the historian's trust that unless the registers specifically say otherwise, no materials have been left uncatalogued or otherwise concealed, and that the collection was not distorted to begin with by an originating agency that held back important records. Again, verification other than by archivists themselves is almost always impossible, a circumstance that further shapes and delineates the complicated politics of shaping an enduring record.

Especially with digital materials and the managerial demands of our post-custodial age, the organizational structure of a record group also involves a further level of trust, since the complex question of how documents should be organized involves important assumptions about how they relate to each other. Here one encounters important epistemological issues, since the analytic categories that structure the ways documents have been assembled and catalogued necessarily reflect a series of assumptions about what needs to be known, and hence what is knowable. This was always a problem in the process of the generation and retention of paper records, but in the days when there was a convergence of historical understanding between archivists and historians, and when this convergence was paramount in the archival process as a whole, scholars could reasonably assume materials were catalogued within well-defined and for some subjects at least, analytically useful categories. In principle, this could always be verified in historical archives by looking at all the documents themselves, even if this was almost always impractical in any but very small collections. With the shift away from history and historical authorities that marked the opening of the archival divide and with the advent of new digital finding aids and searchable databases, the historian has had to confront the possibility that he or she may not find any useful directional information in these essential resources at all. The "moment of truth" must await the delivery of actual files, digital or otherwise, and the use of the documents themselves. Even here, however, almost every use the historian can make of the material is still contingent on a set of assumptions, each difficult or impossible to verify: that through its agents, the archive has provided an authentic record that will verify some specific historical idea; that nothing has been held back; that the record is an adequate representation of the activity of the person or office; that digital or other reproductions have captured the original as well as technologically possible; and especially that the documents themselves have not been falsified or distorted in any way.

It is at this point that the user may also have to confront directly the critical issue of restricted access, where power over the dissemination of knowledge about the past as stored in the archives is most clearly and problematically reflected. However necessary in principle to protect individual privacy or sensitive interests of the state, the very process of restriction creates a unique sphere of privileged knowledge, accessible only to a "trustworthy" few with appropriate clearances. Always among them, of course, are a select group of archivists themselves, whose professional codes of practice and responsibility require them to uphold the laws as written and to protect confidentialities as determined by the established processes for determining restrictions. The archivists' control over the past in this capacity is not only very great in absolute terms, but again reflects potent relations of power. The researcher without access to restricted files knows he cannot see the "entire picture," that is, understand particular events or state behaviors that are defined as sensitive by the very act of restriction itself. He or she can only rely on the professional integrity of the process of restricted access—that material is being withheld because of clear national security or other stated priorities. These processes may be contained within an agency or may be in the hands of a documentary review board of some kind. There must also be assurances that what is restricted as classified in the archives conforms to the law and that material scheduled to be declassified is done so in an expeditious manner.

In states where Freedom of Information Acts can be used to pry loose materials that are being withheld, the issue is even more graphic. The researcher will commonly receive a document that is partially blacked out, and where access to the redacted material is not subject to any ready legal appeal. The black ink of the redactor explicitly reduces the legalities of state control to a relationship of trust. The researcher can only hope that the archivist has handled his material in a knowledgeable, professional, and responsible manner, knowing the many reasons why this might not necessarily be so. In this case the archival function of documentation may be delegated to a specifically trained legal staff whose responsibility is to the letter of the law in the determination of exemptions to FOIA.

Here again are fundamental practices in which archival politics, which in essence reflect a kind of power over the past, are not fully understood by historians because they derive from a system of values and categories that are not at all historical. If a state archivist's position is as that of a professional civil servant, the employees of a collecting archival institution are also subject to the legal and conceptual parameters that govern the agency and its records. Thus the archivist is always necessarily a broker of interests that derive from the sponsorship of the archive, itself a political function. When their roles as servants both of the public and the state conflict, archivists find themselves confronting difficult ethical dilemmas.

What is the archivist's responsibility, for example, when he or she knows that the relationship of classified materials to related unclassified documents clearly distorts the public's understanding of an important past event? All of the sanctions created by law to prevent the revealing of classified documents or information are predicated on the assumption that secrecy protects vital state interests or safeguards individual privacy, and hence human rights and the welfare of society more broadly. But no laws, even the most progressive, allow the release of classified documents to demonstrate the state officials are allowing a misrepresentation of an event to stand, even if their falsification is obviously harmful to recognized state and social interests.

The Daniel Ellsberg case is most often cited in this regard. A former government official who illegally leaked secret Pentagon materials during the Vietnam War, Ellsberg created a national debate on the appropriateness of the disclosure and legality of publishing secret information. Many applauded his efforts. Indeed, they had a major effect on the American public's view of how the Vietnam conflict was being conducted. An archivist, however, would face the severest of sanctions for taking such an activist role. The action would be a violation of institutional policy governing the archive, as well as a violation of professional ethical requirements that restrictions and closures of material be respected and consistently applied. To take on the responsibility as arbiter for historical truth with the intention of doing what is ethically right is a matter fraught with tensions and ambiguities. While it cannot be taken lightly, it also cannot in any very useful way be codified.[44]

Moreover, in purely practical terms the idea that archivists can know and understand the content of the vast series of records under their control is an anomalous throwback to the nineteenth century, when curators could read a greater portion of manuscripts entrusted to their institutions. With today's complex bureaucratic records, piecing together a story or a discovery takes an inordinate amount of time and deliberation. Rarely is a single document in a single file in a single collection sufficient to bolster a case for a narrative counter to a well-crafted official position. This kind of discovery is a research function that falls outside the boundaries of normal archival interventions.

Sometimes research can expose wrongdoing, creating a moral imperative that transcends many established professional procedures. For archivists, this raises the question of whether social loyalties or personal values should supersede subordination to official representations known to be false. For historians it gets to the integrity of scholarship itself, since any collusion with government falsification in the creation, retention, and disposition of records undermines the integrity of all scholarship being done on the issues or events being falsified or concealed. At the same time a broader public must trust that the historian has read the documents carefully and has understood that the archival record is the product of multiple layers of intervention, both in the creation of documents and in the processes leading to their retention. In the end it is the community of users, that is of readers and viewers of the products of archival research, for whom these works must reflect the highest standard in the accountability and veracity both in terms of the historical interpretations they present as well as the standards by which the records themselves have been created and retained.[45]

In terms of the opening of the archival divide, one must also emphasize, however, that if the archivist in his or her proclivity to do the "right thing," is in fact used for particular and partisan purposes, trust in the archivist as a professional broker among multiple and contending interests will rapidly erode. In the post-custodial age, when the interests and responsibilities of the archivist and the historian are fundamentally different, the archivist must be particularly attentive to balance institutional interests with those of broader communities of users to assure the retention of the record over the long term, and whatever its form, its effective access for future generations.

The Limitations of Law

By now it should be apparent that the law itself has its limits in terms of assuring free and open access to archival documentation: what we know as the historical record always derives from the convergence of the attributes the historian understands in the record and the interventionist processes through which it is shaped by the archivist. With the onslaught of the digital age, archivists like Richard Brown, Brien Brothman, Terry Cook, Verne Harris, Eric Ketelaar and others themselves became increasingly aware of this convergence, challenging and even rejecting in some instances their profession's traditional claims to objectivity and neutrality regardless of the laws and regulations governing archival practice.[46]

At the same time, it is certainly not the case that laws and regulations governing archives are in any sense unimportant—just the opposite. Archival laws and regulations that assure open access to essential records and guarantee their preservation are absolutely essential to the ability of any society to understand itself and assure this understanding in the future. Laws encapsulate a vital set of standards. They represent social values and provide an explicit, as well as implicit, set of administrative directives. Together with an effective judicial process, they can provide an essential restraint on efforts to conceal information or otherwise restrict access, however costly and time-consuming their enforcement may sometimes be. Effective laws also codify processes, define roles, affect values and attitudes, and help set administrative styles. They represent a set of standards against which the administration of particular archives can be measured. Efforts to correct weaknesses and limitations in archival law also provide a valuable opportunity for focusing concern on the contending and interrelated interests of individual persons, society, and state, to which all state archives in democratic societies must be responsive.[47]

Still, the relationship of formal laws and regulations to actual archival practices is a limited one: the fundamental relationship between the archivist and the scholar in terms of processing the past is founded on trust, not on law. It is essentially an ethical, not a legal one. In the context of the archival divide, moreover, when the basic relationship between what comes to be called historical and the processes of preserving its documentary fragments still remains fundamental despite the distance between historian and archivist, those who create and maintain the record carry a high degree of moral, as well as social, political, and legal responsibility. This is best achieved, perhaps, through a self-conscious understanding of the way their work affects how the past can and will be understood.

In this respect, the complex processes of digitization we turn to in the following chapter have created the need for a much greater degree of accountability for decisions affecting archival practice. In open societies committed to broad public access to archives, the politics of appraisal, acquisition, access, preservation, reproduction, and even the training and management of archivists themselves may not involve the high politics of blunt ideological manipulation or concealment that characterize authoritarian regimes but they are vital fields of politics and power in both. In this respect as well, it is hardly surprising that one of the principal conclusions of the 1994 conference in Bellagio with which this chapter began was that even with the best of intentions on the part of well-trained archivists, access issues—the relations of power over the past—have always and everywhere been intrinsically problematic.

10

Archives and the Cyberinfrastructure

Some years ago in a brilliant analysis of the impact of the printing press, Elizabeth Eisenstein proposed that while the invention proved "an agent of change," its consequences were not evident quickly or dramatically, but unfolded initially in a slow and almost imperceptible way. Over time, of course, moveable type changed modes of communication, the nature and forms of discourse, and ultimately even seats of power.[1]

Whether historians will see Bill Gates, Steve Jobs, and Michael Dell as having affected seats of power remains to be seen. In striking contrast to moveable type, however, the personal computer and its own revolutionary effect on modes of communication and discourse has been sudden, all embracing, and global. As an agent of change, it has worked its presence into the fabric of nearly every human activity virtually overnight, recording and transmitting information in ways entirely unimaginable only a few years earlier. Like moveable type, the last great revolution in written communication, computers have changed fundamentally the ways records and documents are constructed, transmitted, and archived.

Even the word "archive" has taken on a specific meaning on the PC. No doubt millions of users employ it with little or no conception of what archiving means in a formal and institutional sense. Yet the computer revolution has dramatically affected formal archives as well, even if much that has happened is barely perceptible to historians. How archivists think about records, as well as the very notion of what "properly" constitutes an archive, have been challenged in fundamental ways.

What scholars know best is the computer's impact on book publishing, libraries, and traditional print culture. When Google announced in 2003 that it would embark on a project to digitize the holdings of several major research libraries in a plan to assemble more than ten million volumes by 2012, it was obvious that dramatic changes were underway, even if their implications were not—and could not be—fully comprehended. What was clear was that this new "cyberinfrastructure" would create radical new possibilities for scholars, and like moveable type, permanently change the culture of scholarship itself.

The possibilities of digitized archives have seemed very exciting. Expectations regarding access have been particularly high: historians would be liberated from the burdens and costs of travel; documents would be accessible by personal computer; full text searching would open the possibility of uncovering particular documents in obscure places, and even cross-referencing them with others. Perhaps most important, historians have imagined that the new cyberinfrastructure—without in most cases the slightest understanding of how it actually works—would finally grant them their deepest and most cherished wish: that every document and record of possible use to future historians could now be saved. The cursed destruction of documents would finally cease once and for all—the "bulk" problem finally solved! All this presumably required was vast columns of servers and substantial amounts of money.

These imagined possibilities belie a basic paradox of the new cyber age: more may actually turn out to be less. In fact, cyberinfrastructures do not have the capacity to preserve certain aspects of traditional scholarly environments. In our view, they may well affect traditional disciplinary certainties and practices as much as they open new opportunities and possibilities. While the march of information technology is transforming information resources, emerging digital archives are also permanently dependent on system designs, as we have seen. These are derived not from the needs or values of scholarship or the authorities that have, in various ways, historically governed archival processes and retrieval. They are structured instead by the principles of "data curation," a new conception of archival practice based on processes of information technology and computer engineering. The documents in digital archives are digital not only in terms of their formats. The processes of their generation, acquisition, appraisal, description, and preservation are also engineered technologically through the design of information management systems.

Aside from historians interested in the history of technology, scholars have had little reason to engage the thinking or research of cyber engineers about these or other matters important to archival scholarship. Since these systems are being developed in response to challenges in the flow of institutional information and to problems with retaining digital records, historians are essentially passive consumers of new digital products and services. One could also say, of course, that once archival administration emerged as a distinct profession, historians have had very little say about what paper records were preserved. Yet the cyberinfrastructure places the issue of nonengagement on an entirely new plane. The engineering of new information environments affects how the future historical record will endure in ways entirely outside the historian's control.

What, then, can we expect from the cyberinfrastructure for historians and the archives that still give authority to their work? What is its impact on archival institutions as we have known them? What will it mean to have enhanced access, using one's own computer instead of an archival reading room? How will scholars and archivists engage these new structures in processing the past? What are the challenges in preserving digital materials? While our questions look to an unclear future, the structures and managerial demands of digital archives are almost certain to reinforce the separation between historians and archivists—between historical understanding and archival administration—that characterize the archival divide.

Cyberinfrastructure/Cyberspace

In its relation to archives, cyberinfrastructure gained much of its present currency and meaning in a 2003 National Science Foundation report prepared under the direction of Dan Atkins, Professor of Engineering and Dean of the School of Information at the University of Michigan. The Atkins report saw computer-based information technology as a revolutionizing force in science and engineering. It defined cyberinfrastructure as the "layer of enabling hardware, algorithms, software, communications, institutions, and personnel" that lies between "base technologies—the integrated electro-optical components of computation, storage, and communication" and "software programs, services, instruments, data, information, knowledge, and social practices applicable to specific projects, disciplines, and communities of practice." Atkins and his colleagues emphasized that this was more than a consideration of the ways the computer would aid research in engineering and the sciences. Rather, they saw this powerful technology as transformative of all scholarship in significant and basic ways. Immediate access to information—the speed of access itself—would affect the pace of research and discovery while the breadth of access would transform the basis of discovery and the authority of findings. The speed and character of communication would transform the very notion of collaborative research.[2]

As a National Science Foundation report, the Atkins study was read with interest in the sciences, engineering, and science-oriented medicine. It also gained considerable attention in the social sciences. Within the humanities, however, there was very little if any interest, and perhaps surprisingly, little reaction among archivists either. There were other initiatives underway at the time that seemed to signal more interesting change. Most notable for historians and other humanists was the Journal Storage Project (JSTOR), initiated by the Andrew W. Mellon Foundation that digitized the most important journals in the humanities and social sciences. JSTOR was the first large-scale project presenting the transformational possibilities the cyberinfrastructure held for these disciplines. Whole runs of journals were suddenly searchable in full text from a personal computer.

As Atkins might have put it, JSTOR exactly reflected combinations of hardware/software institutions and communities that could transform patterns of scholarship, communication, and knowledge generation. Not only would access be radically simplified in terms of finding individual articles or the corpus of individual scholars, but users would be able to use JSTOR's powerful search functions to connect instantly to work in other disciplines, to voices from decades earlier, and to obscure references embedded within individual articles and otherwise inaccessible in any rapid, comprehensive, and hence practical way. Moreover cited works could be easily pulled up from the database, sent to a colleague, incorporated into a syllabus, or downloaded to a bibliography—all quickly linked to the full text. Almost overnight, many scholars cleared their shelves of weighty and yellowing journal runs, no longer needed physically at hand.[3]

Did cyberinfrastructure then carry broader meanings for scholarship in the humanities and social sciences? Was this the reading room of the future, absent the well-worn tables, comfortable chairs, and silent companions? This aspect of the new technologies was more fully explored in a report prepared in 2005 by the American Council of Learned Societies on "Our Cultural Commonwealth." To its credit, this study situated the cyberinfrastructure as a series of broad challenges, even as it recognized the potential for radical changes in source bases and delivery mechanisms that could transform the culture of scholarship. It explored these issues in terms of public accessibility, "inter-operability," standards, copyright, and new scholarly methodologies, suggesting that the grand challenge to scholars in the humanities and the social sciences would be to collaborate with the products and processes that emerged from the cyberinfrastructure. Yet the report did not directly address how libraries and archives, both as institutions and as modes of thought, were also likely to be transformed. The ACLS study simply recommended, rather unhelpfully, that humanists and social scientists had to be "engaged," without suggesting how.[4]

Archives and the New Institutional Repositories

The ways in which cyberinfrastructure will supplant the traditional "infrastructures" of humanist scholarship remain unclear. Archives and libraries are being challenged to adjust, without fully comprehending what exactly they are adjusting to. The challenges are both technical and cultural. The most significant response in recent years has been the establishment of electronic "institutional repositories" in a variety of locations, especially at universities. Some are campus specific, such as DSpace@MIT at the Massachusetts Institute of Technology and Deep Blue at the University of Michigan. Others are more cooperative, utilizing electronic-archiving services such as PORTICO or open source software such as FEDORA.[5]

This was partly a consequence of the extensive work done in the sciences in the 1990s on the use of technology to support collaborative research. Universities began to experiment with new forms of repositories in order to capture and circulate the "content," as they called it, derived from their faculty's research. These new repositories were archival in nature, since they derived from a core function of the university. In the words of information scientist Clifford Lynch, they were "essentially an organizational commitment to the stewardship of these digital materials, including long term preservation where appropriate, as well as organization and access or distribution."[6] With DSpace, Deep Blue, and similar systems, scholarly output was no longer limited to the structures of journals and monographs. It could be mounted and circulated directly without the mediating processes of editorial or peer review that have long been part of scholarly publication.

Central here was the new concept of "content management," in which content can be text, voice, visualization, or data depending on, and based in, a variety of software. The established descriptive and organizational concepts and models for archives that have emphasized genre, origin, and authenticity, and that have focused on the integrating functionality of documents and files, were now challenged by new electronic systems for holding content. As with the holdings of electronic institutional repositories, these new kinds of artifacts have had an entirely different relationship to print-oriented notions of authorship, edition, and the fixity of text. They constitute a new kind of "information artifact," one that is very much system dependent.

They also blend the notion of archives and libraries, since the repositories that hold them are essentially cyberspaces engineered specifically for content. The idea of book or manuscript has little value here because these artifacts are not objects with specific physical attributes and because their forms do not affect content or its delivery. In essence, they are new digital objects mounted in cyber repositories—digital accumulations that for better or worse will constitute the historical archives scholars will need to explore the social, intellectual, cultural, political, and other historical patterns of the future.

As information in various forms is ingested into these systems, multiple links take users to specific parts or items in an instant or two. But in contrast to paper-based archives, what is easily lost in the process is an understanding of the structures that bind the parts or items together. In effect, the item that appears on a computer screen appears as a specific and discrete "product." It is "released" from its relationship to other materials or files unless the user deliberately tries to uncover its larger contextual meaning. In the hard copy world, these attributes are far more obvious. They are preserved by the physical need to pull an item from a box, a box from a shelf, or simply by seeing the file or item listed in a structured finding aid. In digitalized institutional repositories it is possible to search through Google and pull up an archival document or item without full indication of its date, version, relationship to other relevant documents, or the authenticity of its connection to particular administrative processes.

While some involved in managing these systems have worked to map these attributes in ways that make context more readily apparent, a danger has been that one part of a digital site could be moved to a different storage site or erased, and the original links completely severed. Just as paper archives are vulnerable to theft, fire, and misplaced files, digital repositories have thus raised security issues that also require new definitions, applications, and procedures. What these will be, how they are known, in what way they will be applied, and the extent to which these applications are part of the archival system design, are fundamental to an understanding of the content of these repositories. They are hence important concerns for digital archive users.

Moreover, the management of traditional historical archives has been based on perspectives developed some time after the creation of the documents from the outside looking in as it were. A variety of authorities—administrative, legal, cultural, and even notions of the historical—may have formed the evaluative models for ascribing value to the archive's holdings but such models have been almost entirely retrospective, engaged at the end of the life cycle of the record. In new "content management" systems, the perspective (and process) may be thought of as being from the inside looking out. The systems have to be engineered to capture all sorts of communications in all sorts of formats. Of necessity, the emphasis here has had to be on the "capture" at the point of the origin of the record. As a result most of the administrative systems that have come into place by the time of this writing turned out to be stressed by the sheer volume of information they accumulated, in great part because, in contrast to traditional archives, they have not fully established procedures to determine what was and was not of "enduring value." This problem forced institutions like Ohio University to completely redesign its administrative information systems, and IBM itself to begin work on solutions to e-mail "overload." Of necessity, however, the focus of these efforts has been on efficient, as well as rapid, information flow and on effective computer response, not on issues of value or archival preservation.

While working "from the inside out" thus has the possibility of capturing more content, even the best system designs cannot ascribe meaning to what institutions or societies produce, or discriminate among what is socially useful to retain. For example, the Internet Archive assembled as a result of the huge investment by entrepreneur Brewster Kahle holds some 85 billion web pages, but at least in its initial stages its material was accessible only to users with knowledge of specific URLs.[7] On one hand, the vastness of this repository is something unimaginable in the print world. On the other, the absence of any physicality has created equally unimaginable challenges to the tasks of access, and perhaps even more to the processes of producing historical knowledge, since the repositories are engineered to capture vast amounts of content in indiscriminate ways. Archivists have no role to play in its appraisal and even in its retrieval, at least in the ways that have made traditional archives the essential foundations of modern historical scholarship.

Will projects like the Internet Archive and Google Books further transform the patterns and styles of reading, replacing books and documents with their virtual counterparts? Most important for our purposes, what do these transformations mean for historical archives of the present and future, those sometimes grand physical monuments that permanently retain the artifacts of historical knowledge creation? There is little doubt that the cyberinfrastructure is changing the processes of records creation and the authority of documentary evidence in fundamental ways.

Although much is uncertain in this continually changing cyber world, we can say with some confidence that individual scholars and scholarly communities will have to be active in gaining an understanding of, and even active in the shaping of, the ways these new digital archives will function if scholarly research and communication itself are to remain relatively transparent. This is equally the case for institutionally based archives and for the rapidly growing number of those that are institutionally independent. The archival divide will only deepen if scholars are unable to interpret what they find in these vast accumulations of digital content. It is clear, though, that "the train has left the station," as our Russian colleagues might put it. With little if any "input" from historians and other scholars, the source formats in archives are already changing. Complex new programs are already being designed or in place. New protocols for access are already being engineered. How this will affect the ways future historical research is conducted remains an open, and very worrisome, question.

Digital Archives and the Retention of Records

The transformations of cyberspace have had a profound effect on archival practice and thinking. Although far from a reality in 2010, the very idea of a paperless office has stimulated archivists to reexamine the ways institutional activities and processes have traditionally been connected to records.

Throughout the twentieth century, the processes of paper records generation in an institutional setting involved an "infrastructure" of their own, one consisting of secretaries and filing clerks who transformed texts of record into archivable formats like "letter," "memorandum," "form," "report," or "minutes." These record keepers took care to prepare the required number of copies, file them systematically, and create what eventually became a permanent record, provided they deemed the documents to be valuable enough to preserve. The physical repository of these records and an essential element of the information flow was the prosaic filing cabinet, a "structural element" of paper records processing that commonly found room for less formal materials like notes, drafts, reference materials, or even an occasional doodle or two like those discovered in the cabinets maintained by John F. Kennedy's secretary.[8] The active intervention in an ideal situation of professional archivists in determining records of enduring value was assured when the contents of the file cabinet were packed up and sent to a permanent repository. At this point, theoretically at least, the expectation on the archivist's part was that the documentation reflected a complete or nearly complete record of individual, office, or agency processes and transactions.

Information technology has already challenged this culture of record keeping in radical ways. Indeed, the file cabinet as a system for preserving the record is largely obsolete. In up-to-date offices, documents "of record" are now prepared mostly on computers that are the property of the institution or agency itself and connected to broad internal information systems. Such systems not only have their own particular formats and templates but also carry their own set of record-keeping parameters and expectations. To understand them, the archivist requires a seat at the table at the time they are designed as well as when they are managed.

Each of the agreements, commitments, contracts, memoranda, reports, even significant "winks and nods" generated and distributed electronically in these systems also carry their own sets of attributes. They have authors, recipients, dates, and often the equivalent of a letterhead embedded within their operating systems and applied to all documents automatically. The identity of a recipient or their office is also a function of the institution's electronic directory, which in turn is dependent on technicians to assure it is accurately and systematically maintained. In many cases, of course, documents are prepared and kept outside these systems—on laptops, mobile devices, private e-mail accounts and the like. In effect, these are the equivalent of the unofficial diaries and private records that have been so important in the past to historical understanding apart from official records. Here, too, the medium for the retention of this kind of digital information is very unstable, even more so than with institutions.

The termination or retirement of individuals also raises a different set of problems. "Cleaning out the office" means dealing with the contents of a personally assigned computer that often needs to be left behind. It is not uncommon now to find laptops that can connect to tens of thousands of e-mail messages and a countless variety of word and other documents, the elements of an essential record and accessible only through a particular account. Companies like Ford Motor have policies that prohibit personal use of company e-mail accounts. The policies of universities and other institutions are more ambiguous. Often personal, professional, research, and business matters are conflated in a single e-mail system. In any case, to "clean out the office" someone either has to go through the accumulation of material and decide what to retain, clean and reboot the computer, or simply wait "until later"—in essence, ignore whatever need or value might derive from an archival evaluation. Even the delete key, however, does not usually erase all traces of what one might want to destroy.

While retention was not a perfect science in paper-based information systems, the challenges of digital materials thus present significant problems for the archives because the varied elements that define the context and authorities of digital records are located in particular and often quite individualized technological systems. These in turn are linked by specific and equally individualized kinds of computer applications. The attributes of the digital records themselves are essentially unsystematic "tags of retrieval." While they give a particular order to the records, allowing them to be filed in digital environments by common categories like date, recipient, or subject, what in the paper world would have been a discrete memorandum is now typically created and found in a string or trail of e-mails, text attachments, or other kinds of malleable formats. In some offices these documents may be copied to an assistant or secretary, and even printed out and filed in the old-fashioned way. Standards and commercial systems such as Documentum are only now emerging as the challenges of managing content is addressed in large institutions. Still lone authors or advocates have their personal computers and generate their own archives in ways that are still dependent on very particular software and hardware.

The cyber world challenges even the idea of a permanent record. The specificity of individual formatting and style sheets to certain kinds of computers or computer networks effectively ties records to formats that themselves undergo constant and sometimes quite rapid transformations. Floppy disks become hard drives; hard drives become thumb drives; thumb drives get larger in capacity as they shrink in size; and since pockets still have holes, relatively large batches of records can often disappear on an airplane seat or taxicab even if they are someplace (and sometimes) backed up. What high school student now remembers what a 5¼ inch floppy disk even looked like, much less has the capacity to read its contents? Even the encased 3½ inch disks—a real innovation a few short years ago—are now museum pieces.[9]

In effect, records are now commonly "archived" internally in large, relatively undifferentiated, and often precarious files that commonly contain documents of potential historical value that are specific to one machine, hard drive, or server, even if they are systematically, intentionally, and institutionally preserved. Even backup files are two-edged swords for the archivist. While they carry the implication that data once thought unimportant and therefore deleted can possibly be recovered, the delete key also implies that what is not needed or wanted is truly gone. Its recovery therefore distorts the more accurate record reflected in what has been saved. Finally, and perhaps most important, users typically have their documents on computers that they think of as their own, especially in institutions that tolerate use of their systems for both personal and official purposes. This inevitably creates a tension between what is personal and what is official, between what is properly the responsibility of institutional archive in the selection and retention of documentation and what is at an individual's discretion.

As cyberinfrastructures have rapidly spread, these matters began to get a good deal of attention. Danish technicians, for example, moved aggressively to create comprehensive systems that both monitor and collect the records generated by governmental processes at the city and national levels. The Danish national archives began to require the content of all government information systems to be transferred to them every five years for full evaluation and review. There were significant variations in how individual offices responded to the program, but Denmark had at least defined a comprehensive approach.

Where no such initiatives have begun the difficult issue for archives and archivists has been the absence of any transparent understanding or systematic institutional control over the way records are generated and kept. In effect, the individual creating a record is now more often than not the curator of that record. Any solutions to the task of systematic record keeping—the preservation of those materials worthy of becoming a part of the enduring record—rest squarely on the generator of the documentation. In some places, such as the Bibliothèque Nationale in Paris, archivists themselves have tried to address this challenge by asking that those generating records "declare" their content, especially in terms of whether a document is a final ("official") one or only a draft. At the point of "declaration," the document can be transferred intact to a central institutional "holding" cyberspace. The formal archival functions of arrangement and description then become a function of the how the system itself is designed. Residual documents not "declared" remain on individual computers and can be destroyed (or not) at their user's desire.

Here too, however, the appraisal of records becomes a function of the system, rather than one made by professional archivists if and when the documents are transferred to a formal repository. The ascription of enduring value still necessarily reflects quite individualized concerns. Even where guidelines are prepared to prescribe what should be saved or destroyed, their implementation still rests with the generator of the record, whether this is a person or the systems design itself, not with an archivist professionally engaged in and informed about the quite different tasks and needs of preservation. If preservation guidelines are embedded in the system itself to determine automatically what is saved or destroyed, the record that is ultimately preserved in the archive may be even more dependent on the provisional frameworks of records management rather than any consideration of potential future use.

In other environments, notably corporate ones, content management systems are in place (or rapidly being developed) that try to limit or remove the authority of the individual to control information. When the Sarbanes-Oxley legislation set formal mandates concerning corporate responsibility in the aftermath of the Enron scandal, systems were developed that can troll through corporate e-mail and other communication systems, pick up certain documents, and move them directly to a central file with fixed requirements for disposition. While these systems have been carefully engineered to meet legal and administrative requirements, they have no regard at all for the needs of historical or scholarly research. Indeed, they are typically structured so that the system provider itself has full possession of their content. In some cases, use of the information they gather is actually leased back at a cost by data management companies to its creators themselves.

As the accumulated content eventually becomes part of the historical archives of the future, understanding what the records contain, and why, will thus require on the part of archivists and scholars alike some real understanding of their systemic origins, as well as the how and why they were used. Much more so than with their paper counterparts, the archival grain that comes to reflect what was encouraged or discouraged in the production of these materials is likely to be extremely difficult to read by anyone not familiar with how the document gener-ating systems actually worked. In these circumstances, technical guidebooks out-lining whatever information the archivist can obtain in this regard may be an even more important "finding aid" than sophisticated search engines. Creators of the search engines themselves, meanwhile, may well need to consider the nature of their archives' grain in engineering their retrieval programs if they are to assure that the materials they access accurately reflect the historical circumstances of their creation.[10]

Even with the best search engines, however, historians and others can hardly expect cyber archives to include anything resembling a complete record any more than they can in paper-based archives. Almost certainly to be gone are most if not all of the ancillary material that historians have often found so informative: the digital equivalent of penciled musings taken at a meeting, preliminary designs or thoughts, or documents like the notes former U.S. Supreme Court Justice Frank Murphy took at the Court's weekly meetings and which remain one of the princi-pal sources for insights into its working. Even if the creators of documents saved their various musings, these are not likely to be "declared" individually or by a gathering system as records of enduring value. Matching paper content of desk drawers to digital files will be even more complicated—if someone thinks to clean out the desk! While some items may find their way to the archives through the personal donation, most will never become a matter of record.

Nor could they be, given that the new digital world has only escalated the prob-lems of "bulk." The University of Michigan, for example, was generating more than 12 million e-mail messages a day by 2008, a number that is exponentially higher in large and complex organizations like governments and international corporations. As the Bush administration prepared to leave office in 2009, the National Archives had to devise an emergency plan because officials doubted its new $144 million computer system could cope with the 70 terabytes of digital material it would receive. Although millions of White House e-mail messages created between 2003 and 2005, appeared to be missing from these files, and not recoverable, more than 200 million messages were still received.[11] The total volume proved to be some 10 times larger than the Clinton White House left behind in 2001 and some five times greater than the contents of all 20 million catalogued books in the Library of Congress.[12] Historians and other scholars of the Clinton and Bush years now risk being drowned in a sea of data.

Responses in the Archival Community

Understandably, these challenges have been at the center of concern in almost all the major world archives and scores of lesser ones as well. As the realities of digitization became clear, archivists at the U.S. National Archives and Records Administration (NARA), for example, began working to develop a comprehensive system to manage federal electronic records. Archivists there recognized that given the flood of digital materials arriving at their doorstep—and at archival doorsteps all over the world—one of the principal challenges they faced was identifying the mix of software, hardware, and institutionalized cultural practices needed to construct programs to capture, organize, and make accessible records "born digital." Reflecting the Archives' 2006–2016 strategic plan, the NARA 2006 Performance and Accountability Report emphasized that the development of any effective Electronic Records Archives (ERA) system would have to include "a comprehensive, systematic, and dynamic means for preserving electronic records, free from dependence on any specific hardware or software." It would also have to have the capacity not only to store materials in effective ways but also to improve preservation of and access to computer-based records into the future.[13]

As with paper records of the past, a fundamental concern of archivists is that an electronic record be authoritative and reliable in its relation to its original purpose—that it be an authoritative and authentic archival document in the traditional senses of these terms. At the same time, the new technological context of records production has further stimulated archivists to think about what is "essential" and "authentic" about digital records in terms of their archives' own requirements. A leading thinker on the subject, Luciana Duranti, has called this relationship the "archival bond." In her words,

> At the core of archival science is the idea that every record is linked to all the records belonging in the same aggregation by a network of relationships, which finds its expression in the archival bond. The archival bond is originary, because it comes into existence when a record is created; necessary, because it exists for every record (i.e., a document can be considered a record only if and when it acquires an archival bond); and determined, because it is qualified by the function of the record in the documentary aggregation in which it belongs. . . . With electronic records, this understanding also allows us to identify means of representing the record's relationships in a way that an electronic system will be able to recognize and maintain them intact.[14]

Duranti's idea has had broad resonance. Since the "archival bond" in her approach is the basis for determining reliability and authenticity, it also serves theoretically as a foundation for constructing digital archives. For example, it has helped NARA create a design for electronic records management that assigns a profile for every record type, and assembles these profiles in repositories that become the basis both for access and retrieval. In order to ensure the reliability, integrity, and authenticity of profiled records, NARA's program also establishes its own agency wide control over all records under its administrative purview. It also creates special protocols to establish and implement access. Nonelectronic records can be similarly tracked and located, again with an emphasis on control.

In reviewing the enormity of the challenge, NARA archivists have concluded that controls over the use and styles of annotation, confidentiality, records transmission, copying and especially over schedules and forms of retention are essential to make an electronic archive work.[15]

Having worked through some of the basic theoretical issues, NARA awarded a contract to build its Electronic Records Archive system to the Lockheed Martin Corporation, not generally known for its engagement with the humanities. Lockheed Martin was to "deliver to NARA an initial version of the ERA system that will enable NARA to test the hardware and software on which all business processes related to electronic records will run. Early installation and testing of the infrastructure will ensure basic capacity and operability of the system before NARA staff depends on it in their work."[16] Over time, NARA's efforts may well provide key components for historical and other scholarship in digital archives.

NARA archivists themselves have anticipated this, noting in their 2006 Report that "just as electronic records have forever changed the way Government does business, the ERA system will change how NARA cares for Government records and how the public gains access to our holdings."[17] Given the relatively large resources at its command, NARA's approach may well become the standard for digital archive structures in the same way the Library of Congress has standardized so much in the library world. It is important to note, however, that three years after NARA signed its contract with Lockheed Martin, the National Archives ERA was still in the process of being engineered. In addition to Lockheed, other technology firms, schools of information, engineering associations and universities with significant engineering capacities had become NARA's partners in this endeavor, but even as the access phase of its ERA moved into its final phases, the role historians and other academic users might play in its final design had yet to be announced.[18]

Other archives and archival collections have addressed these challenges as well. The system we have referred to at the Bibliothèque Nationale in Paris actually assembles its own digitized archives. Although only 3,000 employees generate its records, the Bibliothèque's system has implications for much larger organizations. It does not attempt to harvest all of the documentation that its staff creates, but recognizes the actual practices of electronic records creation by formally assigning the task of final selection to the document's creator. To counter the effects of the random ways digital records are created, amended, reformatted, and further amended in circulation, all of which threatens the integrity of collective authentic and authoritative records in digital archives, the system of authorial "declaration" in the French system determines which particular documents are transferred into the archival system. "Declaring" an e-mail, text file, or other document "validates" it as a record. The system itself then captures the metadata that is embedded in the record in the form of its essential tags: "from," "to," "department received," "department sent," and "date." Additionally, the creator of the document must also assign a descriptive classification to the record to preserve some sense of the file relationship of one document to another. Thus authenticated, classified, and transferred, the document is automatically tagged to remain in the archives for a set amount of years, and then, on further review, either destroyed or marked for permanent preservation.[19]

Both the NARA and Bibliothèque Nationale systems still depend on the originator of the record rather than the archivist to appraise value—a significant departure from the established appraisal processes in paper records. The archivist's activism here is concentrated instead in the design, management, and development of the electronic records system as a whole. Again, there is no provision for specific user communities, including professional historians, to inform the guidelines for retention or disposition. It is not even clear that this would be practicable or even desirable, given the number of different communities interested in the content of the archive. Without this kind of mediation, however, digital archives will continue to be "system dependent" rather than "archive dependent," which means that the authority of their records will depend on the degree to which the electronic programs that create and house them can respond to shifts in the basic informational needs of their institutions as well those of its users.

Under these circumstances, it is again not clear how systems of this sort, whether or not they are called archives, will be easily understood by historians and other scholars—a requisite both for reading the archival grain and for contextualizing historically the materials preserved. However excited historians might be about the retrieval possibilities of digital archives and the ways they can potentially extend access to everyone with a computer, they must be concerned as well about the equally great uncertainties of the digital future, especially in terms of the authority of digital documents and the processes of their retention or disposition. As Eisenstein demonstrated regarding the impact of print, the transformative agency of this new technology, whether engineered badly or well, is inexorably altering patterns of scholarly communication, information accumulation, community definition, and the production of knowledge itself.

The Interconnectedness of Preservation and Access

The historians' dream that everything can be saved is certainly appealing to anyone who has ever walked expectantly into an archive and discovered that what they were looking for was not there. When the telephone changed the ways people communicated, it discouraged time-honored practices of writing things down. While every piece of electronic communication can at least theoretically be saved, saving does not necessarily imply the possibility that it can be retrieved. Even in well-constructed digital archives where tags and other metadata designations allow materials to be identified, there remains the cursed problem of bulk. Google-like systems are not terribly useful when they return tens of thousands of hits.

What, then, should be preserved? Archiving huge amounts of electronic records of different and complex sorts requires particular archival and technical sensitivities. Digital records now include complex databases, digital photographs and videos, satellite imagery, audio files, HDTV files, web pages, geospatial information systems, and other huge aggregates of data, in addition to more common office files. Among archivists at the U.S. National Archives, the governing vision for their ERA system has complemented NARA's official mission of "safeguarding and preserving the records of our Government, ensuring that the people can discover, use, and learn from this documentary heritage." To do this, NARA affirms it must also "ensure continuing access to this essential documentation of the rights of American citizens and the actions of their government . . . and facilitate historical understanding of our national experience."[20] But how, then, can preservation and access be ensured? Because digital documents are invisible until retrieved, any preservation system is useless without a corresponding access system that enables the display of its documents. Access and preservation are now two sides of the same coin.

The National Science Foundation in the United States has been actively seeking solutions that would provide "reliable digital preservation, access, integration, and analysis capabilities for science and/or engineering data over a decades-long timeline" and would be able to "continuously anticipate and adapt to changes in technologies and in user needs and expectations." Margaret Hedstrom, Seamus Ross, and other leading archivists engaged with these questions have pointed out that preservation is not just a matter of scale and capacity.[21] Most important is the challenge of making metadata archivally viable by describing digital objects with various kinds of tags: descriptive categories set within the language structures used in the descriptive or tagging process. The conceptual frameworks used in creating these descriptions that go beyond the most essential institutional linkages thus need to be explained. For purposes of transparency, directories need to be maintained that are capable at a minimum of identifying the provenance of particular digital documents, which like paper materials are products of the social processes and knowledge structures current at the time they were created—the historical contexts that help explain their meaning. Since such time-specific descriptors worked into the cyberstructures of metadata will affect how it is arranged and retrieved, they involve critical issues of retrieval and access that are foundational to all archival systems.[22]

Hedstrom and Ross have pursued these matters in the Digital Library Initiative, a commission they chaired for the National Science Foundation, and in the European Framework Programme of the Network of Excellence for Digital Libraries.[23] Their recommendation has been to automate the metadata in ways that allow it to change over time. While the technological complexities here might well be resolved, implementing the concept requires archivists to engage fully with the knowledge communities involved in developing and redeveloping sophisticated applications of artificial intelligence. At the same time, losses in archived data are inevitable. In May 2009, for example, the *New York Times* reported on a "huge loss" at a National Archives record center of computerized data from the Clinton administration as a result of an "apparent security breach."[24] The Hedstrom–Ross report therefore also explored the idea of "acceptable loss" and the notion of "repurposing archives." It suggested that consideration must be given to the question of how much loss in cyberspace is "tolerable." Is a "system failure," in other words, to be thought of as something like a fire in a paper repository, or is acceptable loss even a sensible concept to deploy in designing huge digital repositories?

A related issue here, of course, is that the digital environment is very much dependent on the stability of the digital storage media itself. Hedstrom and Ross have further suggested that "future user communities" might therefore "exploit stored assets" depending "on the analytic tools they have available to find relevant information patterns in the collection."[25] These tools might also allow historians and other scholars to find historically valuable material in what was digitally saved or even discarded by accessing cyber "voices" that are either evident or submerged within the system itself. Again, however, finding these voices will require at least a minimal understanding of how the digital repository was designed, produced, and engineered.

While the possibilities of sheer capacity in digital archives are enormous, digital preservation is thus far from a simple matter of storage. In the very necessity of discerning "relevant information patterns" in digital archives, there is an implicit call to archivists, historians and other scholars to engage the fundamental processes of description here, just as they once did with paper materials in the long gone era of mutual interests, training, and scholarly commitment.

Changing Institutional Infrastructures: The "Soft" Consequences of Digitization

Most archives and archival holdings have existed historically within formally established institutional repositories whose function it has been to store and provide access to their documentation. Each archive has had both a physical and conceptual presence. By their very names, the National Archives in the United States, the Russian State Historical Archive, or the Archives Nationales in Paris suggest that they house the historical corpus of their nation's records. Even local collections convey similar meaning: the Massachusetts Historical Society holds important manuscripts and archives whose very retention in that institution connotes their enduring value. The same can be said with regard to historically vital institutions like the Bienecke Library at Yale University or the Houghton Library at Harvard as well as other equally important repositories and specialized library collections all over the world.

Each of these collections is not only associated with a particular specialization but with a particular (and often very impressive) physical space. Researchers consequently develop associations with their buildings, as well as their documents. These join the experiences researchers are also likely to have as they journey to the location, register as a user, find a good place in the reading room, and open their document boxes. Experiences like hefting the early inventories of the Archives Nationales or the Archivio Segreto Vaticano are also likely to make a distinct impression. In other words, there is a distinct physicality in the use of these repositories, as well as a broad range of subjective associations that, among other effects, establish bonds with previous generations of scholars and deepen scholarly commitments. Few who sit in grand places like the First Reading Room of the Russian State Library across from the Kremlin in Moscow, the grand rotundas of the Library of Congress or British Museum, or the elegant reading room of the Vatican Library can fail to feel somewhat "in touch" with the experiences, achievements, and struggles of earlier generations of scholars.

We do not want to romanticize the experience of visiting great repositories. No matter how grand the building or how important the collections, archival research has always had its challenges. Still, the importance of these settings to scholarship has never been cause for much reflection. They have simply seemed to be a permanent part of the scholarly and cultural landscape, their very architecture serving as testament to the enduring scholarly values they reflect and the permanent importance of their resources.[26] Visits to these places, the very physical process of entering their space and feeling engaged in the institutional histories and cultures of their collections, has thus served to strengthen the humanistic foundations of traditional archival and library research, lending a particular gravitas to the research experience.

Even in its infancy, it became clear that cyberspace would have a deep impact not only on the definition and use of archival materials and other artifacts but also on these defining aspects of traditional scholarly research. For many, the first sign of momentous digital change, akin to the end of their known research worlds, came with the demise of the card catalog, a fixture in almost all libraries throughout the world for more than a century. Reports that the information contained on millions of cards would be transformed into a single massive digital database caused even the baldest of scholars in some places to tear their hair.[27] The gradual discovery that the virtual information provided by new Online Public Catalogs (OPACs) was essentially the same as what was on the card was some relief, but some early users of OPACs regarded the acronym itself as something of a profanation and clearly missed the physical experience of using real cards. The browsing function of the new databases seemed particularly inadequate in comparison to the "serendipity" of finding a card that pointed to an unanticipated holding.

At first these bibliographic databases were commonly placed in the same room as the card catalog, even existing side by side. (At the University of Michigan, and undoubtedly scores of other research libraries as well, who used which resource quickly marked the differences in scholarly generations!) The virtue of this positioning was that the new tools were set within the venerable old space. They also required the same physical trip to the library. As we know, however, this changed rather rapidly. The emergence of an easily accessible Internet and a new, distributed computer technology soon made the trip to the library unnecessary, at least to use the catalog. The physical catalogs themselves completely disappeared. Soon, of course, it became possible to search thousands of libraries from the comfort of one's own desk, but here too, in a way, was a generational marker: current and future generations of students and young users had no awareness of even what using a "card catalog" was like and how it structured research.

More important, neither young nor older users have much understanding of the conceptual contribution of the card catalog to the structure and limitations of current on-line access systems. As a result, users do not have full understanding of the limits and possibilities of on-line access. The quality of the on-line search experience is almost entirely dependent on the quality of the OPAC and what "comes up." Not only has on-line access become completely independent of conceptual links to the access cultures of the card catalog days; the physicality of the experience has also been completely transformed—absorbed, as it were, into the cyberinfrastructure. As a result, most physical connections that scholars may have are with collections themselves. Large complex integrated search databases still point individuals to specific places where a physical object is housed. Although there are increasing numbers of digitalized exceptions, searches in archives are still by and large focused on finding a physical manuscript, document, map, or video.[28] On-line access systems essentially remain on-line services of convenience for users in remote locations, designed to make the visit to the library or archive more efficient. The physical repository remains the essential research institution.

Now comes the Google project, with its widely heralded capability of capturing millions of library volumes themselves on-line and linking them directly to an on-line search. References to these virtual texts, although in copyrighted cases not the texts themselves, were already appearing in some library catalogs in 2008. As a result, users could now sit at their laptops in coffee shops, search the on-line catalog through a wireless Internet connection, find a book of interest, call it up if it does not violate copyright restrictions, and read the "book" itself between cappuccinos. At the same time one can pull up all kinds of things, from the mundane to the sordid—all from the same terminal. Gone is whatever stimulation that comes from being sequestered in a particular kind of physical research space.[29]

As many have become aware, the same changes are also happening within the community of manuscripts and archives. The Rose project at the Johns Hopkins University Library, for instance, has brought virtual copies of rare French illuminated manuscripts to a distant (and much broader) user community. A substantial portion of medieval manuscripts of the Morgan Library are also available on-line. Portions of the collections at UCLA and at Oxford University have been mounted. And, recently the Stiftsbibliothek in St. Gallen, Switzerland, and the Vatican Library have announced plans to mount a substantial portion of their medieval and renaissance manuscripts.[30] In some cases, like the Valley of the Shadow project on the American Civil War, there has been an attempt to create something like the physical experience of visiting an archive. On-line users are guided to a virtual floor plan that shows "where" in the "building" the materials are housed. Here the artifacts of historical knowledge have been transplanted from physical places in real, sometimes centuries-old institutions, to cyberstructures with no three-dimensional characteristics whatsoever.[31] Indeed, the footnotes to this paragraph illustrate the point. Rather than pointing to artifacts that exist physically on the shelf, the authority of the paragraph rests on information housed in cyberspace and derived entirely from a laptop.

As of this book's writing, all these digital-based innovations may still be seen as enhancements to the work of existing institutions and part of efforts to better serve their users. They are still largely tied to specific institutions and play a supporting role to the work of libraries and archives that are located in specific buildings in specific places. Their on-line catalogs enhance access. Digitization enhances accessibility. All of this is widely and properly seen as important to research, historical and otherwise. The problem looming ahead, however, can be discerned from the fate of the card catalog. What will happen when the institutional links are less clear, or even fade away entirely, when the web presence itself becomes the institution and the physicalities of the traditional research experience disappear? What will happen, in other words, when the digital-based delivery of content subordinates the perceptions, identities, and very physicality of the institutions themselves to the virtualities of cyberspace?[32] While the cyberinfrastructure is unquestionably a tsunami-like force in transforming library and archival transactions and their cultures, it also has the capacity to transform the roles these institutions have historically played themselves in the production especially of historical knowledge.

Transformations of the Artifact

Change in the institutional infrastructure of historical research also has implications for how we understand the artifact itself. The ways historians and archivists have traditionally processed the past has depended on physical interactions with its physical traces. While these often have taken the problematic forms of memory and experience, they have also been grounded in documents, manuscripts, images, and books—the traditional artifacts of historical knowledge. We must therefore be concerned about the implications of an emerging cyberinfrastructure on the authorities these artifacts reflect. Does the transfer from one technology to another diminish the authority of their content?

In this connection we must remember that the migration of texts from one technology to another is not itself a new occurrence. Current projects to digitize content rely heavily on both the existence of real books and our understanding of the legacies in print of reflection and scholarship. Yet many of the most authoritative of these books themselves, including the Bible, Thucydides, Xenophon, Plato, Cicero and others, were assembled, defined, and printed in large quantities on the basis of contradictory manuscripts copied (and corrupted) many times over before the discipline of print defined their texts.

Early explorations into the applicability of on-line systems to archives focused on library-based print elements like author, title, and page, since these were not only specific identifying and cataloguing markers, but provided sure links for citations. The hope was that similar characteristics could be defined for archived materials. Newer archival systems have tried to adjust these categories to the particular qualities of digital records, but the essential goal of on-line archival access systems has still been to bring the user as efficiently as possible to the physical artifact, again allowing its use and citation. As with JSTOR and Google books, the finding aids of some digital archives have even been structured to deliver the artifact itself in digital form, relieving researchers of the need to even encounter the original, along with decades of archival dust and the burdens of travel.

Up to this writing, however, these projects have all been linked to an understanding of the physical attributes of the artifact. JSTOR delivers journal content in picture images of the physical pages from scanned issues of published volumes. The author, title, page numbers, volume and date derive directly from the object's print forms. Google similarly delivers a digital surrogate of a book with an image of its spine and endpapers. Its latest technology even tries to simulate the experience of turning pages. Although Google books rarely have reference to its library setting, interested researchers can still search for a stamped title page to find out where the book was located. Nevertheless, the authority vested in this evidence now derives from its "existence" on-line. The nature, structure, culture, politics, and history of the institution that holds the hard copy—indeed its very existence—is irrelevant to the user. The situation is a bit different for manuscripts whose original copies can be consulted in only one place. For splendid illuminations and texts from the Rose project or from the manuscript digitization projects at the Morgan Library, their on-line markers points to a specific repository where the original can be seen and physically examined. The authority vested in these on-line digital versions is thus derived from their links to real artifacts in actual institutional locations.

Does this matter in terms of understanding the nature of the artifact? And even if it does, do users really care? Most users of on-line documentation from Michigan's Bentley library on the U.S. intervention in Russia's civil war will never visit the library. Nor may they even be conscious that it exists. For the original rare medieval manuscripts digitized in the Rose project, it is not even certain that a visit to the library would provide an opportunity to view the original, since access to these very rare, fragile, and light-sensitive materials is very difficult in any case to obtain.

Increasingly, however, web-based information resources have no institutional home at all. Like Wikipedia, they are inhabited by a cyber community of information providers that freely assemble, post, edit, and even invent information. Among other problems, their materials are difficult to authenticate. They are also hard, although not impossible, to classify as sources. Totally detached from the discipline and thus the traditional authority of print cultures that fixed text to paper in the framework of a specified document or edition, they are also released from the institutional authorities that once assured their validity. The complex associational networks including institutions, buildings, descriptive materials, and even the underlying collection principles are in most cases totally nonexistent.

In conception and authority, production of an encyclopedia like Wikipedia in this way is obviously completely new. Gone is any sense of edition, guarantee of fixed entries, clear authorship, or expert oversight that historically has given authority to the encyclopedia genre. Most important from an archival perspective, the constantly changing content of these sources cannot be archived in any conventional way. Snapshots might be taken at different points in time and archived as sequences of the material, but the archived result will still be a new category of "documents" structured apart from ˙he contexts of their creation and even their creators.[33]

Of course, there will always be those who will find "content" of perceived historical value and preserve it for the future, as specialized historical collecting institutions have always done. But archivists understandably struggle with how this might be done when content is created digitally, stored in digital form in various kinds of systems, and communicated only through the programmed mechanisms of web-based access. Does it matter that a content item is a part of a particular collection? Can an item stand on its own outside that context? Is it important that a collection is a particular part of an institution-based program of accumulating certain kinds of historical materials based on particular understandings of the past? Again, the Leo Baeck Institute and its holdings on the history of the German Jews are instructive. Can a letter of the sort found in this rich repository be set usefully outside the broader collection of which it is a part? If it is important for scholars to understand the purposes of the Institute in order to fully comprehend the historical significance of its objects, does not the digital transposition of the document also deprive it of important kinds of historical meaning?[34]

The Legacy of Print, the Threshold of Adequacy, and The Potential of Cyber Archives

The vault of the Vatican Library contains some 70,000 manuscript volumes that represent a significant record of the transmission of textual knowledge from the end of the Roman Empire to the Renaissance. For the better part of a millennium, up to the advent of printing in the west, these volumes represented the infra-structure of a manuscript culture, one that supported small but vigorous centers of learning all over Europe. This culture was supplanted over time by the emer-gence of print and the availability of texts in multiple copies. Over time, there-fore, and only over time, the importance of this manuscript-based accumulation of textual knowledge receded. Scholarship increasingly could rely on printed sources alone. The need to access manuscript materials directly in order to inform and authenticate different kinds of inquiries and claims passed through what we would call a "threshold of adequacy," where printed sources proved sufficient to support arguments, foster inquiry, and produce and sustain knowledge. Many of the texts in manuscript form "joined" the print world, migrating in their published forms from one "knowledge infrastructure" to another. Others that did not migrate remained well cared for in select repositories. Although largely unknown, they were still available for scholars and scholarship.

A similar process may be happening in the early twenty-first century. The growth of digital archives, only in their infancy in the 1990s, has obviously been prodigious. In the U.S. National Archives, electronic holdings have grown 100 times faster than holdings in paper. One can only think that at some point, schol-arship and scholarly discourse may well pass another "threshold of adequacy," where digital resources will eclipse paper-based resources as an adequate basis of historical and other kinds of authority. While there may always be concern that a particular print or manuscript source might contain important details that its digital form cannot capture, or that a paper watermark obscured in a digitalized archival document may be of historical significance, the corpus of digital surro-gates is likely to assume the same role as their paper-based predecessors and prove fully adequate to authenticate most research. Like the Vatican manuscripts, the paper materials may well be stored for many years in select repositories, but historical understanding of the current and future centuries will derive primarily from documentation that exists purely in digital form.

Is this a good thing? The new epoch has provoked intense scholarly debate about the legacy of print. What will happen to the scholarly monograph, taking a degree of its authority from the distinction of its published form, identified by its appearance, heft, and sometimes even its smell? Through the Google project and others, a great portion of previously printed works will soon be in digital form. Older works may then be "rediscovered," as "full text searching" pulls out citations that might never have been found through traditional catalog searches. Works that remain undigitized may well find themselves almost entirely out of reach. A few major print repositories, perhaps still known as libraries, may still hold stature for the print world comparable to the stature that the Vatican Library holds for the world of manuscripts, but while their actual holdings may survive, these will not be nearly as accessible or as used as their digital surrogates.[35]

It is harder to assess the impact of digitization on archives. As of this writing, there is no project currently underway for archives and manuscripts comparable to the Google book project. One reason is prosaic: for archives, the transfer of paper documents into digital form is more labor intensive and slower.

Archives, however, also pose different and more difficult tasks. The connection of one item to another still needs to be maintained. Both large and smaller files and fonds need to be kept intact. While all documents are unique as individual items, they are also part of files with their own characteristics and ancillary materials. The technological advances of microfilming served archival preservation needs quite well because of its inherent linearity: documents were simply filmed in the sequences of their files, with appropriate markers to delineate separate files, missing pages, and the like. In contrast, digitized archives need to specify these links and delineators by assigning metadata parameters that are unique to each item. While not impossible, the task is complex, laborious, and slow. It also requires the close attention of professional archivists.

Moreover, since archives are by nature unique collections with unique records, there is no comparable scale of efficiency in their digitization. In contrast, say, to the JSTOR project, where digitizing journals allowed thousands of back copies to be discarded, few archival artifacts preserved for their enduring value are likely to go to the shredder. There is also the question of scale. The Google project may involve more than 3 billion images if one estimates its results on the basis of 10 million books averaging 300 pages each. Although 3 billion is a daunting number, the U.S. National Archives estimates that it would take 9 billion images to digitize its paper holdings alone. Paper-based archives and archival collections will thus be with us for some time. As a result, the attention of archivists of necessity is turning toward the challenges of assembling and maintaining archives of documentation "born digital," and bearing the potential of transforming historical scholarship in ways we cannot fully envision.

Of course, the paper world has never been perfect. All sorts of people in the past destroyed letters, burned memoranda, and shredded files. Such is the stuff of the history of archives, of history itself. Still, the digital age holds the possibility of records entirely unmediated by long-established processes of records appraisal, a quintessential function of the archives and at the core of archival professional practice despite its complex and often controversial aspects, as we have seen. There is also the possibility, as Arden Bement, Director of the U.S. National Science Foundation, suggested in 2007, that any current digital records management system might prove totally inadequate for future needs. In his view, we may be "entering a second revolution in information technology, one that may well usher in a new technological age that will dwarf, in sheer transformational scope and power, anything we have yet experienced in the current information age."[36]

These conditions effectively bring to a head all of the issues that have captured our attention in this volume: the authority of the record, how historical meaning is ascribed to documentation, points of contestation in the access and use of archives, and, of course, archival politics. In the future, the most significant mediations of the record are likely to occur before it is even created, the consequence not of serious reflection among archivists and historians after documents come to the archives, but of the way electronic systems are structured and records retention policies are articulated.

Out of this breathtaking flurry of innovation, however, there is reason to hope that new possibilities will emerge to effectively collect and store archival materials, as well as provide efficient access. Historians will surely benefit from this, but their full possibilities will only be realized through an understanding of how these systems are constructed, not simply through awareness of what records they hold. The mutual burdens of archivists and historians are thus to understand the technical processes now shaping their materials and to engage the processes of digital access in mutually supportive ways. Both will need to have a reasonably clear idea of their systems' limitations, as well as their real possibilities, for historical scholarship. In sum, only if future scholars are well informed about the processes involved in creating electronic archives can they realize the full potential of digital records for historical research and take full advantage of these new ways to process the past.

11

Can History and Archives Reconnect: Bridging the Archival Divide

Archivists in many repositories remain dedicated to assisting historians in their work. As in the past, they continue working with scholars to link the nature of their collections to the complexities of historical analysis. Moreover, there are many instances where historians and archivists continue to come together on specific issues: the quest for institutional independence for the National Archives of the United States in the 1980s, for example, or the PROFS case in the 1990s. Still, the new conceptual directions in historical study and in archival work have moved historians and archivists apart, opening an archival divide. Given the current thrusts of archival work and historical scholarship, the respective underlying developments within the two professions are conceptually incompatible.

In fundamental ways archivists have reached a new professional frontier. Of necessity, they have found themselves drawn closely into the process of digital records generation and the institutional values, priorities, uses, practices, and needs that shape their creation—the central processes touching the design and circulation of information within specific institutions and organizations. They have had to be sensitive to the problems of "migrating" records, when the latest shift in technology forces stored materials to be adapted to new forms in order to be readable; and to electronic "viruses," the contemporary version of Michelet's archival dust that damaged the health of archivists and users as well as the documents.[1] With the possibility of preserving everything imagined to be of value to future research in electronic repositories with virtually unlimited capacities, digitization has also brought with it the prospect of instant, ultimate, and sometimes entirely unintended records destruction.

The digital agenda for archivists—utilizing digital technology for description and access along with the complexities involved in managing the digital record itself—has thus come to dominate the professional discourse and identity of the contemporary archivist. It is important to note that this focus has not necessarily limited the interdisciplinary reach of archival concepts. Rather it has opened doors for archivists to engage problems in fields like medical informatics, documentary forensics, data curation, museology, complex systems, and artificial intelligence. Given all of this, it is hardly surprising that the role of historians in the professional activities of managing the archival record has ended.

Moreover, the distance that has emerged between historians and archivists is also more than a separation between circles of professional interaction and training. As historians have opened new areas of exploration by reconceptualizing fundamental aspects of the historical process, their analytic categories have themselves moved far from the historical authorities that structured earlier archives, as we have seen, and even more so from the structural bases of new electronic records. The archival divide thus reflects a division between divergent conceptual frameworks for understanding and using historical documentation. The days when historians and archivists considered themselves colleagues addressing problems of records with a common view of their historical significance has become part of archival history itself.

Does the Divide Have to be Bridged?

Should historians be concerned about bridging the divide? Should archivists? One could argue that archives have and always will exist in one form or another. The problems of access to, reliability of, and authority provided by records have always been part of serious archival research. Still, even in the digital age it is up to historians and other scholars to dig into the materials as best they can to find the material they need, just as they have always done. As we have tried to demonstrate throughout this volume, however, good archival history—indeed, good archival scholarship of any kind—cannot be done without a clear understanding about the ways a repository has assembled and administered its material. In other words, archives are not only places where historical narratives are woven from the documentation at hand. They have narratives of their own that need to be carefully if figuratively "read" before their materials can be fully appreciated and most effectively used.

These archival "stories" are also multiple and unfixed. It is relatively easy to understand how and why state archives are reflections of the self-perceptions of state officials. As we have tried to show with our discussions of the Soviet and Russian archives, these perceptions can also change radically, either through radical changes in the state itself, or more gradually, through the evolution of new values, practices, laws, and conceptions of civil purpose. Documents and records that might have been considered marginal in one context can suddenly have "enduring value" in another. One need only think of the changing contexts in which the archives of China, Japan, France, Germany, and virtually all of the states of Eastern Europe have been variously located over time, along with those of the former Soviet Union. The archives of South Africa are another case in point, while similar if less radical changes have also affected the nature of American and Canadian archives as the turn to identity politics and changing conceptions of the importance of ethnicity, gender, and multiple pasts altered the practices of appraisal and disposition.[2]

Narratives embedded in the archives can also relate to particular kinds of social memory whose purpose might be to "forget" as well as to "remember," preserve and inform. Appraisal decisions in these repositories must be understood in terms of objectives that are sometimes unspecified, sometimes quite specific. Silences in the archives can also be a consequence of social memory practices, while in carefully managed "identity archives," how memories themselves change over time and are reflected through a cycle of what John Randolph has called "production, exchange, and use," is an important issue, in which "their evolving historical presence makes certain kinds of actions and meanings possible."[3]

We know that archives are related as well to particular historical moments and derived from historically specific sets of emphases and the authorities governing practices and discourses at particular points in time. The authorities used by archivists in acquisition and preservation decisions are thus themselves temporal in form and conception. Times may change and the readings of archival holdings may evolve as conceptual frameworks change, but the archives' descriptive apparatus remains rooted in particular understandings of the kinds of documentation that archivists and their institutions thought had enduring value, historical or otherwise, at the moment of their appraisal. When the dynamics of this process are obscured or concealed over time, archives can understandably seem simply to be inert places of record.

Sometimes these conceptions are bared through the processes of social and historical confrontation, especially when foundational interpretations of the past are directly and forcefully challenged. This has been the case particularly with archives of colonial administrations, as we have described, where reading the archival grain becomes a particularly important aspect of studying imperial and colonial histories. The social processes of "truth and reconciliation" also illustrate the issue, as they have especially in South African archives. In these cases, not only are the narratives underlying established archives destabilized; the very nature and value of their records can come into question, both in terms of how and of why they were produced. Even in the most democratic of societies, where both state and nonstate archives have a civil (public) purpose, understanding the practices that have given their collections "enduring value" is necessary to understand the histories their narratives engage.

The archives' own narratives are therefore always more than "stories." They constitute the foundation for understanding archival documentation in all of its forms. Even with historical collections whose original documents are entirely in paper form, these constructions are almost always invisible to an uninformed user who arrives, signs in, and begins to search through neatly arranged finding aids. In digital archives, they may be totally opaque, disguised by elegantly designed web-based locators and catalogues that are easy to "surf." And unlike traditional archives, where the archival narrative is also created by the archivists' own conceptions of purpose and value, we know that digital archives currently allow no point of entry into the principles and practices underlying their formation, other than what the computer screen itself reports.

In sum, understanding archive practices and processes and how they have developed over time is fundamental to ascribing historical meaning to archival holdings. The common notion that historians can understand these practices intuitively is a recipe for poor scholarship. To write good history, scholars must bridge the archival divide by acquiring specific knowledge about archival processes, reading their archives as well as their documents, and by once again understanding what their now distant archivist colleagues actually do. In important ways, this approach constitutes a new historical methodology in which the "source of the source" is carefully considered and explicated. While we have seen that a few scholars in anthropology and ethnography have already moved in this direction, academic historians are still largely unaware of the importance in training their graduate students to comprehend the conceptual and cultural milieu in which their archival sources are created, structured, processed, appraised, discarded, and preserved.

Can the same be said about archivists? Is the archival divide something about which they, too, should be concerned? Or is it simply the inevitable consequence of technology's ineluctable flow, with its stringent and complex requirements for digital records management? It is fair to suggest that from the moment archivists separated professionally from historians, and in the United States, Europe, and Russia, at least, formed their own professional organizations, a professional resistance to the presumptions of many historians that they know best how archives should be administered has been part of the archivists' mindset. Why, then, should archivists be concerned about extending their professional hands across the new divide, especially when administering modern digital repositories requires such different forms of training, and when the postmodern tasks many historians now set for themselves defy easy understanding?

We believe there are two important reasons. The first concerns the links between archives and scholarship generally, and relates to the basic archival issue of provenance. The second, perhaps more important in practical terms, has to do with the help historians and other scholars can provide in easing what has become a critical problem for the curators of digital archives: how to describe their holdings in ways most useful to their users.

Despite the great transformations in archival processes and technologies we have explored, understanding and documenting "what happened" still remains for most archives a core part of their institutional mission. The past may be as recent as a year or two ago, or more historical in terms of its relation to past processes, behaviors, and the age of archived material. As we have argued, even the administration of current records, paper or digital, requires a process for their temporary retention. How long "temporary" turns out to be may depend on many factors outside the archivists' control, but even the most brief retentions require some perspective on "what happened" in order for the records to be effectively used. In other words, the underlying purposes of all archival institutions remain historical in the broadest sense of the concept, however little they may be focused on the interests and needs of historians.

Many archivists schooled in the technologies of information management may resist the idea, but the inherent historicity of all archives leads us to suggest that understanding the kinds of questions scholars might want to put to the documents may be as important as assessing their evidentiary and institutional value. Records in digital archives clearly have to be understood in these terms if they are to have some value beyond their current use, if they are to serve as future testimony to past processes and practices. Those who create, manage, and administer digital repositories are no less exempt from these concerns than their more traditional predecessors. Moreover, archivists will only be able to maintain their important roles as reference counselors and curators if they have some understanding of the historical issues implicit in their materials. This will also help assure that their repositories remain at least partially connected to the needs and cultures of all of their users, a position of civic responsibility that also has practical implications for their necessary support.

Private or "collecting" archives are no less exempt from these responsibilities and concerns than institutional or state repositories. One might imagine corporate archivists in those few firms that maintain research-oriented archives having little interest in these matters. "If someone wants to look at our documents, let them come" has certainly been an unwritten credo for many in the archival world. Yet rapid transformations can affect the corporate and institutional worlds as suddenly and unexpectedly as they affect the state. Institutional and corporate records may suddenly be of importance to those interested in the relationship between gender bias and productivity, efficiency and cultural diversity, mentalities or morals, and the ability of a firm or organization to retain an effective workforce.

The difference between repositories managed by those who understand the kinds of issues their records might be called on to address and archives managed solely by those focused on the internal order and technologies of their holdings might compare to the difference between history written by scholars who are archivally aware and that produced by those who are unable to read the archival grain. The question of provenance is central here. Provenance situates the record in the contexts of their creation without evaluating the relationships between these contexts and the kinds of questions scholars might want to ask of them.

Bridging the Archival Divide

It has never been the archivist's responsibility to provide a descriptive finding aid that is responsive to all of the questions of all of their users all of the time. Such a degree of responsiveness has always been well beyond the capacity of paper-based repositories, much less digital ones. Nor is the responsibility of historians to assure that the historical archives of the future can migrate to newer technologies, remain accessible, and contain the documentation needed for significant historical research.

We believe, however, that archivists and historians can work together to assure that the historical archives of the future are reasonably transparent in the nature, form, subjects, and origins of their materials. The challenges of technology have brought estrangement, but its constantly changing applications also offer some intriguing new possibilities for cooperation. One can imagine, for example, the extensive implementation of what might be called "parallel but linked" access systems, in which communities of scholars or scholarly associations construct their own standards or systems for assigning value to archival material, or otherwise layering them with particular kinds of scholarly historical understanding. In other words, one can imagine principles being deployed here that operate very much like those in "You Tube," where access to videos is determined not simply by specific categories of metadata but also through a parallel system of commentary contributed by users who rate the value of what they have seen. Historians and other users could play a similar role in developing and maintaining comprehensive interactive archival finding aids in which documents and funds are identified and evaluated by well-defined communities of users in terms of their importance to specific kinds of historical enquiry. This approach was considered at the University of Michigan in connection with its Vatican Archives Project, and recently some web oriented "archivists" like Tim O'Reilly and Peter Van Garderen have been exploring the idea in more systematic ways.[4] The Michigan initiative focused on providing a formal computer-based descriptive system for the archives of the Holy See using standard archival descriptive categories. In addition to the needs of the archive, however, the project also tried to understand and accommodate the information needs of the research community and to facilitate researchers' access to the records in terms of the kinds of questions they might bring to the documents.

When the Vatican project was initiated in the 1990s, the Archivio Segreto Vaticano still relied on traditional conceptions of provenance in determining systematic data categories and constructing the archival infrastructure of its holdings. In order to provide new, digitalized access to the Vatican materials, archivists working on the project, began to meet with scholars actually using the archives and discuss how they were approaching their topics. Many came from fields not closely associated with the history of the Holy See. As social and cultural historians, art historians, and students of political science and theory, their research interests were focused not so much on the institutional processes underlying the archives' formation and development as on those related to cultural, aesthetic, and social changes in the history of Catholicism: how, for instance, one could understand the identities of religious women in the nineteenth century, the nature of power relationships between colonial administration and indigenous populations, or the artistic patrimony of a particular church or shrine.

These kinds of questions were not readily researchable using the existing categories that identified and described the documents. Scholars more often stumbled upon the documentation they needed through the footnotes of other studies, rather than through a systematic examination of formal Vatican access tools. They then probed the same or similar sources in more depth, or in terms of their own research questions. In effect, these researchers were not so much searching for specific records as for the historical "voices" embedded in the documentation itself, to return to a nineteenth-century Rankean metaphor. These were more often "heard" by reading them against the "grain" of their bureaucratic contexts. To address this problem, the Vatican Project developed a system of identifying past research projects that had used particular kinds of documentation. Using these bibliographic links, "scope and content" notes were prepared to assist researchers in tracing earlier citations and made available on-line. By today's standards these were rather primitive efforts and rested on technologies that have long since been outdated. Still, they served to incorporate the breadth of scholarly interests in the ways these archives were accessed, and met an obvious and important scholarly need.

Digital or web-based access has clearly opened the possibility for developing similar kinds of parallel finding aids more broadly. In addition to the official registers prepared by the responsible archivists, scholars using materials could make their own contributions to interactive scope and content notes. These notes could also link to major bibliographic references or use the search capacities of a repository like JSTOR to find additional citations in scores of different works. In effect, scholars themselves could then participate in the processes of archival description. In the Vatican case again, bibliographies of work based on the Archivio Segreto holdings have been issued since 1962, organized according to the individual fonds that were used. These could easily be scanned into the archive's existing digitized access tools.[5]

Digitization allows for other access innovations as well. Internet-based social networking technologies like "Web 2.0," have the capacity to incorporate the experiences of researchers and archivists into the mix of more formal access descriptions. Annotations and even document "tags" to materials that researchers have used or archivists think are particularly interesting could readily become part of new interactive finding aids. So could longer comments from users. If readers can post their own reviews of books on Amazon.com, there is no reason why interactive finding aids cannot be put in place that allow researchers and archivists to report on their particular discoveries, note errors or problems with documents or files, or provide additional document references and citations.

If these innovations are developed as parallel aids in ways that preserve the authority of the official archival descriptions and are closely monitored by archivists, they would be of enormous value to historians. They also could enable the sharing of access information among quite broad communities of researchers as well.[6] The coming "Web 3.0" technology, the so-called "semantic" web, may also make it possible for a researcher simply to ask a question in a parallel finding aid that will be transformed through a battery of other reference tools, bibliographies, and word searches to produce a cluster of documentary "hits" that are presented with appropriate contextual information. However improbable this might seem at the moment, given the inherent complexity of both the technological challenge and archives themselves, such a system may well become commonplace in the future, providing the number of "hits" is actually manageable for the researcher.

What is most important about the possibilities of such interactive parallel finding aids in terms of the archival divide is that they require the active engagement of historians together with archivists to make them effective. Since the infrastructures of digital archives rest on technical archival methodologies, archivists can use them to post information about how these methodologies may have affected the ways different kinds of documents were prepared, accessed, or grouped. Historians and other scholars who use the materials can suggest the kinds of keywords or other searching categories they found particularly useful. Others can then expand these lists. While the technologies used to create digital archives do not accommodate historical categories or authorities, as we have seen, the frameworks of understanding in all of history's many new and traditional forms could still become an integral element of such parallel descriptive systems and guide researchers more effectively through complex digital materials.

Different kinds of interactive finding aids based on specific historical interests could also be developed by archivists and historians who best understand those subjects, especially in identity archives or other more focused public archives or collecting institutions. Such "history-based" access systems could rest on understandings of specific disciplinary languages, conceptualizations, and literatures. If scholars were willing to share their interests in an on-line finding aid, they could be particularly useful to other scholars working in the same or similar areas. As interests and conceptualizations shifted over time, along with disciplinary boundaries themselves, these notes could easily be augmented or modified by new users. The construction and maintenance of these parallel systems would then become the responsibility primarily of their communities of scholarly users whose work was based on particular sets of archival holdings or derived from particular approaches to archives more generally. In this way, historians and other scholars could again be drawn into historiographical descriptive processes that professional records managers and many archivists have, of necessity, abandoned.

In our view, this would constitute a major shift in the relationship between historians and archivists. To contribute most effectively in these parallel systems, historians would have to learn more about the fundamental archival relationship between record and activity that continues to center the ways archivists process the past. They would need to be attentive to the complexities of appraisal, cataloging, classification, and preservation, whether these are hidden in digital archives or more readily perceptible in their paper-based predecessors. Communities of scholars would need to take on a much larger role in the processes of providing archival access. In effect, this would also represent a fundamental shift in how historians see their connection to archival repositories. Given the extraordinary complexities of historical research in the twenty-first century, however, and the extraordinary demands on the institutions that hold the archival record, we think this level of engagement by scholars in archival descriptive processes will not only be essential to the conduct of future historical research, but also, we would predict, intellectually quite rewarding.

For their part, curators of these collections will have somehow to reengage with the scholarly interests of their users if they are to understand the full capacities of their vast holdings and continue their traditional roles as research counselors and guides. Few historians would deny the value (and pleasures) of their interactions with knowledgeable archivists in archival reading rooms of every sort and in every conceivable locality. While historical documentation in the future may be entirely in digital form and accessible from great distances, the archivist will still have a vital role to play in the creation of historical knowledge. In this and other ways, the archival divide remains a set of challenges that archivists and historians must both work to overcome.

NOTES

Introduction

1. Jacques Derrida, *Mal d'archive: Une impression freudienne* (Paris: Éditions Galilée, 1995), published in English as *Archive Fever: A Freudian Impression* (Chicago: University of Chicago Press, 1996).

Chapter 1

1. Leonard Krieger, *Ranke: The Meaning of History* (Chicago: University of Chicago Press, 1977), 5.
2. Ibid., 4.
3. See the extensive discussion in Fritz Ringer, *Decline of the German Mandarins: The German Academic Community, 1890–1933* (Cambridge, Mass.: Harvard University Press, 1969).
4. As Moses Finley has observed in a skeptical piece about Ranke, Thucydides relied on oral testimony and traditions but was also deeply committed to getting his facts right, as much as Ranke. Thucydides wrote with authority only about what he quite self-consciously believed was true. His own stories were verifiable by others. See Moses Finley, *Ancient History: Evidence and Models* (London: Chatto and Windus, 1985), 48 ff. and his "Myth, Memory, and History," *History and Theory* 4:3 (1965): 281–302. For a more extended discussion of the continuities between Ranke and his predecessors, see J. G. A. Pocock, "The Origins of the Study of the Past: A Comparative Approach," *Comparative Studies in Society and History* 4:2 (1962): 209–46.
5. *Encyclopédie, ou, Dictionnaire raisonné des sciences, des arts et des métiers* [electronic resource] (Geneva, Paris, Neufchatel, 1754–72), 220–21, 223.
6. See, e.g., Ernst Posner, *Archives in the Ancient World* (Cambridge, Mass.: Harvard University Press, 1972).
7. On the reasons for creating records, see esp. James O'Toole and Richard Cox, *Understanding Archives and Manuscripts* (Chicago: Society of American Archivists, 2006), 1–43.
8. See, e.g., M. Clanchy, *From Memory to Written Record: England, 1066–1307* (London: Edward Arnold, 1979); Ernst Posner, *American State Archives* (Chicago: University of Chicago Press, 1964); and esp. Thomas Osborne, "The Ordinariness of the Archive," *History of the Human Sciences* 12:2 (1999): 51–64.
9. Anthony Grafton, *Forgers and Critics: Creativity and Duplicity in Western Scholarship* (Princeton: Princeton University Press, 1990), 116.
10. Jean Mabillon, *De re diplomatica* (Paris, 1681). The full title of this important work is *De re diplomatic libri vi. in quibus quidquid ad veterum instrumentorum antiquitatem, materiam, scripturam, & stilum; quidquid ad sigilla, monogrammata, subscriptiones, ae notas chronologicas;*

quidquid inde ad antiquariam, historicam, forensemque disciplinam pertinet, explicatur & illustratur. Accedvnt Commentarius de antiquis regum Francorum palatiis. Veterum scripturarum varia specimina, tabulis LX comprehensa. Nova ducentorum, & amplius, monumentorum collectio. Operâ & studio domni Johannis Mabillon . . . (Luteciæ Parisiorum, sumtibus # L. Billaine, 1681).

11. See Michel Duchein, "The History of European Archives and the Development of the Archival Profession in Europe," *American Archivist* 55 (Winter 1992): 16. See also Elizabeth Eisenstein, *The Printing Press as an Agent of Change* (Cambridge: Cambridge University Press, 1979), 1:80–88, 113–26.

12. Ibid.

13. Francis X. Blouin, Jr., General Editor, with Leonard Coombs, Elizabeth Yakel, Claudia Carlen, and Katherine J. Gill, *Vatican Archives: An Inventory and Guide to the Historical Documentation of the Holy See* (New York: Oxford University Press, 1998), xvi–xxi.

14. In addition to Duchein, "History of European Archives," see Jennifer Milligan, "The Problem of *Publicité* in the Archives of Second Empire France," in *Archives, Documentation, and Institutions of Social Memory*, ed. Francis X. Blouin, Jr. and William G. Rosenberg (Ann Arbor: University of Michigan Press, 2006), 20–36.

15. Duchein, "History of European Archives," 14–25.

16. Lara Moore, "Restoring Order: The École des Chartes and the Organization of Archives and Libraries in France, 1820–1870" (Ph.D. diss., Stanford University, 2001). See also Eric Ketelaar, "Muller, Feith and Fruin," in *The Archival Image: Collected Essays*, ed. Eric Ketelaar (Kilversum: Verloren, 1997), esp. 45.

17. See Beatrice Bartlett, "Qing Statesmen, Archivists, and Historians, and the Question of Memory," in Blouin and Rosenberg, *Archives*, 417–26. See also Duchein, "History of European Archives," 22.

18. F. Bonnie Smith, "Gender and the Practices of Scientific History: The Seminar and Archival Research in the Nineteenth Century," *American Historical Review* 100:4 (1995): 1150–76.

19. Leopold von Ranke, *The Secret of World History: Selected Writings on the Art and Science of History*, ed. and trans. Roger Wines (New York: Fordham University Press, 1981).

20. Leopold von Ranke, "Autobiography," in ibid., 50, 259. Leonard Krieger suggests there was even a sexual quality in Ranke's involvement with his sources. His close reading of Ranke's letters has unearthed some telling passages, including allusions to his lust for data and his communion with his materials. In his forties, Ranke wrote of a closed archive, "It is still absolutely a virgin. I long for the moment I shall have access to her and make my declaration of love, whether she is pretty or not." Twenty years later, he could still affirm, "I study the archives with the greatest imaginable pleasure. There is some gleam of youth or rather of youthfulness in these studies, where one always learns something new and important, with the idea of communicating it to the world—a sentiment which makes one forget a little that one is getting old." See Krieger, *Ranke*, citing *Briefwerk*, 441.

21. Jules Michelet, *Histoire de France* (Paris, 1833, 1869) from his *Oeuvres complètes*, ed. R. Casanova (Paris, 1974), 4:613–14, 736–27, as cited and translated by Carolyn Steedman in her critical essay "The Space of Memory: In an Archive," *History of the Human Sciences* 11:4 (1998): 68. See also Steedman's "Archival Methods" in *Research Methods for English Studies*, ed. Gabriele Griffin (Edinburgh: Edinburgh University Press, 2005), 21–24.

22. Benedict Anderson, *Imagined Communities* (New York and London: Verso, 1991 [1983]), 198.

23. Stephen J. Milner, "Partial Readings: Addressing a Renaissance Archive," *History and the Human Sciences* 12:2 (1999): 101–2.

24. The seminal texts are E. Hobsbawn and Terence Rangers, eds., *The Invention of Tradition* (Cambridge: Cambridge University Press, 1984), and Anderson, *Imagined Communities*.

25. Herbert Baxter Adams, "Special Methods of Historical Study," as quoted in Peter Novick, *That Noble Dream: The "Objectivity Question" and the American Historical Profession* (New York and Cambridge: Cambridge University Press, 1988), 33. See also Robert Weibe, *The Search for Order, 1877–1920* (New York: Hill and Wang, 1967).

26. Owen Chadwick, *Catholicism and History: The Opening of the Vatican Archives* (Cambridge: Cambridge University Press, 1978), 97 ff.

27. Letter of August 18, 1883, in *Acta Apostolica Sedes III*, 264–65, as quoted in Chadwick, *Catholicism and History*, 101–3.

28. Ludwig von Pastor, *The History of the Popes from the Close of the Middle Ages. Drawn from the Secret Archives of the Vatican and Other Original Sources*, 40 vols. (London: J. Hodges, 1891–1953).

29. Indeed, Guizot was a passionate and devoted historian and threw himself into the archives after being overthrown as French premier in 1848. Among his many achievements was his six-volume *History of the English Revolution (1826–56)* and his unfinished *General History of Civilization in Modern Europe*, which centers, not surprisingly, on France.

30. Alfred D. Chandler, *The Visible Hand: The Managerial Revolution in American Business* (Cambridge, Mass.: Harvard University Press, 1977).

31. S. Muller, J. A. Feith, and R. Fruin, *Manual for the Arrangement and Description of Archives*, 2d ed., trans. Arthur H. Leavitt (Chicago: Society of American Archivists, 2003), drawn up by direction of the Netherlands Association of Archivists.

32. See the discussion in Terry Cook, "Archives in the Post-Custodial World: Interaction of Archival Theory and Practice since the Publication of the Dutch Manual in 1898," Paper presented at the XIII International Congress on Archives, Beijing, 1996; P. J. Horsman, F. C. J. Ketelaar, T. H. P. M. Thomassen, eds., *Tekst en Context van de Handleiding voor het Ordenen en Beschrijven van Archieven van 1898* (Hilversum: Verloren, 1998).

33. Chandler, *Visible Hand*.

34. Nancy Bartlett, "*Réspect des Fonds*: The Origins of the Modern Archival Principle of Provenance," in *Bibliographical Foundations of French Historical Studies*, ed. Lawrence J. McCrank (New York: Haworth Press, 1992), 107–15.

35. See Jo Anne Yates, *Control through Communication: The Rise of System in American Management* (Baltimore: Johns Hopkins University Press, 1989).

Chapter 2

1. See Walter Whitehill, *Independent Historical Societies: An Enquiry into their Research and Publication Functions and Their Financial Future* (Boston: Boston Athenaeum, distributed by Harvard University Press, 1962).

2. An excellent discussion is in Gary Nash, *First City: Philadelphia and the Forging of Historical Memory* (Philadelphia: University of Pennsylvania Press, 2002). An example of this pervasive kind of local history close to the heart of one of us is John P. Farrow, *History of Islesborough Maine* (Bangor, Maine: Thomas Burr, 1893), and continued by the Islesboro Historical Society's volume *History of Islesboro, Maine, 1893–1983* (Islesboro, Maine: Islesboro Historical Society, 1984). The first volume centers almost entirely on prominent local families, ranked in terms of importance by their wealth and their contributions to local welfare. The new version is organized around important community activities and the families involved in them, but it still lists only names in its sixteen-page index. Here, a clear vision of robust individualism building a free, generous, and solid community is quite clear, although unspoken, in both volumes.

3. See, e.g., the interesting discussion on the founding of the Mississippi State Archives in Patricia Galloway, *Practicing Ethnohistory: Mining Archives, Hearing Testimony, Constructing Narrative* (Lincoln: University of Nebraska Press, 2006), 58–60.

4. See Bonnie Smith, "Gender and the Practices of Scientific History: The Seminar and Archival Research in the 19th Century," *American Historical Review* 100:4 (1995): 1150–76.

5. Alfred D. Chandler, *The Visible Hand: The Managerial Revolution in American Business* (Cambridge, Mass.: Harvard University Press, 1977); Jo Anne Yates, *Control Through Communication: The Rise of System in American Management* (Baltimore: Johns Hopkins University Press, 1989).

6. A full discussion can be found in Jennifer Milligan, "The Problem of *Publicité* in the Archives of Second Empire France," in *Archives, Documentation, and Institutions of Social Memory*, ed.

Francis X. Blouin, Jr. and William G. Rosenberg (Ann Arbor: University of Michigan Press, 2006), 20–35.

7. Quoted in Victor Gondos, Jr., *J. Franklin Jameson and the Birth of the National Archives, 1906–1926* (Philadelphia: University of Pennsylvania Press, 1981), 11.

8. Ibid.

9. Ibid.

10. See Timothy Walch, ed., *Guardian of Heritage: Essays on the History of the National Archives* (Washington, D.C.: National Archives and Records Administration, 1985), 17; Gondos, *Jameson*, 17.

11. Gondos, *Jameson*, 15.

12. Kevin Guthrie, *The New York Historical Society: Lessons from One Nonprofit's Long Struggle for Survival* (San Francisco: Jossey-Bass, 1996), esp. 12–13.

13. Ole Kolsrud, "The Evolution of Basic Appraisal Principles," *American Archivist* 55 (1992): 30.

14. Hilary Jenkinson, *A Manual of Archive Administration* (Oxford: Oxford University Press, 1922; rev. ed., London: P. Lund Humphries, 1937). See also Margaret Procter, "Consolidation and Separation: British Archives and American Historians at the Turn of the Twentieth Century," *Archival Science* 6:3–4 (2006): 361–79.

15. Jenkinson, *Manual*, 123–24.

16. Mark A. Greene and Dennis Meisner, "More Product, Less Processing: Revamping Traditional Archival Processing," *American Archivist* 68:2 (2005): 208–63.

17. Frank Boles and Mark A. Greene, "Et Tu Schellenberg? Thoughts on the Dagger of American Appraisal Theory," *American Archivist* 59:3 (1996): 298–311.

18. Donald McCoy, *The National Archives: America's Ministry of Documents, 1934–1968* (Chapel Hill: University of North Carolina Press, 1978), 72.

19. *Fourth Annual Report of the Archivist of the United States* (Washington, D.C.: National Archives, 1939), 5, cited in H. G. Jones, *The Records of a Nation: Their Management, Preservation, and Use* (New York: Atheneum, 1969), 18.

20. Milton O. Gustafson, "The Empty Shrine: The Transfer of the Declaration of Independence and the Constitution to the National Archives," *American Archivist* 39:3 (1976): 271–85; James M. O'Toole, "Between Veneration and Loathing: Loving and Hating Documents," in Blouin and Rosenberg, *Archives*, 44–45.

21. Jones, *Records of a Nation*, 39.

22. J. Franklin Jameson, *The American Historian's Raw Materials; An Address by J. Franklin Jameson . . . With the Presentation and Other Exercises at the Dedication of the William L. Clements Library of Americana, June 15, 1923* (Ann Arbor, Mich.: William Clements Library, 1923), 48. See also Randall Jimerson, "American Historians and European Archival Theory: The Collaboration of J. F. Jameson and Waldo G. Leland," *Archival Science* 6:3–4 (2006): 299–312.

23. *Ninth Annual Report of the Archivist of the United States* (Washington, D.C.: National Archives, 1944), as cited in Jones, *Records of a Nation*, 30.

24. Jones, *Record of a Nation*, 32.

25. David Lowenthal, "Archives, Heritage, and History," in Blouin and Rosenberg, *Archives*, 195.

26. P. C. Brooks, "Current Aspects of Records Administration: The Archivists' Concern in Records Administration," *American Archivist* 6:3 (1943): 164.

27. Hilary Jenkinson, "British Archives and the War," *American Archivist* 7:1 (1944): 1–17.

28. Editorial entitled "A Proposed Model Act to Create a State Department of Archives and History," *American Archivist* 7:2 (1944): 130–33.

29. Paul Lewinson, "The Archives of Labor," *American Archivist* 17:1 (1954): 19–25.

30. Fritz Epstein, "Washington Research Opportunities in the Period of World War II," *American Archivist* 17:2 (1954): 225–37.

31. Oliver W. Holmes, "Some Reflections on Business Archives in the United States," *American Archivist* 17:4 (1954): 291–304; Eldon Scott Cohen, "French Archives in Indochina," *American Archivist* 17:4 (1954): 313–17; Seymour V. Connor, "Legal Materials as Sources of History," *American Archivist* 23:2 (1960): 157–67.

32. See, e.g., Thornton W. Mitchell, ed., *Norton on Archives: The Writings of Margaret Cross Norton on Archival & Records Management* (Carbondale: Southern Illinois University Press, 1975); Theodore Schellenberg, *Modern Archives: Principles and Techniques* (Chicago: University of Chicago Press, 1956), and Schellenberg's *The Appraisal of Modern Public Records* (Washington, D.C.: U.S. Govt. Printing Office, 1956).

33. E.g., Jacques Barzun and Henry Graff, *The Modern Researcher* (New York: Harcourt Brace, 1957), a popular book published in several subsequent editions over many years; Marc Bloch, *The Historian's Craft* (New York: Knopf, 1953); Louis Gottschalk, *Understanding History: A Primer of Historical Method* (New York: Knopf, 1969).

34. See, e.g., F. B. Evans, "Archivists and Records Managers: Variations on a Theme," *American Archivist* 30 (1967): 45–58.

35. *Final Report of the Joint AHA–OAH Ad Hoc Committee to Investigate the Charges against the Franklin D. Roosevelt Library and Related Matters* (Washington, D.C.: American Historical Association, 1970). See also Francis X. Blouin, Jr., "The Two Dimensions of Professional Service: A Reflection on the Life of Robert M. Warner," *American Archivist* 70:2 (2007): 405.

36. Robert M. Warner Papers, Bentley Historical Library, University of Michigan, box 29, files: AHA/OAH/SAA.

37. Robert M. Warner Papers, loc cit.

38. F. Gerald Ham, "Archival Strategies for the Post-Custodial Era," *American Archivist* 44:3 (1981): 207–16. This article was among the first to predict the importance of standardization for archival practice.

39. See Frank G. Burke, *Research and the Manuscript Tradition* (Chicago: Society of American Archivists and Scarecrow Press, 1997), and his "The Future Course of Archival Theory in the United States," *American Archivist* 44:1 (1982): 40–46. See also Elizabeth Lockwood, "'Imponderable Matters': The Influence of New Trends in History on Appraisal at the National Archives," *American Archivist* 53:3 (1990): 394–405.

40. Lester J. Cappon, "What, Then, Is There to Theorize About?" *American Archivist* 45:1 (1982): 23.

41. Richard J. Cox, ed., *Lester J. Cappon and the Relationship of History, Archives, and Scholarship in the Golden Age of Archival Theory* (Chicago: Society of American Archivists, 2004).

42. See, esp., "The Society of American Archivists: Description and Brief History" (Chicago: Society of American Archivists, 2003), as cited on the SAA Website <http://www2.archivists.org/about/introduction-to-saa. Hans Booms, "Society and the Formation of a Documentary Heritage: Issues in the Appraisal of Archival Sources," *Archivaria* 24 (Summer 1987): 69–197; and Terry Cook, "An Archival Revolution: W. Kaye Lamb and the Transformation of the Archival Profession," *Archivaria* 60 (Fall 2005): 185–234. For an overview of the evolution of appraisal concepts, see Cook's "Macroappraisal in Theory and Practice: Origins, Characteristics, and Implementation in Canada, 1950–2000," *Archival Science* 5:2–4 (2005): 101–61.

43. Compare, e.g., changes in the language of the reports from the New York State Archives. In the 1984 report the emphasis was on "historical records," a term used throughout. See *Toward a Usable Past: Historical Records in the Empire State: A Report to the Governor and Citizens of New York by the State Historical Records Advisory Board, January, 1984* (Albany, N.Y., 1984). In the 1988 report, the language shifts to a broader consideration of "research resources" of "enduring" value. See *Our Memory at Risk: Preserving New York's Unique Research Resources: A Report and Recommendations to the Citizens of New York by the New York Document Conservation Advisory Council* (Albany, N.Y., 1988).

44. Terry Cook, "What Is Past Is Prologue: A History of Archival Ideas Since 1898, and the Future Paradigm Shift," *Archivaria* 43 (1997): 17–63.

Chapter 3

1. See Meyer Fishbein, "The 'Traditional' Archivist and the Appraisal of Machine Readable Records," in *Archivists and Machine-readable Records: Proceedings of the Conference on Archival*

Management of Machine-Readable Records, February 7–10, 1979, ed. Carolyn L. Geda, Erik W. Austin, Francis X. Blouin, Jr. (Chicago: Society of American Archivists, 1980), 56–61.

2. See "About ICPSR," at the website of the Inter-University Consortium for Political and Social Research, <http://www.icpsr.umich.edu>.

3. Richard J. Cox, *Archives and Archivists in the Information Age* (New York and London: Neal-Schuman, 2005), 211.

4. Margaret L. Hedstrom, *Archives and Manuscripts: Machine-readable Records* (Chicago: Society of American Archivists, 1984); David Bearman, ed., *Archival Management of Electronic Records* (Pittsburgh: Archives & Museum Informatics, 1991).

5. Among the first articles to focus on the importance of standardization for archival practice was F. Gerald Ham, "The Archival Edge: Archival Strategies for the Post-Custodial Era," *American Archivist* 44:3 (Fall 1981): 207–16.

6. Frank G. Burke, *Research and the Manuscript Tradition* (Chicago: Society of American Archivists, 1997), 93. This quotation is from a 1941 manual on archival practice prepared by the National Archives and Records Service.

7. Ibid., 100.

8. Ibid., 100–101.

9. For a full discussion, see Lyn M. Martin, "Viewing the Field: A Literature Review and Survey of the U.S. MARC-AMC in U.S. Academic Libraries," *American Archivist* 57:3 (Summer 1994): 482–97. See also David Bearman, *Towards National Information Systems for Archives and Manuscript Repositories: The National Information Systems Task Force (NISTF) Papers, 1981–1984* (Chicago: Society of American Archivists, 1987). Canadian Archivists were also working on this problem at the time. See Bureau of Canadian Archivists, *Toward Descriptive Standards: Report and Recommendations of the Canadian Working Group on Archival Descriptive Standards* (Ottawa: Bureau of Canadian Archivists, 1985).

10. See, e.g., Steven Hensen, *Archives, Personal Papers, and Manuscripts: A Cataloging Manual for Archival Repositories, Historical Societies, and Manuscript Libraries* (Chicago: Society of American Archivists, 1989); Avra Michelson, "Description and Reference in the Age of Automation," *American Archivist* 50:2 (Spring 1987): 192–208.

11. Randall K. Berry, "Development of the Encoded Archival Description DTD" (Washington, D.C., 2002) at <http://www.loc.gov> (the EAD official site). See also the two volumes of *American Archivist* that were devoted to a discussion of EAD: "Encoded Archival Description: Context and Theory," 60:3 (Summer 1997), and "Encoded Archival Description: Case Studies," 60:4 (Fall 1997).

12. Ibid.

13. This project was generously funded by the Andrew E. Mellon Foundation, the National Endowment for the Humanities, and the Earhart Foundation.

14. Daniel Pitti, "Encoded Archival Description: The Development of an Encoding Standard for Archival Finding Aids," *American Archivist* 60:3 (Summer 1997): 268–83.

15. David Bearman, "Archives and Manuscripts Control with Bibliographic Utilities: Challenges and Opportunities," *American Archivist* 52:1 (Winter 1989): 26–39; Adrian Cunningham, "Harnessing the Power of Provenance in Archival Description: An Australian Perspective on the Development of the Second Edition of ISAAR(CPF)," in *Respect for Authority: Authority Control, Context Control, and Archival Description*, ed. Jean Dryden (forthcoming). In some respects, these ideas were not entirely new, since several Australian archivists had been promoting similar ideas in ways not related to the new digital technologies for many years. See, e.g., Ian Maclean, "An Analysis of Jenkinson's 'Manual of Archive Administration' in the Light of Australian Experience," in *Essays in Memory of Sir Hilary Jenkinson*, ed. A. E. J. Hollander (Chichester: Moore and Tillyer, 1962), 128–52; and Peter J. Scott, "The Record Group Concept: A Case for Abandonment," *American Archivist* 29:4 (October 1966): 493–504, both reprinted in Peter Biskup et al., ed., *Debates and Discourses: Selected Australian Writings on Archival Theory 1951–1990* (Canberra: Australian Society of Archivists, 1995).

16. David Bearman, "Record Keeping Systems," *Archivaria* 36 (1993): 35.

17. David Bearman, "Archival Principles and the Electronic Office," in *Information Handling in Offices and Archives*, ed. Angelika Menne-Haritz (Munchen: Saur, 1993), 177–99.

18. International Council on Archives, *International Standard Archival Authority Record for Corporate Bodies, Persons and Families (ISAAR(CPF))*, 2d ed. (Paris: International Council on Archives, 2004). See also International Council on Archives, *International Standard on Activities/Functions of Corporate Bodies (ISAF)* (Paris: International Council on Archives, 2007).

19. See, e.g., the discussion in Anne Gilliland-Swetland, "Testing Our Truths: Delineating the Parameters of the Authentic Archival Electronic Record," *American Archivist* 65:2 (Fall/Winter 2002): 196–215; Francis X. Blouin, Jr., "A Framework for a Consideration of Diplomatics in the Electronic Environment," *American Archivist* 59:4 (Fall 1996): 466–79.

20. Terry Eastwood, "Introduction," in Luciana Duranti, Terry Eastwood, and Heather MacNeil, *Preservation of the Integrity of Electronic Records* (Dordrecht: Kluwer Academic, 2002), 1. See also Luciana Duranti, ed., *The InterPARES Project: The Long-term Preservation of Authentic Electronic Records (Findings of the InterPARES Project)* (San Miniato: Archilab, 2005); and "Reflections on InterPARES 2: The InterPARES 2 Project (2002–2007): An Overview," *Archivaria* 64 (2007): 113–21. See also Eastwood, "Introduction," in Duranti, Eastwood, and MacNeil, *Preservation*.

21. See Duranti, Eastwood, and MacNeil, *Preservation*, esp. 35.

22. Ibid., 17.

23. See http://nagara.org/displaycommon.cfm?an=1&subarticlenbr=1

24. Ibid.

25. Ibid.

26. See, e.g., Michael S. Hindus, Theodore M. Hammett, Barbara M. Hobson, *Massachusetts Superior Court Files, 1859–1959: An Analysis and a Plan for Action* (Boston: G. K. Hall, 1980); and the elaborations by David Bearman, "Archival Methods," *Archives and Museum Informatics Technical Report* 3:1 (Pittsburgh: Archives and Museum Informatics, 1989).

27. E.g., Robert W. Lovett, "The Appraisal of Older Business Records," *American Archivist* 39:1 (1976): 15–20; Francis X. Blouin, Jr., "A New Perspective on the Appraisal of Business Records," *American Archivist* 4:3 (1979): 312–20; Ralph M. Hower, "Problems and Opportunities in the Field of Business History," *Bulletin of the Business Historical Society* 15 (1941): 17–26; J. Stanley Kimmitt and Richard A. Baker, eds., *Proceedings: Conference on the Research Use and Disposition of Senators' Papers* (Washington, D.C.: Govt. Printing Office, 1978); Patricia Aronsson, "Appraisal of Twentieth Century Congressional Collections," in *Archival Choices: Managing the Historical Record in an Age of Abundance*, ed. Nancy Peace (Boston: Heath, 1984); Paul Chestnut, "Appraising the Papers of State Legislators," *American Archivist* 48:2 (1985): 159–72; Jo Anne Yates, "Internal Communications Systems in American Business Structures: A Framework to Aid Appraisal," *American Archivist* 48:2 (1985): 141–58; Joan K. Haas, Helen Willa Samuels, and Barbara Trippel Simmons, *Appraising the Records of Modern Science and Technology: A Guide* (Chicago: Society of American Archivists, 1985); Candace Loewen, "From Human Neglect to Planetary Survival: New Approaches to the Appraisal of Environmental Records," *Archivaria* 33 (1991–92): 87–103; Mary Ann Pylypchuk "A Documentation Approach to Aboriginal Archives," *Archivaria* 33 (1991–92): 117–24.

28. See, esp., Frank Boles in association with Julia Marks Young, *Archival Appraisal* (New York: Neal-Schuman Publishers, 1991); Frank Boles and Julia Marks Young, "Exploring the Black Box: The Appraisal of University Administrative Records," *American Archivist* 48 (Spring 1985): 212–40; and Frank Boles, "Mix Two Parts Interest to One Part Information and Appraise Until Done: Understanding Contemporary Record Selection," *American Archivist* 50 (Summer 1987): 356–68. See also Barbara Craig, *Archival Appraisal: Theory and Practice* (Munich: K. G. Saur, 2004). The "appraisal debate" literature is extensive. Among the many notable articles are Frank Boles and Mark A. Green, "'Et tu Schellenberg?' Thoughts on the Dagger of American Appraisal Theory," *American Archivist* 59:3 (1996): 298–310; Luciana Duranti, "The Concept of Appraisal and Archival Theory," *American Archivist* 57:2 (1994): 328–45; Terry Eastwood, "How Goes It with Appraisal," *Archivaria* 36 (1993): 111–21; and Terry Eastwood, "Towards a Social Theory of Appraisal," in *The Canadian Archival Imagination:*

Essays in Honour of Hugh Taylor, ed. Barbara Craig (Ottawa: Association of Canadian Archivists, 1992), 71–89; Mark Greene, "'The Surest Proof': A Utilitarian Approach to Appraisal," *Archivaria* 45 (1998): 127–69; Elizabeth Lockwood, "'Imponderable Matters': The Influence of New Trends in History on Appraisal at the National Archives," *American Archivist* 53:3 (1990): 394–405; Barbara Craig, "Doing Archival Appraisal in Canada: Results from a Postal Survey of Practitioners' Experiences, Practices, and Opinions," *Archivaria* 64 (2007): 1–46; and Verne Harris, "Postmodernism and Archival Appraisal: Seven Theses," in *Archives and Justice* ed. Verne Harris (Chicago, Society of American Archivists, 2007): 101–106.

Chapter 4

1. Anthony Grafton, *The Footnote: A Curious History* (Cambridge, Mass.: Harvard University Press, 1997). The citation to the authority of the magistrate's decrees is as old as the *arkheion* itself, in its earliest Greek and Roman forms as repositories of the law.

2. Ibid., 204–5, 221.

3. S. Shapin, *A Social History of Truth* (Chicago and London: University of Chicago Press, 1994). This epistemological issue is the subject of a substantial literature, especially in the American journal *History and Theory*. See also the important contributions by Richard Campbell, *Truth and Historicity* (New York and Oxford: Oxford University Press, 1992); Donald Davidson, *Inquiries into Truth and Interpretation* (New York and Oxford: Oxford University Press, 1984); Michel de Certeau, *L'Écriture de l'histoire* (Paris: Gallimard, 1975, English ed., New York: Columbia University Press, 1988); and Mary Poovey, *A History of the Modern Fact* (Chicago and London: University of Chicago Press, 1998).

4. Marc Bloch, *The Historians Craft* (New York: Knopf, 1953).

5. See Carole Fink, *Marc Bloch: A Life in History* (New York and Cambridge: Cambridge University Press, 1989).

6. Fernand Braudel, "L'Histoire et les sciences sociales: La *Longue Durée*," *Annales. E.S.C.*, 4 (1958): 725–53. The English translation is his *On History*, trans. Sarah Matthews (Chicago: University of Chicago Press, 1980), 25–55. Citations are to this version.

7. Ibid., 25–27.

8. Ibid., 43.

9. Ibid., 39.

10. Patrick H. Hutton, *History as an Art of Memory* (Hanover, N.H.: University Press of New England, 1993), xiv.

11. Published in English as *The Order of Things: An Archeology of the Human Sciences* (London: Tavistock, 1970).

12. Theodor Adorno, *The Jargon of Authenticity* (Evanston, Ill.: Northwestern University Press, 1973); Clifford Geertz, *The Interpretation of Cultures: Selected Essays* (New York: Basic Books, 1973); Jürgen Habermas, *Technik und Wissenschaft als "Ideologie"* (Frankfurt: Suhrkamp, 1968), *On the Logic of the Social Sciences* (Cambridge, Mass.: Harvard University Press, 1988), *The Structural Transformation of the Public Sphere* (Cambridge, Mass.: Harvard University Press, 1989); Hayden White's essays are collected in *Tropics of Discourse: Essays in Cultural Criticism* (Baltimore: Johns Hopkins University Press, 1985), and *The Content of the Form: Narrative Discourse and Historical Representation* (Baltimore: Johns Hopkins University Press, 1987).

13. Leopold Haimson, "The Problem of Social Stability in Urban Russia, 1905–17," *Slavic Review* 23:4 (December 1964): 619–42 and 24:1 (March 1967): 1–22; E. P. Thompson, *The Making of the English Working Class* (New York: Vintage, 1963).

14. Francis Fukuyama, *The End of History and the Last Man* (New York: Free Press, 1992).

15. For extended discussions, some quite critical, see Peter Stearns, "Social History Update: Encountering Postmodernism," *Journal of Social History* 24:2 (Winter 1990): 449–52; James A. Henretta, "Social History as Lived and Written," *American Historical Review* 84:5 (1979): 1293–1322; Christopher Lloyd, "The Methodologies of Social History: A Critical Survey and

Defense of Structuralism," *History and Theory* 30:2 (1991): 180-219; and the contributions by Richard T. Vann, "The Rhetoric of Social History," and Michelle Perrot, "The Strengths and Weaknesses of French Social History," to the *Journal of Social History* 10 (1976), 221-36; 166–77.

16. Hayden White, *Metahistory: The Historical Imagination in Nineteenth Century Europe* (Baltimore: Johns Hopkins University Press, 1973).

17. See E. J. Hobsbawm, *Labouring Men* (London: Weidenfeld and Nicolson, 1964), *Bandits* (London and New York: Delacorte Press, 1969), and with George Rude, *Captain* Swing (London and New York: Pantheon, 1968); Michelle Perrot, *Les Ouvriers en grève, 1871–1890* (Paris: Mouton, 1974); Benedict Anderson, *Imagined Communities* (London: Verso, 1983); and Frederic Jameson, *The Political Unconscious* (Ithaca, N.Y.: Cornell University Press, 1981), among other works.

18. Robert Berkhofer, *Beyond the Great Story* (Cambridge, Mass.: Harvard University Press, 1995).

19. See, e.g., Geertz, *The Interpretation of Cultures*; Mary Douglas, *Cultural Bias* (London: Royal Anthropological Institute, 1978); Victor Turner, *Dramas Fields and Metaphors: Symbolic Action in Human Society* (Ithaca, N.Y.: Cornell University Press, 1974); and Victor Turner and Edward Bruner, eds., *The Anthropology of Experience* (Urbana: University of Illinois Press, 1986).

20. James C. Scott, *Domination and the Arts of Resistance: Hidden Transcripts* (New Haven: Yale University Press, 1990). See also, Kerwin Lee Klein, "In Search of Narrative Mastery: Postmodernism and the People without History," *History and Theory* 34:4 (1995): 275–98.

21. See Karl Polanyi, *The Great Transformation* (Boston: Beacon Press, 1957).

22. Berkhofer, *Beyond the Great Story*, 2–3. See also the discussion in Geoff Eley, *The Crooked Line: From Cultural History to the History of Society* (Ann Arbor: University of Michigan Press, 2005).

23. Lawrence Stone, "History and Postmodernism," *Past and Present* (May 1991), as reprinted in Keith Jenkins, ed., *The Postmodern History Reader* (London and New York: Routledge, 1997), 242–43.

24. Ibid.

25. See, esp., among the many studies Alessandro Ferrara, *Modernity and Authenticity: A Study of the Social and Ethical Thought of Jean-Jacques Rousseau* (Albany: State University of New York, 1993), 112 ff., and his *Reflective Authenticity: Rethinking the Project of Modernity* (London and New York: Routledge, 1998).

26. M. Foucault, *The Archeology of Knowledge* (London: Tavistock, 1972), *Discipline and Punish* (New York: Pantheon, 1977), *Power/Knowledge*, ed. C. Gordon (New York: Pantheon, 1980), and the discussions in G. Burchell, ed., *The Foucault Effect: Studies in Governmentality* (Chicago: University of Chicago Press, 1991).

27. Bruce Lincoln, *Authority: Construction and Corrosion* (Chicago: University of Chicago Press, 1994), 1–3.

28. *Postmodern History Reader*, 107.

29. Ibid., 85.

30. Gertrude Himmelfarb, "Telling It as You Like It," *Times Literary Supplement*, October 16, 1992, 14–15. Himmelfarb's and Fox-Genovese's passion was echoed at the time in many places in and outside of print. See, e.g., Perez Zagorin, "Historiography and Postmodernism: Reconsiderations," and the rejoinder by F. R. Ankersmit, *History and Theory* 29:3 (1990): 263–96.

31. Joan W. Scott, "Gender: A Useful Category of Historical Analysis," *American Historical Review* 91:5 (1986): 1053–75.

32. See, e.g., Gerda Lerner's discussion about the exclusion of material on gender in traditional archives in her *The Creation of Feminist Consciousness: From the Middle Ages to Eighteen Seventy* (New York: Oxford University Press, 1993). See also Berkhofer, *Beyond the Great Story*.

33. Stone, "History and Postmodernism," 242-43; Patrick Joyce, "History and Postmodernism," *Past and Present* 133 (Nov. 1991): 208. The article is reprinted in the *Postmodern History*

Reader, 244-49. See the full debates in *Past and Present* and *Critical Theory*, 1991-92. Joyce expresses his debt here to our colleague Geoff Eley for his "spirited and informed defense of the 'linguistic turn,'" in "Is All the World a Text? From Social History to the History of Society Two Decades Later," in *The Historical Turn in the Human Sciences*, ed. T. McDonald (Ann Arbor: University of Michigan Press, 1996).

34. Richard Vann, "The Reception of Hayden White," *History and Theory* 37:2 (1998): 143-61. See also his "Louis Mink's Linguistic Turn," *History and Theory* 26:1 (1987): 1-14; Carlo Ginzburg, *Clues, Myths, and the Historical Method* (Baltimore: Johns Hopkins University Press, 1989). See also Hans Kellner, "Narrativity in History: Post-Structuralism and Since," *History and Theory* 26:4 (1987): 1-29.

35. Thomas Richards, *The Imperial Archive: Knowledge and the Fantasy of Empire* (London and New York: Verso, 1993).

36. Joyce Appleby, Lynn Hunt, and Margaret Jacob, *Telling the Truth about History* (New York: Norton, 1994).

Chapter 5

1. Preben Mortensen, "The Place of Theory in Archival Practice," *Archivaria* 47 (1999): 2.

2. Ibid.

3. <http://www.sims.monash.edu.au/research/rcrg/> accessed August 21, 2008. See also S. McKemmish, "Yesterday, Today and Tomorrow: A Continuum of Responsibility," in *Naar een nieuw paradigma in de archivistiek*, ed. P. J. Horsman, F. C. J. Ketelaar, and T. H. P. M. Thomassen (Gravenhage: Stichting Archiefpublicaties, 1999), 210; S. McKemmish, "Are Records Ever Actual?," in *The Records Continuum: Ian Maclean and Australian Archives First Fifty Years*, ed. S. McKemmish and M. Piggott (Clayton: Ancora Press, 1994), 187-203; Julie McLeod and Catherine Hare, eds., *Managing Electronic Records* (London: Facet, 2005), 70.

4. F. Gerald Ham, "The Archival Edge," *American Archivist* 38:1 (January 1975): 8.

5. L. Duranti, "The Concept of Appraisal and Archival Theory," *American Archivist* 57:2 (Spring 1994): 344. See also her "Reliability and Authenticity: The Concepts and Their Implications," *Archivaria* 39 (1995): 5-10; and Richard J. Cox, *Managing Records as Evidence and Information* (Westport, Conn.: Quorum, 2001).

6. Rebecca Scott, "The Provincial Archive as a Place of Memory: Confronting Oral and Written Sources on the Role of Former Slaves in the Cuban War of Independence (1895-1898)," in *Archives, Documentation, and Institutions of Social Memory*, ed. Francis X. Blouin, Jr. and William G. Rosenberg (Ann Arbor: University of Michigan Press, 2006), 284. See also Tom Nesmith, "Archives from the Bottom Up: Social History and Archival Scholarship," *Archivaria* 14 (1982): 5-26.

7. Helen Willa Samuels, *Varsity Letters: Documenting Modern Colleges and Universities* (Chicago: Society of American Archivists, 1992).

8. Ibid., 2.

9. Margaret Hedstrom, "Building Record-Keeping Systems: Archivists Are Not Alone on the Wild Frontier," *Archivaria* 44 (1997): 63. See also her "How Do Archivists Make Electronic Archives Usable and Accessible?" *Archives and Manuscripts* 26:2 (1998), 6-22.

10. Rand Jimerson, "Embracing the Power of Archives," *American Archivist* 69:1 (Spring–Summer 2006): 19-32.

11. See, esp., Joan W. Scott, "The Evidence of Experience," Thomas C. Holt, "Experience and the Politics of Intellectual Inquiry," and Joan W. Scott, "A Rejoinder to Thomas C. Holt," in *Questions of Evidence: Proof, Practice, and Persuasion across the Disciplines*, ed. James Chandler, Arnold I. Davidson, and Harry Harootunian (Chicago: University of Chicago Press, 1994), 363-400. See also Elizabeth Kaplan, "We Are What We Collect, We Collect What We Are: Archives and the Construction of Identity," *American Archivist* 63:1 (Spring–Summer 2000): 125-51.

12. Gabrielle Spiegel, "History, Historicism, and the Social Logic of the Text in the Middle Ages," in *The Postmodern History Reader*, ed. Keith Jenkins (London and New York: Routledge, 1997), 264.

13. John C. Carlin, "The National Archives: Issues for Historians," speech delivered at the annual meeting of the American Historical Association, January 9, 1999, and republished in *Perspectives* (September 1999). For a Canadian perspective on these issues, see Tom Nesmith, "What's History Got to Do with It? Reconsidering the Place of Historical Knowledge in Archival Work," *Archivaria* 57 (2004): 1–28.

Chapter 6

1. Daniel Sherman, *The Construction of Memory in Interwar France* (Chicago: University of Chicago Press, 1999), 1.

2. "Memory industry" is from Kerwin Lee Klein, "On the Emergence of *Memory* in Historical Discourse," *Representations* 69 (Winter 2000): 127.

3. See, e.g., *Journal of Modern History* 75:4 (1989): 1; Allan Megill, "History, Memory, Identity," *History and the Human Sciences* 11 (August 1998): 37; Alon Confino, "Collective Memory and Cultural History: Problems of Method," *American Historical Review* 102:5 (1997): 1386. See also the special issues of *History and Anthropology* 2:2 (1986) and *Representations* 26 (Spring 1989). One of the best general studies of social memory is Paul Connerton, *How Societies Remember* (Cambridge: Cambridge University Press, 1989). Other important work on this subject published at this time included Keith Baker, "Memory and Practice," *Representations* 11 (Summer 1985): 134–59; James Fentress and Chris Wickham, *Social Memory* (Oxford: Oxford University Press, 1992); Amos Funkenstein, "Collective Memory and Historical Consciousness," *History and Memory* 1 (Spring 1989): 5-26. The University of Michigan Library lists more than 1,000 titles alone on memory itself from the period 1975 to the present, and some 610 entries for "social memory." See the somewhat cynical but interesting discussion by Kerwin Lee Klein, "On the Emergence of *Memory* in Historical Discourse," *Representations* 69 (Winter 2000): 127–50.

4. This is addressed very well from an archival perspective by Joan M. Schwartz and Terry Cook, "Archives, Records, and Power: The Making of Modern Memory," *Archival Science* 2 (2002): 1–19. See also Cook's important article, "Remembering the Future: Appraisal of Records and the Role of Archives in Constructing Social Memory," in *Archives, Documentation, and Institutions of Social Memory*, ed. Francis X. Blouin, Jr. and William G. Rosenberg (Ann Arbor: University of Michigan Press, 2006), 165–68.

5. Allen Weinstein, Archivist's Column in *NARA Staff Bulletin*, May 2005, at http://www.archives.gov/about/speeches/staff-bulletin/2005-bulletin/nara-staff-bulletin-archivist-column-may05.pdf. The insertion of the implied "still" is our reading of his remarks. The argument that for archivists, the "idea of archives as memory is more than metaphor," and help to sustain collective memory is made by Kenneth E. Foote, "To Remember and Forget: Archives, Memory, and Culture," *American Archivist* 53 (Summer 1990): 378–92. See also Cook, "Remembering the Future," 169–81.

6. Karl Marx, *The Eighteenth Brumaire* (1852), as cited in Robert C. Tucker, ed., *The Marx–Engels Reader*, 2d ed. (New York: Norton, 1978), 595; John McCumber, ed., *Endings: Questions of Memory in Hegel and Heidegger* (Evanston: Northwestern University Press, 1999).

7. Jeffrey K. Olick and Joyce Robbins, "Social Memory Studies: From 'Collective Memory' to the Historical Sociology of Mnemonic Practices," *American Review of Sociology* 24 (1998): 106.

8. See, e.g., A. M. Alonso, "The Effects of Truth: Representation of the Past and the Imaging of Community," *Journal of the History of Society* 1 (1988): 33–57.

9. M. Halbwachs, *Les Cadres sociaux de la mémoire* (Paris: F. Alcan, 1925); M. Halbwachs, *Les Mémoire collective* (Paris: Presses universitaires de France, 1950), trans. and ed. Lewis Coser as *On Collective Memory* (Chicago: University of Chicago Press, 1992).

10. See, esp., David Lowenthal, *The Heritage Crusade and the Spoils of History* (Cambridge: Cambridge University Press, 1998).

11. For an important discussion of documentary film in this regard, see Paula Rabinowitz, "Wreckage upon Wreckage: History, Documentary and the Ruins of Memory," *History and Theory* 32:2 (1993): 119–37.

12. Philippe Aries, *Centuries of Childhood*, trans. Robt. Baldick (New York: Knopf, 1962).

13. E. P. Thompson, *The Making of the English Working Class* (New York: Vintage, 1963), 12–13.

14. Roy Medvedev, *Let History Judge*, trans. C. Taylor, ed. D. Joravsky, and G. Haupt (New York: Knopf, 1971).

15. Alex Haley, *Roots* (New York: Doubleday, 1976); Eric Hobsbawm and Terence Ranger, eds., *The Invention of Tradition* (Cambridge: Cambridge University Press, 1983); Benedict Anderson, *Imagined Communities* (London: Verso, 1983).

16. See, esp., U. Neisser, *Cognitive Psychology* (New York: Appleton-Century-Crofts, 1967); Daniel Schacter, *Searching for Memory: The Brain, the Mind and the Past* (New York: Basic Books, 1996), and *The Seven Sins of Memory: How the Mind Forgets and Remembers* (Boston: Houghton Mifflin, 2001).

17. See the discussion by Jonathan Boyarin, "Space, Time, and the Politics of Memory," in his edited volume *Remapping Memory: The Politics of Timespace* (Minneapolis: University of Minnesota Press, 1994), 1–37.

18. Michael Lambek, "The Past Imperfect: Remembering as Moral Practice," in *Tense Past: Cultural Essays in Trauma and Memory*, ed. Paul Antze and Michael Lambek (New York: Routledge, 1996), 240. See also Reinhard Koselleck, *The Practice of Conceptual History: Timing History, Spacing Concepts* (Stanford, Calif.: Stanford University Press, 2002). See also Eviatar Zerubavel, *Time Maps: Collective Memory and the Social Shape of the Past* (Chicago: University of Chicago Press, 2003).

19. An especially good discussion of this problem by Tom Holt, Joan Scott, and others can be found in James Chandler et al., *Questions of Evidence* (Chicago and London: University of Chicago Press, 1991), 363–509.

20. I. Lotman, *Universe of the Mind: A Semiotic Theory of Culture* (Bloomington: Indiana University Press, 1990), 221.

21. C. Caruth, "Introduction to 'Trauma and Experience'," in *Trauma*, ed. C. Caruth (Baltimore: Johns Hopkins University Press, 1995), 151–57. See also, among many other works, Laurence Krimayer, "Landscapes of Memory: Trauma, Narrative, and Dissociation," in *Tense Past: Cultural Essays in Trauma and Memory*, ed. Paul Antze and Michael Lambek (New York: Routledge, 1996), 173–98.

22. Among the more interesting works in this extensive literature are Yosef Yerushalmi, *Zakhor: Jewish History and Jewish Memory* (Seattle: University of Washington Press, 1982); James E. Young, *The Texture of Memory: Holocaust Memorials and Meaning* (New Haven: Yale University Press, 1995); Yael Zerubavel, "The Death of Memory and the Memory of Death: Masada and the Holocaust as Historical Metaphors," *Representations* 45 (Winter, 1994): 72–100; Ilan Avisar, *Screening the Holocaust: Cinema's Images of the Unimaginable* (Bloomington: Indiana University Press, 1988); G. Hartman, ed., *Holocaust Remembrance: The Shapes of Memory* (Cambridge, Mass.: Blackwell, 1994); Jane Kramer, *The Politics of Memory: Looking for Germany in the New Germany* (New York: Random House, 1996); Dominique LaCapra, *Representing the Holocaust: History, Theory and Trauma* (Ithaca, N.Y.: Cornell University Press, 1994); Lawrence Langer, *Holocaust Testimonies: The Ruins of Memory* (New Haven: Yale University Press, 1991); Charles, Maier, *The Unmasterable Past: History, Holocaust, and German National Identity* (Cambridge, Mass.: Harvard University Press, 1988); Cathy Caruth, *Unclaimed Experience: Trauma, Narrative and History* (Baltimore: Johns Hopkins University Press, 1996); Michael S. Roth, *The Ironist's Cage: Memory, Trauma and the Construction of History* (New York: Columbia University Press, 1995); Henry Rousso, *The Vichy Syndrome: History and Memory in France since 1944* (Ithaca, N.Y.: Cornell University Press, 1990); Dominique LaCapra, *Writing History, Writing Trauma* (Baltimore: Johns Hopkins University Press, 2001); Joan Wolf, *Harnessing the Holocaust: The Politics of Memory in France* (Stanford,

Calif.: Stanford University Press, 2004). See also the interesting article by Andrea Smith, "Social Memory and Germany's Anti-Foreigner Crisis: A Case of Collective Forgetting," in *The Labyrinth of Memory: Ethnographic Journeys*, ed. R. Josselson and A. Lieblich (Westport, Conn.: Sage, 1995), 61–94; and Krimayer, "Landscapes of Memory," in Antze and Lambek, *Tense Past*, 173–98.

23. Lara Moore, "Putting French History in Order: Archivists and Archival Classification in the 1840s," paper presented for discussion at the Sawyer Seminar, based on her "Restoring Order: Archives, Libraries, and the Legacy of the Old Regime in Nineteenth-Century France" (Ph.D. diss., Stanford University, 2001).

24. Halbwachs, *Collective Memory*, 38. For a more current sociological approach (and a full range of references), see also David L. Morgan and Michael L. Schwalbe, "Mind and Self in Society: Linking Social Structure and Social Cognition," *Social Psychology Journal* 53:2 (1990): 148–64. There is also an extensive discussion in I. Irwin-Zarecka, *Frames of Remembrance: The Dynamics of Collective Memory* (New Brunswick, N.J.: Rutgers University Press, 1993); and Susan Crane provides an excellent general summary in "Writing the Individual Back into Collective Memory," *American Historical Review* 105:5 (1997): 1372–85.

25. See the insightful discussion by Crane, "Writing the Individual," 1375–76.

26. Jacques Derrida, *Mal d'archive: Une impression freudienne* (Paris: Éditions Galilée, 1995), published in English as *Archive Fever: A Freudian Impression* (Chicago: University of Chicago Press, 1996). See also Michel de Certeau, *L'Écriture de l'histoire* (Paris: Gallimard, 1975), published in English as *The Writing of History*, trans. M. Conley (New York: Columbia University Press, 1988).

27. Francis Yates, *The Art of Memory* (Chicago: University of Chicago Press, 1966); Jacques LeGoff, *History and Memory* [1977] (New York: Columbia University Press, 1992). See also Patrick H. Hutton, "The Art of Memory Reconceived: From Rhetoric to Psychoanalysis," *Journal of the History of Ideas* 48:3 (1987): esp. 373–85; and Janet Coleman, *Ancient and Medieval Memories: Studies in the Reconstruction of the Past* (Cambridge: Cambridge University Press, 1992). Keith Baker, "Memory and Practice: Politics and the Representation of the Past in Eighteenth Century France," *Representations* 11 (Summer 1985): 134–64, takes issue with Halbwachs in arguing that documentary materials can retain "prescriptive force within the social order" (156) and thus belong to memory rather than history as Halbwachs's understands it. See also Patrick H. Hutton, "The Role of Memory in the Historiography of the French Revolution," *History and Theory* 30:1 (1991): 56–69.

28. Paul Ricoeur, *Memory, History, Forgetting* (Chicago and London: University of Chicago Press, 2004).

29. Yerushalmi, *Zakhor*. See also Michael Kammen, *Mystic Chords of Memory: The Transformation of Tradition in American Culture* (New York: Knopf, 1991).

30. Tom Brokaw, *The Greatest Generation* (New York: Dell, 1998).

31. See, e.g., the many reviews and discussions of Sheila Fitzpatrick, *Education and Social Mobility in the Soviet Union* (Cambridge: Cambridge University Press, 1979) and Daniel Goldhagen, *Hitler's Willing Executioners* (New York: Knopf, 1996).

32. See, esp., Iris Chang, *The Rape of Nanking: The Forgotten Holocaust of World War II* (New York: Basic Books, 1997) and Yoshida Takashi, *The Making of the "Rape of Nanking": History and Memory in Japan, China, and the United States* (New York: Oxford University Press, 2006).

33. Boyarin, *Remapping Memory*, 23–24.

34. See Eric Hobsbawm, *On History* (New York: Norton, 1997): 7.

35. For the American experience, see, e.g., John Bodnar, *Remaking America: Public Memory, Commemoration, and Patriotism in the Twentieth Century* (Princeton: Princeton University Press, 1992).

36. See, esp., Robert Nelson and Margaret Olin, eds., *Monuments and Memory, Made and Unmade* (Chicago: University of Chicago Press, 2003).

37. Pierre Nora, "Between Memory and History: *Les Lieux de mémoire*," *Representations* 26 (1989): 9.

38. Ibid., 13.

39. Ibid. For a full discussion, see his *Les Lieux de mémoire*, 7 vols. (Paris, 1984–92). An excellent analysis of Nora's work is Nancy Wood, "Memory's Remains: *Les Lieux de mémoire*," *History and Memory* 61 (1994): 123–48.

40. See, esp., Jay Winter and Emmanuel Sivan, eds., *War and Remembrance in the Twentieth Century* (New York and Cambridge: Cambridge University Press, 1999); Jay Winter, *Sites of Memory, Sites of Mourning: The Great War in European Cultural History* (New York and Cambridge: Cambridge University Press, 1995); and Paul Fussell, *The Great War and Modern Memory* (New York: Oxford University Press, 1975).

41. Hayden White, *Metahistory: The Historical Imagination in Nineteenth-Century Europe* (Baltimore: Johns Hopkins University Press, 1973), 1–42.

42. See, esp., Kristin Hass, *Carried to the Wall* (Berkeley: University of California Press, 1998); Robin Wagner-Pacifici and Barry Schwartz, "The Vietnam Veterans Memorial: Commemorating a Difficult Past," *American Journal of Sociology* 97:2 (September 1991): 376–420. An excellent discussion of commemorative practices is John Gillis, "Memory and Identity: The History of a Relationship," in *Commemorations: The Politics of National Identity*, ed. John R. Gillis (Princeton: Princeton University Press, 1994). See also Barry Schwartz, "The Social Context of Commemoration: A Study in Collective Memory," *Social Forces* 61:2 (1982): 374–402; Gerald Sider and Gavin Smither, eds., *Between History and Histories: The Making of Silences and Commemorations* (Toronto: University of Toronto Press, 1997); and Koselleck, *The Practice of Conceptual History*, esp. chap. 17.

43. David Lowenthal, *Possessed by the Past: The Heritage Crusade and the Spoils of History* (New York: Free Press, 1996); see also his *The Past is a Foreign Country* (New York and Cambridge: Cambridge University Press, 1985); and "The Timeless Past: Some Anglo American Historical Preconceptions," *Journal of American History* 75 (1989): 1263–80. For a lively study of American reenactment practices, among other elements of civil war remembrance, see Tony Horwitz, *Confederates in the Attic* (New York: Pantheon, 1999).

44. Lambek, "The Past Imperfect," in Antze and Lambek, *Tense Past*, 235–54. See also Richard Harvey Brown and Beth Davis-Brown, "The Making of Memory: The Politics of Archives in the Construction of National Consciousness," *History and the Human Sciences* 11:4 (1998): 17–32; Henry Rousso, *The Haunting Past: History, Memory and Justice in Contemporary France* (Philadelphia: University of Pennsylvania Press, 2002), and the extended discussion in Ricouer, *Memory, History, and Forgetting*, esp. 412–56.

45. See, e.g., Teski and Climo, *Labyrinth of Memory*, esp. 2–8. This volume of essays had its origin in a panel at the American Anthropological Association meetings in 1992, where the subject was widely discussed. Two interesting case studies are Anne Christine Taylor, "Remembering to Forget: Identity, Mourning, and Memory among the Jivaro," *Man* 28:4 (1993): 653–78 and Janet Carsten, "The Politics of Forgetting: Migration, Kinship and Memory on the Periphery of the Southeast Asian State," *Journal of the Royal Anthropological Institute* 1:2 (1995): 317–35.

46. See Robert J. Donia, "The New Masters of Memory: Libraries, Archives and Museums in Postcommunist Bosnia-Herzegovina," in Blouin and Rosenberg, *Archives*, 393–401; Jeffrey Burds, "Ethnicity, Memory, and Violence: Reflections on Special Problems in Soviet and East European Archives," in ibid., 466–79; and the more general discussions in John Lampe, *Yugoslavia as History* (Cambridge: Cambridge University Press, 1996) and Norman Naimark, *Fires of Hatred: Ethnic Cleansing in Twentieth-Century Europe* (Cambridge, Mass.: Harvard University Press, 2001).

47. See, esp., Jochen Hellbeck, *Writing a Diary in Stalin's Time* (Cambridge, Mass.: Harvard University Press, 2007); Catriona Kelly, *Comrade Pavlik: The Rise and Fall of a Soviet Boy Hero* (London: Granta, 2005).

48. See the discussions in Elizabeth Yakel, "Archival Representation," in Blouin and Rosenberg, *Archives*, 150–61 and Seven Hensen, "The Evolution of Archival Description," *American Archivist* 60:3 (1997): 284–95.

49. See the general discussion by Richard J. Cox, "The Concept of Public Memory and Its Impact on Archival Public Programming," *Archivaria* 36 (1993): 122–35.

50. See, e.g., the discussion in John Keegan, *The Face of Battle* (New York: Viking, 1976).
51. L. Passerini, "Memory and Totalitarianism," in *International Yearbook of Oral History and Life Stories*, ed. L. Passerini (Oxford: Oxford University Press, 1992), 8. See also Kathleen E. Smith, *Mythmaking in the New Russia: Politics and Memory During the Yeltsin Era* (Ithaca, N.Y.: Cornell University Press, 2002); and James V. Wertsch, *Voices of Collective Remembering* (Cambridge: Cambridge University Press, 2002).
52. Irwin-Zarecka, *Frames of Remembrance*, 54.
53. Mikhail Bakhtin, *The Dialogic Imagination*, ed. and trans. Michael Holquist, with Caryl Emerson (Austin: University of Texas Press, 1981), 342–48.
54. See, e.g., Brian Williams and William K. Wallach, "Documenting South Africa's Liberation Movements: Engaging the Archives at the University of Fort Hare," in Blouin and Rosenberg, *Archives*, 321–31.
55. On this point, see, esp., Susan Crane, "Writing the Individual Back into Collective Memory," *American Historical Review* 102:5 (1997): 1372–85, which in addition to its other virtues has an excellent review of the literature.
56. See the brief but important discussion by Inge Bundsgaard, "The Question of Access: The Right to Social Memory versus the Right to Social Oblivion," in Blouin and Rosenberg, *Archives*, 114–20.
57. Hobsbawm, *On History*, 8.

Chapter 7

1. See the Air Force Association website <http://www.afa.org/media/enolagay>.
2. The fullest discussions of this incident are Robert Newman, *Enola Gay and the Court of History* (New York: P. Lang, 2004) and Charles T. O'Reilly and Wm. A. Rooney, *The Enola Gay and the Smithsonian Institution* (Jefferson, N.C.: McFarland, 2005).
3. In 1999 a new center to house the exhibition materials and other Aeronautic and Space Museum archives, the Steven F. Udvar-Hazy Center, was made possible by a gift of $65 million.
4. See <http://www.afa.org/media/enolagay>.
5. Carolyn Steedman, *Dust: The Archive and Cultural History* (New Brunswick, N.J.: Rutgers University Press, 2002), 68.
6. These issues here are deftly examined by Boris V. Ananich in his discussion of the materials concerning the 1929–31 trial of Soviet academicians, where the fabrications of information in the documents was made all the more problematic by the realities of the trial's victims asserting they were true, a set of issues that could only be understood by historians fully cognizant of the historical context. See Boris V. Ananich, "The Historian and the Source: Problems of Reliability and Ethics," in *Archives, Documentation, and Institutions of Social Memory*, ed. Francis X. Blouin, Jr. and William G. Rosenberg (Ann Arbor: University of Michigan Press, 2006), 490–96.
7. Ann Stoler, *Along the Archival Grain* (Princeton: Princeton University Press, 2009). We are grateful to Stoler for sharing her ideas with us during our preliminary discussions about this project and participating in their elaboration at an early seminar on archival matters in St. Petersburg.
8. Ann Stoler, "Colonial Archives and the Arts of Governance: On the Content in the Form," in Blouin and Rosenberg, *Archives*, 267–79 and her *Along the Archival Grain*; Thomas Richards, *The Imperial Archive: Knowledge and the Fantasy of Empire* (London: Verso, 1993); Nicholas Dirks, *Castes of Mind* (Princeton: Princeton University Press, 2001). Thomas Holt also explores the idea of the reading against the grain in his "Experience and the Politics of Intellectual Inquiry," in *Questions of Evidence: Proof, Practice, and Persuasion across the Disciplines*, ed. James Chandler, Arnold Davidson and Harry Harootunian (Chicago: University of Chicago Press, 1994), 388–400.
9. Stoler, "Colonial Archives," 271–72.

10. Dirks, *Caste of Mind*, 122.

11. Ibid., 122–23.

12. Ibid., 103. On the MacKenzie collection, see H. H. Wilson Esq., *A Descriptive Catalogue of the Oriental Manuscripts and Other Articles Illustrative of the Literature, History, Statistics and Antiquities of the South of India Collected by the late Lieut.-Col. Colin MacKenzie*, Vol. 1 (Calcutta: Asiatic Press, 1828).

13. Michel de Certeau, "History: Science and Fiction," in *Heterodologies: Discourse on the Other*, trans. B. Massumi (Minneapolis: University of Minnesota Press, 1986), 203.

14. Florencia Mallon, *Peasant and Nation: The Making of Post Colonial Mexico and Peru* (Berkeley: University of California Press, 1995).

15. For a description of Record Group 75, see <http://www.archives.gov/research/guide-fed-records/groups/075.html>. For examples of work that use official archives in interesting ways, see Richard White, *The Middle Ground: Indians, Empires, and Republics in the Great Lakes Region 1650–1815* (Cambridge: Cambridge University Press, 1991) and Phil Deloria, *Playing Indian* (New Haven: Yale University Press, 1998).

16. James Sanders, *Contentious Republicans: Popular Politics, Race, and Class in Nineteenth Century Colombia* (Durham, N.C.: Duke University Press, 2004); Paul Eiss, "Redemption's Archive: Remembering the Future in a Revolutionary Past," in Blouin and Rosenberg, *Archives*, 301–20; Marcus Rediker and Peter Linebaugh, *The Many-Headed Hydra: Sailors, Slaves, Commoners, and the Hidden History of the Revolutionary Atlantic* (Boston: Beacon Press, 2000); S. Sarah Chambers, *From Subjects to Citizens: Honor, Gender, and Politics in Arequipa, Peru, 1780–1854* (University Park: Pennsylvania State University Press, 1999); Rebecca Scott, "The Provincial Archive as a Place of Memory: Confronting Oral and Written Sources on the Role of Former Slaves in the Cuban War of Independence (1895–98)," in Blouin and Rosenberg, *Archives*, 280–91.

17. See the NARA Website: <http://www.archives.gov/declassification/>

18. The National Security Archive is an independent nongovernmental research institute and library located at George Washington University. The Archive collects and publishes declassified documents obtained through the Freedom of Information Act, and it also serves as a repository of government records on a wide range of topics pertaining to the national security, foreign, intelligence, and economic policies of the United States. See <http://www.gwu.edu/~nsarchiv/nsa/the_archive.html>.

19. Stoler, "Colonial Archives," 271; Patricia Galloway, *Practicing Ethnohistory: Mining Archives, Hearing Testimony, Constructing Narrative* (Lincoln: University of Nebraska Press, 2006), 10.

20. Dirks, *Castes of Mind*, 107.

21. See, esp., Larry Hackman, ed., "Presidential Libraries: Programs, Policies, and the Public Interest," *Public Historian* 28 (Summer 2006): 7–184 and Benjamin Hufbauer, *Presidential Temples: How Memorials and Libraries Shape Public Memory* (Lawrence: University Press of Kansas, 2005).

22. Nancy Bartlett, "Past Imperfect: Mediating Meaning in the Archive," in Blouin and Rosenberg, *Archives*, 123.

23. Lara Moore, "Putting French History in Order: Archivists and Archival Classification in the 1840s," paper presented for discussion at the Sawyer Seminar, based on her "Restoring Order: Archives, Libraries, and the Legacy of the Old Regime in Nineteenth-Century France" (Ph.D. diss., Stanford University, 2001).

24. See the discussion in Michael Kammen, *Mystic Chords of Memory: The Transformation of Tradition in American Culture* (New York: Knopf, 1991), 36.

25. These materials largely came from the formerly heavily restricted Central Party Archive, as well as the State Archive of the Russian Federation (formerly the Central Archive of the October Revolution), but in contrast to previous documentary publications, they included materials drawn from western repositories, as well as newspapers and other sources. More than forty thick volumes documenting the history of Russian political parties at the end of the old regime were been published between 1995 and 2005 alone, along with a number of remarkable collections of archival materials on peasant rebellion during the civil war,

collectivization, the secret police, the international communist movement, and correspondence between state leaders. Western and Russian scholars and archivists were jointly
involved in most of these efforts.

26. For an extended discussion, see Hufbauer, *Presidential Temples*.
27. Frederick Cooper, "Memories of Colonization: Commemoration, Preservation, and Erasure in an African Archive," in Blouin and Rosenberg, *Archives*, 257–66.
28. Jacques LeGoff, *History and Memory* (New York: Columbia University Press, 1992), 31.
29. Bonnie Smith, "Uncontrollable Archive: Visual Culture and the War in Iraq," paper presented to the Workshop on Gender in the Archives, University of Michigan, September, 2004.
30. As cited by Joan Schwartz, "We Make Our Tools and Our Tools Make Us: Lessons from Photographs for the Practice, Politics, and Poetics of Diplomatics," *Archivaria* 40 (1995): 60.
31. See, e.g., the various discussions in Joan Neuberger and Valerie Kivelson, eds., *Visualizing Russia* (New Haven: Yale University Press, 2008).
32. Joan Schwartz, "'Records of Simple Truth and Precision': Photography, Archives, and the Illusion of Control," in Blouin and Rosenberg, *Archives*, 61–83.
33. An excellent discussion is Geoff Eley, "Finding the People's War: Film, British Collective Memory, and World War II," *American Historical Review* 106:3 (2001): 837.
34. Jonathan Boyarin, "Space, Time and the Politics of Memory," in his edited volume *Remapping Memory: The Politics of Timespace* (Minneapolis: University of Minnesota Press, 1994).
35. Ibid., 12–13.
36. Reinhart Koselleck, *The Practice of Conceptual History: Timing History, Spacing Concepts* (Stanford, Calif.: Stanford University Press, 2002): xii.
37. In a large forum on the Enola Gay episode at the University of Michigan, historians were accused of putting the National Aeronautics and Space Museum curators in an impossible (and vulnerable) position by believing nothing was really true about the past, and being unable to say it intelligibly.
38. Steven Shapin, *A Social History of Truth* (Chicago: University of Chicago Press, 1994), 5.
39. David Abraham, *The Collapse of the Weimar Republic: Political Economy and Crisis* (Princeton: Princeton University Press, 1981).
40. As cited in the discussion by Peter Novick, *That Noble Dream: The "Objectivity Question" and the American Historical Profession* (Cambridge: Cambridge University Press, 1988), 612–21.
41. *New York Times*, December 23, 1984, in reviewing decisions made by the Council of the American Historical Association.
42. As cited by Novick, *That Noble Dream*, 616.
43. Ibid., 619.
44. Joyce Appleby, Lynn Hunt, and Margaret Jacob, *Telling the Truth about History* (New York: Norton, 1994).
45. Eric Wolf, *Europe and the People without History* (Berkeley: University of California Press, 1982).
46. Patrick Geary, "Medieval Archivists as Authors: Social Memory and Archival Memory," in Blouin and Rosenberg, *Archives*, 106–13 and his *Phantoms of Remembrance: Memory and Oblivion at the End of the First Millennium* (Princeton: Princeton University Press, 1994). See also Chris Given-Wilson, *Chronicles: The Writing of History in Medieval England* (London and New York: Hambledon, 2004).
47. James Hevia, *English Lessons: The Pedagogy of Imperialism in Nineteenth-Century China* (Durham, N.C.: Duke University Press, 2003), 234.
48. Richards, *Imperial Archive*, 6.
49. Hevia, *English Lessons*, 242.
50. Hosea B. Morse, *Trade and Administration of the Chinese Empire* (Shanghai: Kelly and Walsh, 1913); *The Chronicles of the East India Company Trading to China, 1635–1834* (Oxford: Clarendon Press, 1926–29); *International Relations of the Chinese Empire 1834–1911* (Shanghai: Kelly and Walsh, 1910).

51. See Terry Cook, "Macroappraisal in Theory and Practice: Origins, Characteristics, and Implementation in Canada, 1950–2000," *Archival Science* 5.2–4 (2005): 101–61.

52. See the interesting discussion on this issue by Atina Grossman, "Out of the Closet and into the Archives? German Jewish Papers," in Blouin and Rosenberg, *Archives*, 89–100.

Chapter 8

1. Jacques Derrida, *Mal d'archive: Une impression freudienne* (Paris: Éditions Galilée, 1995).

2. *History of the Human Sciences* 11:4 (November 1998) and 12:2 (March 1999).

3. Caroline Steedman, *Dust: The Archive and Cultural History* (New Brunswick, N.J.: Rutgers University Press, 2001).

4. Derrida, *Mal d'archive*; Michel Foucault, *Archeology of Knowledge* (New York: Harper and Row, 1976).

5. Steedman, *Dust*, 67.

6. Jules Michelet, Preface, *Histoire de France*, new ed. (Paris: A. Le Vasseur, 1876–78), 613. It is interesting that digital and data archives carry no similar negative and unclean associations.

7. Steedman, *Dust*, 68.

8. Ann Laura Stoler, "Colonial Archives and the Arts of Governance: On the Content in the Form," in *Archives, Documentation, and Institutions of Social Memory*, ed. Francis X. Blouin, Jr. and William G. Rosenberg (Ann Arbor: University of Michigan Press, 2006), 272.

9. Ann Pederson (ed.), *Keeping Archives*, (Sydney: Australian Society of Archivists, 1987), 285.

10. Ibid., 285. See also Terry Cook, "What Is Past Is Prologue: A History of Archival Ideas since 1898 and the Future Paradigm Shift," *Archivaria* 43 (Spring 1997): 18–63.

11. See Ian E. Wilson, "The Gift of One Generation to Another: The Real Thing for the Pepsi Generation," in Blouin and Rosenberg, *Archives*, 333–42; Donald McCoy, *The National Archives: America's Ministry of Documents, 1934–1968* (Chapel Hill: University of North Carolina Press, 1978).

12. See, e.g., Theodore R. Schellenberg, *The Management of Archives* (New York: Columbia University Press, 1965); Association des archivistes français, *Manuel d'Archivistique* (Paris: S.E.V.P.E.N., 1970); James O'Toole and Richard Cox, *Understanding Archives and Manuscripts* (Chicago: Society of American Archivists, 2006). The Louis Armstrong Archives is a good case study. See Ben Alexander, "'For Posterity': The Personal Audio Recordings of Louis Armstrong," *American Archivist* 71 (Spring–Summer 2008): 50–87.

13. See David Bearman, "Archival Methods," *Archives and Museum Informatics Technical Report* 3:1 (1989): 10–11.

14. See Michael Stephen Hindus, Theodore M. Hammett, and Barbara M. Hobson, *Files of the Massachusetts Superior Court, 1859–1959: An Analysis and Plan for Action* (*Report of the Massachusetts Judicial Records Committee of the Supreme Judicial Court*) (Boston: G. K. Hall, 1979).

15. Tom Nesmith, quoted in Robert McIntosh, "The Great War, Archives, and Modern Memory," *Archivaria* 46 (Fall 1998): 17.

16. See Barbara Craig, *Archival Appraisal: Theory and Practice* (Munich: K. G. Saur, 2004). Brien Brothman, however, offers a somewhat contrary view, drawing on a wide range of sources. He argues that while one can put records into evidence, one cannot put evidence into records. See his thoughtful "Afterglow: Conceptions of Record and Evidence in Archival Discourse," *Archival Science* 2 (2002): 311–42. Terry Cook's "Appraisal Methodology: Macro-Appraisal and Functional Analysis" reflects a more comprehensive view of appraisal: <http://www.collectionscanada.gc.ca/government/disposition/007007-1035-e.html>. See also the discussions by Frank Boles and Julia Marks Young, "Exploring the Black Box: The Appraisal of University Administrative Records," *American Archivist* 48 (Spring 1985): 121–140; Frank Boles, "Mix Two Parts Interest to One Part Information and Appraise Until Done: Understanding Contemporary Record Selection," *American Archivist*, 50 (Summer 1987): 356–68; Richard Cox, "The Documentation Strategy and Archival Appraisal Principles: A Different

Perspective," *Archivaria* 38:2 (1994): 11–36; Helen Willa Samuels, "Who Controls the Past," *American Archivist* 49:2 (1986): 109–24; Luciana Duranti, "The Concept of Appraisal and Archival Theory," *American Archivist* 57:2 (1994): 328–44; Timothy Ericson, "At the 'Rim of Creative Dissatisfaction': Archivists and Acquisition Development," *Archivaria* 33:1 (1991–92): 66–67.

17. For a contemporary analysis of the challenges in archival processing, see Mark A. Greene and Dennis Meissner, "More Product, Less Process: Revamping Traditional Archival Processing," *American Archivist* 68:2 (Fall/Winter 2005): 208–63.

18. We are grateful to Nancy Bartlett for this observation and for her many insights into various elements of archival mediation.

19. See Nancy Bartlett, "*Respect des Fonds*: The Origins of the Modern Archival Principle of Provenance," in *Bibliographical Foundations of French Historical Studies*, ed. Lawrence McCrank (New York: Haworth Press, 1992), 107–15 and her "Past Imperfect (l'imparfait): Mediating Meaning in Archives of Art," in Blouin and Rosenberg, *Archives*", esp. 123–24; Elizabeth Yakel, "Archival Representation," in Blouin and Rosenberg, *Archives*, 151–63.

20. Yakel, "Archival Representation," 151–63.

21. See Ugo Baldini, ed., *The Catholic Church and Modern Science: Documents from the Archives of the Roman Congregations of the Holy Office and the Index*, 4 vols. (Rome: Libreria Editrice Vaticana, 2009).

22. Vladimir Lapin, "Hesitations at the Door to an Archive Catalog," in Blouin and Rosenberg, *Archives*, 480–89.

23. Yakel, "Archival Representation," 159.

24. Tamar G. Chute and Ellen Swain, "Navigating Ambiguous Waters: Providing Access to Student Records in the University Archives," *American Archivist* 62:2 (2007): 212–33; Marjorie Barritt, "The Appraisal of Personally Identifiable Student Records," *American Archivist* 49:3 (1986): 263–76.

25. See, esp., Nancy Bartlett, "*Respect des Fonds*," 107–15 and "Past Imperfect," esp. 123–24.

26. See Helga A. Welsh, "Dealing with the Communist Past: Central and East European Experiences after 1990," *Europe–Asia Studies* 48:3 (1996): 413–28, and the discussion of the Bad Arolsen materials in the *New York Times*, April 19, 2006.

27. Quoted in Alasdair Roberts, *Blacked Out: Government Secrecy in the Information Age* (Cambridge: Cambridge University Press, 2006), 208.

28. See the discussions by Mary Jo Pugh, "The Illusion of Omniscience: Subject Access and the Reference Archivist," *American Archivist* 45:1 (Winter 1982): 33–44; Kathleen Marquis, "Not Dragon at the Gate but Research Partner: The Reference Archivist as Mediator," in Blouin and Rosenberg, *Archives*, 36–43.

29. See in particular Lara Moore, "Restoring Order: The École des Chartes and the Organization of Archives and Libraries in France, 1820–1870" (Ph.D. diss., Stanford University, 2001); Bartlett, "*Respect des Fonds*," 107–15; Vladimir Lapin, "Hesitations at the Door to an Archive Catalog," in Blouin and Rosenberg, *Archives*, 480–89; Jonathan Spence, *The Memory Palace of Matteo Ricci* (New York: Viking, 1984); and Beatrice Bartlett, *Monarch and Ministers: The Grand Council in Mid-Ch'ing China, 1723–1820* (Berkeley and London: University of California Press, 1991).

30. National Archives and Records Administration, *Preserving the Past to Protect the Future* (Washington, D.C.: National Archives and Records Administration, 2007), 1.

31. Lucie Favier, *La Mémoire de l'état: Histoire des archives nationales* (Paris: Fayard, 2004).

32. These issues are nicely brought out in the film *Lives of Others*, which examines among other things the various ways archives can represent contemporary and historical lives. See also Abby Smith, "Russian History: Is It in the Archives?" in Blouin and Rosenberg, *Archives*, 451–58. See also Serhy Yekelchyk, "Archiving Heteroglosia: Writing Reports and Controlling Mass Culture under Stalin," in the same volume, 459–65.

33. Joan Schwartz "'Records of Simple Truth and Precision': Photography, Archives, and the Illusion of Control," in Blouin and Rosenberg, *Archives*, 77–79.

34. See, e.g., Alessandro Portelli, "Lookin' for a Home: Independent Oral History Archives in Italy," in Blouin and Rosenberg, *Archives*, 219–24; Andor Skotnes, "People's Archives and

Oral History in South Africa: A Traveler's Account," *South African Archives Journal* 37 (1995), and John Bodnar, "Power and Memory in Oral History: Workers and Managers at Studebaker," *Journal of American History*, 75:4 (1989): 1201–21, both of which have a good discussion of methodological issues.

35. United States. Congress. Senate. Select Committee on Ethics, United States. Congress. Senate. Ethics Counsel, *The Packwood Report* (New York: Times Books, 1995).

36. P. J. Horsman, "Abuysen ende desordien: Archiefvorming en archivering in Dordrecht, 1200–1920" (Dissertation, University of Amsterdam, 2009), 335–39.

37. Theo H. P. M. Thomassen "Instrumenten van de macht: De Staten-Generaal en hun archieven 1576–1796" (Dissertation, University of Amsterdam, 2009), 457–58.

38. "National Archives Responds to Reclassification of Documents," NARA press release, February 22, 2006 at http://www.archives.gov/press/press-releases/2006/nr06-63.html.

39. Roberts, *Blacked Out*, 215–16.

40. Alfred D. Chandler, *The Visible Hand: The Managerial Revolution in American Business* (Cambridge, Mass.: Harvard University Press, 1977). James M. O'Toole, ed., *The Records of American Business* (Chicago: Society of American Archivists, 1997).

41. JoAnne Yates, *Control through Communication: The Rise of System in American Management* (Baltimore: Johns Hopkins University Press, 1989).

42. Gary B. Nash, *First City: Philadelphia and the Forging of Historical Memory* (Philadelphia: University of Pennsylvania Press, 2002).

43. See <http://hiphoparchive.org/>.

44. See Frank Mecklenburg, "German Jewish Archives in Berlin and New York: Three Generations after the Fact," in Blouin and Rosenberg, *Archives*, 101–5; Tanya Chebotarev and Jared S. Ingersoll, eds., *Russian and East European Books and Manuscripts in the United States: Proceedings of a Conference in Honor of the Fiftieth Anniversary of the Bakhmeteff Archive of Russian and East European Culture* (New York: Haworth Information Press, 2003); Anatol Shmelev, *Tracking a Diaspora: Emigrés from Russia and Eastern Europe in the Repositories* (New York: Haworth Information Press, 2006).

45. Christopher Klemek, "Gary Nash, *First City*," H-Book Review, H-Urban@n-net.msu.edu (March, 2002).

46. See, Terry Cook, "Mind over Matter: Towards a New Theory of Archival Appraisal," in *Archival Imagination: Essays in Honour of Hugh A. Taylor*, ed. Barbara Cook (Ottawa: Association of Canadian Archivists, 1992) and his discussion in "Remembering the Future," in Blouin and Rosenberg, *Archives*, esp. 175–79; Richard Brown, "Records Acquisition Strategy and Its Theoretical Foundation: The Case for a Concept of Archival Hermeneutics," *Archivaria* 33 (1991–92): 34–56 and his "The Value of 'Narrativity' in the Appraisal of Historical Documents," *Archivaria* 32 (1991): 152–60.

47. Terry Cook, "Remembering the Future," in Blouin and Rosenberg, *Archives*, 172. See also, Shirley Spragge, "The Abdication Crisis: Are Archivists Giving Up Their Cultural Responsibility," *Archivaria* 40:3 (Fall 1995): 173–89. See also John Bodnar, *Remaking America: Public Memory, Commemoration, and Patriotism in the Twentieth Century* (Princeton: Princeton University Press, 1992).

48. Robert McIntosh, "The Great War, Archives, and Modern Memory," *Archivaria* 46 (Fall 1998): 18.

49. Terry Cook and Joan Schwartz, "Archives, Records, and Power: The Making of Modern Memory," *Archival Science* 2 (2002): 1 and Joan Schwartz and Terry Cook, "Archives, Records, and Power: From (Postmodern) Theory to (Archival) Performance," *Archival Science* 2 (2002): 171–73. See also Paule René-Bazin, "The Influence of Politics on the Shaping of the Memory of States in Western Europe (France)," in Blouin and Rosenberg, *Archives*, 353–60.

50. Jacques Le Goff, *History and Memory* (New York: Columbia University Press, 1992 [1977]): xvii. See also Nan Enstad, "Fashioning Political Identities: Cultural Studies and the Historical Construction of Political Subjects," *American Quarterly* 50:4 (1998): 745–82.

51. McIntosh, "The Great War," 19.

52. Nancy Bartlett, "Mediating Meaning in Archives of Art," in Blouin and Rosenberg, *Archives*, 121–33.

53. Ann Stoler, *Along the Archival Grain: Epistemic Anxieties and Colonial Common Sense* (Princeton, Princeton University Press, 2009): 32.

54. Derrida, *Archive Fever*, 17.

Chapter 9

1. *American Historical Association et al. v. Trudy Peterson as Acting Archivist of the United States and George H. W. Bush* (94.2671), Complaint for Declaratory and Injunctive Relief, as cited in David A. Wallace, "Preserving the U.S. Government's White House Electronic Mail: Archival Challenges and Policy Implications," Paper presented to the Sixth Delos Workshop, Lisbon, Portugal, June 19, 1998: footnote 36 (http://www.ercim.eu/publication/ws-proceedings/DELOS6/wallace.pdf) and David A. Wallace, "The Public's Use of Federal Recordkeeping Statutes to Shape Federal Information Policy" (Ph.D. diss., University of Pittsburgh, 1997), 502.

2. A version of this address appeared as William G. Rosenberg, "The Expectations of Scholars Concerning Archival Access," *Janus: Revue Archivistique/Archival Review* (1994:1): 79–85.

3. Thomas Osborne, "The Ordinariness of the Archive," *History of the Human Sciences* 12:2 (1999): 54.

4. Patrick Joyce, "The Politics of the Liberal Archive," *History of the Human Sciences* 12:2 (1999): 35–49.

5. Some archivists, especially those currently entering the field, seem well aware that their colleagues need to explore further the state-based framework of their profession and understand more fully the ways even state archives may be grounded in societal values. Lara Moore explores aspects of this issue in her Ph.D. dissertation, "Restoring Order: Archives, Libraries, and the Legacy of the Old Regime in Nineteenth-Century France" (Ph.D. diss., Stanford University, 2001), as does Jennifer Milligan, esp. in "The Archives Nationales and the State–Citizen Contract in Modern France," unpublished paper presented to the Sawyer Seminar on Archives, Documentation, and the Institutions of Social Memory, University of Michigan, November, 2000. See also Hans Booms, "Society and the Formation of a Documentary Heritage: Issues in the Appraisal of Archival Sources," *Archivaria* 24 (Summer 1987): 69–107, translation by Hermina Joldermas and Richard Klumpenhouwer, who provide a brief introduction and discussion as well of Booms's 1972 original article, published in *Archivalische Zeitschrift*, 68; and esp. Terry Cook, "What Is Past Is Prologue: A History of Archival Ideas since 1898, and the Future Paradigm Shift," *Archivaria* 43 (Spring 1997): 17–63.

6. See NARA, *Protecting the Past to Preserve the Future: The Strategic Plan of the National Archives and Records Administration 2006–2016*, <http://www.archives.gov/about/plans-reports/strategic-plan/2009/nara-strategic-plan-2006-2016-final.pdf>.

7. See Patricia Kennedy Grimsted, "Lenin's Archival Decree of 1918: The Bolshevik Legacy for Soviet Archival Theory and Practice," *American Archivist* 45:4 (1982): 429–43.

8. William Rosenberg attended that meeting on behalf of the AHA.

9. *Washington Post*, May 26, 1995; *New York Times*, May 5, 1995.

10. See Robert M. Adler, "The Public Controversy over the Kennedy Memorabilia Project," in *Archives, Documentation, and Institutions of Social Memory*, ed. Francis X. Blouin, Jr. and William G. Rosenberg (Ann Arbor: University of Michigan Press, 2006), 230.

11. "*Glasnost*' in the Archives? Commentary by Soviet Historians and Archivists," *American Archivist*, 53:3 (1990): 469, 472, 474–75.

12. Ibid., 472.

13. Iu. N. Afanas'ev, "Chasnye fakty i chestnye otsenki," [Private Facts and Honest Evaluations] *Moskovskie Novosti* 25 (June 19, 1988): 8.

14. See Patricia Kennedy Grimsted, "Beyond Perestroika: Soviet-Area Archives after the August Coup," *American Archivist* 55:1 (1992): 94–122; A. N. Artizov et al., "Osnovy zakonodatel'stva Rossiiskoi Federatsii ob arkhivnom fonde Rossiiskoi Federatsii i arkhivakh: Idei, printsipy, realizatsiia," [The Fundamentals of Legislation in the Russian Federation on the Archival Collection and the Archives of the Russian Federation: Ideas, Principles, and their Realization], *Otechestvennye Arkhivy* 4 (1996): 3–8. Separate laws were adopted at this time on state secrets, on external state secrets, on Russian federal security agencies, and on the rehabilitation of victims of political repression. See *Sobranie aktov prezidenta i pravitel'stva Rossiiskoi federatsii* [The Collection of Presidential and Government Acts of the Russian Federation] 51 (Moscow, 1993), 4936.

15. B. V. Ivanenko, "Ukrainian Archives: Statutory and Ethical Problems," *Janus: Révue Archivistique du Conseil International des Archives* 1 (1994): 84–86.

16. In October 1999, the "Public Interest Declassification Act" was introduced in the U.S. Congress to address this problem, sponsored by Senator Daniel Moynihan, who had been known as a supporter of broad declassification reform. This bill addressed only special searches around specific incidents, such as the records related to Pinochet, the American church women murdered in Central America, and the Kennedy assassination. The declassification authorized by this bill was only of selected documents, not entire record groups. It was strongly opposed by the Association of American Historians and the American Historical Association, which argued that it would not in any productive way "advance the imperative of agencies to declassify all but the most sensitive of their older records that are of historical significance." See *NCC Washington Update* 6:3 (February 4, 2000), and the further discussion by Bruce Craig in his contributions to the newsletter of the American Historical Association: "Records Withdrawn from Public Access," *AHA Perspectives* 40:5 (2002); "State Secrets, Advisory Committees, and the CIA," *AHA Perspectives* 42:2 (2004); and "Combating Government Secrecy—An Update," *AHA Perspectives* 42:7 (2004). See also Bruce P. Montgomery, *Subverting Open Government* (Lanham, Md.: Scarecrow Press, 2006).

17. See http://atxp.choicepoint.com/> which

18. The policy was later said to be based on a misunderstanding and was amended, but a number of new restrictions still applied. See Federation of American Scientists, *Secrecy News: From the FAS Project on Government Secrecy*, posting of May 24, 2007, at <http://www.fas.org/blog/secrecy/2007/05/page/2>.

19. See the discussion by David Wallace, "Archivists, Recordkeeping, and the Declassification of Records: What We can Learn from Contemporary Histories," *American Archivist* 56 (1993): 794–814.

20. *New York Times*, August 26, 2004. See also Bruce P. Montgomery, *The Bush–Cheney Administration's Assault on Open Government* (Westport, Conn.: Praeger, 2008).

21. *NCC Washington Update*, 6:2 (January 19, 2000).

22. See *Otechestvennye Arkhivy* 6 (1998): 9–38.

23. Ibid., 21. See also "*Proekt. Federal'nyi zakon. O vnesenii izmenenii i dopolnenii v Osnovy Zakonodatel'stva Rossiiskoi Federatsii ob arkhivnom fonde Rossiiskoi Federatsii i arkhivakh.* [Draft. Federal Law. On Changes and Additions to the Basic Legislation of the Russian Federation on Federation Archives and Archival Holdings]," in ibid., 22–33.

24. "Declaration on the Right of Access to Information," *Treaty of the European Union, February 7, 1992*, as published by the Pennsylvania State University, *Electronic Classics Series* (University Park, Pa.: Pennsylvania State University Press, 1999), 200.

25. Alasdair Roberts, *Blacked Out: Government Secrecy in the Information Age* (Cambridge: Cambridge University Press, 2006), 15.

26. See, e.g., Athan G. Theoharis, "The FBI and the FOIA: Problems of Access and Destruction," *Midwestern Archivist* 5:2 (1981): 61–74 and his "FBI Files, the National Archives, and the Issue of Access," *Government Publications Review* 9 (1982): 29–35.

27. See the discussion in ibid., pp. 26–30.

28. Ibid., p. 205. At the same time, however, the National Archives and Records Administration has been working to provide on-line access to a variety of databases under its control. There

are now a variety of sources on-line and fully available. Among the most popular are the Second World War enlistment records and the records of immigrants arriving at the Port of New York because of famine in Ireland. NARA recently has posted central foreign policy files for the period 1973–1975 that includes a great deal of declassified information, and military contract files 1968–1985 documenting the period 1959–1985. In June 2007 the CIA released nearly half a million pages declassified and made available for research. This material is searchable and on-line through the CREST access system and the NARA website.

29. See the further discussion in Roberts, *Blacked Out*, passim, and Osborne, "The Ordinariness of the Archive," 56 ff.

30. Wallace, "The Public's Use of Federal Recordkeeping Statutes," 11–12.

31. See <http://www.archives.gov/>. The material on recovering from disasters includes guides to taking a "pro-active rather than re-active approach," institutional procedures, "saving family treasures," and salvage procedures.

32. See 44 U.S.C. Chapter 33 at <http://www.archives.gov/about/laws/disposal-of-records.html>.

33. Ibid. See also Wallace, "The Public's Use of Federal Recordkeeping Statutes," 146 ff.

34. See the discussion in Elizabeth B. Drewry, "Records Disposition in the Federal Government," *Public Administration Review* 15:3 (Summer 1955): 218–21.

35. See the discussion in Roberts, *Blacked Out*, 177–90; Athan Theoharis, *Culture of Secrecy: Government vs. the People's Right to Know* (Lawrence: University Press of Kansas, 1998).

36. The Professional Office System for managing electronic communications was menu driven and had a number of important features pertaining to records. See Wallace, "The Public's Use of Federal Recordkeeping Statutes," 1–2.

37. See the extended discussion in Wallace, "The Public's Use of Federal Recordkeeping Statutes," on which much of the following is based.

38. Ibid., 419–20.

39. As cited in ibid., 433.

40. Ibid., 502–5. See also Montgomery, *Subverting Open Government*, passim.

41. Ibid., 504.

42. Ibid., 430 ff. Tensions over the nature and release of presidential records continued in the United States in ways that further restricted access. For a caustic critique of the entire presidential library system, including this order, see

43. See Department of Justice FOIA Post, February 2009, item #1 "Courts of Appeal, Stewart v. Dept. of Interior 554 F. 3d 1236" (10th Cir. 2009) (Henry C.J.) <http://www.usdoj.gov/oip/foiapost/2009foiapost4.htm>. See also Department of Justice, *Freedom of Information Act Guide, March 2007 Edition*, ed. B.A. Cleveland (GPO: Washington, D.C., 2007).

44. This matter is discussed in detail in Rand Jimerson, *Archives Power: Memory, Accountability, and Social Justice* (Chicago: Society of American Archivists, 2009).

45. Jimerson, *Archives Power*.

46. Many historians might be surprised by, for example, the discussions on these important issues in the *South African Archives Journal, Archivaria, Archives and Manuscripts, Archival Issues*, and other archival journals. See, e.g., Terry Cook, "Mind Over Matter: Towards a New Theory of Archival Appraisal," in *The Archival Imagination: Essays in Honor of Hugh Taylor*, ed. B. Craig (Ottawa: Association of Canadian Archivists, 1992); "Electronic Records, Paper Minds: The Revolution in Information Management and Archives in the Post-Custodial and Postmodernist Era," *Archives and Manuscripts* 22 (November 1994): 300–329; and his "What Is Past Is Prologue," already cited. Brien Brothman and Richard Brown raised the postmodernist issue in Brien Brothman, "Orders of Value: Probing the Theoretical Terms of Archival Practice," *Archivaria* 32 (Summer 1991): 78–100; and Richard Brown, "The Value of 'Narrativity' in the Appraisal of Historical Documents: Foundation for a Theory of Archival Hermeneutics," *Archivaria* 32 (Summer 1991): 152–56; "Records Acquisition Strategy and its Theoretical Foundation: The Case for a Concept of Archival Hermeneutics," *Archivaria* 33 (Winter 1991–92): 34–56; and "Death of a Renaissance Record-Keeper: The Murder of Tomasso da Tortona in Ferrara, 1385," *Archivaria* 44 (Fall 1997): 1–43. Derrida's writing and

especially the publication of his *Mal d'Archive: Une impression freudienne* (Paris: Éditions Galilée, 1995), evoked penetrating commentary from archivists. See, esp., Brien Brothman, "The Limit of Limits: Derridean Deconstruction and the Archival Institution," *Archivaria* 36 (Autumn 1993): 205–20 and his review in *Archivaria* 43 (Spring 1997): 189–92; Verne Harris, "Claiming Less, Delivering More: A Critique of Positivist Formulations on Archives in South Africa," *Archivaria* 44 (Fall 1997): 132–41; and esp., "Postmodernism and Archival Appraisal: Seven Theses," *South African Archives Journal* 40 (1998). More recent work has included Preben Mortensen, "The Place of Theory in Archival Practice," *Archivaria* 47 (Spring 1999): 136–50; Eric Ketelaar, *The Archival Image* (Hilversum: Verloren, 1997), which contains among other essays thoughtful work on archival theory, and his "Archivalisation and Archiving," *Archives and Manuscripts* 27 (May 1999): 54–61; Francis Blouin, "Archivists, Mediation, and Constructs of Social Memory," *Archival Issues* 24:2 (1999): 101–12; and Bernadine Dodge, "Places Apart: Archives in Dissolving Space and Time," *Archivaria* 44 (Fall 1997): 118–31. A number of important contributions to this discussion were presented at the University of Michigan Sawyer Seminar. See Blouin and Rosenberg, *Archives*.

47. See, e.g., Roland M. Baumann, "The Administration of Access to Confidential Records in State Archives: Common Practices and the Need for the Model Law," *American Archivist* 49 (Fall 1986): 439–69; T. I. Bondareva, "Arkhivy Rossii na sluzhbe lichnosti, obshchestva, gosudarstva," [The Archives of Russia in the Service of Individuals, Society, and the State] *Otechestvennye arkhivy* 1998:6.

Chapter 10

1. Elizabeth L. Eisenstein, *The Printing Press as an Agent of Change: Communications and Cultural Transformations in Early Modern Europe* (Cambridge: Cambridge University Press, 1979).

2. National Science Foundation, *Revolutionizing Science and Engineering through Cyberinfrastructure: Report of the National Science Foundation Blue-Ribbon Advisory Panel on Cyberinfrastructure* (Washington, D.C.: National Science Foundation, 2003), i, 5, 6, and passim.

3. Roger Schonfeld, *JSTOR: A History* (Princeton: Princeton University Press, 2003).

4. American Council of Learned Societies, *Our Cultural Commonwealth: The Report of the American Council of Learned Societies Commission on Cyber-infrastructure for the Humanities and Social Sciences* (New York: ACLS, 2006).

5. PORTICO began with a 2002 grant from the Mellon Foundation in conjunction with JSTOR. Its aim was to design a sustainable electronic-archiving model. In 2004, the initiative became a part of Ithaka Harbors, Inc., a nonprofit organization with a mission "to accelerate the productive uses of information technologies for the benefit of higher education around the world." PORTICO emerged in 2005 designed for and by academic libraries and publishers. See <http://www.portico.org>. FEDORA (Flexible Extensible Digital Object and Repository Architecture) is a free, Linux-based operating system designed for various users by a community of contributors. See <http://fedoraproject.org>.

6. Clifford A. Lynch, "Institutional Repositories: Essential Infrastructure for Scholarship in the Digital Age," *ALR* 226 (February 2003): 2.

7. See <http://www.archive.org>.

8. See the interesting discussion by Robert M. Adler, "The Public Controversy over the Kennedy Memorabilia Project," in *Archives, Documentation, and Institutions of Social Memory*, ed. Francis X. Blouin, Jr. and William G. Rosenberg (Ann Arbor: University of Michigan Press, 2006), 225–37.

9. Cal Lee at the University of North Carolina is working on the application of forensics technologies to the problem of recovery of archives on outmoded technological platforms.

10. A cooperative project of Tufts and Yale universities conceived in 2005 illustrates this problem of "content management." Using FEDORA architecture for their electronic records preservation systems, these universities have adapted their respective institutional repositories for their university archives. The emphasis here is in ensuring through proper architecture

and storage programs that the records generated by university administrative systems can be effectively transferred into a designated digital archival repository in a way that assures the records to be trustworthy, authentic, and reliable. Broader issues concerning description and use have not yet been fully worked through. The resulting separate archival repositories at Tufts and Yale remain primarily the product of institutional information flow. How these "content managed" repositories become resources for historical research will depend on the descriptive systems archivists develop and how they can be accessed.

11. Robert Pear and Scott Shane, "Bush Data Threatens to Overload Archives," *New York Times* (December 27, 2009), A8–A9.

12. Ibid.

13. National Archives and Records Administration (NARA), *Performance and Accountability Report FY 2006* (Washington, D.C.: National Archives and Records Administration, 2007), 14–15. See also National Archives and Records Administration, *Preserving the Past to Protect the Future: The Strategic Plan of the National Archives and Records Administration 2006–2016* (Washington, D.C.: National Archives and Records Administration, 2006), 8–9, 20–21.

14. Luciana Duranti, Terry Eastwood, and Heather MacNeil, *Preservation of the Integrity of Electronic Records* (Dordrecht and Boston: Kluwer Academic, 2002), 11.

15. We are grateful to Rita Cacas of the NARA ERA Communications Office, who provided us with an overview of the ERA initiative.

16. *Performance and Accountability Report FY 2006*, 15.

17. Ibid., 16.

18. Given these challenges it is interesting to note here that on November 6, 2009 the US Senate confirmed David Ferrio as tenth Archivist of the United States. His experience as a prominent director of major research libraries and his background in library science was further indication that the challenges of information technologies had emerged as the central concern for the agency.

19. Bibliothèque Nationale de France, *Manuel de production documentaire: Utilisation des bases de production documentaire BnF Lotus Notes V6* (Paris: BNF, 2007).

20. National Archives and Records Administration (NARA), *Preserving the Past to Protect the Future: The Strategic Plan of the National Archives and Records Administration, 2006–2016* (Washington, D.C.: National Archives and Records Administration, 2006), ix.

21. <http://www.nsf.gov/dir/index.jsp?org=OCI>.

22. NSF-DELOS, *Invest to Save: Report and Recommendations of the NSF-DELOS Working Group on Digital Archiving and Preservation prepared for the National Science Foundation Digital Library Initiative and The European Union under the Fifth Framework Programme by the Network of Excellence for Digital Libraries* (Washington, D.C.: NSF-DELOS, 2003). See also *It's About Time: Research Challenges in Digital Archiving and Long-term Preservation. Final Report on a Workshop on Research Challenges in Digital Archiving* (Washington, D.C.: NSF-DELOS, 2002).

23. *NSF-DELOS Working Group on Digital Archiving and Preservation*, viii.

24. *New York Times*, May 20, 2009, 22.

25. *NSF-DELOS Working Group on Digital Archiving and Preservation*, 19–20.

26. See James O'Toole, "On the Idea of Permanence," *American Archivist* 52 (Winter 1989): 10–25.

27. Nicholson Baker, "Discards," *New Yorker*, April 4, 1994, 64–86.

28. One notable exception is the Making of America project, where a search points to a particular text on line. See <http://quod.lib.umich.edu/m/moagrp/>.

29. Jay David Bolter, *Writing Space: Computers, Hypertext, and the Remediation of Print* (Mahwah, N.J.: Lawrence Erlbaum Associates, 2001).

30. Stephen G. Nichols, "An Artifact by Any Other Name: Digital Surrogates of Medieval Manuscripts," in Blouin and Rosenberg, *Archives*, 134–43, esp. 142; <http://rose.mse.jhu.edu/; http://polarbears.si.umich.edu/>.

31. See <http://valley.vcdh.virginia.edu/>. An important discussion is in Edward Higgs, ed., *History and Electronic Artifacts* (Oxford: Oxford University Press, 1998), esp. Seamus Ross, "The Expanding World of Electronic Information and the Past's Future," 5–28. An interesting

discussion of the metaphors by which electronic databases like Profile, a continuously updated bank of British newspaper texts, are conceived as archives, is George Myerson, "The Electronic Archive," *History of the Human Sciences* 11:4 (1998): 85–101.

32. Aaron Swartz's experiment with a free on-line book catalog that anyone can update illustrates the problem. His goal was a "comprehensive Web page about any book ever published . . . with links that direct users to the nearest library." See *Chronicle of Higher Education*, 54 (February 22, 2008): 24.

33. See Brewster Kahle's Internet archive at <http://www.archive.org/index.php>. See also M. Day, "Preserving the Fabric of Our Lives: A Survey of Web Preservation Initiatives," in *Research and Advanced Technology for Digital Libraries: Proceedings of the 7th European Conference* (Berlin: Springer, 2003), 461–72.

34. Atina Grossman, "Out of the Closet and into the Archives? German Jewish Papers" and Frank Mecklenburg, "German Jewish Archives in Berlin and New York: Three Generations after the Fact," both in Blouin and Rosenberg, *Archives*, 89–105.

35. See Council on Library and Information Resources, *The Evidence in Hand: Report of the Task Force on the Artifact in Library Collections* (Washington, D.C.: CLIR, 2001); Rob Blackhurst, "Will History End Up in the Trash?" *Financial Times*, March 17, 2007. See also Robert Darnton, "The Library in the New Age," *New York Review of Books* LV:10 (June 12, 2008): 72–80.

36. Arden L. Bement, "Cyberinfrastructure: The Second Revolution," *Chronicle of Higher Education* (January, 2007), as quoted in former University of Michigan President James J. Duderstadt's "The Navigation of Universities through a Flat World," unpublished paper presented to the European University Association in Barcelona Spain, March 16, 2008.

Chapter 11

1. See Carolyn Steedman's spirited discussion of this in "'Something She Called a Fever': Michelet, Derrida, and Dust (or, In the Archives with Michelet and Derrida)," in *Archives, Documentation, and Institutions of Social Memory*, ed. Francis X. Blouin, Jr. and William G. Rosenberg (Ann Arbor: University of Michigan Press, 2006), 4–19.

2. See, e.g., the insightful discussions by Peter Fritzsche, "The Archive and the Case of the German Nation," in *Archive Stories: Fact, Fictions, and the Writing of History*, ed. Antoinette Burton (Durham, N.C.: Duke University Press, 2005); Brian Williams and William K. Wallach, "Documenting South Africa's Liberation Movements: Engaging the Archives at the University of Fort Hare," in Blouin and Rosenberg, *Archives*, 321–32; Verne Harris, "Redefining Archives in South Africa: Public Archives and Society in Transition, 1990–1996," *Archivaria* 42 (1996): 6-27.

3. John Randolph, "The Bakunin Family Archive," in Burton, *Archive Stories*, 211.

4. See, e.g., Rand Jimerson, *Archives Power: Memory, Accountability, and Social Justice* (Chicago: Society of American Archivists, 2009): esp. 323.

5. See the series *Bibliografia dell'Archivio vaticano* (Vatican City: Vaticano presso l'Archivio Segreto Vaticano e Biblioteca Apostolica Vaticana, 1962–2003). Nine volumes have been published to date.

6. Libraries at the Universities of Michigan and Pennsylvania have also explored new technologies for assigning user "tags" specific items in their catalogs. These "M-Tag" and "Penn-Tag" programs should permit an on-line conversation about sources apart from the formal descriptive systems, which itself will be searchable. Institution-specific systems like these, however, are unlikely to allow broader discussion about their materials that goes beyond their own institutional users, although the potential to do so is clearly there.

INDEX

Abbey of Saint-Germain-des-Près, Paris, 18
Abu-Graib, 128, 138
access, 4–5, 7, 20, 22–23, 28–29, 31, 33–34, 36–39,
    41, 45–46, 48, 51, 52, 53–56, 58, 60, 64,
    66–67, 69–70, 86–87, 89–92, 101–2, 105,
    111, 114, 119, 123, 132, 138, 140, 144–45,
    147, 149–51, 155, 161–72, 176–79, 181–82,
    184–90, 193–98, 200–208, 212–15
  on-line, 3, 52–53, 55–56, 128, 188, 199–203,
    213–14, 238–39n.28, 241n.28, 242n.6
acquisition, 6, 31, 33–34, 37, 46, 49, 57, 60, 63, 69,
    83, 98, 103, 111, 113–15, 121, 124, 129–30,
    133, 137, 143–45, 149–50, 156–60, 163–64,
    182, 184, 209
Adams, Herbert Baxter, 27
administration. *See* archival administration
administration, colonial, 209
Adorno, Theodor, 70
Aeronautic and Space Museum, 106, 116–18, 130,
    231n.3
Afanasiev, Iuri, 166–67
affirmative action, 107
Africa, 71, 82, 100, 113, 126, 133, 208–9
African-Americans, 82
African National Congress (ANC), 113
agencies, 9, 20–21, 27, 30, 33–35, 42–43, 48–49,
    55–56, 60, 72, 86, 89, 91, 114, 121, 132, 134,
    142–43, 147–48, 150–52, 168–70, 173, 175,
    177, 179–80, 190, 194
  originating, 38, 57, 144–45, 148, 150, 169, 178
Air Force Association, 116–17
Alperovitz, Gar, 117
Amazon.com, 213
AMC. *See* Archives and Manuscript Control)
American Archivist, 39, 41, 43–44, 46–47, 54, 159,
    164, 167, 175, 217
American Anthropological Association, 230n.45
American Historical Association (AHA), 8, 36–37,
    39, 43–44, 91, 161, 164, 175–76, 238n.16
American Historical Review, 36, 131

amnesia, social, 32, 99, 106–8, 110–12, 114–15,
    135, 138, 154, 209
Amsterdam, 157
Ananich, B.V., 70, 231n.6
Anderson, Benedict, 26, 75, 100, 107
Annales, 67–71, 73, 83, 99
Ann Arbor, Michigan, 56
anthropology, 7, 13–14, 68, 78, 110, 134–35, 210
Appleby, Joyce, 132
appraisal, 8, 10, 33, 38–39, 41–42, 45, 50, 58,
    60–62, 69, 87–88, 91, 98, 114, 118–19,
    133–34, 140, 145–47, 149, 152, 158, 163,
    182, 184, 188, 192, 196, 205, 209–10, 214
appraisal debates, 61–62, 140, 158, 223n.28
archival divide, 7, 10–11, 38, 85, 87, 89, 91–93,
    101, 117–18, 132, 137–38, 140, 152, 161,
    179, 181–82, 185, 189, 207–11, 213–17
archival grain, 118–22, 192, 196, 209, 211
archival theory, 13, 16, 39, 44, 46, 52, 57, 59, 62,
    66, 75, 83, 85, 88, 90, 93, 117, 130–31, 166,
    189, 212, 217, 239–40n.46
archive and archives, definitions and meanings of, 4,
    6–7, 17, 21, 31, 117–19, 138, 140–41, 183, 196
archives, 3–10, 13–26, 28–34, 38–60, 63–66, 69,
    71, 73–76, 78, 80–82, 84–92, 97–99, 107–15,
    117–38, 140–69, 171–80, 182–214, 217
  absences in, 118–19, 123, 209, 225n.32
  administration, 4, 7, 16, 20–23, 29, 34, 38–41,
    43, 59, 85, 89, 92, 111, 120, 124, 127, 136,
    143, 150, 154–55, 162–67, 171–72, 176–77,
    182, 184–85, 210
  arrangement and description, 38, 41, 52–53, 86,
    119–20, 133, 135, 147, 149, 152, 192
  authoritarian systems, in, 80, 106, 113–14, 122,
    152–53, 163–64, 168, 177, 182
  authoritative, 13, 15, 17, 19, 21, 23, 25–27, 29,
    31, 33, 38, 65, 68, 74, 78, 84, 99, 103, 133,
    136, 185, 189, 213
  authorities in, 8–9, 19–20, 32–34, 39–41, 50–63,
    65, 67, 69, 71–73, 75–77, 79, 81, 83, 86–87,

archives (*Continued*)
    92, 97, 107, 113, 118, 132, 134, 143, 153,
    158, 169, 172, 188, 204–5, 208–9
  authors, as, 135
  British, 18, 21, 38, 42, 71, 168, 217
  business and corporate, 29, 38, 46, 50–51, 89,
    150, 154, 156, 169–70, 190, 195
  Canadian, 138, 144, 146, 158, 208
  capacity of, 24, 35, 51–52, 87, 91, 97, 108, 147,
    149, 179, 184, 191, 194–95, 197–98, 201,
    211, 213
  catalogues and cataloguing in, 5, 19, 23, 33–35,
    42, 51–55, 59, 64, 75–77, 84, 93, 111–12,
    114–15, 120–21, 123, 135–36, 146, 160,
    169–70, 178–80, 193, 199–202, 204, 212–14,
    242n.32
  changing conceptions of, 4, 6–7, 17, 21, 31,
    117–19, 138, 140–41, 183, 196
  Chinese, 17–18, 23, 32, 34, 36, 110, 136–37,
    152, 208
  church, 17, 21, 28, 34, 166
  city, 4, 153
  classification in, 22–23, 30, 53, 90, 111, 118, 122–
    23, 140, 149–50, 164, 167–68, 170, 195, 214
  colonial, 23, 120, 122, 137, 209
  community, 6–7, 45, 47, 53, 55, 63, 88, 129,
    155, 193
  constituencies of, 47–49, 61–62, 158
  contexts of, 34, 58, 61, 90, 103, 119, 121, 123,
    134, 143, 153, 157–58, 160, 197, 203, 208,
    211, 213
  counter, 128, 138
  cultures of, 108, 120, 136, 142, 152, 156–57, 189
  data, 51, 234n.6
  declassification in, 123, 168–69, 238n.16,
    238–39n.28
  description, 10, 27, 30, 33–34, 38, 41, 46, 52–54,
    57, 63, 68, 70, 77, 80, 86, 91, 100, 113–14,
    119, 122, 133, 136, 143, 147–50, 152, 160,
    178, 184, 192, 197, 207, 213–15, 240–41n.10
  diaspora, 133
  digital (electronic), 10, 50, 52, 58–59, 89, 139,
    151, 184–85, 187–90, 193, 195–96, 198–99,
    202–5, 209–11, 214, 232n.6, 240–41n.10
  Dutch, 29–30, 38, 53, 153–54, 174, 181, 219n.31
  East European, 208
  essentialism in, 10, 54–55, 85–89, 91, 93
  European, 8, 13, 17–21, 23, 26–27, 30–33, 35–
    37, 64, 71–72, 75, 83, 90, 97, 100, 102, 104,
    107, 125, 135, 148, 150, 161–62, 166–67,
    171, 204, 208, 210
  files and filing, 19–20, 34, 38–39, 91, 122, 141,
    146, 148–49, 171, 173, 178–79, 187, 189,
    193, 197, 205, 213
  film, 128, 228n.11
  French, 4, 20–22, 25, 33–34, 36, 42, 64, 67, 104,
    108–9, 124–25, 143, 152, 159, 166, 195,
    198–200, 208

future, 4, 6–10, 14, 21, 40, 48, 51–52, 57, 60, 66,
    71, 83, 86–89, 92, 98, 104, 108–9, 112, 121,
    127, 135, 137, 139–40, 142, 145, 147, 150,
    152–53, 158–60, 166, 170, 172, 174, 181–82,
    184–89, 192, 194, 196, 198, 200, 203–7,
    211–12, 214–15
gender in, 225n.32
German, 20, 25, 27, 30, 37, 67, 114, 125, 132,
    151
Greek, 7, 17
historical, 3, 6–7, 22–23, 32–33, 38, 42, 44,
    51–52, 60, 63–84, 89, 92, 98, 114, 124, 129,
    133–35, 137, 152, 156–57, 166, 179, 187–88,
    192, 209, 212
identity, 117–18, 121, 132–35, 137–38, 143,
    156, 209, 214
as information systems, 54, 59, 86, 89, 188,
    190–91, 197
institutional, 5, 43, 75, 121, 157, 186–87, 189,
    191
internet, 117, 188, 238–39n.28
Israeli, 138
Italian, 19
Japanese, 208
management, 30, 39, 46
mediation in, 58, 72, 102, 119, 143–45, 147,
    149–53, 158, 160, 163, 168, 187, 196, 205
memory, as, 227n.5
monumental, 124, 126–27
music, 234n.12
national and state, 4, 9, 21–22, 32–33, 36–37,
    39–43, 45, 51, 64, 76, 92, 98, 124–25, 133,
    138, 143, 146, 152–53, 159–63, 165, 170,
    172–76, 191, 193, 195, 197–98, 204–5, 207,
    237n.5
neutrality of, 16, 38, 79, 104, 117–18, 124, 128,
    134–35, 142, 146–47, 154, 156, 158, 163,
    181
omissions in, 118–19, 123, 209, 225n.32
photographic, 128
politics in, 161, 163–65, 167, 169, 171, 173, 175,
    177, 179–81, 205
practices and principles, 3, 5–11, 24, 26, 31, 33,
    37, 39–40, 42–46, 52–53, 62, 80, 85–87, 89,
    92, 98, 101, 108–9, 111, 113–14, 117–19,
    123, 125, 132, 136–38, 140, 142–44, 152,
    156–57, 161–63, 166, 170–73, 177–79,
    181–82, 184–86, 189, 194, 205, 207–10,
    214–15
public, 36, 48, 64, 138, 155, 162–63, 176, 182,
    214
registers, 53, 56, 64, 82, 141, 148, 164, 178, 199,
    213
romance of, 24–26, 218n.20
Russian and Soviet, 6, 14, 19–21, 111–12, 122,
    124, 126, 133, 136, 149, 151, 163, 166–68,
    171, 198, 208, 232n.25, 238n.14
searching in, 23, 52, 56, 184, 187, 204, 213

sources, 14, 40, 53–55, 57, 63–66, 80, 93, 115, 117–19, 122, 125, 131–32, 171–72, 195, 210
South African, 181, 208–9
Spanish, 21
standards, 28, 186
state, 7, 17–18, 20–22, 24–26, 29–30, 32–36, 38, 42, 45, 61, 64–65, 69, 72, 77, 79–80, 83, 89–91, 114–15, 119, 121, 123–27, 129, 132, 135–36, 138, 150–52, 154, 156–58, 160–64, 166, 168–69, 171, 173–74, 179–80, 182, 208–9, 211, 217
survey, 39, 41, 46, 52, 62, 85, 88, 144–45
transfers to, 5, 58, 144, 161, 169, 175–76, 201, 205
transparency in, 142
university, 4, 7, 88, 240–41n.10
U.S., 4, 9, 21, 32–33, 35–37, 39–43, 45, 76, 98, 125, 133, 138, 143, 152–53, 159, 162, 165, 170, 172–76, 191, 193, 197–98, 204, 207
users of, 48–49, 52–53, 57, 121, 123, 126, 128, 133, 141, 147–52, 154, 159, 162, 166, 169, 173, 178–79, 181, 183, 185, 187–88, 191–92, 196–97, 199–202, 207, 210–15
value systems in, 163
Vatican, 18–20, 27–28, 148, 165, 199, 212–13
verification in, 8, 14, 16, 18–20, 27–28, 31, 34, 64–67, 73–74, 80, 103–4, 107, 112–13, 160, 178–79, 217
women's history, 134
Archives and Manuscript Control (AMC), 54
Archives and Museum Informatics, 58
Archives for the Congregation of the Doctrine of the Faith (CDF), Vatican, 148
Archives Nationales, Paris, 4, 20–22, 25, 33–34, 36, 42, 67, 104, 108–9, 124–25, 159, 166, 195, 200
Archivio Segreto Vaticano. *See* archives, Vatican
Archivist of the United States, 8, 39–40, 91, 98, 143, 154, 161, 164–65, 175–76, 241n.18
Archivists
accountability of, 22, 30, 152, 181–82, 194
as activists, 5, 10, 77, 117, 140–43, 145, 147, 149, 151–61, 165, 180, 196
American, 39, 43–44, 47, 54, 159, 164, 175, 217
Australian, 142, 222n.15
British, 18, 21, 38, 42, 71, 168, 217
Canadian, 138, 144, 146, 158, 208, 222n.9, 227n.13
Chinese, 17–18, 23, 32, 34, 36, 110, 136–37, 152, 208
Dutch, 29–30, 38, 53, 153–54, 174, 181, 219n.31
French, 4, 20–22, 25, 33–34, 36, 42, 64, 67, 104, 108–9, 124–25, 143, 152, 159, 166, 195, 198–200, 208
German, 20, 25, 27, 30, 37, 67, 114, 125, 132, 151
objectivity of, 147, 149, 171, 181
professional identities of, 31, 38, 42–45, 49, 51, 62, 86, 92, 100, 124, 138, 142–43, 147,

149, 152, 154, 156–58, 160, 162, 170, 172, 179–80, 189, 192, 205, 208, 211, 215
research consultants, as, 150–51, 176, 178
Russian and Soviet, 6, 14, 19–21, 111–12, 122, 124, 126, 136, 149, 151, 163, 166–68, 171, 198, 208, 232–33n.25
South African, 181, 208–9
Spanish, 21
training of, 43, 89, 152, 164
Aries, Philippe, 99
arrangement and description, 38, 41, 52–53, 86, 119–20, 133, 135, 147, 149, 152, 192
Arthur, Chester, 164
artifacts, 5, 15, 25, 57, 84, 103, 108–9, 112–13, 117, 127–28, 131, 134, 140, 160, 187–88, 199, 201–2, 205
Association of Records Managers and Administrators (ARMA), 49
Atkins, Dan, 185
Australia, 142
authenticity, 8–9, 15, 17–19, 24–25, 28, 30–32, 35, 38, 47, 60, 64–65, 67, 70, 80, 99, 127–30, 134, 187, 194, 203–4, 240–41n.10
authoritarianism, 80, 106, 113–14, 122, 152–53, 163–64, 168, 177, 182
authority, meanings of, 5–6, 33–34
authority and authorities
in archives, 8–9, 19–20, 32–34, 39–41, 50–51, 53, 55, 57–63, 65, 67, 69, 71–73, 75–77, 79, 81, 83, 86–87, 92, 97, 107, 113, 118, 132, 134, 143, 153, 158, 169, 172, 188, 204–5, 208–9
bibliographic, 55
contextual, 35, 143
counter, 87, 98
in digital records, 190, 194–96, 202, 204, 214
in history, 3, 5–8, 10, 15, 21, 24–26, 32–37, 39, 41–43, 45, 47–50, 58, 63, 65, 67, 69, 71, 73–84, 90, 97–103, 107–13, 115, 125, 127–33, 135, 143–44, 146, 151, 179, 199–202, 205, 208, 213, 217n.4
institutional, 82, 203
political, 7, 26, 75, 82–83, 134, 164
authors, 19, 25, 30, 53–54, 106, 118, 127, 132, 135–37, 148, 159, 187, 190–91, 202

B

Bacon, Roger, 16, 64
Bakhmeteff Archive, New York, 157
Bakhtin, Mikhail, 113
Baldini, Ugo, 148
Balkan wars, 110
Bantin, Philip, 86
Bartlett, Nancy Ruth, 124, 160, 235n.18
Barzun, Jacques, 43
Bayle, Pierre, 64

Bearman, David, 52, 58–59, 89
Belgium, 21
Bellagio, Italy, 161, 176
Bentley Historical Library, Ann Arbor, 56, 202
Berkhofer, Robert, 76–77
Berlin, 66, 99
Bernstein, Barton, 117
bibliographies, 53, 55, 186, 199, 213–14
Bibliothèque Nationale, Paris, 192, 195–96
Bienecke Library, New Haven, 198
biography, 106, 135
Bloch, Marc, 43, 67–68
Boles, Frank, 62
Bolkovitinov, N.N., 166–67
Bolsheviks, 14, 112, 122, 164
Boston City Archives, 4
Boyarin, Jonathan, 107, 129–30
Braudel, Fernand, 67–69, 74
British Museum, 199
Brokaw, Tom, 105
Brooks, Philip C., 41
Brothman, Brien, 181
Brown, Richard, 181
Buck, Solon J., 41
Bukharin, Nikolai, 122
bulk. See records, growth of
Burckhardt, Jacob, 26–27, 74
Burke, Frank G., 45–47, 53
Bush, George H.W., 161, 165, 175–76
Bush, George W., 128, 154, 161, 165, 175–76, 193

C

Cambodia, 74
Campbell, Ann Morgan, 49
Canada, 99, 138, 144, 146, 158
Cappon, Lester J., 46–47, 57
Cacas, Rita, 241n.15
Carlin, John, 91–92, 164–65, 176
catalogs, 5, 19, 34–35, 53, 64, 84, 114, 135–36,
    178–79, 193, 199–201, 204
    bibliographic principles in, 53
    card, 199–201
    machine reading, 54
    on-line, 52, 199–202, 213–14,
    242n.32
Catholicism, 212
Central Party Archive, Moscow, 232n.25
celebrations and memorialization, 107, 109
censorship, 155, 166, 179
Center for Electronic Records, 176–77
Center for Public Integrity, 171
Central State Archive of the October Revolution,
    Moscow, 125
Certeau, Michel de, 105, 121
Chandler, Alfred, 29, 155
charters, 18, 21, 135

Cheney, Richard, 165
Chicago, 36, 46, 74, 217
China, 17–18, 23, 32, 34, 36, 110, 136–37, 152, 208
ChoicePoint corporation, 169
CIA, 14, 17–21, 23, 30, 36, 38, 40, 46–47, 66, 72,
    76, 109, 112, 121–23, 128, 144, 153–55,
    158–59, 168, 174–75, 180–81, 190–93, 197,
    208, 213, 238–39n.28
citations, 14, 64–65, 67, 74, 132, 148, 202, 204, 213
citizenship, 71
city archives, 4, 153
civil rights, 71, 74, 77, 173
Civil War, Russian, 136, 232n.25
Civil War, U.S., 32, 35, 49, 109, 136, 156, 201–2,
    230n.43
class, social, 68, 71, 81, 83, 90, 98–99, 110
classification, 22–23, 30, 53, 90, 111, 118, 122–23,
    140, 149–50, 164, 167–68, 170, 195, 214
Clinton, Bill, 164–65, 176
Clinton Presidential Library, 154
Coca Cola Company, 154
Cohen, Eldon S., 42
Cold War, 71, 79, 116
collections, unique, 52, 205
collections and collecting institutions, 4–5, 32–33,
    36, 46, 53–54, 56–57, 59, 68, 107, 111, 115,
    119–22, 125–26, 134–35, 144–45, 148–51,
    156–57, 162–64, 168, 178–80, 198–201, 203,
    207, 209, 214–15
collective identities. See indentities
collective memory. See social memory
Collingwood, R.G., 8
colonial and postcolonial studies, 120, 122, 212
Columbian Exhibition 1893, 36
Columbia University, 150, 157
commemoration, 17, 40, 98, 104–5, 108–9, 124,
    127, 130, 230n.42 See also reenactments
computers, 4–6, 51–53, 55–56, 59, 62, 93, 176,
    183–85, 187–88, 190–94, 196, 198, 200–201,
    210, 212
Comte, Auguste, 27
Congress, U.S., 37, 40, 45, 52–56, 116–17, 164,
    173, 193, 195, 199
Connor, R.D.W., 30–31, 39–42, 49, 59, 61, 89, 120,
    150, 155–56, 192, 211
Connor, Seymour V., 42
Conrail Corporation, 145
Constitution, U.S., 40, 108–10, 113, 173
content management, concept of, 187–88, 192,
    240–41n.10
contexts and contextualization, 33–34, 42, 58,
    61, 90, 103, 119, 121, 123, 134, 143, 153,
    157–58, 160, 197, 203, 208, 211, 213, 231n.6
Cook, Terry, 49, 138, 158–59, 181
Coolidge, Calvin, 164
Cooper, Frederick, 43, 126, 169, 186, 212
copyright, 186, 200
courts, 5, 15–16, 18, 21–22, 27, 31, 34, 42, 45, 49,

61, 64, 67, 80, 103, 105, 123, 134, 143–46,
150–51, 153, 155, 158, 161–67, 169–71,
173–82, 188, 192–93, 208
CREST access system, 238–39n.28
Critical Theory, 131
Cuba, 87
cultural turn, 74–77
culture and cultural studies, 9, 13–14, 57, 70, 73,
76–77, 93, 98–99, 108, 110, 120, 134, 136,
149, 152–53, 155–57, 183, 186, 189, 199,
201–4, 211–12
cultures of records production, 152, 154–55
Cunningham, Adrian, 58
curators, 44, 47, 116, 124, 130, 142, 151, 161, 180,
192, 210–11, 215
custodial tradition, 9–10, 20, 35–36, 38–40, 45–48,
50, 62–64, 85–86, 88, 93, 98, 118, 143, 172,
177–78, 181
cyberinfrastructure, 183–89, 191, 193, 195, 197,
199–201, 203, 205
cyberspace, 187, 189, 191, 198–99, 201
Czechoslovakia, 75

D

D'Alembert, Jean-Baptists, 16
Darwin, Charles, 27, 29, 79
databases, 51, 151, 171–72, 186, 238–39n.28,
241–42n.31
    bibliographic, 199
data mining, 151
Declaration of Independence, U.S., 40, 167, 173
declassification, 123, 168–69, 238n.16, 238–39n.28
decolonialization, 71
deconstruction, 75–76, 78, 132
Deep Blue, University of Michigan, 186–87
Dell, Michael, 183
de Maupassant, Guy, 74
democracy and democratic practices, 23, 27, 29,
35, 46, 66, 71, 74–75, 114, 124, 128, 143,
152–53, 163–64, 166–68, 171–72, 177, 182,
209
demographers, 68
Denmark, 191
Department of Defense, U.S., 91, 143
Department of Justice, U.S., 171
Department of State, U.S., 174
Derrida, Jacques, 7, 70, 76, 78–79, 84, 103, 115,
119, 130, 140–42, 160, 217
Descartes, Rene, 16, 64
description, 10, 15, 27, 30, 33–34, 38, 41, 46,
52–54, 56–59, 63, 70, 77, 82, 86, 91,
100, 113–14, 119, 122, 133, 135, 143,
147–49, 152, 184, 192, 198, 207, 209, 213,
240–41n.10 *See also* archives, description;
records, description
d'Haussonville, Baron, 36

Dickens, Charles, 97
Dien Bien Phu, 69
digital archives. *See* archives, digital
digital records. *See* records, digital
digitization and digital technologies, 4, 6–7, 9–10,
50–53, 57–62, 85–89, 91–93, 117, 123, 127,
144–47, 151, 154–55, 158, 170–71, 174–75,
177–79, 181–82, 184–85, 187–90, 193–99,
201–15
diplomatics, 7, 18–19, 30, 41, 59–60, 125
Dirks, Nicholas, 47, 120–22, 124, 136–37
disposition, 57, 87, 119, 143, 151, 174, 176, 181,
192, 196, 209
documents and documentation, 3–4, 6–10, 14–26,
28–30, 32–39, 41–42, 45, 47–48, 50, 52–56,
58–63, 65, 69, 78, 80, 83–90, 92, 99–100,
103, 107, 110–11, 113–38, 140–46, 148,
151–52, 154–55, 157–60, 165, 167–75,
177–81, 183–84, 187–215
    archival, 3–4, 6–8, 15, 18–19, 23–24, 30, 32, 36,
42, 51, 53–57, 65, 68, 72, 78, 82, 97, 111,
114, 116, 120, 123, 125, 127, 129–32, 136,
141–42, 147–50, 152, 157, 162, 164–65,
167–68, 177–78, 181, 183, 187, 195, 198–99,
203–6, 209–12, 215
    authentic, 15, 31, 47, 59–60, 240–41n.10
    authoritative, 7–9, 14–20, 22–25, 28, 30, 32, 35,
37–38, 47, 60, 64–65, 80, 83, 91, 129, 136,
153, 179, 194–95
    authority of, 130
    classification of, 22, 53, 118, 122, 150, 164,
167–68, 170, 180, 214
    content, 20, 24–25, 30, 38, 41, 54, 60, 66, 69, 76,
115, 119, 122, 125, 131, 135, 144, 147–51,
156–58, 162, 169, 172, 178, 180, 186–93,
196, 201–3, 213
    contexts of, 16, 18, 27, 30, 33–34, 42, 47, 53–54,
58–59, 61, 72–73, 76, 88, 123, 134, 136,
152–53, 156–58, 160, 163, 172, 174, 182,
187, 190, 194, 203, 208, 211, 231n.6
    creation of, 164, 181
    destruction of, 23, 37, 48, 83, 87, 92, 110, 114,
123, 145, 151, 160, 164, 167, 171, 173–76,
184, 187, 192, 196, 205, 207
    digital, 4, 9, 50–53, 57–61, 86–87, 89, 91, 123,
127, 144, 146–47, 154–55, 170, 176–78, 182,
184–87, 190, 193–98, 201–8, 210, 213–15
    enduring value of, 174, 221n.43
    evaluation of, 143, 146
    as evidence, 89, 234n.16
    generation of, 178
    historical, 4–9, 15–17, 21–22, 24–26, 31–33, 35,
37–43, 46, 48, 52, 55, 60, 62–64, 69, 80, 82,
86–87, 91–92, 97, 102, 115, 118, 125–26,
132–33, 140–43, 147, 152, 156–58, 160, 163,
166–67, 172–73, 176, 188, 191, 197, 201,
203, 208, 214–15, 221n.43
    memory, 229n.27

documents (*Continued*)
  nature of, 129
  photographs, 51, 84, 110, 112, 126–30, 138, 153,
    173, 187, 197
  preservation and retention, 6, 8–9, 17, 20, 26,
    33, 35–41, 43, 48–50, 52, 58–63, 65, 68, 83,
    86, 88–89, 92, 98, 108, 111, 114, 117, 124,
    126–27, 129, 133–34, 137, 140, 143, 154,
    156, 163–65, 167, 170, 172–75, 181–82, 184,
    187–92, 194–98, 205–6, 209–10, 214
  production of, 41, 45, 47
  retrieval of, 4, 23, 31, 38–39, 45, 48, 52–53, 56,
    87, 89, 170–71, 184, 188, 190, 193–97
Documentum content management system, 191
donors, 144–45, 151, 163
Dordrecht, Netherlands, 153–54
Douglas, Mary, 77
DSpace@MIT, 186
Duchein, Michel, 22
Duderstadt, James, 170
Duranti, Luciana, 59–60, 86, 194
Dutch Manual, 29–30
Dutch States-General archives, 154

E

EAC. *See* Encoded Archival Context
Eastern Europe, 8, 75, 83, 107, 150, 161–62,
    166–67, 208
East India Company, 120, 137
École des Chartes, 22, 28, 30
Edison, Thomas A., 27
Einstein, Albert, 130
Eisenstein, Elizabeth, 183, 196
electronic-archiving services, 9, 52, 57–59, 89, 91,
    170, 176, 186, 194–97, 208
Electronic Records Archive System (ERA), 195, 197
electronic. *See* digital, 183
Eley, Geoff, 222–26n.33
Ellsberg, Daniel, 180
e-mail, 145–46, 155, 165, 174–75, 188, 190–93, 195
empires, 19, 29, 36, 115, 120, 136, 142
Encoded Archival Context (EAC), 59
Encoded Archival Description (EAD), 56–57, 59
Encyclopédie, 104, 217
enduring value, 17, 24, 48, 55, 60–61, 85–91, 141,
    147, 156, 158, 172, 174, 178, 184, 188–89,
    192–93, 198–99, 205, 208–9, 221n.43
England, 18, 21, 27, 37–38, 59, 104, 120–21, 136,
    140, 168, 199, 217
Enlightenment, 16, 23–24, 65, 79–80, 104
Enola Gay, 106, 116–18, 130, 233n.37
Enola Gay Archive, 117
Enron corporation, 192
epistemology, 8–9, 78, 110, 132, 136, 140, 178,
    224n.3
Epstein, Fritz, 42

essentialism, 9–10, 17, 55, 85, 87, 89, 91, 93, 137,
    143, 146, 157, 172
  in archives, 85, 87, 89–91, 93, 137, 143
  in history, 9, 90
ethics, 5, 18, 23, 38–40, 46–47, 49, 60–61, 64, 87,
    89, 99, 102, 104–6, 109–10, 112, 114, 117,
    120, 130–31, 138, 151, 161–62, 173–74,
    176–82, 191, 194–95, 211–12, 214
ethnicity, 8, 51, 75, 77–78, 81–84, 90, 100, 107,
    110, 115, 134, 209
ethnographers, 68
Europe, 8, 13, 17–21, 23, 26–27, 30–33, 35–37, 64,
    71–72, 75, 83, 90, 97, 100, 102, 104, 107,
    125, 135, 148, 150, 161–62, 166–67, 171,
    204, 208, 210
European Framework Programme of the Network
    of Excellence for Digital Libraries, 197
European Union, 171
events, historical, 6, 8, 14, 19, 24, 27, 32, 34,
    66–69, 74, 77–78, 80–82, 88, 90, 100, 102–3,
    119, 128, 141–42, 160, 166, 180
evidence, 7, 16, 19, 24–25, 28, 31, 41–42, 51, 58,
    64–65, 82–86, 89–91, 99, 101, 104, 107, 110,
    112, 114–15, 118, 121–22, 128, 130–31, 136,
    146, 153, 160, 165, 172–73, 189, 202, 217
  archival, 51, 82, 107, 112, 115, 130
  historical, 7, 114, 160
exhibitions, 36, 116–17, 130, 159
experience, authority of, 3, 5–6, 8, 24–25, 73–74,
    76–78, 82–83, 90, 98–103, 108–13, 125,
    127–30, 132, 135, 144, 151, 199–202, 213
explanation, in history, 9, 16, 21, 23, 26, 34, 42, 48,
    66–67, 72–74, 85, 87, 90–91, 97, 99, 101–3,
    106, 129, 133, 157, 163, 173, 181, 212

F

Family Educational Rights and Privacy Act, U.S., 150
Favier, Lucie, 152
FBI, 149, 165, 168, 173
Febvre, Lucien, 67
Federal Records Act (FRA) of 1950, 164, 173,
    175–76
Federal Records Disposal Act of 1943, 173
FEDORA electronic archiving service, 186,
    240nn.5, 10
Feith, J.A., 29
Feldman, Gerald, 131
Ferrio, David, 241n.18
files. *See* archives, files
films, 99, 110, 127–29, 205, 235n.32
finding aids, 3, 22, 31, 34, 38, 53–54, 56–57, 78,
    82, 148–49, 160, 167, 170–71, 177, 179, 187,
    199, 202–3, 209, 211–14
  interarctive, 56, 170, 213–14
Finley, Moses, 83, 217n.4
First Nations, 78

Fishbein, Meyer, 51
FOIA. *See* Freedom of Information Acts
fonds, 30, 42, 76, 147, 149, 178, 205, 213
footnotes, 14, 64–65, 67, 74, 132, 148, 202,
    204, 213
Ford, Gerald R., 47
Ford Motor Company, 154, 190
Foreign Office, Great Britain, 168
forgery and fraud, 18, 25, 28, 65, 83, 131, 180
forgetting. *See* social amnesia
Foucault, Michel, 70, 79, 140
Fourier, Jean Baptiste Joseph, 27
FRA. *See* Federal Records Act
France, 4, 18, 20–22, 25, 27, 29, 33–34, 36–37,
    42, 67, 74, 78, 100, 104, 108–9, 124–25,
    138, 143, 152, 159, 165–66, 195, 200, 208,
    219n.29
Franklin D. Roosevelt Library, 44
Freedom of Information Acts (FOIA), 123, 155,
    163, 165–66, 168–69, 171, 174, 176–77,
    179–80
French Revolution, 20, 33–34, 104, 166
Freud, Sigmund, 27
Fruin, Robert, 29
Fukuyama, Francis, 71, 84
functional analysis, 88–89

G

Galloway, Patricia, 123
Gance, Abel, 110
Gates, Bill, 126, 183
Geary, Patrick, 135, 137
Geertz, Clifford, 70, 77
gender and gender studies, 8, 51, 57, 77–78, 81–84,
    90, 97–98, 115, 118, 133, 135, 157, 209, 211,
    225n.32
genealogy, 49, 75, 173
General Accounting Office, U.S., 174
General Services Administration, U.S., 43
Genovese, Elizabeth Fox, 81, 225n.30
Genovese, Eugene, 80
geography, 68–69
Germany, 15, 19–20, 27–30, 37–38, 67, 106, 112,
    114, 125, 131–32, 149, 151, 157, 171, 203,
    208, 217
Gillis, John, 230n.42
Ginzburg, Carlo, 83
George Washington University, 232n.18
Goethe, Johann Wolfgang von, 27
Goody, Jack, 104
Google, 183, 187–88, 196, 200, 202, 204–5
Gorbachev, Mikhail, 166
Gottschalk, Louis, 43
governmentality, 120, 163
Grafton, Anthony, 18, 64, 217
grammar of objectivity, defined, 65

Great Britain, 18, 21, 27, 37–38, 59, 86, 104,
    120–21, 136, 140, 168, 199, 217, 241–42n.31
Guizot, François, 29, 219n.29

H

Habermas, Jürgen, 70
Hackman, Larry, 48
Hagley Museum and Library, 156
Haimson, Leopold, 71–72
Halbwachs, Maurice, 99, 103, 108, 229n.27
Haley, Alex, 100
Ham, F. Gerald, 9, 45–47, 86, 88, 132
Harris, Sir Arthur "Bomber," 106
Harris, Verne, 106, 181
Harvard University, 157, 198, 217
Harwit, Martin, 116–17
Hedstrom, Margaret, 52, 89, 197
Hegel, Georg Wilhelm Friedrich, 24, 98
Heidegger, Martin, 79
Herder, Johann Gottfried von, 27
heritage and heritage industry, 21–22, 40, 99–100,
    109, 152–53, 197
Hevia, James, 136
Himmelfarb, Gertrude, 80–81, 131, 225n.30
Hiphop Archive, Harvard University, 157
historians, 3–10, 14–16, 22–23, 25–28, 31–34,
    36–37, 39–40, 43–44, 46–48, 51–53, 55, 57,
    63–65, 70–71, 73, 75–93, 97–99, 101, 103–5,
    114–15, 117–19, 121–23, 125, 129, 131–42,
    145–46, 148–49, 152, 157–58, 160–64,
    166–70, 172–73, 175, 177–85, 189, 193, 196,
    198, 201, 206–8, 210–15
    academic, 13, 15, 78, 84, 105, 132, 157, 210
    archival, 24, 26, 31, 46, 63–64, 68, 81, 99, 150,
        167, 169–71, 177, 182, 208
    art, 212
    cultural, 9, 13–14, 57, 70, 73, 76–77, 93, 98–99,
        108, 110, 120, 134, 136, 149, 152–53,
        155–57, 183, 186, 189, 199, 201–4, 211–12
    interests of, 10, 62, 88
    professional, 9, 14, 20, 22, 24, 36, 44–46, 70, 75,
        79, 81–82, 90, 106, 125, 129–30, 151, 156,
        173, 196, 208
    social, 50–51, 69, 71–73, 77, 83–84, 100, 131, 157
historical anthropology, 13–14
historical archives. *See* archives, historical
Historical Records Surveys, U.S., 41
historical societies, 15, 19–20, 27–30, 32–35,
    37–38, 41, 67, 106, 112, 114, 125,
    131–32, 149, 151, 157, 171, 203, 208, 217
historical sociologists, 70, 75
historicism and historicity, 8, 24, 27, 46, 74, 78,
    131, 134, 137, 144, 211
historiography, 6, 14, 27, 29, 42, 46, 57, 66, 68, 70,
    80, 83, 85–86, 105, 125, 136, 138, 140, 156,
    163, 214

history, 3–8, 10, 14–16, 20, 22–23, 25, 27–29,
  32–33, 36–40, 42–43, 45–49, 52, 54, 63,
  65–73, 75–88, 90–93, 97–98, 100, 102,
  104–8, 113, 115–17, 119, 121–22, 125–29,
  131–32, 134–35, 137, 142, 152–53, 156–57,
  160, 170, 176, 178–79, 184, 191, 197, 202–3,
  205, 207, 209, 211–12, 214, 217
  academic, 9, 16, 21, 23, 26, 34, 42, 48, 66–67,
    72–74, 85, 87, 90–91, 97, 99, 101–3, 106,
    129, 133, 157, 163, 173, 181, 212
  American, 131
  archival, 31, 63–64, 68, 208
  authoritative, 6–8, 13–17, 19, 21, 23, 25, 27, 29,
    31–32, 37, 62–63, 72–74, 76, 80, 83, 97, 99,
    118, 130, 133, 184, 201
  authorities in, 3, 5–8, 10, 15, 21, 24–26, 32–37,
    39, 41–43, 45, 47–50, 58, 63, 65, 67, 69, 71,
    73–84, 90, 97–103, 107–13, 115, 125,
    127–33, 135, 143–44, 146, 151, 179,
    199–202, 205, 208, 213
  from below, 73, 77–78, 84, 90, 135, 167
  Chinese, 136–37
  critical, 106
  cultural, 51, 97, 123, 140
  end of, 71, 84
  French, 21
  German, 35
  idea of progress in, 15, 20, 24–25, 35, 63, 66–67,
    70–71, 74–77, 79–80, 100, 137
  institutional, 10, 82, 135, 199
  Jewish, 99, 102, 105, 110, 133, 138, 157, 203
  Latin American, 35, 122
  local, 121, 219n.2
  meaning in, 55, 66–67, 73, 77, 82, 87, 102, 104,
    110, 115, 118–19, 121, 130, 137–38, 203,
    205, 210
  medieval, 77, 133, 200, 202
  methodology, 6, 8, 18, 23, 28, 31, 43–44, 52, 57,
    61–63, 66, 77, 85, 92, 129, 134, 186, 214
  Mexican, 122
  national, 8, 28, 35, 75, 133
  new approaches in, 7, 10, 13, 43, 52, 54, 58, 60,
    67, 71, 73, 76, 78–81, 84, 86, 98, 100, 105,
    123, 132, 134–35, 158, 194, 210, 212
  oral, 16, 35, 84, 104, 125, 127, 134–35, 153, 211,
    217n.4, 235–36n.34
  political, 7, 15, 26–27, 68–69, 75, 82–83, 118, 164
  popular, 15, 105
  quantitative, 51, 70
  Russian and Soviet, 6, 14–15, 21, 36, 70, 72, 78,
    100, 124, 126, 136, 149–50, 165–66, 171,
    189, 198–99, 208, 231n.6, 232n.25
  scholarship in, 4, 8, 10, 15, 31, 37, 46, 63–65,
    67, 70, 75–76, 78, 83, 92, 105–6, 108, 115,
    121, 125, 134, 152, 162, 188–89, 201, 205–7,
    212, 215
  scientific, 14–15, 24, 26–27, 33–34, 37, 63,
    65–67, 70, 79–80, 104, 135

  social, 50–51, 69, 71–73, 77, 83–84, 100, 131, 157
  traditional, 81–82
  understanding in, 3, 5–7, 9–10, 13–14, 16,
    23–24, 33, 35, 41, 43–44, 46–47, 62, 66, 68,
    72, 80, 84, 92–93, 97–99, 121, 127, 129–31,
    140, 142, 160, 165, 172, 177–79, 185, 190,
    197, 204
  women's, 81, 156
History and Theory, 83, 217
History of the Human Sciences, 140
History of the USSR., 14
Hitler, Adolf, 106
Hobsbawm, Eric, 75, 100, 106
Holmes, Oliver W, 42
Holocaust andlocaust museums, 99–100, 102, 138
Holt, Thomas, 228n.19
Hoover, Herbert, 39
Horsman, Peter, 153–54
Houghton Library, 198
humanists and humanities, 4–5, 9, 68, 185–86, 195
Humphrey, Hubert, 74
Hunt, Lynn, 84, 132

I

IBM, 175, 188
identity, 8, 44, 49, 55, 57, 82–83, 97, 99–100,
    104–7, 110–11, 114, 128–29, 133–34, 141,
    156, 158, 162, 190, 201, 207, 212
  national, 72, 76–77, 115, 158
  social, 5, 97, 103–4, 106–7, 113–14, 118
identity archives. See archives, identity
identity narratives, 115
identity politics, 77, 107, 110, 114–15, 208
identity theft, 151
Ilizarov, B.S., 166–67
Illinois, 42
images, 52, 108, 112, 128, 201–2, 205
immigration, 5, 156, 238–39n.28
Immigration History Research Center, University of
    Minnesota, 5, 156
Index of Forbidden Books, 8, 20, 148
India, 86, 110–11, 120–21, 137
Indiana University, 86
Indochina, 42, 77
industrialization, 29, 35, 155
information flow, 30, 49, 89, 188–89, 240–41n.10
Information Management Journal, 49
information science, 4, 55–56, 85, 88, 93
information technologies, 49–51, 57, 61, 71, 79,
    85–86, 93, 112, 152, 170, 177, 184, 186, 197,
    201–2, 210–14, 241n.18
Institute for Social History, Amsterdam, 157
institutional values, 86, 151, 158, 160, 207, 211
institutions, social and political, 4–6, 8–9, 17, 19,
    21, 26, 30–31, 34–35, 37, 39, 42, 47–48, 52,
    54–56, 58–60, 64–67, 72, 74–75, 77, 79–80,

86, 88–91, 100, 103–4, 111, 113, 117–18, 120–23, 127, 133–34, 136, 138, 142, 147, 151, 156–57, 169, 171–72, 181, 185–86, 188, 190–91, 196, 201–3, 207, 215
interdisciplinarity, 10, 138, 140, 207
International Council on Archives (ICA), 59
International Organization for Standards (ISO), 59
International Standard Archival Authority Record (ISAAR), 59
International Standard on Declassification (1968), 168
International Tracing Service, Bad Arolsen, Germany, 151, 235n.26
internet, 3, 52–53, 55–56, 128, 188, 197, 199–203, 209, 213–14, 238–39n.28 *See also* sources, on line
InterPARES Project, 223n.20
Inter-University Consortium for Political and Social Research (ICPSR), 51
inventories. *See* finding aids
Iran-Contra scandal, 175
Iraq, 128
Ireland, 238–39n.28
Ithaka Harbors corporation, 240n.5
Israel, 138
Italy, 19, 27–30, 67, 157, 161, 168

J

Jacob, Margaret, 84, 132
James I, 18
Jameson, Fredric, 36–38, 40, 75
Jameson, J. Franklin, 36–37, 40
Japan, 34, 67, 106, 110, 116, 208
Jenkinson, Hilary, 38–39, 41, 46–47, 133
Jews, 99, 102, 105, 110, 133, 138, 157, 203
Jobs, Steve, 183
Johns Hopkins University, 200
Joint Committee on Historians and Archivists, 44
Joyce, Patrick, 82, 163
JP Morgan Chase Corporation, 154
JSTOR, 185, 202, 205, 213

K

Kahle, Brewster, 188
Kansas, 91
Kant, Emannuel, 24
Kennedy, John F., 74, 165, 189, 238n.16
Kennedy, Robert, 74
Ketelaar, Eric, 30, 181
King, Martin Luther, Jr., 74
Kissinger, Henry, 174
Klemek, Christopher, 157
Korea, 110

Kovalchenko, I.D., 70
Krieger, Leonard, 15, 218n.20

L

Lambek, Michael, 102, 110
language, 6, 8, 13, 34, 42, 53–54, 56–57, 61, 64–65, 68–71, 73, 76–79, 83, 91–92, 100, 102, 107, 130, 141, 148, 197
Laos, 74
Latin America, 35, 122
laws and regulations, 5, 15–16, 18, 21–22, 27, 31, 34, 42, 45, 49, 61, 64, 67, 80, 103, 105, 123, 134, 143–46, 150–51, 153, 155, 158, 161–67, 169–71, 173–82, 188, 192–93, 208, 224n.1
archival, 41, 124, 150, 167, 169–71, 173, 177–78, 182, 238n.14
Lee, Cal, 240n.9
Lefebvre, Georges, 70
LeGoff, Jacques, 104–5
Lenin, V.I., 15
Leningrad, 70
Leo Baeck Institute, New York, 134, 157, 203
Leo XIII, Pope, 28, 165
Lesbian and Gay Archives, San Francisco, 134
Lévi-Strauss, Claude, 67–68
Lewinson, Paul, 42
liberalism, 66, 71, 74–75, 81, 151, 163, 176
libraries and librarians, 5, 18, 37, 40–41, 44–46, 52–57, 69, 124–26, 134, 138, 144, 150, 154, 156, 161, 165, 173, 175, 183, 186–87, 193, 195, 197–204, 242nn.6, 32
presidential, 124–25, 154, 175, 239n.42
searching in, 200
Library and Archives Canada, 144
Library Model, 52
Library of Congress, U.S., 40, 45, 52–53, 55–56, 193, 195, 199
Lifton, Robert J., 117
Lincoln, Abraham, 105
Lincoln, Bruce, 80
Lincoln, Evelyn, 165
linguistics and linguists, 6, 13, 16, 19, 48, 55, 57, 68–69, 74–77, 83, 89, 91
linguistic turn, 13, 74–77, 91, 225–26n.33
Lives of Others, 235n.32
literary criticism, 99, 131, 134
Literaturnaia Gazeta, 166
Lithuania, 135
Lockheed Martin Corporation, 195
Lodge, Henry Cabot, 37
Loewenheim, Francis, 44
Los Alamos National Laboratory, 169
loss, of information, 109, 131, 172, 197–98
Lotman, Iuri, 102
Louis Armstrong Archives, 234n.12
Louis Napoleon, 36

Lowenthal, David, 41, 109
Lynch, Clifford, 112, 186

M

M-Tag (University of Michigan), 242n.6
Mabillon, Jean, 18
Machine Reading Cataloging (MARC), 54
Mackenzie, Colin, 121
Making of America Project, 241n.28
Mallon, Florencia, 122
management. *See* records, management; archives, management
manuscripts, 15, 19, 37, 44–45, 53–56, 77, 121, 133, 141, 181, 187, 198, 200–204, 217
Marx, Karl, 27
marxism, 66, 68
Mason, Philip, 44
Massachusetts Historical Society, 23, 32, 198
Massachusetts Institute of Technology, 186
mathematicians, 68
McIntosh, Robert, 158–59
meaning, in history, 55, 66–67, 73, 77, 82, 87, 102, 104, 110, 115, 118–19, 121, 130, 137–38, 203, 205, 210
mediation, 58, 72, 102, 119, 143–45, 147, 149–53, 158, 160, 163, 168, 187, 196, 205
Medvedev, Roy, 100
Mellon Andrew W. Mellon Foundation, 185, 222n.13, 239–40n.46, 240n.5
memoirs, 153
memorials and memorialization., 17, 98, 104–5, 108–9, 124, 127, 130 *See also* commemoration
memory, 4, 17, 78, 82–83, 97–117, 119, 121, 125, 127–30, 135, 138, 141, 156, 158–60, 162, 167, 201, 209, 217
  historical, 43, 98–99
  historical authority of, 103
  individual, 101, 103, 107, 110–13, 115, 119, 130, 141, 160
  social, 7–8, 10, 93, 97–101, 103–15, 117, 125, 129–30, 138, 144, 158–61, 209
Mensheviks, 122
mentalities, 16, 27, 68–70, 72, 99, 128, 211
metadata, 52, 85, 144, 195–97, 205, 212
methodology, 6, 8, 18, 23, 28, 31, 43–44, 52, 57, 61–63, 66, 77, 85, 92, 129, 134, 186, 214, 235–36n.34
Mexico, 122
Michelet, Jules, 25–27, 74, 81, 84, 141
Microsoft Word, 170
Middle East, 71, 102
migration. *See* records, migration of
Minnesota, 5, 32, 156
Mississippi State Archives, 219n.3
Mitchell, W.J.T., 128
modernity and modernization, 13–14, 20, 29, 31,

34, 66–67, 71, 73, 75, 77, 79–80, 108–9, 130–32, 140
Monash University, 85
Montesquieu, C.L. de, 16
monuments and monumentality, 8, 107–8, 124–27, 188
Moore, Lara, 22, 102, 237n.5
morals and morality, 5, 18, 38–40, 46–47, 49, 61, 87, 89, 99, 102, 104–6, 109–10, 112, 114, 117, 120, 130, 138, 151, 162, 173–74, 176–77, 179–82, 191, 194–95, 211–12, 214
Morgan Library, 200, 202
Morse, Hosea B., 136
Mortensen, Preben, 85
Moscow, 15, 70, 126, 162, 165–66, 169, 171, 199
Moscow State Historical Archival Institute (MGIAI), 162, 166
Moskovskie Novosti, 167
Moynihan, Daniel Patrick, 238n.16
Muller, J.A., 29–30
multiculturalism, 99
multiple pasts, 87, 98, 111, 117, 129–30, 134, 209
Murphy, Frank, 193
museums, 5, 56, 58, 99, 116, 156, 165, 191, 199

N

NAGARA. *See* National Association of Government Archives and Records Administrators
Nanking, 106
Napoleon Bonaparte, 36
NARA. *See* National Archives and Records Administration
narration and narrativity, 9, 14–15, 35, 66, 70–75, 77–78, 80, 83, 99, 101–2, 104–8, 112, 115, 119, 121, 123, 128, 134–37, 157, 163, 208–9
Nash, Gary, 157
National Archives, U.S., 4, 9, 21, 32–33, 35–37, 39–43, 45, 76, 98, 125, 133, 138, 143, 146, 152–53, 159, 161–63, 165, 170, 172–76, 191, 193, 197–98, 204–5, 207
National Archives and Records Administration, Performance and Accountability Report, 194
National Archives and Records Administration (NARA), 51, 92, 98, 122, 124, 143, 146, 159, 161, 163, 165, 170, 173–75, 193–95
National Archives and Records Service, 64, 222n.6
National Association of Government Archives and Records Administrators (NAGARA), 61
National Declassification Center, U.S., 123
National Historical Archive, Madrid, 20–21
National Information Systems Task Force (NISTF), 54
nationality, 90, 133–35
National Science Foundation (NSF), 185, 197, 205
National Security Archive, Washington D.C., 123, 232n.18

National Security Council (NSC), 123, 161, 169, 175–76

Native Americans, 106, 110, 122, 135

Nazism, 106, 114, 131, 151

Nesmith, Tom, 146

Netherlands, 29–30, 38, 53, 153–54, 174, 181, 219n.31

Netherlands Association of Archivists, 219n.31

neurology, 101

Newberry Library, 46

Newton, Sir Isaac, 16, 66

New York, 15, 36–37, 48, 132, 134, 145, 164, 198, 221n.43, 238–39n.28

New York Central System, 145

New York Historical Society, 37

New York Public Library, 134

New York State Archives, 221n.43

New York Times, 132, 164, 198

Nietzsche, Friedrich, 79

NISTF. *See* National Information Systems Task Force

Nixon, Richard, 74, 153, 164, 173, 176

Nora, Pierre, 105, 107–9

North Carolina State Historical Commission, 39

Norton, Margaret Cross, 42, 48

Norway, 138

nostalgia, 13, 98, 109–10, 128

numismatics, 16

O

objectivity, in scholarship, 6, 15–16, 29, 65, 74, 81, 84, 88, 104–5, 127, 133, 138, 142, 147, 149, 164, 177

Ohio University, 188

Olick, Jeffrey, 99

on-line access, 3, 52–53, 55–56, 128, 188, 199–203, 213–14, 238–39n.28, declassification, 123, 168–69, 238n.16, 238–39n.28, 241n.28

Online Computer Library Center (OCLC), 53, 56

Online Public Catalogs (OPACs), 199

O'Reilly, Tim, 212

Organization of American Historians (OAH), 44, 238n.16

orientalism, 84, 99

Orthodox Church, Russia, 125

Osborne, Thomas, 163, 217

Otto I, 28

P

Packwood, Robert, 153

paleography, 16, 59

Palmer, Bryan, 81

papacy, 17–18, 28–29

papyrology, 16

Paris, 4, 18, 30, 33, 70, 192, 195, 198, 217

Passerini, Louisa, 112

Past and Present, 25, 78, 93, 132, 135

Pasteur, Louis, 27, 29

Pastor, Ludwig von, 29

Paul V, Pope, 18

Pearl Harbor, 102–3

Pederson, Ann, 142

Penn-Tag (University of Pennsylvania), 242n.6

Pennsylvania Railroad, 145

Pentagon, 46, 180

Pentagon Papers, 46

Perrot, Michelle, 75

Peru, 122

Peterson, Trudy Huskamp, 161, 176

Philadelphia, 157

photographs, 51, 84, 110, 112, 126–30, 138, 153, 173, 187, 197

physiology, 101, 113

Pinochet, Augusto, 238n.16

Pitti, Daniel, 56

Pius IX, Pope, 28

politics, 5, 7–8, 10, 20, 26–27, 66, 68–69, 72–73, 75, 81–83, 118, 121, 133–34, 151, 154, 159, 163–64, 168, 172–74, 177, 182, 202

Poovey, Mary, 131

PORTICO electronic archiving service, 186, 240n.5

positivism, 26–27, 29, 35, 66, 70, 81–82, 130

postcolonialism, 84, 118, 120, 122, 126, 142

post-custodial era, 9, 46, 88, 118, 177

post-Marxism, 83

postmodernism, 13, 74, 76, 78–82, 84, 87, 97–99, 117, 130, 137, 210, 224n.15, 239n.46

poststructuralist, 83

Potsdam, 69

Prague, 74

PRA. *See* Presidential Records Act

preservation, 6, 8–9, 17, 20, 26, 33, 35–41, 43, 48–50, 52, 58–63, 65, 68, 83, 86, 88–89, 92, 98, 108, 111, 114, 117, 124, 126–27, 129, 133–34, 137, 140, 143, 154, 156, 163–65, 167, 170, 172–75, 181–82, 184, 187–92, 194–98, 205–6, 209–10, 214

preservation. *See* documents, preservation

Presidential Libraries, U.S., 124–25, 154, 175

Presidential Records Act (PRA), 173, 176

Princeton University, 78, 118, 131–32, 217

print and printing, 19–20, 50, 53, 104, 140, 174–75, 183, 187–88, 191, 196, 202–4

production. *See* records production, documents production

PROFILE Electronic Database, 241–42n.31

PROFS (Professional Office Systems) case, 174–77, 207, 239n.36

progress, ideas of, 15, 20, 24–25, 35, 63, 66–67, 70–71, 74–77, 79–80, 100, 137

Proudhon, Pierre-Joseph, 27

provenance, 34, 42, 54, 58–59, 121, 124–25, 127, 129, 134, 159, 197, 210–12

Prussia, 30
psychology and psychologists, 5, 57, 68, 113, 141
public interest, 22, 162, 165–66, 168–69
Public Records Office (PRO), England, 18, 20–21,
    33, 37–38, 56, 104, 121, 166, 172
Putin, Vladimir, 126

Q

quantitative analysis, 51, 70
Quisling movement, 138

R

race, 51, 77–78, 81–84, 90, 100, 115, 133–35
Radcliffe College, 140, 156
railroads, 155–56
Randolph, John, 209
Ranke, Leopold von, 8, 14–16, 23–29, 33, 64–65,
    74, 84, 131, 213, 217n.4, 218n.20
reading rooms, 3, 122, 126, 150, 178, 184, 186,
    199, 215
Reagan, Ronald, 47, 165, 173–76
records, management of, 4, 45, 50, 61–62, 178,
    185, 211
records and record keeping, 5, 17, 23, 26, 30, 34,
    43, 48, 55, 57, 60, 85–91, 107, 109, 120–21,
    123, 141–48, 151–52, 154–56, 158, 165, 167,
    170, 172, 174, 179, 181–82, 184, 188–89,
    191–96, 198, 205, 208–9, 211, 214
  authentic, 5, 8–9, 16, 19–20, 30, 47
  bureaucratic, 19–20, 22, 30, 38, 40, 42–43, 47,
    80, 93, 120, 137, 164, 167, 169, 181, 213,
    240–41n.10
  business & corporate, 30–31, 42, 49, 59, 61, 89,
    120, 150, 155–56, 192, 211
  creation of, 86, 140, 143, 154–55, 157, 189, 195
  cultures of, 152, 154–55
  definitions and meanings of, 172–75
  description of, 10, 15, 27, 30, 33–34, 38, 41, 46,
    52–54, 56–59, 63, 70, 77, 82, 86, 91, 100,
    113–14, 119, 122, 133, 135, 143, 147–49,
    152, 184, 192, 198, 207, 213
  destruction of, 37, 39, 45, 63, 108, 110, 146, 159,
    173, 175, 190, 205
  digital (electronic), 4, 9, 50–53, 57–61, 86–87,
    89, 91, 123, 127, 144, 146–47, 154–55, 170,
    175–78, 182, 184–87, 190, 193–98, 201–8,
    210, 213–15
  enduring value of, 17, 24, 48, 55, 60–61, 85–91,
    141, 147, 156, 158, 172, 174, 178, 184,
    188–89, 192–93, 198–99, 205, 208–9
  generation of, 20, 86, 143, 162, 184, 189–90, 207
  groups, 31, 34, 42, 53–54, 57, 123, 150, 178
  growth of (bulk), 9, 26, 41, 45, 47, 61–62, 129,
    146, 159, 177, 184, 193, 196, 204

historical, 4–9, 15–17, 21–22, 24–26, 31–33, 35,
    37–43, 46, 48, 52, 55, 60, 62–64, 69, 80, 82,
    86–87, 91–92, 97, 102, 115, 118, 125–26,
    132–33, 140–43, 147, 152, 156–58, 160, 163,
    166–67, 172–73, 176, 188, 191, 197, 201,
    203, 208, 214–15, 221n.43
  institutional, 194, 211
  machine readable, 50–51, 54, 191, 194
  management, 6–7, 30, 41, 43–46, 49, 52–53, 59,
    61–62, 72, 86, 89–91, 118, 142, 152, 156–57,
    169, 175, 182, 188, 192, 194, 205, 210, 214
  migration of, 170, 204
  organic relationships in, 4–5, 26–27, 30, 34, 38,
    57, 86, 107–8, 113
  preservation, 6, 9, 17, 20, 26, 33, 35–41, 43,
    48–50, 52, 58–63, 65, 68, 83, 86, 88–89,
    92, 98, 108, 111, 114, 117, 124, 126, 129,
    133–34, 137, 140, 143, 154, 156, 163–65,
    167, 170, 172–75, 179, 181–82, 184, 187–92,
    194–98, 205–6, 209–10, 214
  presidential, 239n.42.
  production, 7, 30, 35, 38, 42, 50, 65, 83, 85, 93,
    120–21, 129, 133–34, 140–41, 143, 145, 147,
    149, 151–55, 157, 159, 172, 192, 194, 201,
    203, 209
  selection, 9, 37, 39–41, 46, 48, 88, 132, 137, 143,
    152, 167, 191, 195
  state, 17, 30, 32–33, 37, 40, 42–43, 48, 51, 61,
    64, 91, 123, 143–44, 146, 150, 159, 170–71,
    173–74, 176, 193, 195, 197
  storage, 4–5, 43, 45–46, 151, 185, 187, 198
  tags, 53, 55–56, 190, 195–97, 213. 242n.6
  transformation of, 20, 29, 38
  vital, 17
Records Continuum Research Group, 85
Records Disposal Act, U.S., 41, 173
records management, 6–7, 30, 41, 43–46, 49,
    52–53, 59, 61–62, 72, 86, 89–91, 118, 142,
    152, 156–57, 169, 175, 182, 188, 192, 194,
    205, 210, 214
reenactments, 49, 109, 230n.43
regulation. See laws and regulation
religion, 28, 81, 104–5, 107, 109, 212
Renaissance, 27, 201, 203
Research Libraries database (RLIN), 53
Research Libraries Group, 56
retention. See records preservation, documents
    preservation
retrieval. See access
revisionism, 72, 116–17
Richards, Thomas, 84, 120, 136
Ricoeur, Paul, 104
Robbins, Joyce, 99
Roberts, Alasdair, 155
Rome, 19, 28, 59, 165, 203
Roosevelt, Franklin D., 37, 39–41, 44, 47, 161, 165
Rose Project, 200, 202
Ross, Seamus, 197–98

Rumsfeld, Donald, 128
Russia, 6, 13–15, 19, 21–22, 29, 32, 34, 36, 67, 70–72, 78, 100, 123–26, 136, 149–50, 152, 158, 165–67, 171, 189, 198–99, 202, 208, 210
Russian State Historical Archive (RGIA), 21, 126, 149, 198

S

SAA. *See* Society of American Archivists
Sakhiet-Sidi-Youseff, 69
samizdat, 100
Samuels, Helen Willa, 88
Sanders, James, 122
Sarbanes-Oxley legislation, 192
Sartre, Jean Paul, 67
Saussure, Ferdinand de, 78
Schellenberg, Theodore, 42–43, 48, 146
Schlesinger Library, 156
scholars, 3–5, 7, 9–10, 13–15, 22–23, 27–29, 37, 43, 49–52, 55, 57, 63, 65, 67, 73, 75, 78, 81–82, 90, 97, 99–100, 106, 109, 111, 113, 117–20, 122–23, 125, 129–32, 136–37, 140–42, 144–45, 148–49, 152–53, 155–56, 158–62, 166–72, 177–79, 181–87, 189, 192–93, 195–96, 198–200, 202–4, 206–8, 210–15
    archival, 24, 26, 64, 73, 99, 129, 151, 167
Schools of Information, 93, 185, 195
Schwartz, Joan, 129, 153, 159
science, 4, 14, 16, 24, 29, 31, 36, 55–56, 61, 63, 65, 71, 77, 79–80, 82–83, 85, 88, 93, 134, 185, 190, 194, 197, 205, 212
scientific history, 14–15, 24, 26–27, 33–34, 37, 63, 65–67, 70, 79–80, 104, 135
scope and content notes, 150, 213
Scott, James C., 90
Scott, Joan W., 81, 228n.19
Scott, Rebecca, 122
searching, full text, 177, 184, 193, 204
self, defining of, 14–15, 36, 82–84, 86, 100, 105, 107, 114, 129, 135, 137, 142, 146, 155, 157, 171, 182, 208, 217
Serbia, 135
SGML. *See* Standard Markup Language
Shapin, Steven, 65, 131
Sherwin, Martin J., 117
Shindler's List, 99
Shoah, 99
Sickel, Theodor von, 28
Slavic Review, 71
Smith, Bonnie Shawn, 128
Smithsonian Institution, 58, 116
social amnesia., 32, 99, 106–8, 110–12, 114–15, 135, 138, 154, 209
social history. *See* history, social
socialism, 66, 71, 74–75, 157

social memory, 7–8, 10, 93, 97–115, 117, 125, 129–30, 138, 144, 158–61, 209, 227n.3, 231n.55
    concept of, 103
social sciences, 9, 29, 36, 51, 55, 61, 63, 68, 70, 77, 82–83, 134–35, 185–86
Society of American Archivists (SAA), 39, 43–44, 49, 54, 61, 132, 164, 175, 217
sociology and sociologists, 45, 68, 70, 75, 99, 134–35, 168, 229n.24
sources, 5, 9, 14–16, 18, 20, 27–29, 31, 33, 36–37, 40–42, 55–56, 60, 64–66, 73, 75–76, 78, 80, 84, 92–93, 97–98, 100, 106–9, 115–39, 143, 147–48, 155, 160, 174, 186, 189, 193, 203–4, 210, 213
    archival, 3–4, 6–8, 15, 18–19, 23–24, 30, 32, 36, 42, 51, 53–57, 65, 68, 72, 78, 82, 97, 111, 114, 116, 120, 123, 125, 127, 129–32, 136, 141–42, 147–50, 152, 157, 162, 164–65, 167–68, 177–78, 181, 183, 187, 195, 198–99, 203–6, 209–12, 215
    authoritative, 80, 97–98, 129
    historical, 4–9, 15–17, 21–22, 24–26, 31–33, 35, 37–43, 46, 48, 52, 55, 60, 62–64, 69, 80, 82, 86–87, 91–92, 97, 102, 115, 118, 125–26, 132–33, 140–43, 147, 152, 156–58, 160, 163, 166–67, 172–73, 176, 188, 191, 197, 201, 203, 208, 214–15
    oral, 16, 35, 84, 104, 125, 127, 134–35, 153, 211, 217n.4, 235–36n.34
South Africa, 113, 208
Southeast Asia, 71, 75
Soviet Union, 6, 13–14, 22, 64, 66–67, 70–72, 74–75, 77–79, 83–84, 90, 100, 110–14, 122–25, 136, 149–52, 161–70, 208
sphragistics, 16
Spiegel, Gabrielle, 91
Spielberg, Steven, 110
Spragge, Shirley, 158
Stalin, J.V., 122
Stalinism, 100, 106
standardization, machine-compatible, 54
Standard Markup Language (SGML), 56
standards and standardization, 28, 40, 43, 49, 53–57, 59, 62–65, 88–89, 93, 120, 124–25, 128, 147, 151, 171–72, 181–82, 186, 191, 195, 212–13, 221n.38, 222nn.5, 9
Stanford University, 150
Stasi archives, East Germany, 171
State Archive of the Russian Federation (GARF), 124, 232n.25
state archives. *See* archives, national and state
State Department, U.S., 122, 169, 174
state secrets, 168, 171
statistics and statisticians, 50–51, 61, 68, 70, 136
Steedman, Carolyn, 119, 140–42
Stephan Shapin's, 131
Stevens, John Paul, 151
Stoler, Ann, 119, 122–23, 136–37, 160

Stone, Lawrence, 78–83, 132
St. Petersburg, 16, 21, 24, 63, 231n.7
subaltern studies, 72, 90, 122, 142
Supreme Court, U.S., 151, 174–75, 193
survey. *See* archival survey
Swartz, Aaron, 242n.32

T

tags and tagging, 53, 55–56, 190, 195–97, 213,
     242n.6
technology, 5–6, 9, 14, 24, 26, 28, 49–52, 57, 61,
     66–69, 71, 75–77, 79–80, 83, 85–86, 93, 112,
     131–32, 134, 152–53, 163, 170, 177, 184–86,
     189, 195–97, 200–202, 205, 207, 210–14
terrorism, 111
testimony, oral, 16, 35, 84, 104, 125, 127, 134–35,
     153, 211, 217n.4, 235–36n.34
texts, 8, 15, 51–52, 57, 64–65, 67, 70, 75–76, 78,
     83, 119, 122, 124, 129–31, 135–36, 141, 144,
     149, 153, 172, 184–87, 189, 191, 195, 200,
     202–4, 241–42n.31
theory, 13, 16, 39, 44, 46, 52, 59, 62, 66, 75, 83,
     85, 88, 90, 93, 117, 130–31, 212, 217 *See also*
     archival theory
Thomassen, Theo, 154
Thompson, E.P., 71–72, 99, 134
Thucydides, 16, 24, 202, 217n.4
time
   concept of, 70, 101
   historical, 69, 73, 129–30
Tolstoy, Leo, 74
transactions, as source of records, 17–20, 22,
     24–26, 34, 42, 51, 58, 60–61, 91, 146, 159,
     172, 174, 189, 201
transfers. *See* archives, transfers to
transparency, 75, 122, 134, 142, 150, 166, 171,
     178, 189, 191, 197, 212
trauma, 102, 111–12
Trotsky, Leon, 122
trust, 5, 18, 23, 38–40, 46–47, 49, 60–61, 64, 87,
     89, 99, 102, 104–6, 109–10, 112, 114, 117,
     120, 130–31, 138, 151, 161–62, 173–74,
     176–82, 191, 194–95, 211–12, 214
   historical, 8, 14–18, 20, 23–24, 28, 33, 35,
     65–67, 74–75, 78–79, 84, 99–100, 104, 107,
     113–15, 130–32, 137, 161, 180, 217n.4
Tufts University, 240–41n.10
Turkey, 110
Turner, Gordon, 131
Turner, Victor, 77

U

Ukraine, 123, 133, 135
UNESCO, 125

United States, 4, 8, 15, 20–21, 32–44, 46–47, 49,
     51, 54, 61, 64–66, 70, 72, 74–75, 77–78,
     81–82, 87, 90–91, 98, 100, 103, 106, 109,
     111–12, 116–17, 122, 124–26, 128, 130–33,
     143, 145, 152–54, 156, 159, 161, 164,
     166–77, 180, 186, 197–98, 201, 207–8, 210,
     217
University of British Columbia, 59
University of California, 56, 169
University of Kentucky, 45
University of Maryland, 117
University of Michigan, 51, 86, 124, 166, 170, 174,
     185–86, 193, 199, 212, 233n.37, 239–40n.46,
     242n.6
University of Minnesota, 5, 156
University of North Carolina, 240n.9
University of Pennsylvania, 242n.6
urbanization, 29, 35, 69, 150
usable past, 22, 113
users, 48–49, 52–53, 55, 57, 64, 121, 123, 126,
     133, 141, 147–52, 154, 159, 162, 166, 169,
     178, 181, 183, 185, 187–88, 191, 195–96,
     199–202, 207, 210–15
U.S. National Archives. *See* National Archives, U.S.

V

values, 14, 17, 34, 36, 40–42, 44, 58, 61–62, 68, 70,
     72, 79, 84, 86–87, 91, 104–5, 115, 117, 121,
     123–24, 126–29, 134, 136, 147, 149, 151,
     153, 158–60, 163–64, 171, 180–82, 184, 188,
     190, 196, 199, 207–13, 215
Van Garderen, Peter, 212
Vann, Richard, 83
Vatican, 18, 20, 28, 148, 157, 213
Vatican Archives Project, 212
Vatican archives. *See* archives, Vatican
Vatican Library, 18, 199, 201, 203–4
verification, 8, 14, 16, 18–20, 27–28, 31, 34, 64–67,
     73–74, 80, 103–4, 107, 112–13, 160, 178–79,
     217n.4
Vichy, France, 100, 138
Vietnam, 71–72, 74, 109, 130, 180
Vietnam war memorial, 109, 130
visual and visuality, 51–52, 84, 108, 110, 112,
     126–30, 138, 153, 173, 187, 197, 201–2, 205
Voltaire, 16

W

Wallace, David, 7, 15, 26–27, 46, 73, 87, 118,
     120–22, 137, 158, 186–87, 198, 213
Walworth, Ellen Hardin, 36
Warner, Robert M., 44
Washington, D.C., 40–41, 159, 166, 168, 175
Washington Post, 164

Watergate, 46, 165
Wayne State University, 44, 150
Web 2.0 & 3.0 networking technologies, 213
Weber, Max, 80
Webster, William, 173
Weinstein, Allen, 98
White, Hayden, 70, 73–74, 81, 109, 130, 161,
    164–65, 174, 176, 193
Whitehill, Walter, 32
White House, 161, 164–65, 174,
    176, 193
Wikipedia, 203
Wilmington, Delaware, 156
Wilson, Don, 161, 175–76
Winter, Jay, 110
Wisconsin, 32, 45, 132
Wolf, Eric, 135
women, 39, 57, 67, 72, 81–82, 134, 156,
    165, 212
Woodrow Wilson Center, 166
Work Projects Administration (WPA), 41
World Trade Center, 103
World War I, 71, 109, 159

World War II, 41–42, 63, 66, 131, 173,
    238–39n.28
Wounded Knee, S.D., 106

Y

Yakel, Elizabeth, 86, 149
Yale University, 44, 131, 198, 240–41n.10
Yalta, 69
Yates, Francis, 104, 155
Yates, JoAnne, 155
Yeltsin, Boris, 124–26
Yerushalmi, Yosef, 105
Young, Julia, 62
You Tube, 212

Z

Zakhor, 105
Zhitomirskaia, S.V., 166–67
Zionism, 138

CPSIA information can be obtained at www.ICGtesting.com
Printed in the USA
BVOW042057221012

303657BV00004B/2/P